How to Write Successfully in High School and College

4th Edition

Barbara Lenmark Ellis, Ph.D.
Former Journalism Professor
Oregon State University
McNeese State University

BARRON'S

© Copyright 2005, 1989, 1981, 1971 by Barron's Educational Series, Inc.

All inquiries should be addressed to:

Barron's Educational Series, Inc.
250 Wireless Boulevard
Hauppauge, New York 11788
www.barronseduc.com

Library of Congress Catalog Card No. 2004056187
International Standard Book No. 0-7641-2822-1

Library of Congress Cataloging-in-Publication Data

Lenmark-Ellis, Barbara.
    How to write successfully in high school and college / by Barbara Lenmark Ellis.—4th ed.
        p. cm.
    Rev. ed. of: How to write themes and term papers. 3rd ed. c1989.
    Includes bibliographical references and index.
    ISBN 0-7641-2822-1
        1. Report writing.   I. Lenmark-Ellis, Barbara. How to write themes and term papers.   II. Title.

LB2369.L385 2005
808'.02—dc22   2004056187

Printed in the United States of America
9 8 7 6 5 4 3 2 1

TABLE OF CONTENTS

Section II   WRITING ABOUT COMPLEX SUBJECTS

Section III   THE TERM PAPER

Section IV   COLLEGE ADMISSION ESSAYS

INTRODUCTION

Most students hate writing and for some rather solid reasons.

At the outset, virtually every piece of writing they have done from first grade on has been returned with the focus almost always on mistakes. These well-meaning, instructive comments are usually couched in charitable terms—at first. As students move from grade to high school, the notations get more demanding and praise is less forthcoming. At the university level, errors are crisply dispatched in code ("awk" for "awkward") or caustic reflections on the student's failure to have learned anything about composition from K–12.

Even the ink is discouraging. Teachers may have switched to purple or turquoise ink after being told that red is such a psychological stopper that it stifles mastery and creativity. But unless they permit students to revise compositions for the grade via such red-letter "private tutoring," mastery of basic writing is all but impossible for ordinary students.

Beyond this, however, unless students are writing a composition per week and have it returned in timely fashion, they get little practice in writing. How can they become proficient on two compositions a month, returned two weeks after being collected? One learns to write by writing—a lot. Worse, if the teacher prefers a literary style few students can match to the bare-bones English that most people use, it's no wonder most students give up at an early age. They know they're neither William Faulkner nor Joyce Carol Oates.

In fairness to composition teachers, however, only colleges can afford to limit classes to twenty students; today's monumental financial shortfalls in K–12 public schools can mean class overloads of up to forty students. If a teacher spends ten minutes per composition with, say, four sections of even twenty-five students, that amounts to nearly seventeen hours assessing assignments after school (nearly three hours per day or an entire weekend).

A major study on how high school English teachers assessed compositions reported that 85% attributed burnout to laboring over student writing; absenteeism was the highest of all the core courses. Many dedicated writing teachers said their home and social life and even mental and physical health were suffering. The findings also revealed that those demanding a life outside school had ingenious teaching systems to prevent accumulating mountains of compositions (a week or two discussing the topic; another week discussing its organization; then, another on a précis or rough draft to be critiqued by classmates, etc.). Even so, the results showed that most teachers assigned no more than two compositions per month and that turnaround time was usually two weeks. Only the gifted or dogged student can master writing under those conditions.[1]

Add to this doleful report the fact that almost no college English department offers a how-to-teach-composition course or proffers high rank, high regard, or high salaries to those teaching Composition 101-102. Most are graduate students, housewives, or retirees who've done no writing for the general public—where mastery is demonstrated.

Few English teachers in that massive study reported they had ever stooped to take a journalism copy-editing class. As someone with copydesk experience on five publications, this author can attest that grading time on the average composition (two pages) can be cut at least in half.

Too, if English majors or teachers had spent a few weeks on a newspaper copydesk, they would have overcome the unsureness many reported in teaching content and organization concerning realms *outside* of literature. They would have picked up speed in spotting technical errors (spelling, grammar) and eliminated that traditional bias for the literary gem instead of the practical, bare-boned writing most students will need in their lifetimes. That some English departments have fought the "writing-across-the-curriculum" mandate from other disciplines— science, technology, history, business, etc.—says much about such insularity, fears, and competence concerning "real-world" writing their students will face.

So much for the reasons why students have feared and even hated writing. Blame is not constructive. Neither is refusal to pick up a pen or to rush to the keyboard when given a writing assignment. This book's intent for over thirty years has been to teach students how to write successfully in high school and college *despite* their past bitter experiences with red ink, *despite* getting little practice at it and *despite* the limitations of their school systems. They'll find, as thousands have, that they can teach themselves to write successful assignments—and quickly. All it takes is willingness to look at a different route presented by a professional writer and editor who started out with the same disadvantages.

An adjunctive purpose of the book is to help teachers who have recognized that old methods of teaching composition needed a fresh approach. Whether veterans or newcomers, hundreds have found the system easy to teach and gained great pleasure seeing even the plodders rejoice in success at basic writing. Assessment is finally surefooted and rapid.

This book is obviously not a grammar or creative-writing textbook. Much of it is focused principally on new ways to master basic writing skills needed for high school and college: composition assignments and term papers, essay tests and SAT/GRE essays, theses and dissertations. But it also includes the latest wrinkles in college-application essays (insight résumés) and the Internet's current best research sources for term papers.

In addition, this new edition offers an updated section on how to write on complex topics in five of the most common fields demanding advanced expertise:

---

[1] Barbara G. Ellis, "Major Inhibitory Factors in the Assessment of Themes by Oregon High School English Teachers: A Study of 503 Schools." PhD diss., Oregon State University, 1990, 4-6, 9-10, 14-20, 177, 182-205.

business, science, technology, statistics, and public finance. Students heading for these areas can't afford to shrug off writing unless they are prepared to be powerless in the hands of a sneering and expensive vendor. One executive at a New York research company that writes reports from the tangled prose and numbers submitted by desperate oil and automobile firms sniggered to me: "If engineers ever learn how to put one word in front of another, we'll be out of business."

Whatever the writing needs, this book will serve as a quick and practical reference tool on organizing and presenting material. The system used has journalistic roots, chiefly editorial writing. It was begun at a Maine high school with average students, most of whom previously hated writing and did poorly at it. Yet even the slowest mastered the system within three weeks. Many at that school subsequently wound up with high scores in the essay portion of the SAT examination.

When several showed such writing proficiency at college entrance examinations that they were exempted from the two required undergraduate courses in composition, the author decided to write this textbook to explain how the system works. In shifting from high school English teacher to being a university professor in journalism, she still found that average students grasped the system quickly and had the joy of earning high grades in writing even in other courses. Significant sales in foreign countries show that the presentation is easy to understand and apply.

Above all, that this book is now in its fourth edition attests to its effectiveness with ordinary students who want only to write successfully in both high school and college.

Barbara Lenmark Ellis, Ph.D.
Portland OR

SECTION **I**

COMPOSITIONS

CHAPTER 1

THE OUTLINE

Who doesn't remember the time when a class was told to work up an outline and *then* to write from it? Someone was bound to do the writing *first* and then, to pacify the teacher, scribble an outline. An A student probably tore up the first draft and rewrote it in keeping with the organization needed in the first place with an outline. Those pulling C's probably brazened it out by outlining whatever they wrote, hoping the teacher would never notice. If classroom speed was at stake, the situation may have become desperate because most students won't invest time on an outline.

In most cases, the composition revealed all too clearly it was a disorganized mess. If caught and given a scolding in red ink, they can scarcely be blamed if they decide to be more devious the next time an outline is required.

No wonder so few students bother with outlines, regarding them as an annoyance.

The Jot Outline

If you want A's or B's on your writing, you're going to have to make some kind of outline. It need not be one of those fussy and elaborate jobs with the Roman numerals before main points, the capital letters before subdivisions, the Arabic numbers in subdivisions and the meek little a's and b's in whatever is left over. Indeed, your outline may be nothing more than some cryptic jottings in the paper's margin, or they may look like a series of hen tracks.

That's why it's called a "jot" outline. Should your instructor later demand a formal outline, you will find it relatively easy to convert a jot outline to the formalities of I, A, 1, etc.

The body, or main part, of the composition will come from the jot outline if you follow the simple procedures in this book. Students who have used it declare it's easy to learn and vital to *any* written work. It takes about ten minutes to learn how to do a jot outline at first—and five minutes, after you get in some practice, when you're writing from that outline.

The jot outline has two simple parts. The first part involves jottings. The second part involves arranging those jottings into some kind of order.

In practice it works something like this: When you get the topic, jot down *every* thought on the subject that comes into your head. It doesn't matter what it is. Put it down. Despite how mixed up, how disjointed the thoughts may seem or how unrelated they are, the thoughts should be scribbled out—in one word or several. If it's a class composition, put the jottings in the margins of a paper or on a separate piece of paper. If the assignment is to be homework, jot down whatever comes into your head when you *first* see the topic. There's a sound psychological reason for the put-it-down-immediately approach. Ideas are fresher and more workable at first than they will be later.

Remember that these are *your* jottings. Nobody else will care about them. Never mind spelling, usage, or legibility. The jottings might involve phrases or a single word. You might write only an abbreviation that is meaningful to you. Perhaps even a number means something. Whatever the jottings are, they should jog your memory about what you're going to put into the composition. To be helpful, of course, your jottings should include some specific examples. Above all, remember that you don't need Roman numerals or other formal outline systems with this method.

Below, you'll find an example of jottings from one such outline. Don't let the topic unnerve you. The students writing on this one already had read the two Russian novels on which the topic was based. The subject assigned was:

> Dostoyevsky's *The House of the Dead* and Tolstoy's *Resurrection* both show the punishments in the 1800's given to political and criminal prisoners in Siberia. What do you think of the punishments given to both classes of prisoners in that era?

One student's jottings looked something like this and lined the top of the first page:

Dead
bribes, chains, barges
20 murders = only exile
no books - Bible
green sticks
roaches
1930 trials
Koestler + brainwash
Stalin - liquidations
1984

Resur.
Vera - books
allow - family - trots; oxar
Larissa (in Dr. Z.)
food
130 no passports
doctors kind
bribes, bureaucrats

(Siberia, beautiful, cold, people stay after release)

If that topic still scared you off, watch what one student did with jottings on a well-worn topic that many teachers still give: "What I Did Last Summer." Here are the jottings:

work—$	MD	play
147 lawns	brace	D.C.
$67	$120	tuba
cannery	Rollins	Goucher girl
Mobil station	C.Q.	tux rent
75¢-hr.	teeth	car ins.
		H. M. pool

To show you just how cryptic you can get, here's one from a student who wrote on the topic "Patterns I Like in Jazz":

B "Bix" mod. B.C. = F.S. = Ed.F. = J.V.
1÷1z and BR + 6. Krupa

♪ = ♪ trump.   1941
    perc.   MR   1945
    woods   1950T
5th Dim.   1968-Beat.
RCA vs. Indies   Ill. Jacquet
radio vs. T.V. — Sullivan 1954

In each outline the jottings made a great deal of sense to the writer even though "outsiders" like you may not understand them. Each item perhaps provided part of the meat for the composition. There's not a Roman numeral, a capital letter, or an Arabic number anywhere. Nor did neatness count.

The next step is to put the jottings quickly into some kind of order.

This step should be a fast one. All you do is sort out the jottings. Some you can delete by running a line through them if the jottings are off the subject. Jottings you want to keep can be put into some kind of order perhaps by numbering them. Or maybe you'll prefer just to circle them. Or maybe checks will work for you. It doesn't matter so long as you find a method of order that takes no more than a minute to do. Remember, however, to put down the most important things first.

You may run out of time to get everything in if you're doing classroom writing. Even if you're writing outside of class, get in the most important points first.

How some students "sorted out" their jottings are shown in the next examples.

> 2 courage - Crane
> 3 coward - Gröss
> 6 suffering - Hasek + Remarque
> 5 friend - Mailer
> 4 ~~enemy - Rem~~
> ① amoral - Cross of Iron

One student with a naturally organized mind needed no numbers. All he did on a topic of "Business Ethics" was to circle the three items he wanted to write about at the outset. He did it like this:

> (Teapot D)   Bobby Baker
>   -NHG   Bell Tel.
> Nader   ~~Wythe~~
>   (Sinclair (Jung))
> (Westing. G.E.)
> Norris - S.P. - Cyclamates -
>   the movers and F.T.C.

Another who couldn't shake off the traditional formal outline used the alphabet to sort out the order for the topic of "The Riches Given by Science."

> ⑧ destruct { A-bomb - Hiro   A'comm. (TV, tel. rad)
>   ship - Savannah   A'home (clocks
>   heated water fish   plumb.
>   stove
> ⓐ const { Jenner, Lister, Pasteur, Salk B'home (tel. TV)
>   pollution (R. Carson, etc.)
>   Barnard and canibaliz.

There was, to be sure, the student writer with half of the ideas on one side of the paper, the other half across the way—who then checked them off. Such was the case for this piece on "In Defense of the TV Western" which was outlined like this:

So no matter what your method is—checks, numbers, circles, squares, or letters—the outline provides the order in which you'll tackle each phase of the composition.

You will notice, by the way, that students had specific examples to illustrate the points they planned to use. That's one of the things this book will emphasize.

Here's how to practice the jot outline:

Give yourself a topic. Any one will do, but it helps if it's interesting to you. Allow yourself 15 minutes on the jottings as they come into your mind concerning the topic. Then, put them into some kind of order with numbers or letters or other notations. That should take about ten minutes for a good reflective job. Add specific examples or even new points as they occur to you.

Then, cut your time in half, seven minutes for the jottings, five minutes to put things in order. Cut your time still more until the two operations are *combined* in five minutes. In classroom themes, five minutes spent this way is the maximum if you want to finish by the end of class.

In the end, no matter what subject is assigned, you'll know what to put into your composition if you use this jot-outline technique. You'll present a specifics-laden piece as well as a well-organized one. Never again will you be that frantic soul who rationalizes an F by complaining, "My mind just went blank, that's all. I couldn't think of a thing to write." With a jot outline, the only trouble you may have is in deciding what to winnow out of the assignment.

The Quick-and-Dirty Outline

A speedy variation of the jot outline is known as the "quick-and-dirty" outline, shown at the end of this chapter. It's just what the name suggests: It can be laid down quickly, and neatness does *not* count. The example uses jottings from a student writing a classroom composition on the topic "What I have Learned From Studying Milton." But those jottings could furnish an outline just as well for a term paper or an essay examination.

Note the graphic structure of boxes to illustrate the content, paragraph-by-paragraph. A box could stand for one paragraph or for several.

With a quick-and-dirty outline, you can visualize—immediately—what goes into each paragraph. It's recommended that you start by quickly throwing down nearly 20 "boxes" of an inch square or larger. Making boxes *smaller* does block thinking. It's vital to feel you have elbow room when working on thoughts that will become a fine composition.

Make the boxes large enough and ensure that they contain no more than one word or symbol in each. To pack more than one word in a box—or a symbol such as "$" or a letter "M"—means that you're more involved in perfection than using an outline for its fundamental purpose: a quick reference tool in writing.

Once you come up with jottings, you can fill each box with what you want and move it wherever you want it. You can see in an instant which topic grows out of another, which topic logically follows another, which topic starts the composition and which ends it. If you change your mind, a quick-and-dirty outline enables you to either erase it or to draw an arrow showing where it's to be moved.

In the Milton example, the student decided to deal with diction *after* imagery. Rhyme and meter were to go toward the end of the piece. She put a brief summation of what she would be writing about in the second paragraph, wrapping it up in two sentences.

From there, she took up the first topic mentioned in that summation and did seven paragraphs on imagery. Next, she took up diction and wrote six paragraphs about it, making a point and illustrating each with an example.

Most writing professionals point out that one of the principal reasons for "writer's block" is not knowing where to go with a load of research or ideas. With that kind of quandary, a writer gets overwhelmed and sits immobilized. As a student, you've probably suffered the same thing. You stare at a piece of paper with a good topic, but you don't know what should go into it; if you've got content, you don't know what to put where. In the end, you begin fretting about the time that's passing and the deadline. That's when you give up.

However, with a quick-and-dirty outline, you know exactly where you're going and the content. Within one or two minutes after your jottings are out of your mind and on a corner of the paper, you know *what* you're going to write and its placement. You can paste that outline on the computer and proceed.

To become proficient at this type of outline, you need to practice for an hour or so on various topics, as suggested previously. Do several. Again, don't worry about neatness. This is not an art project. It's a tool to help you write.

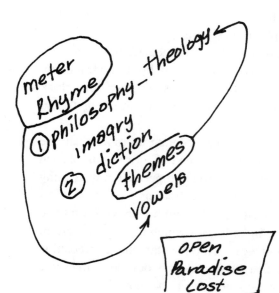

meter
Rhyme
① philosophy — theology
imagry
② diction
themes
vowels

open
Paradise
Lost

Summary
① Phil
② dict.
③ P.Skills

phil — theo

Dict.

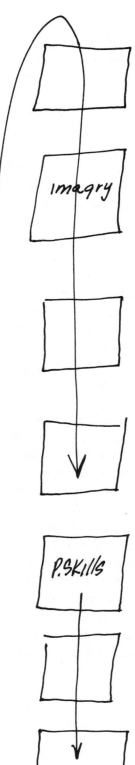

imagry

P.Skills

met.

Rhyme

vowels

close

THE BEGINNING PARAGRAPH

The composition's start is probably the most difficult part of an assignment, as you know only too well. In that opening paragraph, you must reveal the subject and, above all, must not bore while doing it. That's why professional writers take hours and sometimes days to do a superb job of reworking and polishing that opening. They know they must catch the editors' eyes in the first paragraph—and, then, the readers' eyes.

But you don't have hours, days, and weeks for most writing projects. You might have just the 50-minute class period or overnight, or, at most, two weeks. Yet no matter what you think, you do not need to come up with an "opener" on your work that's competition for the best of Steinbeck or Victor Hugo.

Once in awhile you may turn out an opener that truly is magnificent, but few authors can do that regularly. This usually does not happen to students who have many compositions to turn in during the term. You can't shine all the time, but you can do a passable job on openers if you keep reminding yourself that you first want to secure the reader's attention and, second, to supply a brief résumé of the composition.

When to Write the Beginning

You could write the beginning last, strange as that may seem, and mark it for insertion at the beginning of the piece. That way you would have finished and then could present a capsule view of what's in the *entire* composition. Those adroit at this technique know that if writing is being done in class, there's an element of risk in ever getting around to the beginning if it's left until last. What might be left is a body without a head, so to speak.

If you do your beginnings first, as most do, don't agonize over them. Don't spend more than five minutes on them if they involve class work. Those openers written outside class shouldn't involve more than 15 to 30 minutes.

What Goes Into the Beginning (the "Opener")?

Basically, the opener should contain one or two paragraphs telling readers what they're getting into. Such beginning paragraphs should be short, but intriguing—especially if the subject may appear to others to be dull. You want to keep the reader awake. That's why the first sentence of that opener is the most extraordinarily important. To rivet attention, however, don't include such amateurish starts as "Wow!" or "Good news!" or "Wait until you read this!"

No poll among teachers has ever been taken, but it is almost a certainty they would agree that the following six openers are most likely to exasperate them because they've been overused by students. These gems and their variations are:

> "I have been assigned to write about…"
> "Here I sit, pondering what to write…"
> "What is fear? Webster's dictionary defines *fear* as.."
> "What is love? What is it, indeed? What is hate?"
> "Are you affected by feelings of vengeance, H'mmm?"
> "To be artistic or not to be artistic. That is the question."

Why Are These Openers Guaranteed to Bore or Irritate?

No professional writer would start off an article with: "I have been asked by *Sports Illustrated* to write on the subject of…" No editorial writer would begin: "The management of this newspaper said I had to write a 350-word editorial on the subject of…" In short, never hint at the "assignment" aspect or use words indicating that's what it is. Just get into the topic.

Aside from the prepositional ending on the second example, few readers really care what mood or what troubles beset a writer. Perhaps they're too dispassionate, but they want the author to get on with the subject and to stop whining and explaining about writing conditions.

The Webster-dictionary approach in the third example is used by all too many students stumped for a fresh beginning—or because they're insecure. They feel a few words citing Webster will pad out a paragraph or more to procrustean lengths.

The "what-is-love?" lead in the fourth example tells readers they are about to get snarled in a dispute over the definition of words. Such a dispute could go on for pages without coming to grips with the main topic. Writers who back into topics this way not only lose readers at the end of the first sentence, but also reveal that they, too, are about to find a method to pad out a piece by writing *around* the subject. It's true that such an opener is appropriate for a philosophy course where language precision is a prime virtue. But in the ordinary high school or college composition it's not necessary to beat around the semantical bush.

The "*you*" appeal on the fifth example is offensive to many readers. A first reaction often is annoyance at a writer wanting to get familiar. The exception is in explanatory (process) writing, but in that category few writers get too informal as they instruct. They usually employ the "you-understood" form of address and omit that irksome word *you*. The personal touch of *you* is still considered effective by hard-sell advertising copywriters ("Do You Have Bad Credit?"); it may be emphasized in political promotions ("I Want YOU to Support the Democratic Nominee!!"), but the aim here is writing school assignments.

The last example of poor openers—the quotation-paraphrase—is an admission students have so little confidence in themselves that they must lean on another's words. The idea for some is to be classed with Aristotle or Napoleon if those names are dropped in a composition—or that they'll be considered a Shakespearean expert if they paraphrase or use direct quotes from his plays. This dependence is essential only in term papers and professional writing—especially editorial columns and scholarly articles because editors and teachers demand writers produce evidence (sources) to substantiate positions.

The common composition assignment doesn't require sources or dropping names of the famous, particularly if it's written in class. In fact, quotation openers are usually so clumsily done, so inappropriate or so indicative of the "leaning" weakness as to merit low grades or nasty notations. Don't lean. Stand by your convictions.

So what kind of opening sentence should be used?

If we have cited as taboo your favorite openers in the six examples above, don't despair. You have a wonderful opportunity to be a little original. Turn to new openers that will make the reader laugh, or become thoughtful, admire your point of view, or, if you're courageous enough, even provoke anger. Yet don't fall into the habit of using the *same* type of opener ever after, even if it earns an A and a delighted teacher's note in the margin.

Four types of openers you might try involve humor, a startling statement or fact, a fascinating anecdote, or a *new* metaphor or simile.

The Humorous Opener

Below are some examples of humorous openers:

> Does anyone ever stop to think that a horse may have ticklish feet?

Or

> There are three things a woman usually looks for in a husband: He must be as boyish as Matt Damon, as rich as Bill Gates, and as kind as St. Francis of Assisi.

Or

> Just because Polonius pocketed Hamlet's love letters to Ophelia is no reason to criticize the mail service at Elsinore Castle or anywhere else.

The Startling Opener

For the startling statement or fact that is to arrest attention, you'll have to rely on surprising statistics, revelations, or remarks. One such opener on the subject of sports boredom was:

> It didn't surprise me to learn that baseball bores 200,000,000 of 280,000,000 Americans.

A somewhat heretical approach was contained in this opening sentence:

> No matter what The Bible says, vengeance by man is often justified and often sweet.

A college sophomore, countering a popular theory, wrote:

> Only the self-satisfied or the selfish can believe the "fullness of life" philosphies of writers Santayana, Dinesen, or Ibanez.

The Anecdotal Opener

The anecdotal opener has been thought of as the best way to sustain reader interest. Stories per se have always carried an especial weight with readers, no matter what their age. Witness the fact that almost anyone can be intrigued with those familiar words of childhood: "Once upon a time..." With the anecdotal opener, you need not resort to that level of writing. But you certainly could use many of the elements of that popular style.

On the topic of "Predestination," admittedly a heavy subject, one writer began this way:

> When I was a boy, I used to sit on the back porch and wonder if God knew before I did that I was going to scratch my toe.

In profiling a neighbor, one girl wrote:

> There is a little white-haired lady who digs up crab grass in her yard across from us. One day as I passed, she stood up and hollered at me.

Then, there was this "grabber":

> One afternoon, a car drove up in the Square and out stepped Uncle Mike. The car was a 1923 Rolls-Royce, and he informed us he had just bought it for $25 from a breathless man who said he only used it to drive to church.

The Metaphorical Opener

The student desperate to use openers involving similes and metaphors must recognize that they present difficulties. Similes and metaphors are vidid shorthand all right, but they need a colorful and *original* comparison of one thing to another. Students too often go "over the top" or are stumped for something fresh. Thus, eyes are limpid pools. Men are Herculean. Machinery sounds like the roar of the sea. Heroines are like angels.

This is not to say that you should avoid such openers, but you had better be as creative as the student who wrote on "War" with mood and imagery:

> War with its rotting corpses, agonized screams of the wounded, acrid smoke of gunpowder, and terrors of the conquered is seen as a necessity by the philosopher George Santayana in his essay "Tipperary."

Here's a metaphorical opener:

> The faithlessness shown by an Anna Karenina is the Rorschach ink stain on civilized society.

Another student used *Don Quixote*, the Spanish novel, from which he sketched the ideal spouse:

> A wife should be a Rosinante. Although she was not much on looks or health, the loyal steed required little food, little care, little love, and illustrates the qualities of my prospective mate.

Once you seize the reader's attention by an engaging, even daring or provocative opening sentence such as the above, use the rest of the paragraph to provide the composition's overall content. It should be a summation of what will follow.

An explanatory composition needs a sentence or two *after* the opener to explain the topic's scope. Such a sentence may serve as the second in that opener, or it may lead into the second paragraph of the opening *section*.

In a descriptive composition, include a sentence after the *initial* one indicating what's to be described. Readers like to know whether they're to swelter in the Gobi desert or freeze in McMurdo Sound. Or about to read a profile.

For argumentative writing, the reader should be given the topic and your position at the outset. The opening sentence should be both direct and clear. Play fair. Don't be vague or tricky. Readers hate games and are likely to be annoyed with those who believe in a "clever" approach.

Don't use satire in *any* opening sentence or paragraph unless readers know its foundation; otherwise, they'll take you seriously—and react with fury to your cleverness. Famed humor columnist Art Buchwald learned that when he tried to lighten the witch-hunting atmosphere of the 1960s by declaring, tongue-in-cheek, that J. Edgar Hoover, the much-feared FBI director, was a mythical man created to frighten the Bureau's enemies. The column *did* trigger laughter up and down the country from those unhappy with Hoover, but readers unfamiliar with Buchwald's work took him seriously. Doubtless, the proud and humorless Director assigned agents to watch him even when reminded that the columnist had complained he was not on president Nixon's celebrated "enemies list." Serious people do not like to be fooled.

Linking opening sentences to the rest of the initial paragraph is shown in the next examples. Notice that the first sentences are the "hook" of the opening paragraph, designed to intrigue readers into rest of the compositions. The remaining sentences reveal the topic's gist.

The first sample is in the category of argumentative themes and uses a humorous approach to a serious subject:

> Just because Polonius pocketed Hamlet's love letters to Ophelia is no reason to criticize the mail service at Elsinore Castle or anywhere else. A post office is the nerve center of communications in every community and should not be involved in any kind of suppressive act by a governmental leader even when complaints rise about poor service.

Here's the rest of that anecdotal opener, which was attached to a descriptive composition:

> There is a little white-haired lady who digs up crab grass in her yard across from us. One day as I passed, she stood up and hollered at me. But then that was Mrs. Smith's way of inviting us to a party.

The explanatory piece that opened with a startling statement or fact continued this way:

> No matter what The Bible says, vengeance by man is often justified and often sweet. If this weren't so, there wouldn't be almost a murder a minute in the world, half of which are said to be vendetta killings. States wouldn't have capital punishment either if vengeance weren't in the minds of most of the lawmakers and citizens who continue to break The Bible's injunction about vengeance being a province of the Lord.

In each case, the sentences following the openers gave broad hints of the subject matter.

Some writers use a second short paragraph to spell out the issues or terms to be contained in the topic:

> A gerrymander is a slicing of voting areas into districts favorable to one political party.

The second paragraph could be used to explain the need for a reader to know something about the subject:

> Because rabies can strike anyone, people must know how to deal with this disease.

The second paragraph also can point up some recent event that makes the topic timely or important:

> The European Union and the NAFTA trade agreement may put Americans out of millions of jobs eventually, so we must know about both things.

Equally, the second paragraph could tell the reader about the limitations or the scope of the composition:

> Only the hidden charges in time payments will be dealt with.

Or it could be a paragraph explaining how the topic will be handled:

> We will move from the Head Start program to the AmeriCorps.

The points to be covered may be detailed so the reader will know what to expect:

> We must look at the financing, the use, the criticism, the praise, and the ultimate goals of creating a public utility district.

In short, if you decide to use a second paragraph to expand the opening paragraph, write a brief summary of the content. However, with in-class writing, you'll have little time to stretch the beginning to more than two paragraphs.

ARGUMENTATIVE WRITING

The first type of composition to be dealt with in this book is the argumentative piece. Its aim is to convince a reader about something. You might write, for example, on why you think Shakespeare's King Lear is *not* mad. Or why ethanol is a better fuel for cars and the environment than gas. Or why 18-year-olds—men *and* women—should be drafted to serve their community for two years.

Within the argumentative classification are abstract topics, the most common type of subjects assigned. Who doesn't remember topics like "Patriotism," "Friendship," "Humor," and "Duty"? Abstract topics are included in the argumentative category because students usually produce meatier writing if they can argue both the pro *and* con sides of a topic. Working through the advantages and disadvantages of, say, "Duty" or "Friendship," you'll suddenly have plenty to say instead of platitudes (e.g., "Duty is important." "Friendship is wonderful," etc.).

General Topics

The general argumentative topic asks you to surrender your beliefs about an aspect of a subject. One such topic might be this:

> Critics of the play *Our Town* have called the plot sickeningly sweet and dramatically boring. They have called the characters dull and indistinguishable, comparing them to the weakest characters in other American plays. Do you agree with these critics?

Because *Our Town* is sacrosanct in many classrooms, such a topic should provoke strong views. Another evocative topic might be:

> Much criticism has been voiced lately about the method of drafting people into the Army. Do you feel this criticism is merited?

The assignment's wording might be brief, but this topic invites argument when comparisons involve various states:

> Does the American prison system do its job of reforming criminals?

Whether wording is long or short or left open for interpretation, all such topics are designed to pull views from you.

Once you've been given such a topic, it should provide a lot of material for a jot outline. Let's use the *Our Town* topic as an example of how to work up a fast outline. Even if you're not familiar with this play, you'll be able to follow the instructions.

The topic gives you *two* factors to emphasize in the composition: the plot (sickeningly sweet and boring), and the characters (dull and indistinguishable). As you make your jottings, use specific events either from the play or, if you don't know it, from your own experiences to support every point you make. You could also jot down specifics from other plays. Movies and television dramas also qualify as examples.

Once you've made the jottings, put them in some kind of order. Any system that works for you—numbers, circles, letters, checks—is the one to use. You may not use every item you've jotted down, but that's to be expected. Your finished outline may resemble this sophomore's jottings:

open

Plot
   sweet—(no—like all towns—Winesburg
   boring—(no—drunk, wedding, choir,
                     funeral

char
   dull (who isn't—Emily to Excedrin
   indis.(is about town so not need
                  vivid characters—no unity
              if peop. emphasized

end
   critics wrong

A student's jottings on the prison-system topic—and the order used—looked like this:

One student shaped the jot outline for the draft topic this way:

As has been said, use whatever jotting form and organizing system works for you.

Don't be surprised if you change your mind on the order or even the items making up your content. You may have overlooked items or suddenly thought of others. With a jot outline, such shifts and additions/deletions require only a few strokes of your pen.

Introduction

Your first sentence (the opener) may use humor or the startling statement, but the sentences that follow that first paragraph must indicate what the subject is and your viewpoint. You might include the composition's scope, telling the reader you're going to touch only the high spots or only *one* part of a major topic. If you're writing on such gigantic topics as, say, religion, electronics, safety, war or the like, you'll only be able to handle one or two phases of the subject. Classroom compositions or even short essay tests usually average two or three pages so it's doubtful you'll do much more than scratch the surface of *any* topic. Even when you have the luxury of writing at home and access to Internet sources, it's doubtful whether any teacher will expect a mini-term paper.

In that opener, explain the "who" or the "what" of the topic or the topical reference (the "peg") on which the composition hangs. Is it based on a book, a play, politics, religion, sociology or other fields?

How one student handled the start on the *Our Town* topic is shown in the next example. In it, he took the first two sentences from the topic itself and included his viewpoint:

> Critics of the play *Our Town* have called the plot sickeningly sweet and dramatically boring. They have called the characters dull and indistinguishable, comparing them to the weakest characters in other American plays. Such critics obviously are unaware of the reasons why this Thornton Wilder drama has been popular for years all over the United States.

A beginning of another sort, this one on the draft, tied up the composition with an anecdotal opener built on a topical peg:

> When Congress passed the first conscription act on March 3, 1863, John Q. Workingclass rioted in New York City, causing no end of destruction to property and to lives. That law didn't specify whether he was a family man or a bachelor, whether he was 20, 30, or 45. He didn't have $300 to stall off service until the next call-up. And he could hardly hire a stand-in as the rich could and did. Every time this country has set up a draft, the same inequities turn up.

Another student wanted no reader to have difficulty understanding the topic. She also knew how to arrest immediate attention:

> The American prison system today may have institutions similar to Arkansas where whipping is permitted, but it also has enlightened institutions such as in California where men may work at downtown jobs and take job-training courses. Prisons are not all bad in this country.

Nevertheless, don't employ an opener that assumes the reader already knows the topic:

> No, I don't believe the critics are right about *Our Town*.

A beginning paragraph should be able to stand by itself and not hint that it answers only assigned topics. It should leave no doubt as to what the topic is and briefly explain the issues.

What Comes After the First Paragraph

Once you have completed the beginning of the composition, put in a short paragraph that summarizes the reasons or, in debating terms, the "case points," for your conclusions on the overall topic. In other words, itemize the points you are going to make in subsequent paragraphs.

In a take-home assignment, a graduate student's opening paragraph was followed by one that set out four case points that would get elaboration in subsequent paragraphs—and in the order listed in that second paragraph:

> Congress passed the first conscription act on March 3, 1863. In New York City, the first 1,200 numbers were drawn and the names published July 11, just a few days after Gettysburg. The law didn't distinguish between family men or bachelors and included those from 20 to 45. The rich could hire stand-ins or pay the "commutation fee" that enabled them to be passed over until the next call-up. The Irish immigrants were the hardest hit and the most angry. On one hand, they feared blacks fleeing the South would take their jobs. On the other, blacks weren't subject to the draft in a war supposedly to free them. The result was a three-day riot (July 13–15) against police, soldiers, and blacks, $1,500,000 in property damage and 100–1,500 deaths (depending on white or black sources).
>
> Each time this country resorts to the draft, howls about unfairness go up. Too many are exempted from service, in the first place. Secondly, the draft obviously interrupts lives at an important stage. The draft also has been seen as a means to solve unemployment and falls particularly hard on the poor and ignorant.

A second paragraph's summary listing is a great organizational aid because the student knew she would first deal with draft exemptions. Then, the interruption to lives, followed by unemployment and financial inequities.

Now, the paragraph containing the case points doesn't have to be that long, as another student shows in pro-and-con organization:

> Each summer, our community becomes vibrant and violent—not about world affairs or even the fees charged for dog licenses. Like so many other towns across the face of America, my town is caught up in the throes of something called Little League, that baseball circuit for pre-teeny boppers.
>
> Little League *does* teach the game, prevents delinquency, provides fun, but it can be expensive and exclusive. It also teaches competitiveness at too early an age.

The itemization paragraph is emphasized here because it's a guide for the rest of the composition. Make certain when you set up the "case," as you'll be doing in the paragraph after the introduction, that you put the most important points of the topic *first*. What's important is always a matter of opinion, but many times the most telling points of a topic are obvious to any reader who certainly will notice those you failed to include. Aside from this, if you deal with the most important points of a topic first, you'll get them all into the piece before the class bell rings.

What About the Rest of the Composition?

You're ready to roll once you get past 1) the beginning paragraph and 2) the itemization paragraph. From here on, you'll find it relatively easy. Briefly, you'll use one paragraph for each case point. If you were to do the Little League topic, based on the points the writer used above, you would develop a paragraph on the fact that the League teaches baseball fundamentals.

The next paragraph would take up the argument that the League prevents delinquency. The paragraph after that would deal with the fun this organization offers. Following that, would be a paragraph on the fact the League is expensive, then a paragraph on its exclusiveness. The last paragraph would be on the ills of teaching competitiveness at too early an age. Some might add a paragraph on overprotective parents attempting to control coaches and participants.

A simple diagram shows how easy it is to construct each paragraph. Bear in mind that you may use more than one paragraph per case point, but here we're treating the basic organization of the argumentative composition. Embellishments can be added as you gain speed and ease using this composition method.

By paragraphs, the Little League piece would be constructed like this:

Paragraph No. 1	Beginning
Paragraph No. 2	Listing Case Points
Paragraph No. 3	Case Point 1 (teaches game)
Paragraph No. 4	Case Point 2 (prevents delinquency)
Paragraph No. 5	Case Point 3 (offers fun)
Paragraph No. 6	Case Point 4 (expensive)
Paragraph No. 7	Case Point 5 (exclusive)
Paragraph No. 8	Case Point 6 (too competitive)
Paragraph No. 9	Ending

Let's try the same thing with the draft topic. Select the paragraph where the writer presents the case points and number each. Then, set them up for the composition as a whole. Numbering the case points will be in prose, of course, not actual numbers. Examine the following:

> There are four chief drawbacks to the Selective Service system used in the past. Too many are exempted from service, in the first place. Secondly, the draft interrupts life at an important stage. The draft also has been used as a weapon to silence critics of Administration policies, and, in addition, it is a system particularly hard on the poor. But each of these charges can be countered.

The pattern of her composition in those "boxes" would be:

Paragraph No. 1	Beginning
Paragraph No. 2	Listing Case Points
Paragraph No. 3	Case Point 1 (exemptions)
Paragraph No. 4	Case Point 2 (breaks up life)
Paragraph No. 5	Case Point 3 (hard on poor)
Paragraph No. 6	Case Point 4 (used as weapon)

Paragraph No. 7	Case Point 5 (necessary exemptions)
Paragraph No. 8	Case Point 6 (should defend country)
Paragraph No. 9	Case Point 7 (Army gives training)
Paragraph No. 10	Case Point 8 (other systems worse)
Paragraph No. 11	Ending

Once again, this is just a basic one-idea-per-paragraph structure. Many students probably would use two or more paragraphs for each case point. The setup for the words within each paragraph is an easy one to learn. You merely repeat the case point in the first sentence. All other sentences must involve proving that case-point statement. That means specific examples—statistics, facts, anecdotes, and the like. A *specific* example uses names of people, places, and things as well as dates, statistics and identifiable facts. If you diagrammed the paragraph, it would look something like this:

Case Point { The draft system used in the past is hard on the poor, for the most part. The Congressional committee

Example { which did a study on the selective service system reported that 75 percent of the men drafted between 1962 and 1963 were from families whose total income was less than $3000 a year.

That first sentence of the paragraph in which the writer restates the case point can be simple, as it is above, or complex. As long as the case-point statement is made, it does not matter.

Here's another simple starting sentence, followed by the specific example— also simple:

Case Point { Prisons are cruel sometimes. *The Nation*

Examples { magazine recently reported that only about 10 U.S. prisons were without some form of beating of inmates.

An even simpler one is:

Case Point { Little League teams teach good baseball.

Examples { Pitcher Bruce Sutter rates them as best for teaching kids the fundamentals.

A complex case point—statement underpinned by example—is:

Case Point	The ethics of the business community in the 1980s were as bad as today or in the robber baron days of McKinley's presidency from 1896–1900 or when Harding was in the White House during the Roaring Twenties. In the 1980s, 12 savings and loan associations in California were accused of bribing a U.S. senator for a favorable vote on a savings-and-loan bill. Eight executives from both Westinghouse and General Electric were convicted of price rigging on electrical equipment sold to the government.
Examples	In the early days of this century, stock-market scandals of proportions far beyond the 1929 Crash wiped out workers' pensions and jobs. It was small comfort to see big-business manipulators whose million-dollar gains were well hidden, hauled off in handcuffs or, after being convicted in lengthy and expensive trials, sent to minimum-security prisons that had golf courses or house arrest for a year or two. In Portland, Oregon, one executive's company paid his six-figure salary for the 18-month jail sentence and voted him a $2,000,000 bonus that exactly fit the court's ruling for restitution to investors. At least these scandals ended most people's belief that moving their Social Security deposits to stocks and bonds—and even the supposedly safe mutual funds—would guarantee a secure old age.

Whatever your style—simple or complex—the structure for each case point is: 1) the case-point statement, 2) a *specific* example(s) to underpin that statement. As shown above, you can take more than one paragraph to finish off a case point. But don't overdo if you expect to cover all the case points under a writing deadline.

Examples to be Used

Obviously, the example must illustrate the case-point statement. Most readers can spot examples that don't apply even if they're impressive.

While readers might agree with your case point, they may well view the supporting example as nonpertinent, weak, or exaggerated. That's always the peril of examples, but it shouldn't paralyze you from finding a strong and apt one.

Writers of exposés and newspaper crusades are often among those using examples that are exaggerated or one-of-a-kind. An extreme example is called "hyperbole." For instance, a reporter might seize upon finding rats in *one* hospital's kitchen and generalize this is the situation in most hospitals. A crusade against police brutality in jail wouldn't be complete without an example of one cop beating up a handcuffed suspect despite exemplary behavior at the stationhouse.

The use of hyperboles is effective in calling attention to something that's amiss or it wouldn't be traditional in generations of journalists. But whoever grades your work may well conclude that one shattering example scarcely represents the *total* picture.

So if you plan to use hyperboles, be careful. The best course is to lead off with a hyperbole, note that it's a singular situation, and follow it with more typical examples to illustrate a case point. You'll get the reader's attention and be considered fair.

In all examples, be accurate. And don't lift quotations out of context like those promotional blurbs for films or books which might say, "...one of the best films of the year" though the original review that panned it said: "This is not one of the best films of the year." Don't twist statistics to suit your beliefs. Don't make mistakes on dates or facts—not even with in-class compositions.

Too, never forget that some of your source materials aren't holy writ, particularly if they're off the Internet. All search engines are selling their services to organizations who, in turn, want to sell you something—as pop-up or site advertising indicates. Though you might be writing a homework assignment, only the gullible or lazy fail to consider sources just because they're on the Internet. Statistics on organized labor will be far different in a union paper than in the local daily newspaper or magazines such as *FORTUNE* or *Business Week*. Facts on civil rights will be different in *TIME* magazine from those in many Southern publications. Cross-check your sources. Your instructor may put a tart comment about a flawed source and your researching skills.

Even if you're desperate for an example, don't manufacture one. You might be caught by an eagle-eyed, whip-smart instructor who for the rest of the term will draw suspicious conclusions about your honesty—and put your name on the faculty grapevine.

The Ending

Until you develop skill in endings, stick to one or two methods. One way is to summarize the chief arguments or case points you have covered. Tell readers what you've told them, in short. Rephrase your case-point statements. Another kind of ending involves a general statement summing up your position. It's the easier method of the two forms.

Using the *Our Town* topic again, you might handle an ending as did this student, listing the major arguments:

> It has been seen, then, that *Our Town* is not sweet or boring so far as plot is concerned because the play echoes life in a small town. The birth-death cycle gives it lots of action. Perhaps the characters *were* dull and stereotyped, but ordinary people are usually a little dull anyway. If the playwright had singled out every character for emphasis, he would have had to write a play that would last for weeks. He was trying to portray a town as a whole and this he succeeded in doing.

Ending with a general statement covering all corners of the composition might be:

> The naïve playgoer can't help finding charm and small-town naturalism in *Our Town*. That's why we hicks enjoy it so much.

Above all, be brief—no more than one or two *short* paragraphs.

Don't worry if you don't have time to include an ending if you're writing an in-class composition. Few teachers expect that kind of polish. But they do if it's written at home. The ability to end a composition gracefully comes with practice.

Writing Style

The writing style varies for an argumentative composition, but it should be clear and cogent, and the tone fairly serious. If you use humor, be cautious. The humorous approach demands careful handling if it is to avoid offending the reader (principally your instructor) or falling flat.

Perhaps the best tone to adopt in argumentative writing is used in the newspapers. When opposing a case point, don't display anger or use sarcasm. Rather, be "concerned" or "disturbed" that "all the facts are not known" by those with opposing views. This makes you seem fair and open-minded. Let your examples do the talking and you won't have to shout, use exclamation points, or other overstated reactions. Borrow a tool from debate squads and remain cool as you lay out your case points.

It's well to use some choice connective words and "breather" passages as you move from one case point to another, as shown in the section on writing style. Readers may get lost otherwise. Giving them a helping "in addition" or "on the other hand" keeps them on track.

Abstract Topics

The way for you to tackle some all-encompassing or broad abstract topics such as "Discontent," "Courtesy," and "Laughter," is to argue both the pro and con sides. This is the form used by debating teams. You'll be organized and you will say something substantive. In other words, set up your topic on both the pro (or good) and con (or bad) basis. You'll think up those good and bad points about such abstract topics as "Laughter" (laughter is not always a good thing) or "Discontent" (discontent spearheads improvements), and the like.

Every subject *does* have two sides, as anyone in the law profession can attest. On abstract topics, you can use this dynamic as a means by which to expand a portion of any subject.

For the jot outline on abstract topics, split your case points on the "half-and-half" or the "side-by-side" structure. In the half-and-half system, half of the composition will take up one side of the topic (perhaps the pro). The other half involves the opposite view. With the side-by-side order, you give one pro case point and follow it with the con concerning that point. You'll proceed through your composition in this fashion—a pro balanced by a con, a pro balanced by a con, a pro balanced by a con, and so on. Or the structure could be a con balanced by a pro.

Start off with the half-and-half structure. This order will keep your thinking clear and is the easiest way to tackle abstract themes. A diagram would look like this:

Paragraph No. 1	Beginning
Paragraph No. 2	List of Pro Points; List of Con Points
Paragraph No. 3	Con Point No. 1

Paragraph No. 4	Con Point No. 2
Paragraph No. 5	Con Point No. 3
Paragraph No. 6	Con Point No. 4
Paragraph No. 7	Pro Point No. 1
Paragraph No. 8	Pro Point No. 2
Paragraph No. 9	Pro Point No. 3
Paragraph No. 10	Pro Point No. 4
Paragraph No. 11	Ending

If you look at the example above, you'll see that the idea is to take four case points and to argue the con side of *each* during the *first* part of the composition; then, to argue the pro side in the last portion. For example, on the abstract topic of "Nature," here's the way one student built his jot:

Pro	Con
beautiful - New Eng. spring	not beau. - floods, etc.
unconquerable - DDT	not conq. - Salk vaccine
intelligent - survival of fittest	not intel. - breaks line

Or a piece might be developed along the lines of this writer who outlined the disadvantages and advantages for the topic of "Poverty":

disad	adv.
causes disease (N.Y.)	wealthy sick
" discontent (Watts)	doesn't always cause dis. (Denver)
" ignorance (Chicago)	" " " ign. (Lincoln)
kills spirit (Watts)	" " kill sp. (L. B. Mayer)
" morals (drugs, D.C.)	" " " morals (Levenson)
lowers tax base (N.Y. LA)	slumlords still pay taxes

Note that the outline above has six case points for the con side, six for the pro. But five of the points match pro with con. If you were to write on "Poverty" with the side-by-side structure, the jot outline's boxes might look like the example below:

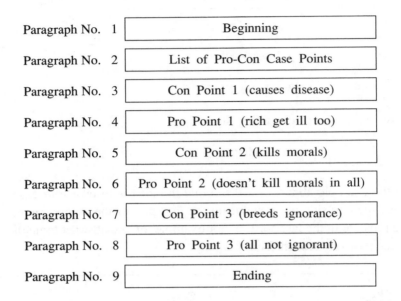

Paragraph No. 1	Beginning
Paragraph No. 2	List of Pro-Con Case Points
Paragraph No. 3	Con Point 1 (causes disease)
Paragraph No. 4	Pro Point 1 (rich get ill too)
Paragraph No. 5	Con Point 2 (kills morals)
Paragraph No. 6	Pro Point 2 (doesn't kill morals in all)
Paragraph No. 7	Con Point 3 (breeds ignorance)
Paragraph No. 8	Pro Point 3 (all not ignorant)
Paragraph No. 9	Ending

In both the half-and-half and side-by-side structures for abstract topics, the case points have been paired by pros and cons. That's because most students find this structure the easiest and quickest way to write an argumentative composition. With two or three basic contentions, you can get four to six case points simply by writing *first* about the pro and then matching it with the con. You don't have to pair contentions, however. You can bring up three or four *pro* case points and follow them with three or four other *con* points that aren't related to the pro. But to do that, you must stick to the half-and-half structure.

Of the two structures, which is better?

To decide this, consider what some call people's "forgetter," the mind's way of shutting off information overload. Even if the first part of what they see or hear is brilliant, much of it won't be remembered by the time a speaker or writer finishes. That explains why some speakers repeat main points in their closing remarks. Lawyers certainly keep this in mind when addressing jurors at the start of a trial and in their "close." Textbook writers try to do the same thing, usually under a subtitle of "Summary." Not for nothing do political candidates jockey to be the last speaker in a forum.

So keep the readers' "forgetter" in mind when you write an argumentative composition.

Take advantage of the "last word" when you're not sure which side of the case to put first—the pro or the con. If you want to convince the reader that the con side is right, put it *after* the pro. If you're supporting the pro side of an issue, ensure that the pro case points come *after* the con.

The openers with the case-point listings and endings are much the same as for the general argumentative form of writing.

The paragraphs that carry the pro and con case points should be set up the same way as those for general argumentative writing. Make the case-point statement in the first sentence of the paragraph and then support it with sentences including the example(s).

Follow the advice given on general topics also because it concerns selection of examples, the tone of your language, the use of humor, and good connective words and phrases. Again, be sure you put the most important case points *first*. In classroom writing, you'll at least have some meaty content on paper if the class bell rings before you get to the other points.

Other pointers for this type of writing need to be mentioned.

If you are to argue well, always anticipate the arguments of the *opposing* side. Whoever reads your composition (especially someone who knows the subject) will wonder why you overlooked an argument crucial to the subject. It's far better to confront a damaging argument than to ignore it. Besides, dealing with such a point will add substance to your composition. You may have to do a lot of thinking to mount a pro argument to a strong con argument, but nothing is impossible for the resourceful student.

Pitfalls

In both types of argumentative compositions—general and abstract—two pitfalls await you. One is the use of syllogistic reasoning; the other is the use of the "either/or" type of black-and-white logic. The two pitfalls are closely related and are indicators of closed minds afraid to venture far from home.

A syllogism is based on a conclusion following a general truth. If the "truth" is sound, in other words, the conclusion seemingly *must* be true. Sounds good, but it's hopelessly flawed. For example, one could reason that every virtue is laudable; kindness is a virtue; therefore, kindness is laudable. But is kindness *always* laudable when it keeps someone from facing responsibilities ("enabling")?

Amusing truths emerge if you carry syllogistic logic to the extreme. For instance, most dogs like most people; most people like television; therefore, most dogs like television. Equally, one could say that the world is round; people are part of the world; so people must be round. Do you now see the folly of this kind of logic?

The either/or type of thinking is far more common in student writing and the general public than syllogisms. In times of crises, we hear leaders—whether of nations or mobs—declare "you're either with us or against us" in an attempt to stampede people into some violent and/or questionable action. Those who refuse to be rushed to judgment are branded cowards or, too often, enemies of a village or nation.

This kind of simplistic reasoning is the concrete bunker of the insecure who fear their position might be undermined if they considered the vast world of grays between black-and-white thinking. Besides, decisiveness is usually held up as an ideal whether it's on the battlefield, in business, or household—unless it results in disaster; then, it's called rash judgment.

Some examples of student writing in either/or logic are these:

We are either going to have war, or we are going to have peace.

Or

Man must make up his mind that if he is not pursuing capitalism, he is following communism.

Or

If he's not working, he must be playing.

Is there sound logic in these examples? Not even writing under deadline pressure in the classroom can excuse the fact that decades of coexistence between the United States and the Soviet Union/Russia have shown that a vast terrain exists between peace and war. Or that much ground is open between capitalism and communism. Or that work sometimes *is* play.

A sure way to avoid this simplistic thinking is to beware of sweeping statements or those black-and-white judgment calls. School is designed to broaden your horizons about life and the world. So show that in your writing.

Sample Argumentative Composition

A complete argumentative composition follows that was written in side-by-side structure by a graduate school student:

Term Papers: Why Neither Plagiarism Nor Copy/Paste Matters

I could hardly believe the headline:

Nearly 40 percent in college cheat off Web, survey finds

The reason I could hardly believe it was that 40 percent seemed so low because the story was about term papers and they interviewed 18,000 students at 23 colleges. Must have been 23 colleges on the honor system out in the boonies, I thought, because here it must be 80 percent. We have four colleges, two universities, two community colleges with three campuses apiece and fifteen high schools. A dozen are church schools, supposedly where morality and ethics are prized.

I figure the term-paper industry makes a killing off 40 percent of the students. The other 40 percent are experts at copying/pasting papers straight off the Net—which means fortunes are being made at the end of terms off subscribers to Comcast or AOL or EarthLink. (You thought it was their new features? Price deals?) The only thing that's remotely worrisome to these kids, I know by their mutterings, is fear of messing up on style in footnotes or bibliographies because some professors dock grades for such travesties. If they book early, though, they can always hire some English major to fix those.

So how come teachers still assign term papers if 80% of those who do them have paid $150 or more for a local nerd's handiwork ($50 off the Net to Term-Papers-R-Us) or turn in the same kind of copy job thrown together the night before deadline by the desperate in junior high?

The rationale is three-pronged. First, term papers offers the opportunity to do some scholarly investigations. Second, those in-depth efforts are supposed to compensate those terrified of reciting—if that's a healthy part of a grade, especially in a seminar or small class. Those who do poorly on tests also get a break. Last, those tomes are supposed to awaken our intellectual curiosity and teach us something that's not in lecture or the textbook.

One reason is that we need to do in-depth stuff in addition to the readings and lectures. Tell that to the Greeks. The only in-depth stuff many in Sigma Phi Nothing have done is reach into house files to thumb through 30 years of term papers to find one ripe for resurrection. Or into billfolds to pay some drone or girl friend to do the job (I know some Moms who'd still do it free just to see that A on the title page). As to the search-engine jocks, "in-depth" research to them is finding a new source before the faculty FBI grapevine does. Even non-Greeks are smart enough to know that a first-day, in-class bit of writing furnishes the prof with style samples that better match what turns up in a term paper.

Yet there's that 20-percent factor made up of grinds and inveterate investigators. They *want* to do in-depth digging! Demand it, in fact! They insist that research is the heart of a university education and the library holdings better be up to snuff or Interlibrary Loan offer one-day service. Not for them just lectures, readings, or weekly interrogations by razor-tongued know-it-alls who publish monthly in at least three peer-reviewed journals here and abroad. You'll never hear groans out of them about a 15-pound $100 textbook and a dozen outside books from which midterms and finals are drawn. They're the only ones in class who don't moan when they see a term paper on the syllabus.

At one institution across town where the GPA is nearly 3.90 and Rhodes scholarships are obscenely common, one new prof feared for her job when *sotto-voce* grumblings of "thin-thin-thin!" greeted her cheery first-day remark of "No term paper in here, Class!" One prof who teaches an on-line chemistry class was overheard griping to another at Starbucks that a clutch of them threatened bad evals because of his slow response to e-mails about mistakes in the text and his poor construction and quality of test questions.

Another reason given for assigning term papers is that students doing poorly in recitations or tests can strut their stuff in research upon which hangs 10–20 percent of the grade. But what about those who can't write a lick, and come up with a paste job a frat brother at far-off LSU bought in the bustling Baton Rouge term-paper mill? That was my roommate, a broadcast major who sweat tacks when his prof grilled him mercilessly about why, if his topic was supposed to be current, all his sources were drawn from the 1970's? Huh? Huh? Only his gift of gab saved him. But the gimlet gaze and a D on the paper will have him hunting for ghostwriters until graduation.

However, there's that 20% factor again. Last term, when I carried 16 hours, three out of those four classes gave from 10–15 percent of the grade for a term paper. That was a relief because I'm a writer and a pretty fair "digger," thanks to a lifetime spent carefully cultivating that talent in compensation for being a tongue-tied, rotten test taker.

Last, those professors and high school teachers making the last stand for assigning term papers tend to argue that curiosity is awakened in the young whose Bunsen burners will be fired up one day to spend 17 years on the monumental discovery leading to a Nobel Prize in physics or the Pulitzer in history. But how is this possible, I ask, when most of my classmates either aren't up to the rigors of such small-scale "scholarly endeavor," or their class schedules are overbooked to maintain a scholarship or to keep pace with student loans off a 40-hour workweek? Most will never use this experience to get a graduate degree, the area where research gets more credit hours than courses—

at least at the doctoral level. Unfortunately, for decades at this school and others at the master's level, while Plan A involves 36 hours of course work and a thesis, Plan B—the choice of 95%—involves 48 hours of course work and *no* thesis.

Yet it is those few whose Bunsen burners *are* ignited by term papers who get all the benefits of a term paper, who become addicted to the hunt for the unknown. They will make the world-shattering breakthroughs to improve life or, at least, to make it more interesting. It is for them that teachers are willing to give round-the-clock attention the week *before* Dead Week, all of Dead Week and sometimes the week *after* Dead Week. They would rather be dead than to paste, plagiarize or resurrect anyone's Lazarus.

Faculty devotion springs from expectations of being the first to read, say, the fledgling findings of a Linus Pauling in physics, an Allan Nevins in history, a Robert Carlson in medicine, a Caroline Spurgeon in literature, or a Marcus Borg in religion. Or knowing that the primary research of average students like me on accident patterns on Sandy Boulevard might change signal-light timing where traffic merges with Burnside Street—and save lives. They and I and others like me get the high of what a term paper is about: Learning something new. Or that breakthrough.

As to the 80%, they'll still be keeping the cottage industry of ghostwriters in cash and boosting egos on those A's and B's. Some might even feel so much guilt when Dad insists on showing off Jimmy's (or Jenny's) purloined paper at family gatherings, they'll swear off these cheat sheets forever. But for almost all, it may be the only piece of reading they do in the class. It's slightly better than nothing, but it's at least *something*. That's why it's important that term papers still be assigned—no matter how much copy/pasting or plagiarism goes on.

CHAPTER 4

DESCRIPTIVE WRITING

When students are assigned a descriptive topic, they ordinarily jump into the subject with little organization. They lay on the poetical allusions and leave incomplete portrayals by omitting important details. Or they focus too much detail on unimportant facets.

To keep from such confusion, a jot outline is a must.

True, descriptives permit creative writers to display their wares and command of prose. But a descriptive piece still requires some kind of order, an organization of features describing the place, the object, or the person.

The key is to work from the *most* important details to the *least* important.

You can work from the top to bottom of the subject (or vice versa), from left to right (or vice versa), or from back to front (or vice versa). The idea is to let your readers know exactly where they're supposed to be looking. They need a guide in written material, and that guide is you. If you are hard put to keep the view in focus, make a small diagram of the subject. Something tangible helps.

Again, the descriptive piece is a composition tailor-made for the creative writer. But even if you're *not* creative, your phrases can sing a little—and without your resorting to a thesaurus. It's not enough to say that Aunt Nellie is beautiful. You've got to illustrate that she is. You could liken her to something beautiful—a flower, a well-known person, or some geographic spectacle. Lead the reader from the known to the unknown with imagery. Imagery involves similes (Aunt Nellie is *like* a rose) or metaphors (Aunt Nellie *is* a rose).

While you're thinking of colorful descriptive terms, avoid trite figures of speech that are called *clichés* or *bromides* ("Her eyes were like diamonds," "She's pretty as a picture"). They are so stale they fail to speak to readers anymore. Many of the trite expressions students use are contained in the Writing Style chapter.

Another tool for good descriptive compositions is the phrase that leads you from one factor to another: connectives ("Behind the shed...," "Above the mountain...," To his left...," "It was fronted by..."). You'll need such expressions to glide smoothly from one element of the object to another.

However, abrupt descriptive jumps confuse readers. If you're moving from the outside to the inside of a cabin, for instance, don't suddenly write about the bed of daisies bordering the building without a link to, say, a spindle chair by the fireplace. One student describing her home's interior had her mother appear in the living room to invite a visitor to taste some Finnish bread in the kitchen. It provided a smooth and interesting transition from one room to another and a human touch.

Let's get specific now about the three major types of descriptive compositions: those on places, people, and things.

Description of Places

To describe places, you'll need that jot outline or a rough sketch.

The sketch should never take you more than five minutes, particularly if you're writing a classroom composition. If you love to dwell on details, you'll run out of time. Outside of class, you'll begin procrastinating. Just include the high spots because few readers savor hundreds of words on one small object of an overall scene. The sketch should keep you on track because at a glance you can pick out the most important items to be described. You'll ignore minor things.

One student with 50 minutes to describe his home, spent no more than three minutes on this sketch:

In handling description of a summer home, another student used this sketch:

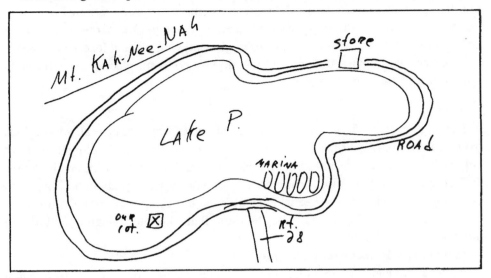

Believe it or not, a sketch will provide the organization of your piece.

In the opening paragraph, try to work people into your description. Give evidence of life, even if it's a discarded potato-chip bag or a smudge left by small fingers on frosty windows. Such touches bring warmth and interest to an otherwise static or dull scene.

Beginning Paragraphs

That opening paragraph should describe the overall scene or at least hint of the area to be portrayed. Reveal the location. And don't get too detailed ("Turn right at the fourth stoplight"). Locations can be indicated by skillful use of the weather, animals, trees (e.g., magnolias are not common in Maine), and so on.

The examples below show how some writers opened a work with descriptives:

The low, undulating Danish landscape was silent and serene, mysteriously wide awake in the hour before sunrise.

And:

The place where everybody would end up before going home was Barden's Drug Store. It was light, bright, and right on the square. A place where a kid could hang out, read a magazine, play the juke box, drown his troubles in Coke floats, and buy his mother a birthday card.

And:

People won't find St. George's Avenue on any city map now. As a result of the terrifying things that happened there, the street was changed to "Kenwood Avenue" by the City Council. It is a decomposing street of 10 Depression-era bungalows with grass unable to make headway against the cars and trucks rusting or resting on what used to be lawns and driveways lined with aspens. The stuccoed Lutheran church where the pastor terrified young and old has become a dance studio.

Or this example:

You can walk from one end of Old Heidelberg to the other and still never escape the musty smells that seep out of this German university town.

As you touch up the place with a few adjectives, ensure that comparisons are familiar to most readers (e.g., "The street is like a corpse," "Small boys came pouring out like ants driven by a hive queen"). If you get too exotic with similes and metaphors, you'll spoil the description by showing off and lose your reader.

Once you've finished the opener, how do you go about placing areas throughout the rest of the composition?

Body of the Composition

Here again, a sketch or outline on a separate piece of paper is vital. As you look over your artwork, the first thing to be decided is which item should get the most emphasis. If you're concentrating on a lake, that and not trees or mountains in the background should get most of the content. If you're writing about a village or a city neighborhood, check to see which part is the most important or the most interesting. If a house is the subject, find the room that's the most singular and devote most of your writing to it.

In other words, focus on *something*.

It's true that each element of a scene, a home, a city, a person may have *equal* worth. But to give the *same* emphasis to everything means that nothing stands out. The piece will be pallid. Good writing has focus. So don't set out one paragraph of equal length and quality to every part of the place being described. The chief aspect should get most of your paragraphs.

A descriptive piece allows you to put that key spot in *any* part of the composition except the opening paragraph. Many prefer to place it at the end as the high point of a journey. Others, especially under a classroom deadline, may use the half-way point and the remainder as "wind-down territory," much as fiction writers use rising and falling action. When you're under the push of a clock or dismissal bell, you can't save the best for last.

The outline below is a portrait of New York City in which the student believed the garment district deserved the most emphasis. He placed it in the middle of the composition:

Paragraph No. 1	Beginning
Paragraph No. 2	Board Bus (rapid transit system)
Paragraph No. 3	Upper Bronx Area
Paragraph No. 4	Colleges (CCNY, Columbia, etc.)
Paragraph No. 5	Harlem, Spanish Harlem
Paragraph No. 6	Central Park, Riverside Drive
Paragraph No. 7	Lincoln Center, RCA, Rockefeller, etc.
Paragraph No. 8	Garment District
Paragraph No. 9	Garment District

Paragraph No. 10	Garment District
Paragraph No. 11	Garment District
Paragraph No. 12	Garment District
Paragraph No. 13	Garment District
Paragraph No. 14	Theatre District, The Village, etc.
Paragraph No. 15	Shopping District
Paragraph No. 16	Financial District
Paragraph No. 17	Ending

A paragraph-by-paragraph examination of another student's description of her home, shows that she put her emphasis at the end:

Paragraph No. 1	Beginning (use Open House Party)
Paragraph No. 2	Landscaping at front of house
Paragraph No. 3	Living Room
Paragraph No. 4	Dining Room and Kitchen
Paragraph No. 5	Stairs and Hall to 2nd Floor
Paragraph No. 6	Parents' Room & Babies'
Paragraph No. 7	Bath and Stan's Room
Paragraph No. 8	Grandma's Room
Paragraph No. 9	My Room
Paragraph No. 10	My Room
Paragraph No. 11	My Room
Paragraph No. 12	My Room
Paragraph No. 13	My Room
Paragraph No. 14	Ending

It should be noted that this writer didn't feel it necessary to mention every nook and cranny of her house. She dealt only with the grounds at the front, omitted the basement, closets, and other areas she believed were of no major importance.

In both examples above, the writers used unifying elements by which to guide readers: a bus ride, an open-house party. Unifying forms are everywhere and are as common as a cat's daily ramble through a house or a portrait of a great-grandmother, from worn shoes and arthritic fingers grasping a walker to the still-twinkling green eyes.

Some student writers are highly creative. This writer has seen them use trappers arriving on the scene to describe a camp, soldiers marching into Rome's Forum, a T-cell's chase of a cancer cell through the lymphatic system, a footsore salesman making his way through an English village, and a TV camera's view of cheerleaders in action. Not only did the unifying element strengthen the piece, but it gave life to what was being described.

Some ways of bringing life to a place shouldn't be difficult to find. Orange peelings on the floor of a theater, notches on a tree, a doll carriage left by a well, and the like have livened many a composition.

How one student handled it is shown below:

> This part of the living room has suffered and rejoiced from the hardwood floors to the beamed ceiling. It's at the piano by the wall where my two sisters wailed—they called it singing—and warbled when they took lessons. And it's where we used to all gather around Saturday nights while Mother played jazz and we sang Christmas carols when my brother Ben came home from the war.

Or take this example:

> The bathroom is where my dad sings, shaves, reads, and practices those speeches for Kiwanis.

And then there is this one:

> The stones here are flat and smooth. The Sisters say it is because the Pilgrims stooped to kiss the ground, but I have seen the flood waters come to that part of town each spring when the mountains were done with the moisture.

Endings

The ending should do justice to all your time and effort spent on the assignment. Don't get near the old close of "as-the-sun-sinks-slowly-in-the-West-we-leave-colorful-Tahiti" of the travelogue. Instead, use a room, a piece of furniture, a person, or some event that captures the *total* mood or atmosphere of the place. One student used poetic imagery:

> When the dusk enfolds the scene with a gray mantle, the lakes wait for the moon to light their fire-like waters.

If you're more practical than poetic, you'll appreciate this example:

> Someday, car collectors will discover that spiffy 1936 Graham-Paige is worth more than $9,000. Until then, it'll stay in the barn up on blocks.

Or one with the human element and some intrigue:

> The fire hid the date of his birth on the wooden chest, the same date that Fullerton fled the same house to escape the mob's wrath.

Description of Objects

To describe objects, follow the same basic instructions as those for describing places, but add factors to them. For example, in the opening paragraph(s), describe the object as a *whole* and include its *purpose* or *significance*, like this:

> A word-processing program can bring joy, laughter, fury, and tears. It's used for emails informing you you've just won the Creepies breakfast food jingle contest and have two weeks of vacation coming in South Bend, Indiana. It's used to send and receive messages from a significant other who likes to send jokes or articles or steamy messages. It's also used to alert you that you're late on credit-card payments ("and unless you contact us immediately...") or annoy you with 150 missives from spammers who are geniuses at coining greetings likely to conceal worms or viruses or items that could get you fired at work or barred from the school library and suspended.

Another student's approach was simpler:

> A J-bar tow is shaped like the letter *J* in steel and when attached to a cable, it pulls you to the top of the mountain where you can ski down—only to get right back on the J-bar tow again.

Once again, inject a human element into the object described. A staircase, for example, might be worn down by generations of use. A desk might have significant carvings or scratchings—or a secret drawer. A jewel might have been cursed and caused deaths.

Humor is certainly permissible if it's not overdone. Wit, lively quotes, or funny stories are never out of place in any kind of descriptive composition so long as they are in good taste and truly illustrative. Perhaps a humorous incident has been connected with the item's invention or use.

The ending of a descriptive piece should avoid the exit that runs something like: "And so now all is known about the sewing machine." You may think of many endings as you gain experience in writing, but one of the best has the object being put to use. One student wrote:

> With a whir, the sleeping computer stirs and the screensaver comes to life.

Another writer wound up with:

> The fishing rod is raised and whipped into the stream, poised for another day's catch.

Description of People

Compositions describing people usually fall into three categories. One is the employee-documentation kind. Another is a simple characterization. The third is a profile.

A descriptive composition does not have to be an adjective-laden or poetic portrait of someone, nor an opus aimed at winning a literary prize. The most widespread and everyday use of this kind of writing in the outside world is *documentation*—in the workplace, on research projects, complaints, accident reports, and the like. The structure is almost always chronological—deed by deed, quote by quote—so that outsiders can reach a verdict on a person or situation. Bosses are taught *not* to insert their opinion. Those are good guidelines to follow because the *reader* is permitted to judge that person by their words and deeds.

Documenting someone is a form of writing you (and everyone else) can do and *will be doing* many times in your lifetime. All it takes is chronological order, honesty, fairness and *scrupulous* accuracy on quotes.

The Characterization

Characterizations deal with personality qualities or quirks. When asked in compositions and essay tests to contrast or compare someone, the emphasis is on what that person *does* or the traits, not about physical looks or a biography. Characteristics might involve cruelty, carelessness, kindness, patience, lovability, a sense of humor (or lack of one), and the like. When you characterize, be sure that the traits cited are fairly common with that person. A selfish person can't be characterized as kind for a single lapse of generosity.

The jot outline for characterizations is simple, as the following example demonstrates on *Everyman*, the leading actor in the medieval morality play by the same name:

```
opener ①
kind = gave money away ⑤
sly - tried stall on D.4
contrite - sought forgiveness from Conf. 6
happy ← 3
pleasure loving ②
end 7
```

When you're given a topic asking you to characterize as many as three people, you could set them up as the student did above so that each character receives a full spectrum of qualities. You'll be pressed for time and space if you have more than one person to characterize, however, so you may not be able to include more than one or two traits.

Another way to write the characterization is to find a common denominator in the people. The persons characterized might have the same traits. One student, reporting on characters from an assigned book, set up the jot outline like this:

1 Beginning (mention all 3)
2 Cruelty (John, slaves; George, girl; Tina, mother)
3 Greed (John, rents; George, life's savings; Tina, insurance)
4 Lovingness (John for Tina; George for Tina; Tina for mother, John, George)
5 Ending

If more differences exist than similarities in the people characterized, combine the qualities and add the difference in traits. Or you might simply organize by moving down the roster of everybody's qualities like this:

1 Beginning (mention 9 traits)
2 Cruelty (slaves; Tina, mother)
3 Greed (rents, savings, insurance)
4 Lovingness (Tina-George-John-mother)
5 Kindness (Tina, George's horse)
6 Faithfulness (George-Tina)
7 Jealousy (Tina's mother)
8 Optimism (John for Tina's love)
9 Pessimism (George on Tina's mother)
10 Carelessness (George, matches)
11 Ending

Beginning

What should you put in the beginning paragraph(s) for a characterization? The best method is to list the *main* qualities of the person. Three traits should be plenty. Identify the person, of course. Here's how a student used a character from a play:

> Eliza Doolittle, the heroine of Shaw's *Pygmalion*, was greedy, loving, and clever as she climbed in three acts from the Lissom Grove gutter to an embassy garden party.

She has identified the person, has spun out the chief qualities, and has completed the sketch with a graceful close to that opening sentence.

If you have two or more people to write about, your introduction might resemble this student's:

> Johnson's creation of Bart and Withers in his book *Wilderness* shows two completely different persons to the reader. Bart's basic decency, idealism, and bravery are a sharp contrast to Withers' treachery, pragmatism, and cowardice.

Most teachers would give high marks to a student with that kind of discernment and that kind of organization. Credit the jot outline.

When the person cannot be characterized by equal contrasts or equal comparisons, you might find this opener helpful:

> When the playwright William Shakespeare wrote *Richard III*, he used the main women characters to be kind, cruel, bossy, and clever. These qualities were shown in his portraits of Anne, Elizabeth, and the Duchess of York.

From all the previous examples, notice that the people have been identified (from books, plays, and the like) and briefly sketched for traits. And the openers are well organized.

Body of the Characterization

What about the body, or content, of the characterization?

You'll notice that in the jot outlines, the writers always included specific examples *after* the traits. This is a good habit to cultivate because it isn't enough to say someone has the quality of kindness. You must follow such a statement with a specific example of kindness. Keep this in mind as you follow the next instructions and examples.

After you've completed the opening paragraph, use one paragraph per trait for one person. You could do more than one, but watch your time.

Let's take the characterization of Eliza Doolittle from the previous example and set up the structure by following the order used by that student. He's declared she was greedy, loving, and clever. We assume that her main trait was one of greediness because he has placed it first. If you follow his example, put the most important traits first. The structure then will look like this:

Paragraph No. 1	Beginning
Paragraph No. 2	Eliza's Greed
Paragraph No. 3	Eliza's Lovingness
Paragraph No. 4	Eliza's Cleverness
Paragraph No. 5	Ending

The composition is not limited to just five paragraphs, of course, because it might take two or three to explain Eliza's greediness and perhaps four to deal with her lovingness. The point is that the qualities are taken up in order. Here's a diagram of a student's piece on the women in *Richard III*:

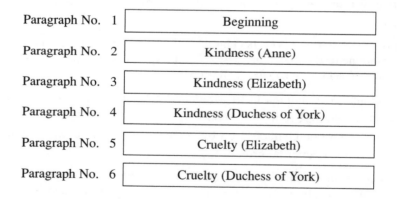

Paragraph No. 1	Beginning
Paragraph No. 2	Kindness (Anne)
Paragraph No. 3	Kindness (Elizabeth)
Paragraph No. 4	Kindness (Duchess of York)
Paragraph No. 5	Cruelty (Elizabeth)
Paragraph No. 6	Cruelty (Duchess of York)

Within each paragraph, she used structure that put the statement of the trait as the first sentence. The rest of the sentences in the paragraph(s) offer proof or specific examples to illustrate that trait. In other words, 1) the first sentence of the paragraph is a statement of the quality the person had; and 2) all other sentences are examples of that statement. Here's how another student put the outline into practice:

Statement ⎰ The Premier is an extreme egoist. He has flown
⎱ around in a black flying suit that makes everyone call
⎛ him Captain Midnight. He has press conferences
⎜ almost everyday to announce his slightest whim.
Examples ⎨ Nobody is allowed to contradict him or that person is
⎜ fired. Four persons alone this month have met this
⎝ fate.

Another, somewhat shorter, version of the 1) statement, 2) specific example set-up is this illustration:

Fearlessness is a quality that Lady Macbeth is not lacking. She's not afraid to dream that her husband might be king or afraid to get him to kill the present king so that her dream will come true.

When you come to the end of a characterization, emphasize either the main point made about the person or else give a short résumé of the many qualities found in that individual. You might use a short sentence pointing out the merits or demerits of the kind of behavior displayed by the person, as this college freshman did:

Ruthlessness and cruelty, sometimes tempered with kindness, were characteristics shown by Richard III. Perhaps these are bad qualities for ordinary people, but for rulers with grave responsibilities of a trouble-ridden state, such traits are necessary.

If one is asked to characterize a state or a city or a group of people in, say, an essay test, the same directions still will apply.

Use humor with care in characterizations. If the person is humorous himself, use as much humor as you like—in good taste, of course. But if the person is humorless, a light touch may brighten the overall dour cast of his personality. When using comparisons, don't overdo either similes or metaphors. They are tiresome to readers.

The Profile

Popularized by *TIME*, *The New Yorker*, and other publications, a profile is a biographical sketch transforming dry résumé-like facts and dull statistics about a person into an interesting composition. It fascinates those who are unfamiliar with that individual. Even unattractive or dangerous people come to life if they are portrayed by an observant and skillful writer.

The profile blends personality traits, physical description, anecdotes, and other biographical data into a full-sized portrait. Its construction, however, *isn't* organized by splitting the composition into those three categories. A far smoother job will result if you base the piece on chronological development. As your subject grows from child to adult, you'll affix the habits, actions, and quotations.

A jot outline for a profile may be filled with items if it's on someone you know well. The more jottings you have, the meatier your piece will be. It might resemble this student's outline profiling his father:

This student's outline used circles as he separated the childhood and youth sections from the adult portion of his father's life.

Another student profiled a president with a different jot outline:

Dividing the life into three parts, she had an easy "sort." Because the profile was written under a classroom deadline, she had to discard some of the points as being too detailed. But note the number of specific items (Harvard, sailing, PT 109, etc.) that helped her flesh out the bare bones of the leader: "boy," "youth," and "man."

Beginning

The profile's beginning paragraph requires more thought and work than compositions describing places, but in many ways it's more interesting. Readers may be hypnotized by a lovely word picture of a city, but it takes some doing to get them interested in your uncle Charley. You need a rousing opening, not "The person I picked to profile is…" That's a sixth-grade writing. Why not use an anecdote, a blunt statement, or a timely tie-in such as this one from a high school senior:

> The big man came running out of the station's warmth, his friendly hand waving at just another customer who would probably want $10 worth of regular and as many courtesies as the fill-'er-up drivers. His hand stopped in mid-wave as he got to the pump banks and he keeled over. My Dad had had his first heart attack.

If you don't want to use the anecdotal opener, try the blunt statement, loaded with revealing details such as this one:

> He shambled across the 18th green like a young grizzly bear, his pudgy face ruddy from the sun, his white cotton shirt soggy with sweat, his cream-colored cap perched on the back of his close-cropped blond head.

Even those who know little about golf might be attracted into such a profile of a golf champion. Moreover, such a beginning covers a multitude of things: physique, the way the man walks, what he's doing, his clothes style, and some personal hygiene.

To rivet attention with a shorter opener, try something like this:

> Just as some people live for the motorcycle, Grandpa Pete lives for the potato cycle.

Motorcycle enthusiasts, potato growers and other farmers—and grandfathers—might be induced to read on. Other readers might like the topical or timely approach shown below from a professional writer:

> The Spaniard with the best chance of unseating the Premier and with the most at stake in the outcome is a six-foot, three-inch blueblood who has not lived in Spain for 31 years.

Here, the subject's physique, his history, and the uncertainty of political life are combined. Yet a topical approach has the disadvantage of losing readers who never pick up a newspaper or who don't care for foreign or current events. Gear your first sentence of the opener to a general audience.

Once you have the first sentence written, the next two or three must identify the person and give some reason why a profile is merited. Such identifications and explanations need not be fancy or lengthy. Sometimes, just a short sentence or a precise appositive will do just as well, as is shown here:

> This dark-haired ex-Miss Maine candidate is currently under fire as the head of the Council.

Once the person is put into focus, you can begin the chronological birth-to-death (or to maturity) portrait.

Organization

The organization of a profile, as has been said, follows the chronological development of your subject. You add facts as you go, the adornments from childhood, youth, adulthood, and the like. A diagram of such a profile would look something like this:

Paragraph No. 1	Beginning (plumber's story)
Paragraph No. 2	Boyhood (poverty, newsboy)
Paragraph No. 3	Boyhood (skinny, scrappy, Brusco fight, hospital)
Paragraph No. 4	Boyhood (always interested in sports, YMCA team)
Paragraph No. 5	Youth (factory work for college) 14 jobs (cafeteria story)
Paragraph No. 6	Youth (sports, broke leg in football, 4 letters, still semi-pro)
Paragraph No. 7	Youth (not so good student in h.s., improved in college, chemistry)
Paragraph No. 8	Youth (tell story of girls, meeting Mom)
Paragraph No. 9	Manhood (Army, sgt., tell story of camp, wound & hospital)
Paragraph No. 10	Manhood (2 jobs always; started in construction, 240 lbs., smokes 2 packs day)
Paragraph No. 11	Manhood (stern but fun, camping story, spanks, story about Tim)
Paragraph No. 12	Manhood (influence on me—career, mate, money, reading)
Paragraph No. 13	Ending

Be careful that paragraphs don't become too lengthy or they'll look formidable to readers. When students write about something familiar, they tend to write at greater length than they ordinarily would. Just don't make paragraphs yards long and don't overwrite an anecdote or one phase of the person's life.

Within the paragraphs in the rest of the profile, it's not too difficult to include those revealing physical and personal details as you move through the person's life cycle. Just remember that such factors should be inserted in a smooth manner and must have a purpose. Use physical description, for instance, when it has a *direct* bearing on the point being mentioned or, possibly, when the person is first introduced. It's important for that reader to know what the person looks like.

Furthermore, physical characteristics have much to do with shaping people's personalities, as Shakespeare once had Julius Caesar observe. Perhaps a woman's plainness has made her strive to be noticed in other ways. A man's short stature might give him a "Napoleon complex." Large hands might have hindered or helped the person. Nails bitten to the quick are most revealing. But it isn't necessary to include Uncle Harry's hat size or Aunt Mary's exact height unless such measurements *are* important parts of their personalities. Professional writers handle the physical aspects adroitly:

> Hastings says his springy stride, crinkly smile, and boxer's wariness come from a boyhood in Minneapolis' toughest neighborhood.

An astute observer of human nature once said: "Never mind the words. Stand back and watch the action." Your subject's deeds do speak volumes. That's why most of your composition should describe those actions. Select deeds highly illustrative or those involving a major turning point. Ways of doing this are:

> Becoming known as "the girl who sings the song about John Foster Dulles," Carol landed the lead role in *Once Upon a Mattress*. The show and Carol were hits. In the middle of its long run, Carol was signed on as a regular with *The Garry Moore Show*.

Another example of actions speaking louder than words is:

> When my mother was given the chance to take a cross-country bus ride to Glendale or to stay at home that summer, she took 15 minutes to pack. Somewhere near Lincoln, Nebraska, the man she was to marry got on the bus.

Or this:

> Pop has always been a joiner. He likes people, which is why he's a member in good standing of the local Masonic temple, Rotary, the Elks lodge, and something called the Rallyboys Bowling Team.

A more elaborate example of deeds reflecting personalities is one from a college senior:

> People like Attiyeh have a lot of elitist arrogance in dealing with other Arabs not so high in society. Once in conference with his Arab shop foreman and with his American editor, Attiyeh offered cigarettes. He handed the American the pack for his choice. But for the foreman, however, Attiyeh yanked one from the pack, tossed it on the floor, and coolly enjoyed the man's groveling to retrieve it.

Habits, those *minor* personality traits, are close relatives to deeds—and monumentally revealing. However, don't bluntly state that the subject has this or that habit. Tell *how* it manifests itself in *what* the subject does. For example, instead of saying that Cousin Joe is nervous, point out that he chain smokes, or drums on tables, bites his nails, or, when sitting, that his foot never stops moving. If you can tie those habits into the major deeds of the person, all the better. Here's how one writer did it:

> Don Juan often escapes the formality that has been thrust upon him by birth. At sea, he does his turn on deck with the crew; he normally wears faded dungarees and sneak-

ers ashore in brief stops at foreign ports. At home in Estoril, he goes to nightclubs, chats with friends until the small hours.

Although the next example has an equally long sentence, it's packed with a workaholic's habits:

> She awakens before seven without an alarm clock, rolls onto her knees for the morning part of the "Daily Dozen" (a short prayer for guidance), feeds Smitty the Kitty, daubs Conceal on a liver spot, downs a bowl of Go Lean cereal and banana slices ("[I'm] working on the HDL levels"), and is out the door for a three-mile powerwalk to the Coffee Cat for scones and coffee to read the paper amid the East Side cops' banterings with regulars over City Hall's latest blunder. No checking emails? No cell-phone calls? "That's nine-to-midnight stuff," she says. "This is my run-up to the day."

The next most revealing aspect about people is what they say or what others say of them. Sometimes using opinions of others about someone (especially enemies) seems unfair when the target is celebrity—politician, sports or film star. But many public figures deliberately seek the spotlight and rarely sue for libel or slander—unless careers are threatened. Our first presidents, especially John Adams, were driven to the same fury or despair by hostile newspaper coverage—deserved or not—as has happened to their successors.

Most readers *do* recognize a hatchet job or, equally, a phony or banal quote ("I just love everybody," she said;" "My dad always said 'it's how you played the game that counts'"). As a student writer, practice fairness in using quotations to describe someone. Quotes should be typical, by the way, not a once-in-lifetime slip of the tongue

By *directly* quoting your subject, you can indicate educational level, background, and attitudes. Presidents and tycoons have provided thousands of such examples, such as millionaire W. H. Vanderbilt's famous remark, "The public be damned," or President Harry Truman's snappy comment about public service: "If you can't stand the heat, get out of the kitchen."

Placement of quotes is an art. Don't drop one anywhere. A quote has the greatest impact if it comes at the *end* of a buildup or follows a point being made about the person—like these two examples:

> Nicklaus has rarely been rattled since his disastrous experience in that U.S. Amateur. Says his father: "Once, when he was 15, I was driving him to a tournament. I started to encourage him and tell him 'You're good enough to win this.' He told me, 'I know it. Now be quiet.' "

And:

> He and another delivery boy, who were both earning six dollars a week for working afternoons and Saturdays, were asked to work Thursday nights, too, just for supper money. They refused and were fired. The long-time union leader said: "I found out that if there's strength in unity, there's got to be more than two people."

Incidentally, unless you want your subject to appear unlettered—sometimes the intent of professional writers—you may have to dress up quotations for a class composition; if your piece is to be published, however, do *not* cosmeticize. A young, smart-aleck Confederate editor was tired of an illiterate, roughneck Rebel cavalry general being revered as a god. The public's reverence for good grammar was seen as the vehicle to cut him to proper size. Accordingly a reporter was ordered to quote—verbatim—the General's address to troops before the battle of Franklin. The result undoubtedly was an "extreme makeover" from the original quote of: "I seen the Mississippi run with blood fer two hun'ert yards, an' I'm gwine tuh see it ag'in," but the repercussions were instant—and deadly. Subscriptions were cancelled by the score, street sales plummeted, the reporter seems to have been killed by friendly fire, and the once-fearless editor soon after put on a disguise and fled to Cincinnati.[2]

<u>Endings</u>

A profile's ending needs impact. It should be brief and include an image guaranteed to remain with the reader. You can do it with a quote, a statement about what might be in store for the person, an anecdote, or a remark about the significance of that individual. In winding up a profile about her grandfather, a student wrote:

> Now, in his old age, he is less active. Only his little dog Pete shares with him the adventures of the past.

Another wound up his profile like this:

> With eight dancing years left, she feels she can reach the top of the profession—with that company. "I'm going to be the best," Anita says.

A college junior, interning at a local newspaper, ended a feature story with:

> Because he was once a rag-tailed tramp who made the rounds of dumpsters, he doesn't forget his past. One night another tramp popped out and nearly killed him in a struggle for a dried-up ham sandwich. Sullivan is still wary of most people, but it's not in evidence when he opens the shop for business each day.

Work at lively writing in profiles. How? Try lead-off sentences with *nouns* (that's active voice). Use strong verbs so you won't have to boost them with unneeded "*verys*" and "*reallys*." Avoid syrupy or sappy adjectives no matter how tempting. If you tend to write long sentences ordinarily, chances are you'll make them even longer. That happens when students are on familiar terrain. If you know that's your problem, track back through the prose when you're finished and circle the sentences. If they're too long, cut them in half or recast the sentence.

Last, the transitional words you'll need to move from paragraph to paragraph as you bridge periods of your subject's life—connectives—are listed in the Writing Style chapter. Such connectives might be like these:

When Simmons was 12, he entered his first rodeo.
Three years after quitting UCLA, he headed for Manhattan and the Copa.
Forty years later, my father doesn't regret his decision to take early retirement.

Sample Descriptive Composition

Of all the descriptive assignments given students, and those included in this chapter, the profile still seems to be the favorite. It offers the freedom to use your

---

2 B. G. Ellis, *The Moving Appeal* (Macon, GA: Mercer University Press, 2003), 330, 341-42.

observations and opinions about someone's words and actions. You may find you're suddenly fired up about writing and doing your best and most interesting work. It might make a gift your subject will keep for a lifetime. A profile may be your lengthiest as well, as is shown in the following composition written outside of class. It uses chronological order, quotations, and simple sentences, but is weighted with subjectivity in describing life on a class project.

Life Behind the Great Man

When Dave and I signed for a joint project in Mr. Rohrman's history class, he was building a reputation as the school's all-around big shot and getting the longest write-up in the yearbook. I was working after school at Kinko's to pay insurance on my pick-up. Nights I was into homework and being the heavy hitter on the debate squad.

Dave's dad was a big-time lawyer and into state politics. Mom was a professor so they already had Dave in Congress by the time he was twenty-five. He didn't need a campaign manager then. He had *them*. His dad hauled him to Toastmasters—which is where I met him. He always got great critiques in content, gestures and decibels, but fell down on impromptu stuff. When I bailed him out once by passing a Post-it with a couple of power points, he got grateful and said a law clerk usually did his research. His mom wrote the speeches. Dad did the coaching. Same thing for <u>all</u> his homework. "Hey, I'm a busy dude," he said. I brought up *Meet the Press* and news conferences and he laughed. "See why I'm not in debate!" Another laugh.

I'd been campaign manager for the guy Dave beat out for Student Council president last spring. My guy was a popular jock, smart, natural leader. Full of big ideas to improve school. A shoo-in, I thought, until his buddies brought him to me because he was sudden-death shy in public and ducked sportswriters for anything more than a couple of words. He went wooden when I made him work the cafeteria and bus stops. I did the research and wrote his speeches. I set them in 72-point bold, but when he looked at the audience, he'd lose his place. He shuffled, his hands never left the pockets, and the decibels never went above 40.

The campaign opened. We put up homemade posters, but Dave's dad bankrolled designer jobs and four-color handouts at Kinko's. Dave worked the cafeteria, buses, halls, baseball games, track meets, and got chased out of two malls. He looked sincere when he went after the unwashed—or the babes. He had buttons and bumper stickers and Snickers with "Vote Dave Prez" stickers. Our guy didn't have that kind of time (scouting trips, the gym, Chemistry II, church) and we were being outspent one-thousand to one.

Dave won in a landslide, but lost so heavy in grades he wound up in summer school. When classes started up last fall, he put the arm on me to partner up for that report. The deal was that Dave pick the topic and do the research. I'd do the writing. Days went by and no topic. Dave came into class on the bell and was gone by the time it stopped ringing *after* class. Either Mom wasn't coming through or Dave was counting on the old group rule that whoever's after an A will do most of the work. The one time I *did* nail him, he went wounded: "We got 'til Christmas. Stop nagging!" he said.

I blinked. By Halloween, I threw a paper together with no research. Twenty-seven pages about getting Dave on City Council, sound trucks, hiring canvassers, using his leftover handbills, cheerleaders in *every* mall handing out Krispy Kreme doughnuts, riding the city buses, shaking hands at plant entrances. It had speech schedules, issue positions—all that stuff. Dave *did* buy me lunch at a Taco Bell for a look before I turned it in. He flipped through it and dripped salsa on Page 25. "Impressive," he said. "You're my campaign manager!"

I turned it in to Rohrman on Monday. Tuesday he held us after and tossed it back to Dave. Writing and organization was first-rate, but "*projected* projects" wouldn't do. He wanted "virtual" or footnoted stuff.

Dave turned on the charisma. How about documenting last spring's election? Rohrman looked at me funny because I'd done that for Mr. Halgren's class and got a district award. I jumped in: How about infiltrating the local campaign of a guy running for president? Rohrman snorted. "Election's a year away! If you get a single page on it, I'd fall down dead." He looked at Dave, the power broker's son. "Infiltrate the opposition. Your father's a primary source."

Dave didn't know what a primary source was. "You leave my father out of this!" he said to Rohrman—who didn't blink. "Whatever," he said. "Thirty percent of your grade, gentlemen!"

That night, I was just about to dump Dave for the class nerd to do the presidential project when his dad called. Project was a great idea. Honored to be a primary source. Dave lucky to have such a smart friend, etc. etc. Would I put on my "blue suit" Saturday and lunch with him and his party's "backroom movers and shakers"—and Dave, too, of course.

I expected some posh hotel suite where *West-Wing* guys watched six TVs, snarfed Chinese take-out and barked into cell phones. But it was just one of those old castle mansions with an upstairs ballroom turned into a dining hall.

The jam-up on the stairs was full of rich old guys and wannabes of thirty and forty that I caddied for at the Minikada Club. Dave and his dad hello-ed this one and that like the old-money somebodies they were. I was like the butler guy counting heads at the dining room—only *he* wasn't in running shoes from Volume Discount. He said something to Dave's dad and nodded at three old codgers in the library watching a red-faced guy do a golf stroke. Dave's dad gave me a look that said to wait while they kissed their rings.

At lunch, nobody talked to me, of course, but they grilled Crown Prince Dave. How was school? Thinking of Yale? Did he know Congressman X had a summer internship? Dave then stunned us—but not his dad who winked at me—by unfurling his run for City Council. The old duffers stopped talking and he dished the drivel to pry open checkbooks on his first step to Washington. I knew then that campaign managers must throw up a lot or get ulcers.

When Dave's engine ran down, Dad stoked Mr. Golfer: "Tell the boys what's being done for the election. They've got some kind of report for school." Mr. Golfer said that the only thing being done was writing the President a check with big numbers. He got laughs. After dessert, Mr. Golfer steered Dave and me to the basement to "get something for your report." Next year's election was going to be a "cakewalk," he said. "Only thing we need are TV ads and mailers. We just landed the party's mailer contract, as you'll see!!"

The basement stink was of old-house mold and poor people in libraries when temperatures hit freezing. And there they were among the three furnaces, hot-water heater, and vacuum cleaners that kept the guys upstairs comfy. A half-dozen space heaters were hooked into three-way sockets by drug-store extension cords. The john and sink were out in the open and being used. Immigrants.

Women and little kids at long tables were jamming campaign stuff into envelopes and tossing them into cardboard boxes. They were picked up and replaced by two skinny girls who ran them back to women sorting and bagging among the humming washers/ dryers and shelves of tablecloths, napkins, and towels. To get to the john, it would be easier to climb over the tables. A clothesline was strung with industrial lamps pumping 40 watts on the assembly line. Nobody looked up because a Big Bertha cruised the room and gave us a dirty look for interrupting. Dave didn't even look shocked as Mr. Golfer gave us the lowdown: "Five dollars an hour. Six if they work after seven. Warmer here than at home, too. Canvassers'll be getting a nickel a doorstep. Worker bees beat volunteer mamas. Most never shut up or show up. Party's efficiency is saving millions."

Mr. Golfer checked Dave nodding away at all the productivity and efficiency. Then, me, the enemy who had breached the bunker. "The party's not just *talking* about creating jobs!" he said. I'd captured stuff for the first part of our report and had nothing to lose.

"President having a hard time getting volunteers, huh?" I said. Mr. Golfer got in my face and shouted: "These people put their pay right back into the economy! They know who butters their bread, as the votes will show next year." I decided not to point that none could vote, but to give him (and the party) a scare. I looked at the lights, the heaters and crammed-up tables. "Where's the fire extinguisher?" I asked Big Bertha which set cheers from the Worker Bees. Dave took it as a cue to shake hands and say he was running for City Council.

On the way to my place, Dave burbled on about what great things the party was doing. Dad went on about what a hit Dave had made with his people. "See ya at that *other* thing," Dave said, and gave me a pal-punch as they dropped me off.

That *other* thing was something called a "meetup" that the opposition party was holding in the back room of Foshay's Steak House, where my dad's union met. Dave said he'd catch the end of the meeting. I knew he'd never show and he knew it was too late for me to hunt up another partner for that report.

I was the youngest guy in that stand-alone mob watching a video of the Candidate in rolled-up shirtsleeves pitching free medical care to kids up to eighteen. They yelled or clapped every sentence which made it hard on the waitresses to take dinner orders. The back table was all laptop. Nerds rushed downloads to a guy and gal up front at a mike. When the lights came up I saw Big Bertha and some of her Worker Bees in the Candidate's T-shirts and baseball caps. She spotted me and yelled: "Hey, Poster Boy for that health deal!" So *I* got cheers and applause—until someone said "Siddown, Kid!"

A guy from Congress stood on a chair and gave the first big-time *live* speech I'd ever heard. He did the two-joke opener, and one WAS funny so I knew I was getting decrepit. He did a rundown of how rundown the country was, thanks to the "income-bent" (big laugh, cheers). Every bad thing the Income-Bent did got boos. Everything the Candidate *planned* to do got cheers.

The couple at the mike did the Q&A and helpers doled out the literature so I had tangibles for the report. At the break, I wandered back to the laptops and then I saw her. A drop-dead beautiful College Babe inputting vitals off the sign-in list. I moved close to look over her shoulder and got brave. Did the Candidate have a chat room? Her eyes shut and she signed. "It's called a blog!" she said, and tapped one open. Would I like to post a question to the Candidate or campaign staff?

Up came Bertha and her Bees to hand us stationery and a list of names. We were to write people in Iowa to vote for the Candidate in next year's caucuses. I begged off on rotten handwriting, mostly because I don't write letters and I didn't know what a caucus was. The College Babe took a batch to write at home, but waved a questionnaire in my face. Which campaign job did I want? I could "host" a house party for people writing big checks. Pass out literature at malls, games, car races, marathons, or bookstore signings. Hold banners on walkways over freeways at rush hour. Design fliers and posters. Work with unions or minorities or write stuff for the papers and TV.

I didn't qualify for any of the above except maybe unions, but she said they'd never listen to a high school kid. "How about canvassing? That's what I do," she said. "Which is how I wound up on Big Bertha's team doing Saturday afternoon doorbelling with registration forms and the Candidate's stuff. Saturday nights it was guerrilla warfare slipping handbills under windshields about the horrible results if the Income-Bent won the election."

For Dave to get his name on the report—we got an A+ and nifty comments from Rohrman—I made him co-host an after-school meetup for the Candidate. He'd been so full of himself for so long, he didn't know the Candidate from the President. Besides, when he reeled off the record and planks, the cheering and stomping went to his head. "Great practice for next year!" he said. I didn't take him seriously.

The day came when his dad called and said he was "sending a car around" to pick me up for Dave's maiden speech for Councilman—at his club. By now, I was not only Dave's friend, but his Karl Rove. When I kept saying "Huh!" his dad kept saying "Isn't it great!" A limo and lunch at the opposition's plushy club didn't sell me. It was bugging out on his Dad's biggest moment and curiosity about Dave flying solo which he had to be doing if his folks thought I was his speechwriter.

So I skipped doorbelling with Bertha the next Saturday and was hugging the fine-paneled back wall in that packed library when Mr. Golfer spotted me. He came over and tried to stare me into leaving. Dave and his Dad made a grand entrance, arm-in-arm, through the door and up to the front. When everyone sat down, Dave saw me, grinned and waved. Mr. Golfer flashed me an evil look.

Dad was introduced to applause and when he turned Dave loose as "the youngest candidate for City Council in history!!!!" his boy got a standing ovation. Mr. Golfer said, "So why is he still associating with the likes of you?" Dave got past the two-joke opener and launched into the greatest presentation I'd ever heard him give. But it was the Candidate's record and planks. He ignored the silence, ended with a grin and little bow, and waited for the cheers and applause. More silence. Mr. Golfer grabbed my lapel and screamed: "This Judas has made that boy into a filthy traitor to our party!"

Dave sucked air and I saw tears. I gave Mr. Golfer an elbow and began to clap. His dad followed and put an arm around his crumpling Crown Prince. Mr. Golfer left.

"You must know your opponent if you're going to run for president someday!" he said. More claps and then cheers! Dave came to, hugged his dad and began working the room like a pro—arm around one while shaking hands with another. When he got to me, he said: "Hey, Dude, are'n'cha glad that Candidate's on our ticket this year?"

Sometimes the hardest job of a campaign manager is *not* to cry—or laugh.

CHAPTER 5

EXPLANATORY (PROCESS) WRITING

Explanatory, or "process," writing is among the easiest compositions for *all* students because it involves the use of *extremely* simple words, short sentences, and should show respect for readers. The last aspect is one too often ignored by professionals dispensing instructions, as any disrespected consumer knows only too well.

Consumers and users are courageous. They are trying to learn something new and willing to put in the money, time, and effort to do so. But they are also apprehensive, impatient, easily confused—and usually infuriated if instructions aren't clear, a step has been skipped, or pieces are missing or damaged.

Like a good teacher, take these consumer frustrations seriously when you write an explanatory composition.

The cardinal rule is so important it should be set in large, boldface type and taped to computers of anyone writing explanatory material. That includes anything from computer manuals and textbooks—especially math or the sciences—to instructions to assemble a birdhouse or a tricycle.

The rule is: **Never *believe* readers are as smart or as experienced as you, nor assume they're as familiar with a process as you.**

Unfortunately, few customers and fewer students ever fire off letters of complaint about lack of clarity, poor examples, or omitted steps. Writing or calling customer service seems a waste of time or money despite the price of product or book. One textbook author heard from McNeese State University media-research students—prodded by their professor—about unclear passages in an otherwise excellent book on statistical research. He may have been irritated at the outset, but considering several students were confused, he wisely kept their suggestions on file for the next edition.

The price tag has never been calculated for contempt of customers who want user-friendly instructions for products costing them hundreds of dollars. But the losses must be in billions, not counting payroll for complaint and legal departments and expensive technical-assistance staffs—all trying to compensate for poorly written materials. Add to this either ignorance or disdain for public relations. Dissatisfied customers poison minds of prospective first-time buyers with tales of long hold periods on the telephone, assessment charges for technical assistance, and "techies" who may be snippy or in Asia. The obvious and chief beneficiaries of such contempt have been telephone companies and publishers of the "Dummies" books.

Nowhere is this more apparent than in electronics whose decision-makers have written off the billion-dollar market of the "technically challenged" or people over fifty. Millions of the rapidly growing seniors' niche, for instance, have the leisure time, interest, and cash to buy everything from computers to high-definition television sets—and their constant upgrades. Most don't buy such goods because of horror stories about sniggering sales clerks or poor instruction booklets, many of which must be downloaded. Poor writing aside, no manuals are set in fonts or type sizes large enough for seniors despite the fact that *The New York Times* and major book publishers with "large-print" editions have tapped into this lucrative customer base.

Thus, you have the challenge, believe it or not, of changing this scene. If you become adept at explanatory writing—beginning with your first try—a career may open to you even while you're in high school. In fact, the younger you are, the better you'll probably be because you generally use simple words and fairly short sentences. If you were to write instructions for Grandma to boot up a computer and e-mail a friend, for example, such a priceless gift could well put you on the road either to high grades on explanatory compositions or a well-paid future because companies and organizations recognize they need your kind of writing talent.

If you're in college, the knack of explaining the complex *does* lead to well-paid internships and even jobs *before* graduation. The chapters on writing about complex subjects (pp. 130–192) were instrumental in doing just that for many Oregon State University journalism students who joined major companies and institutions—high-technology, business, forestry, the sciences, medicine—for careers in those specialties. Several wrote feature stories in science and technology for *The Oregonian*'s science section as undergraduates.

Let's begin.

The best examples of great explanatory writing are still to be found in cookbooks, on frozen-food packages, and in magazines like *Popular Mechanics*. Writers must employ the clearest, most direct prose in the English language: again, simple words, short sentences, short paragraphs. Look at the example below from a package of frozen broccoli spears:

1. Place frozen broccoli in 1/2 cup boiling salted water (1/4 teaspoon salt).
2. Cover pan and bring quickly to second boil, turning solid pack with two forks to hasten thawing.
3. When second boil is reached, reduce heat to keep water simmering. Cook, covering, 5 to 8 minutes. DO NOT OVERCOOK. Overcooking impairs flavor, texture, appearance and food value.
4. Drain, season to taste with butter or margarine, salt and pepper. Serve at once.

Many lucky Internet subscribers demand—and get—easy instructions like this:

1. Quit Netscape.
2. Find the Netscape icon.
3. Click on the icon.
4. From the FILE menu, point to GET INFO. Select MEMORY.

Factory instructions on something as vital as an oven usually are clear and put in equally simple terms, as the manual's troubleshooting section demonstrates:

> To relight oven pilot light, turn thermostat full on. Light match. Press in and hold red button in lower left compartment. Light oven burner through lighter hole. After one minute, release red button.

Before you laugh at the examples above, try writing a set of instructions on something ordinary such as brushing your teeth or making a bed. Then, have someone carry out those instructions.

Two real "killers," a Maine high school class learned, involved explaining how to tie a bow tie and how to put a squirming four-year-old into a snowsuit. They also learned that the writing and organization were easy. What was laborious and boring were all the steps involved, even for the simplest task. But boredom leads directly to lack of clarity, omitting steps—and contempt for the reader.

Once you do an explanatory piece, you'll begin to appreciate the challenges of those explaining the federal budget, or repairing cracked bridges, or putting a space station on Mars, or how tanning leads to skin cancer and death.

Professional writers tackling similar subjects started off just as you're about to do.

Because you'll be writing in step-by-step order, a jot outline is vital to prevent omitting a procedure. Forgetting or "assuming" a step is a widespread problem in this kind of composition. Once again, that happens only if you make assumptions about what your reader should have enough sense to know.

A student explaining mitosis in a paramecium created this outline:

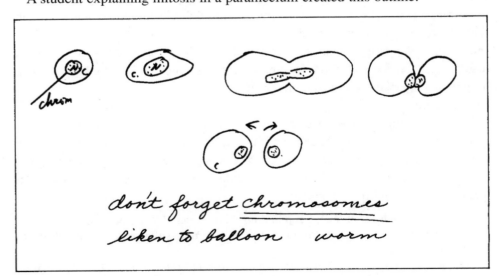

Another student's jot outline, this one for how to brand a calf, was:

> *cut out of head (hand, no horse)*
> *calf on side — use 2 legs throw*
> *sit on side*
> *heated b. iron 30 sec. — haunch*
> *notch ears*
> *vacc. for black leg*
> *castrate some*
> *dehorn (shears or ele. kind)*
> *turn loose — mothers*
> _____
> *can use $ branding stocks*
>   *1. drive calf into*
>   *2. lock ends, turn*
>   *3. brand, v, d, etc.*

Check your jot outline to ensure you have *every* step and that they're *in order*. If you've omitted something, you can always add it anywhere on the outline. Get in the habit of exercising great care in this portion of writing. Think about consumer rage and/or physical endangerment as the result of omitted steps or those that are not in sequential order.

Beginnings

The first sentence in the opening paragraph should be inviting to the reader. It should never be the amateurish "I am going to explain how open-heart surgery is performed" or "My subject is how a frost heave occurs." Show a little more polish than that, even on dry topics.

Examples of inviting leads on rather boring subjects are these:

Girls should know that pole vaulting can brighten up a romance that is fast going sour.

And:

It is the last dance of the night, and I am holding my girl close to me. Her heart is beating fast, and I think that her heart must be pumping an awful lot of blood. Let's examine her heart and see why it beats.

And this:

Jacks is a kid's playground game. But it's good for relaxation and for developing eye-hand coordination.

Or the student whose "reach" from peg to topic *was* remarkable:

> When the sheik's typists wear out a tire, they toss it into the desert and cable the tire-company for a new one. Since it's too expensive for us to do that, we should know how to change a tire.

The opening sentence might be followed by other sentences telling the reader what's to be explained and the need or use of the process. The opener and those sentences might include *both* of these points. The way some university students in a specialty writing course opened their magazine articles is shown below:

> A horse needs new shoes as much as humans do. If a horse exercises without shoes, the animal may crack or break his hoofs.

> Branding calves is a necessary evil among ranchers. Branding hurts the calf for several agonizing minutes, but ranchers have to know what livestock belongs to them so they can ship them to market.

> Atoms are little bits of characters, so small that they can't be seen with the most powerful microscope. These atoms are piled one upon another until there are enough of them that one can see the mass, be it a desk, chewing gum, ink, or Superman. Without this "piling on," everything we see and touch would fall apart.

Organization

The explanatory composition doesn't need the most important aspects included in the opening paragraph(s). But as you move from the opener, you'll still have to keep some balance of material. Don't write so much on one step of an operation that you curtail another. In classroom work, this becomes a deadline danger. If you're writing *outside* class, however, you should be able to include all necessary steps.

You might find it helpful after the opener to use a paragraph summing up major steps and tools. This method tells readers just what they're going to learn and what tools will be needed. Once again, this is a technique used for decades by writers of recipe books and do-it-yourself manuals; they first supply the ingredients or tools and *then* the steps.

In the composition's body, write one paragraph per step. If a step involves one or more operations, give *each* "substep" a paragraph. That will keep the reader on track. Even if it means other paragraphs may have to be shortened, stick to the one-step-per-paragraph formula. You are writing for the utmost in clarity.

How you set up an explanatory piece is shown below in a paragraph-by-paragraph analysis the author did on the composition about branding calves:

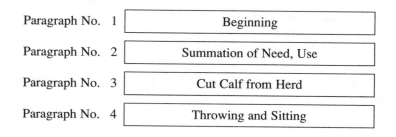

Paragraph No. 1 | Beginning

Paragraph No. 2 | Summation of Need, Use

Paragraph No. 3 | Cut Calf from Herd

Paragraph No. 4 | Throwing and Sitting

Paragraph No. 5	Branding Iron
Paragraph No. 6	Notching Ears
Paragraph No. 7	Vaccinating for Black Leg
Paragraph No. 8	Dehorning
Paragraph No. 9	Turning Loose, Logging z
Paragraph No. 10	Ending

A high school junior organized "How to Change a Tire" this way:

Paragraph No. 1	Beginning
Paragraph No. 2	Tools Needed, Safety Tips
Paragraph No. 3	Jacking Car
Paragraph No. 4	Jacking Car
Paragraph No. 5	Removing Lugs
Paragraph No. 6	Removing, Replacing Tires
Paragraph No. 7	Replacing Lugs, Hubcap
Paragraph No. 8	Letting Down Axle
Paragraph No. 9	Putting Away Tire, Tools
Paragraph No. 10	Ending

Use of Analogies

For first-rate explanatory writing, it must be emphasized once again that you never assume readers know anything about the process you're presenting. You'll have to lead them from things they *know* to things they *don't know*. Why? Because of the "fear factor." Anyone who's ever been thrown into the water as a first step to learning to swim is familiar with that sadistic and dangerous teaching technique. It's often accompanied by laughter at the floundering beginner or ridiculing those who burst into tears at such handling. No matter how successful this method has been to most, many never venture near water again after such a fright, nor respect the teacher who laughs or ridicules.

The best method is still to let novices put a toe into the water until familiarity triggers confidence about safety and success. Then, put out a hand or arm—the *known* security factor in swimming—for the beginner to grip as wading proceeds into the *unknown* of paddling, stroking and, finally, letting go and swimming.

The same fear factor is present when we learn something non-physical. A teacher's impatient sighs, sneering laughter or ridicule also shut down minds. Some labor experts have said the "shock" element lasts for about fifteen minutes in learning a new job or operating a new piece of machinery. Put another way, when an instructor announces "Today we're going to learn about land speculation" and pulls down a map of Mississippi, she might as well dismiss class for the next two days because of both fear of the *unknown* and boredom.

But what if she'd first held up a Monopoly board and asked a half-dozen students which properties they found to be the biggest moneymakers? The game is *known* by most who have favorite pieces of property. But whether they buy Baltic Avenue or Park Place, they are taking a risk to make money on that property. That's land speculation no matter if the map is of Mississippi or Maine. The teacher would be using the centuries-old, super-successful key explanatory tool of the *analogy* or an example—likening the *known* to the *unknown*. Minds not only would be open, but eager to follow where she leads them

The analogy or example has been used by all great teachers: Plato had his hot soup, Jesus his fallen sparrow, math instructors their apples and pies, Robert Frost his two diverging roads, oncology professors likening the popping of popcorn to brain cancer. One writer took a waggish dig at SAT math problems:

> Long separated by cruel fate, the lovers raced toward each other across the grassy field like two freight trains, one having left Cleveland at 6:36 p.m. at 55 mph, the other from Topeka at 4:19 p.m. at a speed of 35 mph.

The simpler the analogy or example, the better. More than one should be used in explaining a complex process. Last, attune them to your audience, either man or woman instructor, the well-traveled or stay-at-home, the wealthy or the poor. Until recently, few math textbooks were ever criticized because word problems were largely male-oriented and stunted most girls' interest in the subject. If they had been female-oriented, of course, publishers would have had a torrent of complaints.

For example, suppose you're assigned to write a composition explaining the stock market. It's a difficult subject with its buying and selling, its references to over-the-counter sales, and areas such as rails, industrials, and commodities. But you could liken the whole thing (an *unknown* thing) to kids running a lemonade stand (a *known* thing). After writing about the parallels between lemonade stand and any business, you might then go on to the purchase of stocks. That means more analogies ("If George decides to buy out Mary's interest in the lemonade stand, he would be doing....").

Below are sample analogies from student compositions on complex topics, all intended to keep a reader's interest by moving from the *known* to the *unknown*:

> Much as the planets of our solar system travel around the sun, electrons fly around the nucleus of an atom in separate circular paths.

> (Explaining half-life)

Imagine an octopus with three polka-dot legs among his normal set of eight. Let's see how many polka-dot legs that *two* octopi have, altogether.

(Explaining the addition of fractions)

The knot should look like a tired spaghetti noodle with its ends overlapping about a half-inch each.

(Explaining how to tie a half-hitch knot)

Think bathtubs. Michelangelo's frescoes are as large as 18 bathtubs put side by side.

(Explaining the Sistine chapel's ceiling)

The average annual income would meet about one car payment on a 60-month plan for a new Ford pickup.

(Explaining Ghana's economic situation)

Another method that helps readers find their way through complex steps is the use of the familiar example. If you're working with an immensely difficult topic, use more than one example on a complex step. Use three or four if you think they're necessary. The most welcome three phrases to readers of explanatory writing are *"for example/instance"* or *"in other words"* or *"putting it another way."* Use them liberally.

Connectives and Breathers

As you move from step to step, choose connective words carefully. Welcomed words here are *"next," "first," "then,"* and the like. A list of connectives is in the Writing Style chapter.

Those short, encouraging, one-sentence paragraphs called "breathers" are equally appreciated. A pause is generally needed between steps of an operation or process. So is encouragement to continue reading. Remember that in this type of writing, a reader does not always have illustrations. Your use of words to paint the steps to be followed is essential. The breather looks like this:

The next step is easier than the last.

Take time out for a coffee break because that's about how long it will take for the glue to dry.

Stir the paint. The next step takes only one fast and easy step.

At this point, the sauce will begin to thicken.

Note psychological encouragement with words such as *"easy"* or *"fast."* Whether the step is difficult or not, the word *"easy"* may make it seem so. Never be facetious with breathers (e.g., "If you're still with me, it's a miracle"). That kind of ill-suited humor antagonizes readers. They're looking for instructions, not snide comments on their abilities to understand what's written.

Mathematical and scientific topics need special care. They are complex with one step usually dependent on a previous one. A poorly written set of instructions in chemistry, or one with omitted steps could cause death or injury—and litigation. It's also well to *overuse* analogies, preferably familiar ones. To write in either of these fields, you must use short sentences and one paragraph per step. Packing too much material into one sentence or paragraph may confuse the reader. Make your writing clear and easy so that a 10-year-old can understand it.

Endings

The ending of the explanatory piece should be brief, surely no more than two sentences and short ones at that. Once you're finished, stop. The graceful ending below is on addition:

> Once you can add two numbers, you can go on to three or more. It's that simple. It should give you a feeling of confidence, especially when your calculator breaks down.

And

> All that remains is to pick up the marbles that have been won and to get home before the boy you beat can try to lure you into another game.

Or this one:

> Now that the bow has been tied, you can go to dinner, to the theater, or to any other formal event.

An ending can show the process in operation or the effects of the process, as the writer did with the bow-tie topic. But let readers know they are at the end of your composition.

Sample Explanatory (Process) Composition

The author of the explanatory composition below was given the guidelines of avoiding the mistakes of those who write high-technology manuals for ordinary people. Many, including this author, blame such mistakes on the contempt many "techies" have for ordinary buyers who have spent billions since the 1980s on both hardware and software as products undergo generational changes almost within months. As noted earlier in this chapter, millions of consumers not only are frustrated by unintelligible manuals, but furious at sales representatives whose jargon and attitude seems designed to intimidate and humiliate "computer illiterates," even though those buyers butter their bread.

The class was told that the rise and high profits of "user-friendly" books with "Dummies" in their titles were the result of poor explanatory writing in manuals and other complex subjects such as filing tax reports. That perhaps the best instructional writing still is that contained on frozen-food boxes or in recipe books. Instructions are in short sentences of simple, one-syllable words and, sometimes, capitalized directions to ensure the user's success or to avoid a lawsuit ("DO NOT BOIL!" "Pre-heat oven to 400°" "Discard after 7/05"). Students also were informed that those who grasped "translations" of the complex to ordinary people would have a lucrative, lifetime career in any kind of instructional writing.

Composition rules were that the piece include prose inserted into a step-by-step style in explaining a process by using "bricklayer's diction." (Words had to be simple, the sentences short.) Students were well aware of the dangers of a reader not having to be told what was obvious. The following composition was written by a graphics sophomore.

Scaling Illustrations Without a Proportion Wheel or Calculator

The illustration you see in a newspaper or magazine may have started either in a much larger or a smaller size. It may also have had people or objects that were unnecessary or detracted from the point the editors were trying to make. Somebody had to figure out how to enlarge or to reduce that illustration so that it fit exactly into a page. That process is called "scaling" because the image must be scaled down or up to fit and parts may have been cut ("cropped out").

One of the easiest, fastest, and most practical methods of scaling can be done without a proportion wheel or calculator. It's based on the oldest method known, still alive and well, and involves a diagonal line. The new twist is that you get an exact-sized stand-in swatch of paper to paste down on your layout sheet.

You'll need a few things: a ruler, rubber cement, a fine-point pen, a felt-tip marking pen, and tissue paper (unglazed yellow "second sheets" are excellent), and paper for mounting the illustration. The transparency of tissue paper permits you to see an illustration as you work atop it.

Here's how to enlarge the illustration:

1. Mount it with rubber cement on that large paper.
2. On that paper, use the felt-tip pen to write one or two identifying words (called a "slug") about the illustration (e.g., "Pittock mansion")—perhaps an alphabetical letter if several pictures are going to be on one page—and the page number if known. The size will be added *after* you scale the illustration.
3. If the illustration needs to be cropped, use the felt-tip pen to put the marks on *all four sides* of the mounting paper. NEVER mark the illustration!
4. Line up the yellow sheet's left side with the left-hand crop marks.
5. Push the yellow sheet up to align its top with the illustration's crop marks for the top.
6. Align the ruler with the crop marks on the *right* side of the illustration.
7. With the fine-point pen, draw a line from the right crop mark and the top edge of the yellow sheet to its bottom.
8. Align the ruler with the crop marks on the *bottom left* side of the illustration.
9. Draw a line along that bottom left crop mark, across the yellow sheet to its right edge.

The hardest work is done. You've now got a cropped original to work with.
Set the illustration aside because that yellow sheet is the key to enlarging the illustration. Get the ruler and let's create the diagonal line vital to scaling the image.

10. To draw that diagonal line, align the ruler from the top left-hand corner of the yellow sheet to the bottom right-hand corner of the "box" you created with those vertical and horizontal lines. Make sure the ruler is laid "corner to corner."
11. Draw the diagonal line from the top left corner to that box's corner. Extend it to the yellow sheet's *outside* edge—right side or the bottom.

Now comes your judgment call on the size of the enlarged illustration. You'll have to decide whether *width* is more important than the "*depth.*" You can't have both unless it's a square illustration.

12. Put a dot on the diagonal line either for your choice of width or depth of the finished enlargement.
13. Draw a straight right-angle line from the dot to the *left* edge of the yellow sheet. That sets the finished *width* of the illustration.
14. Draw a straight right-angle line from the dot to the *top* of the sheet. That sets the finished *depth.*

You now have "scaled up" (enlarged) the illustration. You've also learned the ancient law of using a diagonal line and a dot as a proportioning tool in scaling. It works even if you're enlarging a 35-millimeter contact print to billboard size or those from disposable cameras. Best of all, you have a sized swatch that can be cut (or ripped with a ruler) from the yellow sheet and pasted on the layout.

If you change your mind and want the enlargement even *larger* (or smaller) or *wider* (or deeper) than your first try, tape the box back into the yellow sheet. Move the dot on the diagonal line and repeat Steps 12-14.

The last step is easy:

15. Measure the width and then the depth to enter the sizing information with the other data on the mounted illustration. Whether you give it in inches or picas or centimeters, the *width* always goes first. Thus, if you write "4x5," the production staff will conclude the width is *four* inches.

How do you *reduce* this illustration? It's the same scaling process described above.

Using the same "yellow box" and the diagonal line running from corner to corner, just put the dot *inside* the box and draw those right-angle lines. That works whether the original is as big as a billboard or illustrations taken from a computer's downloaded "PDF" (portable document format).

CHAPTER **6**

ENDING THE
COMPOSITION

Composition endings and beginnings are closely related—much like bookends. The beginning indicates what you're going to *tell* the reader. The ending indicates what you've *told* the reader.

Don't be too concerned with an ending when you first begin to write. The ending is the cake's frosting, to be added in classroom work only if time permits; instructors rarely expect them under the deadline of the bell. If you're writing for homework, however, they'll expect one. Instead, focus on the body of the composition.

Endings obviously depend on the *type* of composition you're writing. The three previous chapters include information on how to write endings specific to each. Yet in general (particularly if you don't think the topic fits these three categories), some points need to be re-emphasized. In argumentative writing, endings should repeat points made in the composition. Descriptive papers don't need a poetic close. Try an anecdote, or a look into the future concerning the topic, or a statement about the subject's overall importance. Explanatory or process compositions too often end with quips that insult either the reader or the author ("If you got through all this, it's a miracle"). Take a tip from those who write copy for computer manuals or frozen-foods and omit a close.

Some Basic Principles

Among the basic principles of writing a good ending for *any* composition is the rule of keep it brief—and somewhat simple and memorable. Your last words should leave no doubt that the composition is at an end.

Among the tightly writtten endings are these examples:

> All in all, many people worked hard and spent much money to accomplish little.

> Once again, we breathe in air. While it's in our lungs, we change it for waste air. Then, we breathe out and get rid of the bad air we have collected. In this way, our cells are fed and stay safe and healthy.

Second, avoid inserting yourself into the ending so that it sounds as if you are bragging about all the magnificent prose and/or research data you've mustered up. Intended or not, this kind of writing irks readers. Many teachers groan when they encounter endings more appropriate to an attorney's closing arguments to a jury, such as this one:

> For these three reasons, I hope I have convinced you that each part of this ridiculous case should be investigated. I have demonstrated well that covering the wellhead is a project of stupidity that should be discarded immediately. I have shown that Mouton's findings are frivolous and unnecessary. And I have proved that some $100,000 of tax-payer money will be required to finance this boondoggle.

To avoid this type of ending, sum up the main points, delete the pronouns and wild-swinging adjectives, and let the facts speak. A better ending might be:

> For these three reasons, it would appear that the matter should be investigated so that the wellhead project should not proceed. Mouton's findings are not convincing, and some $100,000 of public funds are estimated to finance this project.

Third, even if you are emerging from the complexities of an abstract topic, cut a straight and simple path out of the jungle. A senior finished off the *carpe diem* philosophy of life with this ending:

> Regardless of afterlife, ulcers or social clubs, everyone has a responsibility that goes far beyond the stomach or an ability to tango. We all owe the world full use of our talents and imagination—not all of us as Dr. Tom Dooley or the workers at Lambarene; but as thoughtful teachers, social workers, mechanics, and ice-cream vendors. We can't do anything for others without resentments if we haven't first "fed" ourselves.

The quotation ending is tiresome, but seemingly such an indestructible old reliable that it isn't going to vanish from student writing any time soon. One warning about this kind of exit line is that it's a mine field, especially if you use *any* quote out of a source such as Bartlett's.

Quotes must be appropriate to mark the finish of all that you've written—and accurate. For example, if you quote from the Bible as with "Thou shalt love thy neighbor as thyself," be sure you pick up on the word "*as*." If you insist on using axioms such as "all that glitters is not gold," be prepared for your teacher's caustic marginal note that the quote is *not* from the Bible, but from poet Thomas Gray, and it is: "Not all that tempts your wand'ring eyes/And heedles hearts, is lawful prize;/ Nor all, that glitters, gold."

If you venture into obscure or phony quotes, be warned they're usually such stoppers that your reader might just launch an Internet hunt for them.

Last, avoid the banal or trite quote, found daily in a newspaper's sports section:

> It's no wonder that the Trail Blazer center feels that: "I want to be the best. That should be every athlete's goal if sports are really to be competitive and entertaining."

As for humor, students too often feel such pangs of uncertainty when they write seriously about a subject that they believe undermining it with self-deprecating closures will erase the view they're pompous or fanatic ("So much for Ski-U-Mah and Mom"). Humor in good taste or a light touch is tricky and you'd do well to know how your instructor will receive endings such as these:

Wet your thumb, folks. A breeze is rising.

But everyone knows about these swimming meets: They're just so much water over a dame.

CHAPTER 7

WRITING STYLE

As you learn how to use content and how to organize, you'll develop your unique writing style. Beyond suggesting a few things to sharpen your abilities, it's not the intention here to turn out students with lockstep writing patterns. This chapter deals with *various* styles and word usage to adapt and to avoid.

General Writing Style

Write primarily so that your work will be understood. Books that have remained popular for years with the general reader *and* the intelligentsia became classics because the messages were clear. True, each reader might interpret these works differently, but at least a basic understanding of the authors' intent was possible. Such clarity usually stems from simple, unadorned writing, not obscure, cryptic ramblings set in acrobatic grammatical forms or in flossy, flowery gobbledegook favored by insecure showoffs.

Plato and Aristotle are prime examples of clear writers. Dickens is another. So is Steinbeck. Even Dr. Spock, the famous baby doctor, can claim both simplicity and clarity; his *Baby and Child Care* book at one time nearly outsold the Bible because panicked parents could understand his instructions.

How have such writers made themselves so clear? Organization of material helped, but principally it had to do with the use of simple words, short and uncomplicated sentences, and adequate paragraphing.

Because you're writing for class and not for immortality, you don't have to use big words or stud compositions with nonessentials such as "*I think*" to impress an instructor. Use simple words. A writing assignment for most English classes is usually fairly brief anyway so why dress it up? Unless you are majoring in philosophy, where disputes often hinge on the exact definition of such everyday terms as *good* and *truth*, or unless you are writing a term paper (or master's thesis or doctoral dissertation), keep the vocabulary simple. Considering that you're probably headed for a career in which clarity is vital, use a vocabulary that people can understand.

Take the use of foreign phrases—a habit many professional writers overdo to impress readers that they're educated. When challenged, their defense is that the English language is not precise or lacks the same terms. This is doubtful, given the centuries of foreign languages that have poured into English.

It's tantalizing to use a word or an idiomatic expression picked up in foreign language classes or in visits abroad (e.g, "*lagniappe*"="a little bonus") to impress or intimidate readers. If the instructor suspects the purpose is either to show off, tart remarks usually follow. For most English composition classes, plain English will do.

Slang, jargon, and profanity are equally questionable unless such expressions have a definite purpose as, say, in a quotation. Slang and jargon are more permissible around English departments than profanity in assignments. If the intent is to shock the instructor, the subsequent grade might provide corresponding shock to the student. The user of slang or jargon risks not being understood. Slang, for instance, usually is dated in a month or a year. Jargon's result is reader confusion and, for some writers, an attempt to exclude the non-initiated.

Sentence Style

What about overall writing style? Style has to do with *how* you present your material.

The sentence length should vary. Those that continue to be *too short* make for choppy, start-and-stop reading. They're vital chiefly in children's books ("Jump! Jump! Jump, Sally!" said Tommy) or for expressing an action ("He saw the man. He crouched low behind the oil drums. He took aim. He squeezed the trigger"), but it's doubtful you're writing children's books or action-packed fiction.

On the other hand, sentences that continue to be *too long* confuse most readers. You also risk losing control of a sentence and may wander far from its start to its end. That kind of meandering requires a mine field of punctuation. Here's a sample of a long sentence that may take more than one reading to follow:

> Such men will keep you on the way of being contented with yourself, of borrowing nothing of any other but yourself, of restraining and fixing your mind on definite and limited thoughts in which it may take pleasure, and, having recognized the true blessings which men enjoy in proportion as they recognize them, of contenting yourself with them, without desire of prolonging life and name.

Or try this florid example from yesteryear, one topped with ego and confusion:

> My [columns] may have seemed too discursive for the general taste, but I may say, in addition to my own persuasions of duty, I have it in commission from an officer of high rank, and higher intelligence and patriotism——the patriotism which springs from the active sympathy of warm interest and pursuit with the people, as the more general or enlarged sentiment of a love of country, and who has been with the army from the beginning——to press the fact home to the people that nothing will now save us, under

the blessing of God, except ... our army by the oddities of every man, whatever his age, capable of military service.

Contrast them with the blunt, meaty style used to treat a terminal disease:

We alcoholics are men and women who have lost the ability to control our drinking. All of us felt at times that we were regaining control, but such intervals—usually brief—were inevitably followed by still less control, which led in time to pitiful and incomprehensible demoralization....Over any considerable period we get worse, never better.

Another reason for shortening long sentences is that the longer they are, the more punctuation they'll require, as is seen in the example above. You're also likely to have more grammatical errors and misspelled words.

Readership-study experts long ago found that the reader's eye pauses at each piece of punctuation whether it be a comma, a colon, period, parenthesis, or quotation marks. So the more punctuation, the more pauses the reader will take. And many pauses means exhausting or confusing readers. You'll be clearer if you split up long sentences into shorter ones. It may take some rewriting, but the clarity makes the surgery worthwhile.

Try for a balance in sentence lengths.

Other factors interrupting a reader's concentration are too many parenthetical expressions (*however, by the way, I think, to be sure*, etc.). Add to this too many items in too many parentheses, and too many breaks in thought that are set off by dashes. Look at that second example again. Such writing may be harder on readers than tomes loaded with footnotes.

Reread your first draft and use an editing pen liberally to eliminate such expressions. Tighten the material. Perhaps a new sentence will take care of words encased in parentheses or those between dashes. You may be startled to learn that you don't need expressions such as *I think/feel/believe*. Your teacher knows that material in your composition obviously involves something you *think/feel/believe*.

At first, such heavy editing may be agonizing or ego-deflating because most people have such a difficult time writing in the first place. To delete a single word seems to destroy all that they've struggled to put on paper. Worse, they may believe that society—and certainly English teachers—frowns on anyone making a mistake, something that seems to be hardwired into students. Set your ego aside and that myth about Society. Professional writers do even *without* the lash of a flint-eyed editor who slashes away with a red pen.

Think of novelist Charles Dickens, for example. He was famous for racing into publishing houses with yet another marked-up proof to beg the printers to stop the presses for changes. Proofs for new editions of the poetry of John Keats or Walt Whitman are heavy with their self-editing. Writers who sell, edit a lot. So if those who write for a living can edit their "children," you can, too.

Variety

Work at sentence variety, something attained *only* by self-editing your composition. No matter how much active voice is venerated by teachers and a computer's grammar-checker, writing in passive voice is *not* a sin. The exception is in explanatory writing when a series of steps is involved.

Active voice has a structure of subject-verb, subject-verb, and subject-verb sentences. A progression of active-voiced sentences is not only tiring, but boring. Some writers call it the "little-red-hen" writing style, used when you first learned to read or in action-packed fiction of, say, Ernest Hemingway. Remember this:

> The little red hen looked out the window. The little red hen saw the fox. The little red hen closed the doors and windows. The little red hen locked them. The little red hen began to quiver.

Is it any different from the active-voice style in this student's composition?

> The Battle of Murfreesboro was considered a draw by both North and South. General Braxton Bragg, the Confederate field general, claimed he won by strategy even though his army did not hold the field when it was over... Bragg's strategy was frontal attacks by infantry, cavalry, or artillery which initially terrified the Yankees, but drew heavy casualties. General John Breckinridge's division took the greatest number of casualties when Bragg ordered a charge on the battle's last afternoon. His subordinates were furious. They believed all the sacrifices and casualties and loss of equipment went for nothing. He felt he was saving the Army of Tennessee to fight another day.

As you cast about for new ways to form your sentences, avoid the gymnastics of the ostentatious, inverted structure favored at one time by *TIME* magazine writers until it was spoofed in *The New Yorker* magazine with this famous sentence:

> Backward ran sentences until reeled the mind....Where it will all end, knows God!

A good test to check your pattern of sentence lengths and structure is to take two or three of your old compositions and a current one and do some content analysis. Circle the sentences to detect their length. If they're too long or too short for the most part, you can begin to adjust for variety on the next compositions.

To check for voice, mark a big "*S*" above the sentence subjects and a big "*V*" above the verbs. If too many, or too few, reflect the little-red-hen style of active voice, you'll be aware of changing your style for future assignments. Recast a few.

These two simple tests are designed to make you aware of your style. After all, awareness is the first step to corrective action in *anything*, but only if you're willing to change what you're doing. In the case of writing, edit your first draft (and subsequent ones). The result will be a polished final product that will earn you a high grade.

What about the tone or mood to use in a composition?

The atmosphere, or slant, of the piece should match the subject matter. If the topic is a serious one, avoid a humorous or light style. Likewise, if you're working on a light subject, keep it light. Don't rule out *touches* of humor or seriousness, but maintain the predominant mood of the composition.

Place adjectives and adverbs next to, or near, the words they modify. Again, that takes editing the drafts. Proximity of descriptive words keeps the reader from wondering *who* is beautiful or just *what* rock is jagged. The average reader is easy to confuse—and the average English teacher is quick to point that out to students who assume their prose is clear.

One error that few students detect in the fever of writing is the dangling modifier:

> While entering the house, the bell rang.

> Mother put Dad's shirt into the new washer, which was greasy from hours of all that work on the car.

No matter how passionately you may defend such a gaffe with "You *know* what I meant!!" you'll never budge composition teachers any more than professionals who use the same argument with editors. Recognize, too, that dangling modifiers have provided a storehouse of laughter for years in the writing field. Yours may be posted in the faculty lounge to lift spirits or sent off to appear in editing and English journals.

Because dangling modifiers usually start a sentence or are sentences *inside* sentences (subordinate clauses), fine-comb those areas when you edit. Underline those opening phrases or "secondary sentences" to see if they could have double meanings.

The Paragraph

You'll have little trouble deciding what to paragraph if you follow two simple rules:

First, if you're writing on a subject with five aspects, allot a paragraph per aspect.

Second, if your subject has five aspects, each with several aspects, allow a paragraph for *each* subdivision.

Paragraphing has one principal rule: Cluster sentences together in a paragraph if they deal with *one* aspect of the main topic.

Here's how it's done.

Assume that a topic involves a descriptive composition characterizing Don Quixote and Sancho Panza, the leading figures in Cervantes' *Don Quixote*. Obviously, you need to fence off one man from the other.

Because characterizations show personality traits and illustrative examples, the jot outline below shows how to paragraph this topic. Each box represents a paragraph:

Paragraph No. 1	Beginning (2 paragraphs, identify both, give 3 traits each)
Paragraph No. 2	Don Quixote (kindness—to Dorothea)
Paragraph No. 3	Don Quixote (wisdom—advice to Sancho on being a governor)
Paragraph No. 4	Don Quixote (insanity—wineskins, sheep, basin, saw horse, windmills)
Paragraph No. 5	Sancho (practicality—food, shelter, humoring Don Quixote)

Paragraph No. 6	Sancho (wisdom—governor of Barataria)
Paragraph No. 7	Sancho (humor—lashes)
Paragraph No. 8	Ending (sum up 6 traits)

If each trait is complex, say, with two or more aspects, use a paragraph for *each* aspect. This is also how to handle more than one example. Devote a separate paragraph for each example.

Once you've tried a few of these outlines, you'll also understand that in a classroom assignment, you can "reparagraph" by using the proofreader's mark of ¶ to save you time and effort in rewriting that section. Your teacher knows that symbol.

Organization Inside the Paragraph

How do you organize the material *within* each paragraph?

The easiest and quickest method involves using the first sentence of the paragraph as the statement, something emphasized earlier in this book for the various categories of compositions. Subsequent sentences then can offer directions or examples to underpin that statement.

The statement-example/direction organization helps the reader understand the material, whether it's history or literature or in fields such as science and engineering. In the latter two fields, illustrations may be included, but whether they're photographs or pen-and-ink line drawings, pictures are rarely worth a thousand words when they involve instructions.

If you were assigned an explanatory composition on tennis, the paragraph's content on equipment might be handled like this:

Statement	{	Five pieces of equipment are needed for tennis.
Example	{	Players need a racquet, three tennis balls, a net, tennis shoes, and informal clothes.

In an argumentative assignment, your paragraph might be written like this:

Statement	{	Hitler's generals did not have the materiel or the communications to win the battle. In one day alone
Example	{	the Allies pounded the rail center around the area so that the two trains with ammunition, food, and medical supplies were blown up before they could leave the siding. The highways, over which SS trucks had carried artillery shells for months, were heavily laced with bomb craters and were impassable.

Both examples have a first sentence summing up the paragraph's content. Then come the sentences containing examples, or evidence, supporting that first statement.

The Breather

One helpful writing device—the short, one-sentence "breather"—has been mentioned briefly in the chapter on explanatory writing. You've probably seen ones such as these:

> So it will be seen how clever Goebbels was as a master propagandist.
>
> These three reasons demonstrate why Johnson is wrong.
>
> Where could such a policy lead?
>
> The next step is easy.
>
> Kerry wasn't the only Senator taken in by the evidence.

Breathers once were viewed as show-off writing to arrest attention. A computer's grammar-checker will flash "incomplete sentence" on them. Because some professionals have written paragraphs with only one word ("No!"), you might agree they are startling devices. They were permissible perhaps in fiction after the 1920s, but never anywhere else—certainly not in classroom compositions on up to the present. Yet both writers and readers are grateful for this tool. As mentioned previously, it provides a typographical break, a welcome pause from the eyestrain of reading moderate to lengthy works.

Breathers serve many other purposes.

They give readers a moment to catch their breath. You may have silently cheered when encountering this highly effective "pause that refreshes." The over-stuffed mind does balk at absorbing too much material, as any harried student knows. This is particularly true in courses they don't like or in those with heavy reading requirements such as philosophy, political science, the sciences, economics, and the like.

Yet textbook writers who use breathers help students get their bearings on material from previous paragraphs—something that may encourage them to continue reading.

Breathers also can be included *within* a paragraph—at the start, middle, or end—and are in boldface below:

Life got dangerous last summer. Farmers desperate for water surrounded the cut-off valves and went to work opening them with wrenches before federal marshals arrived to shut them off and arrest the ringleaders.

The lumber company's marketing people were absolutely brilliant in knowing how to get us to part with our cash and sell a lot of shop-grade stock in those classes for do-it-yourself dummies. **We suddenly needed a dog house, my mother said.** My dad groaned while getting out the credit card, and my sister and I knew who would be stuck building the blame thing. Next thing, Dad was backing our SUV to the delivery dock while my mother had the clerk look at her calculations and made us follow him to make sure he cut where the knots weren't.

Greenspan sent up two trial balloons within the space of four months to announce at a press conference that huge amounts of the national debt run up by the Administration could be replaced. He strongly recommended that the Consumer Price Index be replaced as a measurement of the cost of living to the "chained price index," which he said was far more accurate. He claimed that if the chained index had been used in the last two years, the federal government would have saved $200,000,000,000 on the regular increases in Social Security cheques. **That index was created by the Administration's Labor secretary.**

If you decide to use the breather, be sure it's not exhibitionism, but that it fulfils one of the purposes listed above. Last, don't overdo using them. Ration them: one per assignment.

Connectives

You may need a word or phrase to indicate you're moving on to a new aspect, section, or case point in your composition. Or perhaps you need a word warning the reader that an opposite viewpoint is to follow. Or that an example will follow illustrating a statement or a series of steps is forthcoming. The most effective tool to guide readers along these paths—or as you shift gears—is with connective words or phrases. They're also called "*transitions*."

You know many of them: *however, next, on one hand, finally*, and the like. If your topic is complex, you'll need a handful, but try not to overdo it. To check the number, go on a "comma hunt" either by circling commas in a classroom composition or by using the FIND feature on the computer. As they say, "If a connective comes, a comma is not far behind."

For optimal effectiveness, put connective words or phrases at the start of a sentence to warn a reader what's coming. Edit the first draft. Not only will you avoid a bad case of too many "*however*'s" and "*also*'s," but you can determine which kind of connectives are necessary to aid reader comprehension.

You undoubtedly have a small store of "old-reliable" connectives. But if you want to expand it, this list should help, especially if you're embarking on a lengthy piece of writing such as a term paper, a master's thesis or a doctoral dissertation.

The connectives are divided by composition categories from this book, but several are interchangeable.

Argumentative Writing

accordingly	for example	on one hand
again	for instance	on the other hand
although	furthermore	otherwise
another	hence	second
as a result	if this be true	similarly
at the same time	in addition	so
besides	in fact	therefore
by contrast	in other words	thus
consequently	in short	too
equally	moreover	to sum up
finally	obversely	whereas
first	on the contrary	

Descriptive Writing

above	beyond	on the left
across from	farther down	on the right
adjacent to	here	opposite
also	in the distance	to the left
before me	nearby	to the rear
behind	next to	to the right
below		

Explanatory Writing

also	for instance	otherwise
another	for this purpose	second
as a result	furthermore	similarly
basically	in addition	such
by contrast	likewise	then
consequently	next	thus
finally	often	too
first	on the contrary	usually
for example	on the other hand	

Pitfalls *do* exist for the unwary with connectives. That's why it's recommended that connectives be *added* (or deleted) when you edit the first draft.

For instance, if you write "there are three reasons why" something is so, make sure you have *three* reasons. If you write *fourth* in listing something, count back to be sure it *is* the *fourth*. If you write *"finally"* (or *"to sum up"*), what follows better be of a final or summary nature.

What follows the connective *"basically"* must be a boiled-down cornerstone, and *"similarly"* needs something *similar*.

In descriptive writing, the words *"in the distance"* can't be in the *foreground*. *"Consequently"* and *"as a result"* have to be followed by the *consequences* or *result* of actions. The terms *"equally"* and *"equally important factors"* must involve *equality* of material. You may have no problem in using the connective phrase *"on one hand,"* but can forget to include what's *on the other hand*. When you write *"by contrast"* or *"on the contrary,"* do show a *contrast* or something that is *contrary*.

Clichés and Bromides

Back in 1892, French printers discovered that if they dipped papier-maché into a chemical, it could be pressed hard against even small metal type and provide a mold for a newspaper page. The result saved type from being worn down by presses, and the metal stereotype (*"clicher"* is French for *"stereotype"*) lasted through thousands of impressions. Thus, was the word *"cliché"* born to define the repetitive use of terms such as *"bottom line"* and today's *"edgy"* that are by now *"history."*

A half century before that, doctors discovered a sedative made of bromine and potassium bromide. In the writing business, therefore, *"bromide"* came to mean tiresome shorthand filling empty conversations ("it never rains but it pours"). So if *cliché* is something repeated and bromides put you to sleep, all it takes is adding a word with an unnecessary adjective ("*hushed courtroom*") for writing to become stale, tiresome, and full of clutter.

In fairness, many of these expressions began life as fresh, memorable, picturesque images in fiction and poetry. But overuse by unoriginal or exhausted writers and speechmakers have turned them into such rubber-stamped terms that when they use the first part of the expression, the audience can fill in the rest.

One of this chapter's purposes is to freshen your writing or at least to make you aware you're using terms as dated as "*hold your horses*" (circa, 800 B.C.), "*twenty-three skidoo*" (the 1920s), "*push the envelope*" (the 1970s), and "*Ground Zero*" (2001). If you shrink from using teenage terms that *are* "so yesterday," you should be ready to bury some aging, favorite clichés and bromides. You have no idea how many have survived until you glance at the list below, which probably contains some of your favorite expressions. It was compiled from composition and grammar textbooks as well as newspaper stylebooks and association bulletins. These old chestnuts are even collected on web pages such as IdiomSite (*http://www.idiomsite.com*) which gives you their origins.

One high school teacher used an excellent method to make students aware of these verbal crutches. She assigned them to write a tale using 25 to 50 clichés or bromides from the list below; the results were hilarious and the burial of "*each and every*" followed. Work on avoiding the following fossils:

abreast of the times	battled cancer
aching void	beat a hasty retreat
acid test	beggars description
after all is said and done	better half
all in all	better late than never
all work and no play	bite the bullet
a long-felt (heart-felt) want	bitter end
along these lines	blind alley
among those present	blissfully ignorant
apple doesn't fall far from the tree	blood is thicker than water
apple of his (her) eye	blushing bride
ardent admirer	bold as brass
armed with a search warrant	bolt from the blue
arms of Morpheus	bottom line
artistic license (temperament)	boys will be boys
as luck would have it	bountiful repast
at first glance	brave as a lion (tiger)
at a loss for words	breathless silence
at one fell swoop	brilliant performance
	briny deep
back to basics (square one)	brown as a berry
back-seat driver	brownie points
bad-hair day	budding genius
balance of power	busy as a bee
baptism under fire	by leaps and bounds
bathed in tears	

captains of industry
carrying coals to Newcastle
caught like rats in a trap
center of attention
charred rubble
checkered career
chip off the old block
choked with emotion
chow down
clear as crystal (a bell)
clinging vine
close to nature
cloudless sky
cold as ice
cold turkey
concerned parents
concerted effort
conspicuous by his absence
conspicuous consumption
copasetic
course of true love
cried like a baby
crisis (epic) proportions
cruel to be kind
cut to the chase
cutting edge
cute as a bug's ear

Dame Fortune
dead earnest
defies description
depths of despair
Devil's advocate
diamond in the rough
dirt poor
discreet silence
doomed to disappointment
drastic action
dressed to the nines
dropping like flies
dry run

early morning hours
easier said than done
edgy
epidemic (epic) proportions

equal to the challenge (occasion)
every parent's nightmare
eyes like diamonds (stars)

face the music
fair sex
fall from grace
familiar landmark
family of origin
feeding frenzy
festive occasion
few and far between
field day
final goodbye
filthy lucre
fit as a fiddle
flat as a pancake
fly on the wall
folded his tent
fools rush in where angels fear to tread
footprints on the sands of time
force of circumstances (destiny)
foreseeable future
from all walks of life

Gen X
general consensus (conclusion)
gilding the lily
golden tresses
goodly number
got my mojo working
grace under pressure (fire)
green as grass (with envy)
gridiron heroes
grim reaper
Ground Zero

hale and hearty
handwriting on the wall
happy as a lark (clam)
happy pair
heartfelt thanks
heart's delight
heated argument (session)
he-man
high five

holy bonds (estate) of matrimony
hushed courtroom

ignorance is bliss
in great profusion
in the last (first) analysis
iron constitution (man)
irony of fate
it never rains but it pours

just desserts

knee-jerk reaction
knock on wood

last but not least
last hurrah
last straw
level playing field
limped into port
loose cannon
love of my life
love is blind

mad as a wet hen (hatter)
make no bones about it
mantel of snow
married bliss
media circus
meets the eye
method in his (her) madness
mind over matter
moment of truth
monarch of all he (she) surveys
more in sorrow than anger
Mother Nature
motley crowd (crew/throng)
Murphy's Law
my brother's keeper
myriad of lights

needs no introduction
nerd
new kid on the block
nipped in the bud
no honor among thieves

none the worse for wear
nothing's certain but death and taxes

off the record (wall)
on the dole
over the top

paramount issue
pending merger
Peter principle
picturesque scene
play by ear (play)
play it again, Sam
pleasing prospect
plot thickens
poor but honest (as a church mouse)
posh
power trip (powers that be)
preaching to the choir
presided at the piano
pretty as a picture
promising future (career)
proud possessor
psychological moment
pull out all stops
pull the plug
push the envelope

quality time
quiet as a mouse (tomb)

ran amok
reading my mail
red as a beet (rose)
reigns supreme
replete with interest
rich or poor, young or old
riot of color
robber barons
rolling in the aisles (on the floor)
rule of thumb
ruling passion
rushed to the hospital

sacred cow
sad to relate

sadder but wiser
sea of faces
seething mass of humanity
self-made man (woman)
sharp as a tack (dime)
short and sweet
sigh of relief
signs of life
silence gives consent
silence reigned supreme (is golden)
sitting in the catbird seat
skeleton in the closet
sleep like a baby (the dead)
smart like a fox
snow-capped mountains
spectacle (show) of humanity
spitting image
staff of life
sterling citizen (character)
strong as an ox (lion/iron)
strong, silent type
struggle for existence
sturdy as an oak
sumptuous repast
sweat of his brow

table groaned
take my word for it
take the bitter with the sweet
taken into custody
tall, dark, and handsome
there (here) goes nothing
thereby hangs a tale
thick as thieves (mud)
thin as a dime
third time's the charm
this day and age
thunderous applause

tie the knot
time marches on
time-out
time of our lives
tired but happy
too clever by half (for words)
too funny for words
too much of a good thing

up a blind alley
upside your head

vale of tears
view with alarm

wag the dog
watery (fiery/murky) grave
weaker sex
wee, small hours
well heeled (connected)
wheel of fortune (destiny)
where angels fear to tread
whistling in the dark (Dixie)
whole nine yards
wide open spaces
wild and woolly
with bated breath
words fail (me) to express
wolf in sheep's clothing
worked like a Trojan (charm, dog)
worse for wear
wreathed in smiles
wrought (cry) havoc

young or old, rich or poor
(a) young man's fancy

zero-based budget
zero tolerance

Similes and Metaphors

Similes and metaphors are closely related to clichés and bromides in that this is where many were created. Perhaps writers of fiction, poetry, and advertising copy have worked the hardest to create expressions that *are* new and colorful.

A simile is *similar* to something else ("Ophelia is *like a rose*").

A metaphor is something that has changed its *form* ("Ophelia *is* a rose"). Think *metamorphosis*.

From ancient times to this morning's sports pages and science magazines, similes and metaphors do yeoman's work in explaining things in *every* language. These valuable, vivid and compact expressions illustrate someone or something for readers or listeners. They make something complicated like brain surgery or earthquakes instantly clear. These two tools use the *known* to define the *unknown*—and in that order. Didn't pies and apples teach you fractions?

Bear in mind that if readers are to understand your expressions, they must know the reference. And you need to employ the reference (the known) first in some areas of writing or you'll lose your audience. Such a reference might be the beauty of the rose that's used above with Ophelia, a supporting character in Shakespeare's play *Hamlet*. She is easily pictured.

Stick to references recognized by most readers. Obscure or cryptic ones go over their heads. You may impress some teachers, but not many. Great teachers and writers use the known to teach the unknown. Socrates used soup to teach a complex philosophical point. Jesus used nature (sparrows and lilies). Shakespeare's works are steeped in nature, too. And poet John Milton likened the sun to the "gilded car of day."

However, similes and metaphors don't have to be touched with that kind of magnificence. They can be geared to your locale or interests—so long as your reader understands the frame of reference. You can create the same kind of imagery as these Maine high school students:

> He was a walking bacteria culture.
> She was a drop of water in a bath tub.
> Russia is a whale, always ready to swallow us.
> She was an echo in a large cavern.
> He was a Svengali.
> She was as gossipy as a landlady with 50 apartments.
> He was as lonely as an alligator with bad breath.
> His thinking was as confused as a potato growing on a tomato's vine.
> If you make popcorn, you'll understand what happens in brain cancer.

The only other danger with imagery—metaphors in particular—lies in using more than one within a sentence and, worse, mixing apples with oranges. *The New Yorker* magazine's staff and sharp-eyed readers have filled the publication's "Block That Metaphor" feature for years. Among their classic gems are:

> Mr. Speaker, I smell a rat; I see him forming in the air and darkening in the sky; but I'll nip him in the bud.

> We keep clipping the wool from the goose that lays the golden eggs until we pump her dry.

> He ripped the novel limb from limb, for it didn't hold water at all.

Generalizations

Generalizations are sweeping statements unsubstantiated by parochial beliefs that usually have no factual basis. They are common elements of student writing. It would seem, too, that the younger or less sophisticated they are, the more sweeping the statement and the more questionable the statistics or "facts" used in compositions, though greater care *is* given to accuracy in term papers or graduate-school assignments. We'll discount students who make up "facts" and "statistics" because they are unlikely to read this book.

The insecure like things to be simple, as has been pointed out in the argumentative-writing section about black-and-white thinking. Students who have led rather sheltered lives often fail to understand "how the other half" survives or are prudent about expressing ideas that are not shared by friends or family—or previous teachers. Yet any political canvasser knows "doorstep blindness" by voters who shut doors against issues or candidates they don't like. Hardened attitudes, whether from teenagers or those drawing Social Security checks, change usually only when life serves up some gray areas.

Some generalities extracted from high school and college writing:

Men are no longer so cruel as they were in the time of Genghis Khan.

The reason the United States fought Germany in World War II was to avenge the deaths of six million Jews in concentration camps.

Women are stupid and grasping when it comes to relationships with men.

If everyone votes, we'll have true democracy.

Pharmaceutical companies have to charge high prices because it pays for all the research and development done on medicine.

Rock climbing offers something for everyone.

In each one of these examples, the statements would collapse even upon elementary research. Most stem from lack of access to the Internet or library resources—or failure to think through such sweeping statements. Or disinterest. However, unless you're a well-trained researcher, you may be fooled by source materials when you write the composition as homework. Or not galvanized to do a search. The chapter on writing term papers will help you ferret out some solid facts from the library or Internet.

If you're going to use statistics or facts, be sure that your data are correct; listing a source will force you to do it. It's easy to mislead with statistics, as its practitioners have reminded people believing polls and surveys are gospel and/or representative of the nation's views.

If you do a straw poll of a few people, you'll see how this is possible. Responses vary when the poll is taken before lunch, in the evening, early in the morning, on a good day or a bad one. You'll also learn that many officials also use half-truths or carefully selected facts. Such facts may be accurate so far as they go, but some material could be deliberately omitted that tells a different story. If thousands of federal dollars rest on getting high reading or math scores, it's been a common practice for schools to find something else to do for those students who would "drag down" the scores. If only men are tested for heart conditions, a research group can't claim that the results are probably true for women and children, too.

That's why it's important to study the *methods* section of any research report and also to know who funded a study and where the trials were carried out. Taking a skeptic's view about a report's results isn't a hallmark of cynicism; it's good scholarship.

Even if you quote facts and are fair about sources used, quote material accurately and without lifting it out of context, as television newscasters, pressed for airtime, often do. Your teacher might have read the same and challenge the composition's accuracy and fairness.

If you can't cite a source, but your position on some topic seems to be sound, admit that shortcoming in the composition. Honesty is highly prized in research, especially in the sciences where a life may hang on unbiased clinical trials. Even if one *does* have solid sources, winners of major research prizes still qualify conclusions with the academic hedges of "*it appears*" or "*it seems*" or variations of those terms. Nothing in life or research is 100 percent.

Platitudes

A platitude shares kinship to generalities. It states the obvious and turns up whenever a lull in conversation occurs or a politician sees that honied or patriotic fervor is more prudent than going out on a limb with a platform plank. Avoid writing the kind of platitudes included below:

The boys and girls of today are the men and women of tomorrow.

It takes two to make a marriage.

Duty is sacred.

Freedom of speech (or assembly, or religion, or the press) is the cornerstone of liberty.

Our cause is just.

If you're not with me, you're against me.

Idioms

An idiom is an expression that may be grammatically unsound and/or figuratively weak, but which has been accepted by the reading public through years of usage. The following idioms are "Americanisms" in general use:

accord with	conform to, with
according to	convince that
accuse of	correspond to
acquitted of	desire to
adverse to	desirous of
aim to prove	die of
among ourselves	different from
angry with	disdain for
as far as (so far as)	dissent from
as regards	doubt whether
at home	enamored of
attend to	feel free from
authority on	frightened by
blame me for it	(was) graduated from
cannot help talking	identical with
comply with	in accordance with

in line	prior to
in search of	provided that
monopoly	sensitive to
jealous of	superior to
kind of	treat of (with)
listen to	try to
oblivious of	unequal to
plan to go	unmindful of
prefer to	vie with

Among the idiomatic expressions used with frequency:

One agrees: *to* a proposal, *on* a plan, *with* a person

One contends: *for* a principle, *with* a person, *against* an obstacle

One differs: *with* a person, *from* something else, *about* or *over* a question

One is impatient: *for* something desired, *with* someone else, *of* restraint, *at* someone's conduct

One is rewarded: *for* something done, *with* a gift, *of* a person

Interrupters

One school of thought about interrupters—parentheses and interjections ("*however*," "*I believe*")—is that writers should use only one in a short piece and but a half-dozen in a lengthy one.

Another viewpoint is that aside from parentheses, interrupters should be placed at the *start* of a sentence to warn readers that something counter to previous paragraphs or sentences is about to be unveiled. It's argued that fairness, if not clarity, demands that courtesy. However, sometimes the motive is to educate, trap, or, in the case of political mailers, to deliberately confuse a reader.

The recommendation here is to abide by both schools of thought.

The best way to monitor placement of interrupters in a classroom composition is to do a quick re-read and circle the words; then, mark them with an arrow if they need repositioning. Assignments written on a computer require only highlighting the entire piece and using the FIND feature to locate interrupters for repositioning or deletion.

You do need to determine whether all your interrupters, including parenthetical expressions, are essential. A superabundance suggests insecurity—or at least contempt for editing.

If you know you're partial to certain interrupters or have the parentheses habit, the monitoring suggested above will help you taper off.

This may be an opportune time to check overreliance on interrupters such as, "*I think/believe/feel, however, nevertheless, naturally, incidentally, of course, by the way*," and the like. That "e-mail language" boils such interrupters as "*by the way*" to "*btw*" says much about how vital they are in written communication. Overuse clogs sentences and confuses readers. When you state a viewpoint, as has been noted, aren't you telling readers what you believe? And if you have an addiction to, say, "*however*," awareness should lead to rationing compositions to two at the most.

Pronouns

The misuse of some pronouns—chiefly *it*—perhaps has earned almost as many scolding notes from teachers as misspellings. Readers have short memories, as has been emphasized. They may have a difficult time understanding to what *it* refers if several nouns come before that pronoun. Pronouns such as *they*, *them*, and *their* do present equal challenges as these classic examples show:

> The students turned the pigs loose on the girls; we had to chase *them* (the girls? the pigs?).

> He gave the books and code to them; *they* were clean of fingerprints (the papers? books? them?).

The best way to avoid the problem is *not* to stop using the chief offenders—*it, they, them, their*—but to come to attention when using them to apply at least one of two remedies. Luckily, the English language has few such pronouns to track.

One student overcame "faulty references" by checking whether these troublesome pronouns appeared in the *last* part of a sentence, the usual place of error. That can be done by circling the pronoun as you use it in a classroom composition or by using a computer's FIND feature on homework assignments. Then, comb the sentence to see if the pronoun refers to more than one noun in the *first* half of the sentence.

The second remedy is to substitute the pronoun with a noun, even if the recast sentence initially seems awkward. In the first example above, the word "*them*" could be changed to "*the animals*." In the second example, "*they*" might be converted to "*the items*." Neither change for clarity creates an awkward sentence.

Redundancies

Another item to eliminate when you edit the first draft is the redundant expression, such as "final goodbye" or beefing up powerful adjectives with unneeded adverbs such as "*very, really, truly*." The terms "*quite*" and "*well-*" are nonessentials, too, but these "Unholy Three" adverbs are perhaps the worst offenders for *any* kind of writing—personal letters and compositions to novels. If you're aware of these three, you'll either begin expunging them when they flow from keyboard or pen, or you'll pick them off when editing.

Aside from this infamous trio, the most common redundancies seem to be the following. The words in parentheses are the corrections:

bare essentials (essentials)	on Monday (Monday)
Christmas Eve evening (Christmas Eve)	recur again (recur)
complete monopoly (monopoly)	repeat again (repeat)
completely destroyed (destroyed)	resume again (resume)
first beginnings (beginnings)	round in form (round)
free gratis (free)	tiny little feet (tiny feet, little feet)
he is a man who (he)	unusually/very unique (unique)
in a hasty manner (hastily)	whether or not (whether)

CHAPTER **8**

EDITING SHORTCUTS

When you've written a composition in class, what happens when you want to delete words or entire paragraphs? Or you want to add a word, a piece of punctuation, a sentence, or need to paragraph? Or shift a sentence, move a paragraph or a page?

Students trained to be neat generally ball up the sheet for a new start on a fresh piece of paper. Those trained to be economical with time and effort (or to "save a tree") usually write additions in the margins with an arrow pointing to where that new material is to be inserted.

But fresh starts *do* waste time, energy *and* paper—something realized decades ago by editors and writers who not only were on deadline, but could not afford to waste paper because it was handmade and costly. They invented a set of editing symbols that could be done with a flick of the pen and shown at the end of this chapter.

Those symbols are still used daily in the publishing field and recognized internationally in the Western world. Most of your instructors—English to history, business to the sciences—use them when editing their own work. So they'll have no difficulty with your version of those symbols.

Even if you use a computer for composition assignments, term papers, or other formal documents, chances are you usually download drafts so you can check them before turning in final copies. It's helpful to know about copy-editing procedures tied to those symbols.

Insertions

Insertions are used for single words, punctuation, paragraphs or whole sections when writers discover they've omitted something important.

Let's look first at inserts for sentences, paragraphs, sections, or entire pages.

The student who uses the margins to add sentences or paragraphs has the right idea. However, because such additions have space limits, it means the instructor will have to suffer from attempting to read cramped longhand. Most teachers prefer having additions on a separate sheet. That gives the student ample room to write additional material as well as the legibility teachers appreciate.

Rather than rewrite the *entire* composition, enclose additions or shifts with a box or bracket both sides of the new material. Either way, mark it "*Insert A.*" If the document has *many* pages, include the page number where it's to be placed.

Next, go to the place where material is to be inserted. Draw a line from the *left* margin to that spot (because the reader sees the *left* side first).

At the start of the line in the left margin, write the corresponding symbol "*Insert A.*" If you have several insertions to make in *different* parts of the document, mark *each* addition with successive letters of the alphabet (*Insert B, Insert C, Insert D,* etc.). You'll find the symbols fast and easy to do.

How to do an insertion on hard copy is shown below. The first part shows the original text, marked for an insert. The second paragraph is marked as the inserted material.

Insert A

The safest way of having no thoughts of one's own is to take up a book every moment one has nothing else to do. Men of learning are those who have done their reading in the pages of a book. Thinkers and men of genius are those who have gone straight to the book of Nature; it is they who have enlightened the world and carried humanity further on its way.

Insert A

It is this practice which explains why erudition makes most men more stupid and silly than they are by nature, and prevents their writings obtaining any measure of success. They remain, in Pope's words: "For ever reading, never to be read!" *Insert*

To insert letters or one or two words on hard copy, use the *caret* symbol, which looks like this: ^ The examples below show how:

When in the course of hu͡an events it becomes
^

To add one or two words, use the caret mark this way:

This ⋏ is especially adaptable to ~~examinations~~ *tests*

Don't use the caret for inserting more words than these because it becomes too difficult to follow.

Never write a lot of material to be inserted on the same page, especially in a classroom composition. You may wind up turning the paper sideways and writing additional material in the margins. It's much better to take a fresh sheet of paper and write the addition. Put a box around it and mark it "Insert A" (use alphabet letters to add more inserted paragraphs). To show the instructor where it's to be placed, mark a corresponding "Insert A" and run an arrow to the spot where the new material is to be inserted.

Deletions

The time will come when you'll want to omit (delete) words, sentences, paragraphs, or whole sections—even something that may have taken hours to find and write or that once seemed essential. Balling up a page in classroom work or repeated downloadings off the computer do waste paper and take time, as noted. Besides, what if you change your mind and want to retain the writing buried in the wastebasket?

If you're writing on a computer, do what professionals do: Create a separate "cutting-room-floor" file to store the words and paragraphs to be deleted. Some writers keep *both* the original and the cutting-room files open on the screen for a quick copy-and-paste transfer.

But if you're writing in class in longhand, the traditional deletion mark is still the most efficient timesaver on hard copy because it requires only quick marking with a pen, like this:

It ~~was~~ was on January 2 that ~~George W. Bush~~.

Here's how to omit sentences *within* a paragraph on hard copy:

> We were further told that we shouldn't try to sell them when we were through with them either. He was writing a new set right then. He asked us if we thought he lived on his salary, and when one boy said he thought so, the professor told us that the third-string quarterback made more money than he did last year alone. Furthermore, we were told to buy eight books that he had written for "outside reading." These weren't available in secondhand stores or even the library.

To delete a whole paragraph, mark it like this:

> A man does not have to match this profile exactly, but it won't help him at all if his line zigs where the chart zags. Take a man who scores considerably higher than the 10th percentile on aesthetic values, for example; such people, Sears, Roebuck notes, "accept artistic beauty and taste as a fundamental standard of life. This is not a factor which makes for executive success. . . . Generally, cultural considerations are not important to Sears executives, and there is little evidence that such interests are detrimental to success." **

If you decide to omit a page or several pages, run a single arrow from the top left-hand corner to the bottom right-hand corner.

Deletions shouldn't be done by scribbling over words or by rolling up the botched page and tossing it away. You might change your mind and want to re-include that page or paragraph. To do this, write the word *stet* (Latin for "leave it as it is") on the margins of what you want to preserve. The *stet* marks look like this:

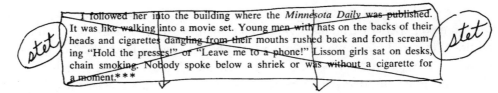

> I followed her into the building where the *Minnesota Daily* was published. It was like walking into a movie set. Young men with hats on the backs of their heads and cigarettes dangling from their mouths rushed back and forth screaming "Hold the presses!" or "Leave me to a phone!" Lissom girls sat on desks, chain smoking. Nobody spoke below a shriek or was without a cigarette for a moment.***

Other Editing Symbols

Another shortcut in checking your rough draft and making small, quick changes is to use other copy-editing symbols from the publishing world. These can be made on your hard copy or on class work. Such symbols pick off minuscule mistakes in the *finished* composition whether it's in longhand or on a computer printout.

Most teachers will accept minor changes on either longhand or computer drafts. So few students know about copy-editing or proofreading symbols, in fact, that you might impress them. If you have too many corrections, you might just as well do what professionals do: Rewrite the composition. You'll find that it's far more polished than what you almost turned in.

The marks shown in this section have been in use for generations wherever the English language is printed. The reason for such timeless and universal popularity is, once again, that that changes require only a flick of a pen.

The symbols are these:

Symbol	Explanation	Symbol in Use
◯	Spell out or abbreviate	N.Y. New York 9 ten
‿	Join separated material	m‿en
/	Separate joined material	old/men
⌣	Insert material	g⌄ld Is ⌃ in (*Not*)
/	No capital letters	/Counties
≡	Use capital letters	m̳e̳mphis
∼ ⌐ ⌐	Transpose words or letters	s⌐o⌐ld are/ firmly/ hit
⌒	Delete or carry-over	are always hit
(stet)	Leave it as it is	are always hit
⌐	Join these parts	flaunt. Not in ↳ Mercy is always strained
⫫	Paragraph within the text	11 men. ⫫ They
NO ⫫	No paragraph	NO ⫫ From all of
⌵	Insert quotation marks	Go! ⌵ he shouted.
⌵	Insert an apostrophe	John⌵s hat
⋀	Insert comma	If he is right ⋀ he should
⊙	Period	one night ⊙ But there is
✗	Delete matter	Johnn was going to

An example of several copy-editing symbols in use is below:

Let me introduce John Q. Paramecium of (N.Y.) He is a happy little fellow, even though he cannot be seen without a microscope. He spends all his time in the water as most tiny one-celled animals do.

When john's body grows so large that he can not take care of it, he divides in half. This is not as easy as it sounds, however.

A Paramecium has two main parts. There is the nucleus, which is something like a brain. And then there is the cytoplasm which is like flesh.

Insert A ———

Now we have seen what a paramecium looks like. The reason why he must divide is too difficult to go into here. But it has much to do with john's being over-weight. The next step is to see what happens.

When John divides, each half must be the same. There must be a nucleus in each half. The chromosomes must in each nucleus also be the same.

It is not hard to see under a microscope.

John's chromosomes unravel as strings would if the ends were not tied. Each chromosome divides into two strings that which have spots that are just alike.

These halves are pulled apart to each side of the nucleus by a strange force. when these groups get to the sides of the nucleus, they keep on going.

Soon the nucleus is pulled apart into two which are just alike. john, then, has a nucleus at each end. The difficult part is over. John Q. simply divides across the middle between the nuclei.

Each half, then, can go on living without the other.

Insert A

The nucleus has many little chromosomes. These are like strings with little colored spots on them. Each spot makes some part of the paramecium work as it should. They, also, are nearly the same in every paramecium so that all of John's relatives look and act the same. This is important. If it did not happen, maybe some would end up looking like trees.

Insert A

BAFFLING WORDS
AND USAGE

Some words and their usage baffle even the language experts. Some insist the last word on *any* confusing term is *Webster's Unabridged Dictionary*. Others insist that English is a "living language" and that "*real hot* " is an acceptable expression in the Deep South. In some circles it takes a courageous grammarian to answer the telephone with "This is she." And who has not wondered whether a hyphen always follows prefixes such as "*non-, anti-, or trans-*? " Or what to do when one must choose between "*who*" and "*whom*" or "*that*" and "*which*?" We've all seen celebrities on talk shows reduced to terror when forced to make a choice between using "*I*" and "*me*" because they suspect all their English teachers might be watching; many retreat into "*myself.*"

This chapter provides a ready-reference tool for most baffling words and usage. The words are listed alphabetically and usage is based on Webster as well as style-books from *The New York Times* and the Associated Press, the author's *The Copy-Editing and Headline Handbook*, and the classic *Elements of Style* by William Strunk, Jr., and E. B. White.

One helpful observation about usage problems is that when you are struggling to keep *two* things straight such as using "*I*" or "*me*," memorize only *one* of them; the other term will be correct by default. For example, memorize the fact that "*I*" is *always* the "actor" in a sentence, not someone "acted upon."

One student sorted them out by memorizing "*me*." "If I'm acted upon, I'm a victim crying 'woe is *me*,'" she explained. Another student conquered the "*to, too*" dilemma by memorizing that "*too*" meant "*also*" and was used far less than "*to*." Some resort to creative, if seemingly illogical, devices such as the coed "majoring" in the word "*between*" instead of "*among*." She used the poetic opening line of "Between the dark and the daylight" (Henry Wadsworth Longfellow's "The Children's Hour") to remember that *dark* and *daylight* were two things.

If high school and college students could figure out solutions for troublesome words, so can you. If they work, share them with your teacher, your classmates, or this author for wide circulation. You'll help those struggling with a written language that baffles almost everyone.

A, An.   The word "*a*" goes before a consonant *sound* in the example (It was a *b*ig game). The word "*an*" goes before a vowel sound and a word beginning with the letter "*h*" (She's an *only* child who has an *h*onored father).

Abbreviations, Acronyms.   When you *first* mention an individual, put the title *before* the name unless it's an academic designation (Dr. Melvin Smith, Sen. Steve Johnson, Gen. Gordon Jones, Mrs. Barbara Roberts, and Irving Story, Ph.D). For the first mention of a business or institution, omit the abbreviation unless it's a trademark, especially the second time you use it (Standard Insurance Company/Co.; The Ohio State University/OSU; *The New York Times*/NYT, etc.).

The *first* time you mention an organization such as government departments (Federal Bureau of Investigation) use the full name. For the second reference, use the acronym (FBI). Publications often prevent reader confusion—and save later space—by sometimes putting the acronym with or without parentheses *immediately* after the first reference as in: The Central Intelligence Agency (CIA) fought back; and in: The *Atlantic Richfield Corporation* was mentioned, but *ARCO* officials denied the allegation.

All-.   When this prefix is *part* of a compound adjective, use a hyphen (all-out effort, all-star game, all-around hero).

Among, Between.   The word "*among*" involves *more than two* elements; "*between*" involves *only two* unless it's a pair with several elements (The meeting was between the group division's legal and underwriting departments and individual-insurance's actuary and policyowner service departments).

Another.   This word doesn't mean something that's *additional*. It's involved with *duplicating* something mentioned *previously* (She earned $15 and lost another $10).

Ante-, Anti-.   Don't hyphenate the prefix "*ante-*" (antecedent), but *do* use a hyphen with all *anti*-words *except* the following:

antibiotic	antihistamine	antipasto	antiserum
antibody	antiknock	antiperspirant	antithesis
anticlimax	antimatter	antiphon	antitoxin
antidote	antimony	antiphony	antitrust
antifreeze	antiparticle	antiseptic	antitussive
antigent			

Anybody, Any Body, Anyone, Any One.   Use *one* word (anyone) when you mean nobody or no one in particular. The words *Any body* can mean any corpse or any group. The rule is the same for "*everybody, nobody, somebody, some-one.*" To avoid confusion when two "*o*'s" meet, make it two words (no one). If you're giving emphasi*s* to *part* of a group, make it two words (Any one of them may be innocent).

Arbitrate, Mediate. An *arbitrator* listens to *evidence* and unilaterally hands down decisions, just as a judge does. A *mediator* also listens to evidence, but tries to get quarreling parties to make a decision.

As Good, Better Than. The first term indicates equality; the second, superiority (Smith's singing was as good as Doe's, but the critics said Doe was better than Smith).

Assassin. An assassin is a *politically* motivated killer.

Average, Mean, Median, Norm. An *average* is the result obtained when the *sum* of all numbers to be added (e.g., 15+20+30+35=100) is divided by the *total* of those numbers (100/4 =25). The *mean* is the *middle* figure between two *extreme* numbers (e.g., 10, 100: 90/2=45). The *median* is the *middle* number in a series (7 in 3, 5, 7, 9, 10). A norm involves the *standard of average* performance previously calculated for a group.

Bad, Badly. The word *badly* is an adverb paired with an adjective (badly worn). The word *bad* is an adjective that's used correctly in statements such as "I feel *bad,*" despite the common fear that it should be "I feel *badly.*" Antidote: Remember that "feel badly" means that your *touch* is poor.

Because, Since. *Because* is part of a specific cause-effect situation; one thing leads directly to another (He flunked out because he was at the Student Union 24/7 instead of classes*)*. Today, the word *since* involves time (Since 1861, skedaddling has become an art in the military).

Bi-. Don't hyphenate this prefix (bilateral, bimonthly, biweekly). Moreover, usage means twice the *period* cited (Biannual means twice per *year*, biweekly means twice per *week*).

Bloc, Block. A *bloc* is a group of people or countries with one goal. A *block* involves either streets or a tangible object (block of ice/cement).

Boycott, Embargo. A *boycott* is an organized movement to get consumers to stop buying goods or services. An *embargo* is a government order or policy prohibiting trade with another country.

But. Help stamp out using this word from the expression "I couldn't help but see/believe/think, etc..." To keep it from becoming an idiom, write: "I couldn't help seeing/believing/thinking.).

But That, But What. Omit the word *but* in sentences that include the word *doubt* so that they become "I don't doubt that he'll do that."

By-. This prefix needs no hyphen (bypass, bylaw) except for *by-election and by-product.*

Cabal, Cable.   The first word means a group of conspirators out to overthrow some entity, a government, company, organization, clique (The cabal at PGE ensured the CEO's downfall). The second word has to do with wire used by communication companies (The trans-Atlantic cable was laid that year; nearly a hundred years later a television cable network came into most American homes).

Co-.   Don't hyphenate prefixes that have outgrown the old rule that a prefix ending in a vowel next to a word beginning with another vowel must have a hyphen (coeducation, coexist, cooperate, coordinate, coessential, coercive, coextensive, coagulate, coalition).

Collective Nouns.   Is it "The couple *was* happy" or "The couple *were* happy?" "The committee is to meet" or "The committee are to meet?" The correct verb is all in the mind of the beholder, remind your teacher, because the verb depends whether you're thinking of the couple/committee as a *whole* or as *individuals* within that unit.

Compared to, Compared with.   The expression *compared to* compares *two or more* similar items. *Compared with* involves putting two things *side by side* to show *similarities and differences.*

Constitute, Compose, Comprise.   *Constitute* is considered the best choice of these three verbs involving a collection of something or people. *Compose* is better suited to something created, as in the arts or sciences. *Comprise* may be more than 200 years old, but language purists have condemned it as an awkward or inadequate verb. *The AP Stylebook* suggests using *comprise* only as an active-voice verb that should be placed next to a direct object (The Panhellenic Council comprises 32 sororities).

Conclave.   A secret meeting.

Connote, Denote.   *Connote* suggests something *beyond* what's on the surface. The word *tithe* connotes obligation. *Denote* deals with what's *on* the surface. (His conduct denotes treason.) Memorize one.

Convince, Persuade.   People are *convinced* about things from some action or realization arrived at by themselves. *Persuade* involves heavy external pressure applied by others.

Discuss.   The Latin root *"dis"* stipulates that *more* than one thing is involved. So *one* person can't discuss anything whether in a speech, essay-test question, or a solo class recitation. Caveat: You won't be popular if you remind people about the correct meaning of this term.

Ex-.   Use this prefix if you mean a former position (ex-convict, ex-governor, ex-husband). But all other applications don't need a hyphen (excommunicate, expropriate).

Extra-.   Use a hyphen if this prefix is part of a compound adjective (extra-base hit, extra-large book). When *extra-* means something *beyond* the norm, omit the hyphen unless it's tied to a capitalized word (extra-Britannic).

Fewer, Less.   Use *fewer* for individual items and *less* for bulk or quantity (Fewer than 18 agents turned up. Paul had less than $30 in his account).

Flounder, Founder.   A fish furnished the origin of a word describing people physically moving around clumsily (Ask my brother to do the dishes and we always lose several because of his floundering). *Foundering* is a maritime term for a ship that's either disabled or is sinking.

Fore-.   Don't hyphenate this prefix except for three nautical expressions (fore-topgallant, fore-topmast, and fore-topsail).

Forego, Forgo.   When one thing is done *before* a second thing, use *forego* and think of the golfer's cry of "fore" or the word "before" (Winning that battle was a foregone conclusion). When you sacrifice something, use *forgo* (I'll forgo chocolate this year).

Fractions.   The AP Stylebook mandates spelling out fractions of numbers *less* than one and using a hyphen (three-fifths, five-sixteenths). If you can't convert fractions into decimals and you don't have a word-processing program that sets "*one-fourth*" as a single numerical character, resort to regular characters with two spaces between the whole number and fraction on people's age or years (Susie was 2 1/2 years old when this portrait measuring 8 3/8 by 12 7/16 inches was painted).

Full Time, Full-Time, Part-Time, Part Time.   The words with the hyphens are compound adjectives (full-time or part-time job) describing the noun that follows. Omit the hyphens when the words are used as nouns (I work part time, but he works full time).

Goodwill.   Spell *goodwill* as one word as a noun (Goodwill is part of selling the company) and as an adjective (It was a goodwill gesture).

Half-.   For this prefix, check the dictionary because its use is illogical (half-dollar, half-hour, half-life, half-truth, half-blood, half brother, half note, half tide, halfback, halfhearted, halftrack).

Half-Mast, Half-Staff.   On ships and naval bases, flags fly at *half-mast*. Everywhere else, flags are at *half-staff*.

Hopefully.   You'll be skewered by purists if you write: "Hopefully, we'll finish soon," instead of "It's hoped we'll finish soon." Common usage has overtaken their prohibition against a word meaning a hopeful attitude.

Hydro-, Hyper-.   Don't hyphenate either prefix.

Imply, Infer.   Writers and speakers *imply* things with their words; their audiences *infer* (think "*in*take") things from those words.

In, Into.   "*In*" involves location (I live in New York City), and "*into*" involves movement (I got into an argument. I went into the next room).

In-.   Don't hyphenate this prefix except for a few compound adjectives (in-depth, in-group, in-house, in-law).

Inter-. Don't hyphenate this prefix except for "*inter-American*" and similar terms whereby the second coupled word is a proper noun.

King, Queen, Prince, Princess, Duke, Baron. Capitalize these royal titles only when they're used before a monarch's name: King George VI on the first reference, King George on the second reference. Don't capitalize the title if it stands alone (The queen didn't die). If you have *several* royals of the same gender in one sentence, make it "*Kings* George, Edward, and Andrew."

Last. Ensure you definitely mean "*last*" and not "*latest.*"

Lay, Lie, Laid. "*Lie*" means to recline, *lay* means to place. Memory devices: "*Recline*" has the same vowel sound as "*lie*" and also an "*i*" and "*e.*" "*Place*" has a long vowel like "*lay*" and an "*a.*" "*Laid*" is the past tense of "*lay.*"

Like, As. "*Like*" is a preposition comparing nouns and pronouns (Sallyanne works like her). "*As,*" however, is a conjunction introducing a clause (Winstons taste good as a cigarette should).

Like-, -like. Use the prefix when one thing is *similar* to something (like-minded, like-natured). Omit the hyphen when the words contain other meanings (likelihood, likeness, likewise). The suffix form (lifelike, etc.) requires a hyphen only if its omission involves the letter "*l*" (bill-like, shell-like).

Magazine Names. Don't capitalize the first letter in "magazine" unless it's part of the official title (I read *Harper's Magazine* and *TIME* magazine regularly).

Majority, Plurality. "*Majority*" means a candidate or measure got more than *half* of the votes; "*plurality*" means an excessive number above the *next highest number* (Woodrow Wilson's plurality was 6.2 million votes over Teddy Roosevelt's 4.1 million).

Mass. *Mass* is a capitalized word that's not given to its adjective (high Mass, requiem Mass). Too, a Mass is celebrated, said, or sung.

May Day, Mayday. "*May Day*" is the May 1 holiday, but the "Mayday" plea for help comes from the French expression "*m'aidez*" ("help me").

Mid-. Don't hyphenate this prefix unless a capitalized word follows or unless it involves a time factor (Nobody changed horses during midterm or in midstream, especially if they were targeting the mid-Atlantic and mid-Africa in the mid-50s).

Mini-. Don't hyphenate this prefix (miniseries, miniconferences, minibus).

Mishap, Holocaust. *Mishap* is an unfortunate, but not fatal, *accident*. Holocaust either involves a major fire or the deliberate effort to exterminate a large number of people as in the World War II treatment of Jews by Nazi Germany.

Ms. This is a term for married or unmarried women. If several are mentioned in a series, use "Ms." It's still used before each name.

Multi-. Don't hyphenate this prefix (multinational, etc.).

Non-. Don't hyphenate this prefix (noncontroversial, nonprofit, nondescript, nonresident).

Nowadays. This word is correct, no matter how much it sounds like "*nowdays.*"

Numbers. Never start a sentence with figures unless it's a year (1976 was a good year). Spell out a number if it starts a sentence (Thirty students passed). Within sentences, spell out numbers *below* 10; use figures for 10 and above. (There were 10 who signed up, but only two passed). Spell out "*first*" through "*ninth*" in time or location (third base, the third step).

For geographic, military, or political designations, abbreviate (1st Marines, 7th Ward, lst Sgt., 2nd Lt.). If a number is *part* of a corporate title, use it (Big Ten, 20th Century Fox, The Thirty Club).

When you spell out large numbers, use a hyphen to link words ending in "*y*" to another word (twenty-four, forty-five, one hundred sixty-seven, seventy-seven thousand four hundred twenty-two).

Odd-. Use a hyphen with this prefix (odd-looking, odd-numbered).

Off-, –off. The authority on this prefix/suffix is Webster's dictionary because too many words contain one of them (prefixes: off-color, off-season, offset, off-side; suffixes: blastoff, send-off, playoff, and stopoff).

One-. When you're writing fractions, use this prefix for clarity (one-half, one-fourth, one-hundredth).

Out-, -out. The authority on this prefix/suffix is Webster's dictionary because too many words contain one of them (prefixes: outpost, output, outfield; suffixes: cop-out, fade-out, hide-out, worn-out, worn out, fallout, pullout, walkout).

Over, More than. "*Over*" does not mean *more* than; it involves space (One Flew Over the Cuckoo's Nest). "*More than*" is used with math (More than 50 took the MBA degree).

Over-, –over. The authority on this prefix/suffix is Webster's dictionary because too many words contain one of them (prefixes: overall, overrate, override; suffixes: takeover, holdover, walkover, makeover, carry-over, etc.).

Pan-. This prefix occurs most often with proper nouns and requires a hyphen as well as capitalization if what follows is a capitalized word (Pan-African, Pan-American, Pan-Slavism). But heavy use with common nouns seems to have worn out the hyphen (Panhellenic, panchromatic, pancratium, panhuman, panmixia, pansexual, pantechnicon, pantheism, pantrophic, etc.).

Pardon, Parole, Probation. A "*pardon*" forgives and releases a prisoner from a sentence; a political pardon is amnesty. A "*parole*" releases a prisoner before the sentence has been completed on condition of good behavior. "*Probation*" suspends the sentence on condition of good behavior.

Percent. Percent now is one word. It takes a plural verb when a plural word completes a prepositional phrase (Only 10 percent of the employees were on the scene).

Post-. The authority on this prefix is Webster's dictionary because too many words contain this prefix (postdate, postgraduate, postscript, postwar, post-bellum, post-mortem).

Pre-. The authority on this prefix is Webster's dictionary, but most usage isn't hyphenated (prewar, prenatal, preheat, preconvention, predawn, preempt).

Prefix Rules. Two chief rules—with a few exceptions—govern most prefixes: 1) Hyphenate if the root word is capitalized (un-American), and 2) hyphenate double prefixes (sub-subcommittee).

Pro-. This prefix requires a hyphen when the word indicates *supportive* conditions (pro-labor, pro-life, pro-war).

Raised, Reared. Only humans are *reared*, but in the Deep South they're also *raised* (The acronym GRITS stands for Girls Raised in the South).

Re-. The authority on this prefix is Webster's dictionary because too many words contain it (re-elect, re-enlist, re-entry, resign, re-sign, reform, re-form, recover, re-cover).

Rebut, Refute. *Rebut* has to do with arguing *against* a point, but *refute* means winning an argument.

Recur, Reoccur. Things *recur*; they never *reoccur*.

Room Numbers. Use: *Room 211*.

Rosary. A rosary is *recited* or *said*; it's never *read*.

Scot, Scots, Scottish, Scotch. A native of Scotland is a *Scot*, and the plural is *Scots*, not *Scotch* which is a form of whiskey. The descriptive term for these nationals is *Scottish*.

Self-. This prefix is usually hyphenated except for *selfless* and *selfish*.

Semi-. This prefix usually takes no hyphen, but an exception or two exist (semi-invalid).

Shall, Will. Determination is shown with the antique term *shall*, but both *shall* and *will* can be used in other situations.

Should, Would. The word "*should*" involves duty. The word "would" is used ordinarily, but it's also correct when something is *conditional* (If Bird had not swung on him, Lucus would not have been hurt).

Skid Road, Skid Row. In the Pacific Northwest, you'll be scolded if you mistake *skid row* (a slum) for *skid road*. A skid road was a chute used to send logs from forest to market, but quickly became a metaphor for a route from wealth to homelessness.

Stanch, Staunch.   If you can *stanch* a flow of blood, you're probably a *staunch* believer in first-aid training.

Straight, Strait.   A *straight-laced* person holds rigid views on moral issues. The word "*strait*" has the same origins, but it has other usages (The Straits of Gibraltar are narrow. The mental hospital uses straitjackets. They wound up in terrible financial straits).

Sub-.   This prefix rarely takes a hyphen.

Super-.   Don't hyphenate this prefix unless it's linked to a capitalized word (Super-Blazer).

Tenterhooks, Tenderhooks.   The proper word is *tenterhook*s.

That, Which.   These two pronouns become troublesome only in a clause. Use "*that*" if the pronoun is *vital* for the sentence to make sense (A refrigerator that doesn't run is useless). If the sentence makes sense without the clause, use "*which*" and put commas around that clause (The refrigerator, which keeps our food cold, is in the shop). Both pronouns are used in writing about inanimate objects and animals.

Titles.   The principal rule is that a formal title is capitalized if it goes *before* the name (Pope John Paul, King Edward VII, Mrs. Mary Smith, President Van Buren, Governor Huey Long, Lt. Col. Hop Harrigan, Secretary of State Bill Bradbury). If the name is fenced off from the title by commas, don't capitalize the title (The vice president, Theodore Roosevelt, went to Vermont that summer. Elizabeth II, the current queen, opened Parliament that year). When titles are *not* linked to proper names, don't capitalize them (The president is expected to speak there. He didn't see the pope.)

If the title is based on a job, don't capitalize it (movie star Rudolph Valentino, astronaut John Glenn, superintendent John Ward.

When someone has held or will hold a title, don't capitalize the adjective (former vice president Al Gore, former governor Howard A. Dean, former prime minister Margaret Thatcher, interim superintendent Carolyn Petersen).

When the title *follows* a name, separate the proper name from that title with commas to help the reader (Max Erntsen, undersecretary for Health, Education, and Welfare, will arrive Monday). Use a comma to separate a lengthy title from the name of the person holding it (The chairman of the subcommittee on rural schools in Montgomery County, Charles J. Evans, was in charge).

Trademark.   A trademark is used by a company that has *exclusive* legal rights to it so that competitors cannot use it. The dictionary indicates whether a word is trademarked. When you write about trademarked products such as Levi's, Coke, Kleenex, or Xerox, capitalize the first letter. The Coca-Cola Company has had a reputation for contacting even high school newspaper editors who fail to capitalize the product's nickname (Coke).

Trans-.   This prefix uses no hyphen except when the word linked to it is a proper noun (trans-Atlantic, trans-Siberian railroad).

Transpire. The word "*transpire*" means to escape from secrecy. It doesn't mean something that *happened*. Memory device: *spire=spy*.

Trustee, Trusty. A *trustee* manages property or the affairs of people, foundations, corporations, and the like. A *trusty* is a convict who has earned special privileges as a trustworthy inmate.

TV. Spell out *television* on the first reference; abbreviate it on the second.

U.S., U.N., UNICEF. A rule helpful to readers is to spell out these words on the *first* reference before resorting to abbreviations or acronyms (United States, United Nations Children's Fund, Union of Soviet Socialist Republics, etc.).

Ultra-. Don't hyphenate this prefix.

Un-. Don't hyphenate this prefix unless the attached word is capitalized (un-American).

Under-. Don't hyphenate this prefix.

Underway, Under Way. The first term is an adjective meaning something *performed* (The play was underway before the sets arrived). The second is an adverb chiefly involved in naval matters (The ship got under way).

Up-, –up. The authority on this prefix/suffix is Webster's dictionary because too many words contain one of them (prefixes: upgrade, uptown; suffixes: walk-up, mock-up, run-up).

Vice. Make "*vice*" a separate word (vice chairman, vice president) without hyphens.

Vital. Because the root of this word means "*life*," use it only in a life-or-death context.

Von, De. These foreign-name particles meaning "*of the*" may be capitalized in their home countries, but in the United States they don't get that (Charles de Gaulle, Ludwig von Beethoven). When the first name is omitted, however, capitalize those titles (DeGaulle headed the army. Von Richthofen flew his missions as the Red Baron).

Well-. This prefix is usually hyphenated because it's part of a compound adjective (He is a well-dressed man). When the adjective **follows** the noun, it's **not** hyphenated (The play was well done). Sometimes it's part of a noun (well-wishers, well-being).

Who, Whom. The pronoun "who" is always a *subject* of a sentence (Who's there? The man who became king was a recluse). *Whom* is the *object* of a verb or preposition (Whom did they want to win? The child to whom the money was left became an overnight millionaire). Use who and whom to refer to humans—*that* or *which* for inanimate objects and animals.

Wide-, -wide. As a prefix, it's usually hyphenated except for *widespread*. As a *suffix*, don't hyphenate it (nationwide).

-wise. Don't hyphenate this suffix except when it's part of a compound adjective (street-wise, penny-wise). Caveat: this particular suffix has drawn heavy criticism in recent years from editors, English purists, and linguists because of what the *AP Stylebook* calls "contrived combinations such as *moneywise, religionwise*." Avoid them by checking the dictionary.

Words as Words. Put words singled out as such in italics (He didn't know the meaning of the word *surrender*). For greater emphasis, add quotation marks around the word (The word "*snickersnee*" comes from India).

Xerox. *Xerox* is a trademark for a photocopying machine. It's not yet accepted as a verb by purists, but its common usage has made it one (Please xerox this for me). The same phenomenon is occurring with the trademarked Google search engine (I *googled* it and found the ship).

CHAPTER **10**

AN EASY GUIDE
TO PUNCTUATION

It's assumed too often that everyone knows the uses of question marks and exclamation points, and certainly the period. The trouble starts when students are faced with deciding, say, whether a comma goes *inside* or *outside* a quotation or whether a semicolon is a dead piece of punctuation. Is it *A*'s and the 20's or As and the 20s? The Jones' or the Joneses? And what about ifs, ands, or buts—or if's, and's, or but's?

Basically, punctuation is designed to help the reader and speaker, though with one main drawback. A little is good, but more is not necessarily better. As has been pointed out, each time readers encounter punctuation—even an apostrophe—their eyes stop. Minds pause to digest what has been written instead of going forward. This is one of the difficulties with long sentences. For comprehension of content, they require commas or semicolons, dashes or parentheses, and often quotation marks—both double and single.

Part of your problem in reading textbooks may be resistance to something mandated in subjects you dislike. But much of it also rests in textbooks authored with an eye to peer approval for publication rather than students. Examine them for vocabulary several levels above your own. Or, more to the point, check for lengthy sentences because they require heavy punctuation for comprehension, thereby creating constant stop-and-start reading.

If you find this to be the case, two good lessons can come from it.

First, you'll learn a lot about punctuation use. Second, you'll become aware of the need for a variety of sentence lengths in your compositions—and the use of punctuation. Mastery depends upon willingness to edit your drafts, even those written in class.

To illustrate the foregoing, try understanding this example on the first reading:

> On the other hand, if we have in view the comprehensibility of a whole of speculative knowledge, which, though wide-ranging, has the coherence that follows from unity of principle, we can say with equal justice that many a book would have been much clearer if it had not made such an effort to be clear.

Eyes tired? Mind wandering? That example doesn't mean going to the opposite extreme, as one reporter did when the managing editor decreed shorter sentences:

> Dead.
> That was the condition of Joe Smith yesterday.

At least the reporter didn't have to worry about punctuation. If you're so unsure of it that you have a bad case of "comma-itis" driving you to drop in commas everywhere ("just to be on the safe side"), shortening sentences is a good *initial* cure. But that only *postpones* broad skills in using punctuation, something you'll need the rest of your life. In starting this chapter, you're showing willingness to use school compositions as the lab to master these "irksome critters," as one student called these 2,000-year-old aids to reading and speaking.

Let's start with the period, the best known, most frequently used and *least* troublesome piece of punctuation.

Periods

The period is nearly 3,000 years old, invented in the fifth century B.C. when speakers of the ancient Western world demanded writers come up with a mark to fence off one sentence from another. The writers decided upon three vertical *points* (imagine an extra period atop a colon). A hundred years later, speakers were demanding writers indicate breaks *between* sections. The writers came up with "*paragraphos*"—horizontal lines between text passages. By 100 B.C., Roman writers were inserting one of those *points* between each word. Sentence endings were denoted by extra spacing and a capital letter on the word starting the next sentence.

If you ever wished punctuation and capitalization had never been invented, this is what you would have had as notes to deliver the opening section of the Gettysburg address around 200 B.C.:

FOURoSCOREoANDoSEVENoYEARSoAGOoOURoFAT
HERSoBROUGHToFORTHoONoTHISoCONTINENTo
AoNEWoNATIONoCONCEIVEDoINoLIBERTYoAND
oDEDICATEDoTOoTHEoPROPOSITIONoTHAToALLo
MENoAREoCREATEDoEQUAL   NOWoWEoAREo
ENGAGEDoINoAoGREAToCIVILoWARoTESTINGo
WHETHERoTHAToNATIONoORoANYoNATIONoSO
oCONCEIVEDoANDoSOoDEDICATEDoCANoLONGo
ENDURE

WEoAREoMEToONoAoGREAToBATTLEFIELDoOFoTH
AToWAR   WEoHAVEoCOMEoTOoDEDICATEoAo
PORTIONoOFoTHAToFIELDoASoAoFINALoRESTINGo
PLACEoFORoTHOSEoWHOoHEREoGAVEoTHEIRoLIV
ESoTHAToTHEoNATIONoMIGHToLIVE

Had you been the writer forced to insert all those dots, enlarge capital letters and remember to put horizontal lines between paragraphs, you probably would have snapped "that's easy for you to say!" at those never-satisfied. Too, it's taken recent typographical studies to show that all-capital letters in text present significant readability problems for most people.

Now that you're aware of punctuation history and limits, you may view a period not only in a different light, but with some appreciation for those sixteenth century French and Italian printers who balked at "Roman form." These men were practical, efficient, and thrifty—and became readability experts because of profits off *readers*, not speakers. They refused to waste time, type, ink, and paper on all those dots and horizontal lines. Periods were placed at the *end* of sentences and paragraphs were indented, guaranteeing clarity and saving space. Capital letters were retained as sentence indicators and proper nouns, and "small," slender letters were born. And, because they were highly visual, they added italic and bold-faced fonts for text requiring emphasis.[3]

Thus, you know what a difficult birth and fight for survival the period had to end sentences. That should make you think twice about discarding it for an exclamation point on a sentence that doesn't need table-banging emphasis.

A period has other functions.

For example, a *series* of periods indicates omitted portions of sentences, whole paragraphs or pages (see "Ellipses" below).

Use periods after initials in people's names (Lyndon B. Johnson, Vikki W. S. Vanderbilt), but not if their initials are famous (FDR). Because a computer may split initials from one line to another, as say, in "P. T. Barnum," don't put a *space*

---

[3] T. Julian Brown, Encyclopaedia Britannica, 15th ed., s.v. "Punctuation."

between the first initial and its period. Make it *"P.T. Barnum," "T.S. Eliot,"* or *"W.C. Fields."*

Brackets

Brackets are those straight-backed cousins of parentheses ([ ]) that you may rarely use in compositions, but do in academic papers.

The death knell for them has been exaggerated for years, particularly in newspapers and magazines. One of the reasons is that the Associated Press has informed newspaper customers that brackets couldn't be "transmitted over news wires. Use parentheses or recast the material." Fortunately, they're still doing yeoman's work in other publications and when newspaper editors add omitted information in quotations:

"I gave those documents to [Tommy] Corcoran."

Ironically, back in the early 1950s, brackets used by three national newspapers played a heroic role in the nation's history. Ever since politicians or other newsmakers learned how to manipulate media with misstatements, lies, or leaks impossible to check on deadline, the bracket has performed a sentinel's duties to the public.

When the infamous Sen. Joseph R. McCarthy began using speeches and press conferences to hurl accusations of treason to advance his political career, the wire services and most newspapers dithered about how to cover this headline hunter and avoid multimillion-dollar slander suits. Not *The Christian Science Monitor*. After each charge it quoted, the editor placed bracketed statements saying the charge was not true, backing it with documentation. It is a successful refutation system used by many newspapers and can be useful for term papers. It looks like this:

Commissioner Smith said: "There were 17 others on that committee who voted to spend $14 million for that boondoggle. I was the only one against it." [Committee records show Smith's silence and vote supporting the reservoir during that October 19 session.]

In 1973 [The World Almanac lists it as 1974], the suit was filed in the Montgomery County Court of Domestic Relations.

Brackets are still on computer keyboards even if relegated to obscurity on the upper right side. It's noteworthy that they don't require shifting, a sign of greater use than even parentheses. You'll also find them helpful in writing term papers, especially in shortening quoted passages:

Galligan says that in 1565: "[Mary Queen of Scots] married the widely hated Lord Darnley, who was murdered two years later."

Another use is in term papers footnotes and endnotes to distinguish material from parentheses:

Bierce, Ambrose. (1956 [1912]). *Ambrose Bierce's Civil War*, (Ed. William McCann). Washington, D.C.:Regnery Gateway.

A bracket's other chief use is for dialect and verbatim quotes of the ungrammatical. The writer puts brackets *after* the "error" and inserts the word "*sic*" (Latin for "*so*" or "*thus*"). It does not need italics:

> The diary says "John went to skole [sic] when he was seven."

> One of the great feature stories about life in those days was in *Publick* [sic] *Occurrences.*

Parentheses

A parentheses' curved, protective walls add material pertinent and even vital, yet separate, to a sentence:

> One ingredient I overlooked (baking powder) probably contributed to why the cake just lay in a heap and my sister-in-law screamed with laughter.

> In reading Smith's declaration of candidacy, it seems to me that he, too, felt someone with clout (10,000+ votes in Texas) needed to keep the pressure on the candidate while draining off votes of unhappy Republicans as an Independent.

If you put a *complete* sentence *within* the parentheses, set it *outside* the sentence to which it pertains, and add a period to that sentence. Then, write the parenthetical sentence—capitalized first word, period at the end—like this:

> So, in another way, nature is the shape and form of things that have a principle of movement in themselves—the form being only theoretically separable from the object in question. (The product of matter and form—man, for instance—is not nature, but does exist by nature.)

One danger in using parentheses is being in such a hurry that you forget to "close the barn door" with the closing parenthesis' mark. One student conquered that habit on the computer by inserting *both* parentheses marks at the start of their use, then dropped in the parenthetical material. You can do the same thing in a classroom composition if you scan it for the first parentheses' mark.

Parentheses enclose clarifications concerning state names, party affiliations, or nicknames:

> She went to Selma (Ala.) High School.
> Senator John A. White (D-OR) attended.
> Lael (Mike) Campbell won the award for applications.

Humor can be slipped into parentheses to brighten dreary passages:

> Three long days, from the 25th to the 28th of January of the year 1077, Henry, dressed as a penitent pilgrim (but with a warm sweater underneath his monkish garb), waited outside the gates of the castle of Canossa.

Caution: Some professional writers overuse parentheses to the point that text is nearly choked to death. You may catch it on computerized compositions, but under the pressure of a classroom composition, you may miss it completely among the thickets of longhand. Readers don't know *why* they're annoyed or having a difficult time trying to follow material, but it's usually because of excessive use of parenthetical interruptions like this:

At first (January 15), I was encouraged to do a good job ("we offer merit raises and bonuses tied to productivity and profits") and took them at their word. (What a mistake that was!). I came in at 6 in the morning and shocked everyone ("what are you doing here!!") and noticed everyone took long lunches and left before 4. Soon, overloads (like that Lockheed contract) were dumped on me. But I really made enemies when I blew the whistle on overruns ($9,000 here, $57,342.10 there) and junkets that should have been teleconferences (five people in Vegas, 4 days=$112,054).

Dashes and Hyphens

No one has to tell you that the hyphen key is used for *both* hyphens and dashes, or that two taps produce that dash. But you might not have understood that a dash is used to show a sudden break in thought *within* a sentence and/or to emphasize something:

> Some perceptions—and I think the best—are granted only to the old soul.
> They have in themselves what they value in their horses—mettle and bottom.

Let's deal with the dash's functions first because they have been increasing of late and threatening to usurp those even of the parentheses. For instance, the quote above about a cynical king and warm sweaters is buried in a parentheses in a lengthy sentence; it may even have been missed by careful readers. Not with a dash:

> Three long days, from the 25th to the 28th of January of the year 1077, Henry, dressed as a penitent pilgrim—but with a warm sweater underneath his monkish garb—waited outside the gates of the castle of Canossa.

If you have to set off a series of unadorned words *within* a sentence, a dash helps clarity so long as it doesn't go beyond a half-dozen words:

> Several qualities—kindness, thoughtfulness, lovingness, trust—were used shamelessly.

A dash goes *before* certain expressions and abbreviations which should be stripped to their essentials:

> — Smith, Jones, White—

> —i.e., that they'd never get better—

Dashes give credit where it's due:

> "When you think you're humble, you ain't."—Henry Haupe

Dashes give added emphasis in a summation:

> The wondering, the waiting, the anxieties—all were over.

If a statement has an internal question, a dash creates greater clarity. It also solves the perplexity of whether to put a question mark at the *end* of the sentence or at the exact point of the question, like this:

> What's all this mean?—you may ask.

Dashes can be substitutes for anonymous last names:

Let's leave this up to George M—

They're essential in interrupted speeches:

> "You—you—you can't just turn in a budget without the Defense Department numbers!"
>
> "I do know that Ashley—did you forget about him?—was modeled after a cousin of hers."

Let's turn now to hyphens.

Hyphens clarify or enhance descriptions in compound adjectives ("comma-pocked sentences,"), but not if the first modifier is an adverb ending in "*ly*" (She was a highly trained operator). Look over the hyphen's role in these examples.

> He'll speak to small-business owners.
> He shot a 150-pound elk.
> They sank a well-known ship.
> She had a know-it-all attitude
> Veronica wore a pair of satin-lined boots.
> They carried full-time jobs with a half-a-loaf philosophy into buying a 15-story high-rise building which was a poorly ventilated tenement with a jury-built foundation.

If the compound adjective follows a form of the verb "*to be*" (is, are, was, were, etc.), the hyphen prevents confusion:

> The reporter was quick-witted.
> The figure is second-rate.
> The well-matched couple was not well-knit.

Editors use hyphens in "suspensive hyphenation" of compound adjectives. Notice the space after the *first* hyphen:

> Jackson got a 15- to 30-year sentence.

Use a hyphen when numbers are spelled out. Consult the chapter on baffling words for three or more digits. Those with only two are punctuated like this:

> One dollar and eighty-seven cents.

A hyphen is needed for *single* letters linked to a noun and/or in colloquial verbs:

> I fear the H-bomb.
> Give me that T-square.
> I posted an e-mail yesterday.
> Rattlesnake Jake an' his pard came a-ridin' and a-shootin' into Lewistown that day.

Use hyphens when spelling a word, showing syllabication, or pronunciation:

> The word on the banner was l-o-s-e-r.
> Pronounce it "*an-thro-po-MOR-phism.*"

Space doesn't permit including *all* words dependent upon hyphens, but Webster's dictionary has them. You'll see ethnic combinations and contradictory ones: Italian-American, French Canadian, *semi-independent, anti-intellectual, semifinal, antitrust,* etc.

Most copy editors at daily newspapers will tell you that the progression of these terms from two words, to hyphenated words, to *one* word all depends on heavy use and reader acceptance. That's how *co-operate* grew into *cooperate* and *co-respondent* became *corespondent* and why *self-less* is now *selfless*, a status not yet conferred on *self-esteem*. In families, half sisters and half brothers still aren't united by hyphens or unions such as *grandchildren* or *stepchildren*. In-laws may have to wait a while—blood being thicker than water—because the term was coined only in 1894; *outlaw* has been with us since 1100.

Ellipses

Ellipses are spaced periods indicating omitted material. Omissions *within* the sentence warrant *three* periods (He was a Yankee. . .whose time has come). Use *four* periods if an omission extends to another sentence or paragraph to paragraph. If you omit *entire* paragraphs, pages or poetic verses, put four spaced periods between the passages:

modern peculiarities of hospitality. So he walked off with the Bishop's candlesticks.

. . . .

Other things will be stated in subsequent volumes. But one of the singular portions

Ellipses also indicate *unfinished* statements or dialogue:

"If you can't see anything good in me…after all this," he snapped, "then leave!"

Unfairness and misleading statements have been blamed on ellipses so you need to be scrupulous in quoting material out of context. For one thing, many readers suspect it the moment they see ellipses, even though you may have omitted only one or two words.

But they have a point. Nowhere is abuse using ellipses more pronounced than in promotional advertisements for films, plays, and books. Terrible reviews become raves. The "fair-use" laws limit lifting copyrighted material to a few hundred words, but have yet to be applied to omitted ones. Here's what a film critic might have written and, below it, the ad copy appearing in the media:

Little Mary Jones is an outrageous desecration of one of the main events in the life of labor agitator Joe Hill. To be funny with unforgettable parts of history of the workingman is to assume what the public likes.

'Little Mary Jones is…outrageous…funny…unforgettable…what the public likes'—Tribune.

Slash (Virgule)

This piece of punctuation has been called a "thingamajig" or "whatchamaycallit" by most people, but a "virgule" by those working with words. It's that slash mark between "*either/or*" indicating either word could be "used by the reader to interpret the sense," as the dictionary defines it.[4]

"Virgule" is Latin for a short whip and was the forerunner of the comma (see *comma*). You know the virgule as restricted, but permissible, shorthand in formal

---

[4] *Webster's New International Dictionary*, 2nd ed., 2848.

composition, though it's also used in some scientific fields. Such is the heavy usage of either/or that keyboard designers demoted the question mark to a secondary position on the key shared with the virgule.

In recent years, the virgule has crept past the either/or boundary and has quickly spread as shorthand for other expressions. A heavy work week became "24/7," an exaggeration of seven 24-hour days. Purists paused in battling the epidemic only because after the terrorist attack on the United States on September 11, 2001, the event instantly was identified around the globe and in official documents as "9/11." But the sanctity of that expression may constrict its overuse. So if you coin a virgule, be prepared to argue that readers will understand it.

Colon

Some functions of the colon at the *end* of sentences lead into a series of items, examples, quotations, or something to be emphasized:

> Among the agencies cited were: Columbia, Hawaii, Siskiyou, Orange, and San Jose.

> The key passage about alcoholism is from Proverbs (23:29): "Who hath woe? Who hath sorrow? Who hath contentions? Who hath wounds without cause? Who hath redness of eyes?"

> They worried about three things: money, health, and power.

In quotations, use a colon for *more* than a dozen words, as is shown above. Use a comma for *less* than that (He said, "What makes you think so?").

Capitalize the first word *after* a colon only if it's a *proper* noun or if it starts a sentence:

> The direction seemed to be successful: Barstow had told the committee he had lined up capital, gained approval on all the city permits, and had 14 construction companies fighting for the bid.

A colon is used with dialogue and question-and-answer material:

> JONES: I won't.
> SMITH: Oh, but you will.

> Q: Mr. President, how will that affect stocks?
> A: How should I know!

Three other functions involve time, racing speeds, and citations from the Bible, statutes, or academic documents:

> It was 8:30 p.m.
> She ran it in 2:24:21.
> Exodus 4:13 notes the same thing.
> They won the case by citing Maryland Code 18: 275-80.
> Marilyn H. Grimes, "A Nation at War," *Journal of Special Events*, 172: 30-32.

Quotation Marks

You first encountered quotation marks when learning to read, but scarcely noticed them perhaps because you were working so hard on the words. But they were there, lurking subliminally in "Jump! Jump! Jump!" said Jane. Once taught that those two raised punctuation marks indicated people talking, you probably had no more difficulty with them—until you encountered *single* quotes and more sophisticated uses.

Single quotes are used when someone being quoted, quotes *another* quotation. Put them *inside* the double quotations:

"Listen to what Shelley wrote," the General was said to have told his subordinates: " 'Round the decay of that colossal wreck, boundless and bare the lone and level sands stretch far away.' "

If you want to ensure your teacher recognizes you know how to punctuate such passages, leave a space *between* the two sets of markers.

Lengthy passages and paragraphs need no quotation marks because the rule is to indent them at the left to show that it's a quotation. In fairness, at least inform the reader about the quotation's source and credentials before launching the passage.

However, if you're writing for a school paper, column widths don't permit indentation. And shrinking the point size for the quotation makes reading difficult.

Here's how to do it: Use a lead-in line to identify the source and provide basic credentials. Then, insert the opening quotation mark. Insert another at the *start* of *each* paragraph so readers will know the quotation is continuing. The closing quote is placed at the passage's end. It should look like this:

John McClanahan set out the charge to his fellow publishers and editors in 1852 when he wrote: ". . . .Newspapers are the principal mediums through which political lessons are learned, and that editor must have but a feeble sense of the importance or responsibility of his position who will give currency to doctrines and opinions calculated to mislead the mind or misdirect the judgment.

"There is a beauty in truth and a sublimity in moral honesty, which not only adorns him who is endowed with them, but which should challenge the adoration of every man wearing the impress of Deity upon him. Properly conducted the press is little lower than the pulpit in the great work of elevating and regenerating the fallen family of Adam, and the editor who properly appreciates his position will see something ennobling in it. It is high privilege to be permitted to hold daily and weekly converse with thousands of our fellow-citizens, and it is one in the abuse of which there is the basest turpitude."

Other uses of quotation marks involving putting them around *words* to emphasize irony or cynicism:

The "riot" consisted of two small boys and a growling dog.

When a word or expression is *new*, especially slang or something coined by the media, quotation marks introduce it to readers, and are removed when it becomes familiar:

He was spaced out on music.
The television was on the fritz again.

Put quotation marks *around* titles of magazine articles, poems, and book chapters (titles of books, periodicals and plays, and the names of ships take italics):

> "Thither the Blue Collar" was in the last issue of *TIME*.
> Whitman wrote "When Lilacs Last in the Dooryard" as a eulogy to Lincoln.
> Read the "Living Solo" part of *Whither Youth Today*.

What about other punctuation, especially periods, *with* quotation marks? The basic rule is that a comma goes *inside* the end of a partial quote when a speaker is interjected, as shown below:

> "I am not a crook," he insisted, telling publishers that "the record looks grim," but extenuating circumstances soon "would explain everything."

The period still goes *inside* quotation marks. It seems complex until you practice a few examples. Try writing them by following the structure below

> "It is a very hot day in the late eighties," Runyon wrote, "when One-Arm Jack Maddox and his gang come a-cussing and a-shooting into town to hold up the Stockgrowers' National Bank."

The dash, semicolon, question mark, and exclamation mark go *inside* the quotation marks, but *only when they apply to the quoted matter*:

> The crowd before the palace shouted, "Assassin! Assassin! Hang the assassin!"
> "Who are those 'ringleaders'?" she asked.
> "Talbot, dey coachman tole me. He wuz shot—"

What if they don't apply to the quoted material? A small war has been fought over this in recent years by grammarians, editors, and other friends of the English language. Because of clarity to readers, this author concurs with those who place other punctuation *outside* quotation marks:

> Imagine Woollcott saying, "I like you"!
> Have you read Frost's poem "Birches"?

The last rule about *both* types of quotation marks is to remember to *close* them, a common failing for those writing with passion, whether students or professionals.

Apostrophe

When letters are omitted from words—forming contractions—insert an apostrophe.

Students generally have little trouble remembering contractions used almost daily (aren't, didn't, here's, let's, we'll, who's, you're). Disuse may make them forget about others (ne'er, o'er, ok'd, 'tis).

The classic use of the apostrophe for omitted letters is seen in the writings of Mark Twain and William Faulkner, who wrote dialect as they heard it. For over two centuries people were convulsed by dialect in humor columns. They had no difficulty translating Twain's "I ain' gwyne to len' no mo' money 'dout I see de security" or, in the Civil War, Henry Wheeler Shaw's helpful definitions for recruits:

> "Militara Straterga"—Tryin' to reduce a swamp by ketchin' the bilyous fever out o' it.

If you plan to write fiction today, you not only will have to have an ear tuned to dialect and colloquialisms, but to realize most readers give up on it as too difficult to follow or perceive it as insulting.

Use an apostrophe when figures are omitted from figures:

> The class of '84.
> The Spirit of '76.
> The '20s.

Include one in the *plural* of a single letter:

> The B's won the trophy.
> He was good on the p's and q's.

However, don't use an apostrophe for plural words, letters, or numbers:

> The company began in the 1920s.
> Temperatures will be in the high 80s.
> There were 14 VPs at the dinner.

One student's memory device on the foregoing was to pick a favorite year and letter: "In the 1970s, everyone got F's."

One of the most bothersome contractions is the word "*it's*" for "*it is.*" The common mistake is to assume "*it's*" stands for the possessive form of the pronoun "*it*" because it contains an apostrophe. Perhaps the best memory device may be remembering that possessive pronouns *don't* take apostrophes:

> The book is neither ours nor yours.
> The baton is hers.
> Its sound was annoying.
> The trip was theirs for the asking.

When anyone *else*, animate or not, possesses something, use an apostrophe:

> It was Boyd's and the girls' motto, and one boy's mantra.

This brings you to the most troublesome possessives involving the apostrophe.

When the words end and begin with an "*s*"—whether singular (Jesus) or plural (boys)—uncertainty begins. Is it "*for conscience' sake*" or "*for conscience's sake?*" Many professionals and editors are sometimes so unsure that they'll recast a sentence before tangling with the apostrophe.

The reason may be that the rule involves the word's *sound*, a test that appalls language purists. Nevertheless, here's the rule: When a word ending in "*s*" is *heavy* with the hissing sounds of other "*s's,*" omit the "*s*" after the apostrophe:

> It was Jesus' lot to be first.

Where the word with the apostrophe ordinarily would require a possessive "*s,*" but the *next* word begins with an "*s,*" don't use an apostrophe:

> For appearance' sake.

Heavy general usage has caused the demise of the apostrophe in some proper nouns:

> St. Elizabeths Hospital is famous.
> The Johns Street hardware store has everything you'll need.

Semicolon

The rise of the short sentence may have been responsible for the phasing out of the semicolon. Until recently, the semicolon had been a favorite piece of punctuation for writers since its birth in eighth-century Greece. Then came the disrespect of one wag dismissing it as "a comma in a tutu."[5]

In the days of historian Edward Gibbon (1737–1794), when epic events deserved epic sentences, the semicolon flourished. Look at his understated explanation of how the exasperated Emperor Justinian finally took Empress Theodora's grisly advice on how to stop riots tied to chariot racing in Constantinople:

> In this narrow space [the Hippodrome], the disorderly and affrighted crowd was incapable of resisting on either side a firm and regular attack; the blues signaled the fury of their repentance; and it is computed that above 30,000 persons were slain in the merciless and promiscuous carnage of the day.

Writers believed using a period might make readers think the *entire* scene or situation had suddenly shifted; a semicolon kept things together. This certainly was true in some works, such as the Bible, where one sentence might describe a lengthy battle and the next, an incident years later.

Purists insist that the semicolon be used just as it was in Gibbons' time, but today's editors favor periods. Yet some compromises *do* exist between the two extreme positions.

A semicolon is needed if commas have been liberally sprinkled throughout a sentence containing several clauses:

> They moved close to the walls, listened for footsteps, watched each other for signs of weakness; but even these efforts drained away their energies.

In a series, semicolons are vital for clarity:

> Production leaders for the year were Dan Corrigan, individual life volume; Bill Zimmerman, disability income; and Mike Campbell, paid applications.

> My grades were A in French; B, algebra; B, English; C, home economics; B, physical education; and D, American history.

If a clause ends with a quotation, put the semicolon *after* the quotation mark:

> He often said his life depended on "one day at a time"; however, he rarely lived that way.

Comma

You may have been told *never* to believe a comma is related to taking a breath when reading aloud. Yet that is how the comma started its ancient journey to complicate today's written English.

It had a simple purpose back in the second century B.C. That's when a staff member at Egypt's magnificent library in Alexandria (Aristophanes of Byzantium) tired of complaints—again from orators about sentences. They wanted to lift quotations for speeches from the great documents of the ancient world

---

[5] Brown.

stored in that building. The dots were still between letters and, by then, the end had a dot placed *above* the *last* letter of a sentence (eyeglasses had yet to be invented). They also demanded marks for pausing *within* those sentences.

Either out of exasperation or inspiration, that librarian decided to use the Roman virgule (/) for pauses in short sentences and the colon for longer sentences. It's easy to see that a dot was added at the top and dropped even with the line so that the tail flagged pauses long before the speaker arrived at them. It's unlikely Aristophanes inserted commas or colons in the library's priceless *past* collections, but given the comma's and colon's instant popularity and long life, he obviously mandated them for new contributors. He became an instant trendsetter.

Today, one function of the comma *does* signal breaks, but only *thought* patterns or sentence structure, not pauses in reading or speaking aloud. Only sheet music contains commas marking pauses; interestingly, it's placed *above* the staff so musicians (with or without glasses) can see it.[6]

Nevertheless, for all of the comma's seemingly perplexing, logical/illogical purposes, its service to writing is so significant, you'll come to be grateful for it and Aristophanes of the Alexandria library.

Let's start with the comma's basic use: clarity.

Nowhere is the need for clarity more crucial than with numbers. They require commas unless *words* separate them, as seen here:

> He was awarded a $5,000,000 settlement.
> Some 100,000 people were out demonstrating.
> The date was July 4, 1776.
> "7 April 1897," was crossed out in the letter.
> By November 2004 it was all over for her.

Commas separate geographical places and/or ages. Notice the confusion in the next examples without commas and the clarity in the corrected versions:

> Our class visited Rheims France and Heidelberg Germany. Although we came from Roundup Montana, we had studied about them all.
> [*Correct*: Our class visited Rheims, France and Heidelberg, Germany. Although we came from Roundup, Montana, we had studied about them all.]

> She was Theresa Richards 18.
> [*Correct*: She was Theresa Richards, 18.]

Commas separate words or people in abbreviations, either in Latin or designations ranging from the academic and religious to the professional and family:

> Names, dates, hometowns, etc., were given.
> Among those honored were James S. Pearcy, Jr.; Timothy Richards, SJ; Pauline Martinson, OSB; Franklin Hurd, IV; Joanne B. Pham, Ph.D.; Janice Hart, CLU, ChFS.

With parentheses, the rule is to put commas immediately *after* parentheses, not before them:

> Mike Tanner, CLU (Los Angeles), 487-1741, led in disability sales.

> J. M. Keating, History of the City of Memphis and Shelby County Tennessee, Vol. I (Syracuse: D. Mason & Company Publisher, 1888), 556-67.

---

[6] Brown.

Commas in a series separate nouns, pronouns, adjectives, adverbs, or phrases and clauses. The purpose is to omit the repetition of "*and*" between each word—except for one before the final item:

> Children teach us how little control we really have in those struggles about eating, naps, homework, friends, money, careers, and spouses.

> He was tall, dark, and handsome, but she was older, wiser, and wary of being a "nurse with a purse."

> Consider that they might be too old to fight, too young to reason, too unfit for duty, too smart to work, too good at finding food and fun, and too dumb to know where all this can lead.

> The castle was up a winding, brick-lined, dimly lighted, traffic-choked, and dangerous route.

One problem area is a series of adjectives that describe *one* thing, as in the example below:

> The strange, off-white, blinking, sizzling, soft, light was part of the phenomenon noted by Dr. Blanding.

The word "*soft*" *shouldn't* have a comma between it and "*light*" because it ends a string of what are called "*accumulative adjectives*" that omit a string of "*ands*." The *last* adjective in the line gets to embrace the noun *without* a comma separating them. As that sentence stands, the writer would mean:

> The strange, AND off-white, AND blinking, AND sizzling, AND soft, AND light was part of the phenomenon noted by Dr. Blanding.

The escape from this familiar trap is an old one: Because each comma in that series stands for the word "*and*," insert an imaginary "*and*" *after* each adjective so that you prevent "soft *and* light."

Sometimes in a series, commas work in tandem with semicolons to distinguish one unit from another:

> Among those honored for that initial performance were Mark Euscher as Hamlet; Brenden Fowell, the King; Suzanne Trimmer, the Queen; Ian Hamilton, Polonius; Shirley Goldsmith, Ophelia; and Eugene Gonzales, Laertes.

Another purpose of a comma is to signal an interruption to the sentence's flow, whether that direct address is placed at the start, middle, or end:

> You, Sir, are a fraud!
> Coach, I'll try it again.
> That's all I know, Mrs. Tubman.

Weak interrupters, such as responses of *yes* or *no*, need commas too:

> Oh, you'll love it!
> Why, I never thought you cared.
> Well, don't ask me that.
> The prize could be, say, Philadelphia for *two* weeks.
> Yes, I've decided to go back to school, she told me.
> The history of Patagonia, as has been noted, has no parallel with Peru.

Some commas signal parenthetical expressions (I think/feel/believe); others indicate transitions, qualifiers, and guideposts (by contrast, however, it seems, first, for instance, next):

> For example, Armstrong trained 10 hours per day.
> On the other hand, the problem is not that simple.
> The result requires longitudinal testing beyond five years, it would appear.
> Moreover, this part of her life was not included in my source.
> Obversely, America's role was not as defined in 1801.

Language purists still insist that certain conjunctions—*yet, but, and, so*—warrant commas when they *lead* a sentence containing conclusions just as if they were as powerful as "*thus*," and "*therefore*." The trend is for many editors and writers to omit commas because they stop a smooth-flowing sentence or significant result—especially when a short sentence follows:

> So when Meriwether Lewis arrived, they rejoiced.
> But Gideon Pillow was unable to back down.
> And no more was heard from any part of Alabama about rerouting the river.

A slightly different interrupter involves commas with attributions to sources, particularly in term papers. This is how a comma should be used:

> The state was the empire, and he was the king, according to Huey Long.
> France would never support the invasion, Chirac indicated, not without evidence of an attack.
> The *Encyclopaedia Britannica* entry on Richard III today admits, "[his] reputation for wickedness originated in sixteenth-century political propaganda."

Yet another kind of interrupter requiring a comma identifies people, places, and events. It's called an "*appositive*." You see them everyday in newspapers:

> The tough questioning was led by Sen. Joe Biden, chair of the subcommittee.
> It was July 14, the day the Bastille fell.
> He bought the car, a 1936 Ford roadster, but found it hard to drive and to get parts without paying a small fortune.

Another kind of appositive often *doesn't* need commas. It depends on whether whatever is being identified is clear or vital. In the sentence, "His daughter Sherri was the top scorer," the man may have more than one daughter, but the use of her name is essential to the sentence's meaning. No comma is needed. The same thing is true for "The play *Waiting for Lefty* won the award." The play's title is *essential* to the sentence.

But when the appositive noun is *unnecessary*, surround it with commas like this:

> His wife, Darlene, worked three jobs that year.
> The Secret Service agents raced after the Secretary of State, Colin Powell.
> Few believe that Margaret Mitchell's only novel, *Gone With the Wind*, was lifted—plot, characters, and even dialogue—from *Vanity Fair*, Henry Thackeray's nineteenth-century classic set in the Napoleonic era.

If you've understood these tips, you now know the comma's function to be a separation device in somewhat short expressions. The same function continues in far lengthier writing passages.

Let's start with those sentences *within* sentences—long *or* short. They've been boldfaced for attention.

The "inside" sentence is called a "*clause*" and *might* be *short* and might also use other words than "*that*," "*which*," and "*who*."

> The bracelet with 23 charms, **which was flung from a Mardi-Gras float**, was mine.
> The girl **who won the geometry prize** got its trophy.
> She has directed several public utilities, **most now thriving**, that gained high marks from their boards.

But many subordinate clauses are yards long and complicated. Thomas Jefferson used a *lengthy* clause—attached to an appositive—in the ringing opening words of the Declaration of Independence; the sentence constitutes an *entire* paragraph. But it was written for well-educated readers accustomed to advanced vocabularies, florid writing styles, and complex sentence structures.

> When in the Course of human events it becomes necessary for one people to dissolve the political bands **which have connected them with another, and to assume among the powers of the earth the separate and equal station to which the Laws of Nature and of Nature's God entitle them**, a decent respect to the opinions of mankind requires that they should declare the causes which impel them to the separation.

Short or long, if clauses can be *omitted* from the main sentence so it *still* makes sense, they may need commas around them for reading comprehension. Some clauses are so far afield from the main sentence's thrust that commas are vital for clarity. Imagine the following examples *without* commas:

> The bridge, **which was grimy**, opened to let the cruiser through.
> That spring, **the season the Trail Blazers won the league title**, New York's budget problems worsened.

Don't be fooled if a clause isn't *within* a sentence, but ends it. It's still subordinate to the sentence itself:

> The coed with the terrible cold and high fever was the one **who should have stayed home that day**.

Knotty questions arise about this kind of clause. Some purists insist at least one comma is necessary. Many editors and writers insist that if the sentence is clear to readers, don't stop the flow with a comma. Even they would insert a comma, however, if the clause's meaning was in doubt or had a double meaning. Here, readers might believe it was fever that was filled because the words are next to each other:

> The coed with the terrible cold and high fever, filled the room with her groans.

A comma also reinforces introductory adverbial clauses or phrases:

> When he moved away, we were all sad.
> Easily fooled, John failed to see it was a practical joke.

However, you *don't* need a comma if the meaning is clear:

> During the morning I made breakfast.

Introductory adverbial clauses (Because this is a major research university, it...) are usually troublesome because students not only forget to drop in a comma *after* them, but often don't remember what an *adverb* is. A chant to remedy both failings was conceived by a student and widely photocopied for peers. The first word, an adverb, and the comma are in boldface:

> **Because** I went to town,
> **If** I go to town,
> **When/whenever** I go to town,
> **Wherever** they go to town,
> **While** I go to town,

Let's move now to using commas as *connections* rather than separators.

In short sentences, errors are easy to detect. Not so with long ones, especially if both clauses seem to be equal and essential for the sentence's meaning. They're almost always linked by a conjunction (and, or, nor, yet, but, because, etc.), like these two examples:

> The three visited Monticello on Thursday, **and** they and the team planned to return by Saturday.
> Haley refused to go to class, **but** everybody else did.

In both examples, boldface type indicates the comma and conjunction coupling the clauses. Now, if the *conjunctions* had been *omitted*, the writers would have been guilty of what's called a "comma splice" or "comma fault" and confused readers with this:

> The three visited Monticello on Thursday, they and the team planned to return by Saturday.
> Haley refused to go to class, everybody else did.

The writers could have taken the coward's way out (comma avoidance) with a semicolon or period, but the result would have been a choppy pair of sentences.

In addition, if the subject of *both* clauses is the same, you won't need a comma:

> The three and the team visited Monticello on Thursday and returned by Saturday.

Let's look next at other areas of writing requiring commas.

You'll have no difficulty in using commas with quotations of less than a dozen words because you've read hundreds of books containing sentences like these:

> Penny said, "Jody, all's been done that was possible."

> "You can't do this to us," Nissan remarked coolly, "not after all the trouble we had financing this film."

When *contrasting* elements are used in a sentence, a comma keeps things clear for readers. The test for the first set of examples shown below is whether commas can be omitted without damaging the sentence's meaning. The second set rests fairness and balance on the words "*not*" and "*but*."

> She's a cunning, yet warmhearted, soul.
> The policy was praised for its morality, if indeed slight, and practical nature.
> It's pertinent, though separated, from the data.
> He's a poor, but honest, businessman.
>
> She should get praise for work, not blame.
> Our team was down, but still proud.

The final point about comma usage is to insert one for clarity when two *successive* words are the same:

> What the question is, is not the real issue here.
> If there's any journalist I've feared for, for over two years, it's Robert Fisk.
> The doctor was in, in the afternoons only.
> Nobody knew where the speaker was at, at the rally.

CHAPTER **11**

A NEW LOOK
AT SPELLING

Unless you're a spelling bee champ, chances are that from the first grade on, you've struggled with spelling the difficult and often illogical English language. You may have decided spelling was unimportant in writing if your teachers have given double grades for content and mechanics—with the fantasy that content is worth 90 percent. Or you may have foisted it off as a humorous personality quirk. Some have talked others into "editing" at first, beginning with sympathetic family members, then helpful friends, and, when both finally balked, hiring help. It's difficult to fault the view that spelling is "no big deal," especially considering most people know that while the business world demands perfect spelling of job applicants and executives, they attain it by the efforts of clerical staffs earning minimum wages.

But you're not yet in the business world. And you may have run out of "editors" willing to check your work with or without pay. Worse, you may encounter a teacher—especially at the university level—who deducts one letter grade for each misspelled word (or punctuation error). The first line of defense in the Information Age is the spelling-check feature of a computer's word-processing program. The second are the hand-held spelling-aid products, some with "sound-based" dictionaries. These have been designed for those still relying on the alibi of "how can I look it up in the dictionary if I don't know how it's spelled?"

True, the spelling checker feature has been a priceless gift to writing of all kinds. But it has serious limitations. The major flaw is that whether it contains a vocabulary of seventy thousand or two hundred thousand words, the spell-checker is *not* an unabridged dictionary. Worse, most spell-checkers ignore two-letter words and "sound-alikes," as this example demonstrates:

The bear bare, who had butt too years two bee long off tooth an to grow hare, filed the woulds with tare or—even the axe-marine an fare made—at the cite with the site when it eight a dear (a dough).

As to the hand-held electronic devices, the leader is a British-made product which means words such as *honor* and *judgment* are spelled *honour* and *judgement* and may set off arguments with your teacher that you'll never win. One with a "sound-based" dictionary contains 100,000 words, but is used only by an age range of 5-13. A top-of-the-line device contains 223,000 words, but without the "sound-based" feature. Prices far exceed a hard-backed dictionary with 13,000,000 words. That sales seem to be drooping is indicated by new add-on features such as a thesaurus, word games, crossword puzzle aids, a calculator and clock, and even a temperature sensor.

At least these checking devices are an improvement over being told you can spell well by merely mastering a few rules such as "*i* before *e* except after *c* and when sounded as *a* as in *neighbor* and *weigh*." The defiant may counter with *seize* and *siege* when pushed to the wall. Add to this those who still insist proficient reading *and* spelling come from "sounding out" syllables. That may explain why millions still spell "*duchess*" as "*Dutchess*" and why we now see "*thru*," "*luv*," and "*nite*."

"Sounding out" words works for Latin, Spanish, or Italian because each syllable *can* be pronounced. It doesn't work for the English language because of words such as *bough, bought, though, through,* and *thorough.* The irony is that for most foreigners learning English, the common word *the* is such a stopper that some have resorted to blowing out a candle to master it. Indeed, those fixated on the sound-out system ought to be reminded that prior to 1500 or so, *night* was not pronounced "*nite*," but "*nicked*." And any Chaucer student knows that most words ending in *e* had that *e* pronounced so that "*herte*" (heart) was rendered as "*herta*."

English started as an unwritten tongue of mostly one-syllable grunts uttered by Germans, Scandinavians, and Saxons bound to plows, not pens. Too, sub-zero winters usually breeds silence in any age because talking admits icy blasts to throats. Their conquerors were from climes farther south with the further advantages of money, leisure and weather to write or speak either elegant Latin or French. Yet neither ridicule of the "unlettered" nor refusing legality to Anglo-Saxon documents could stamp out the colorful simplicity of the earthy English language.

In the end, the unlettered, taciturn peasants won. Latin became a dead language. And though French may make up nearly half our language, their pronouns of *je, moi* and those designators of insiders and outsiders—*tu/vous*—were boiled down to *I, me,* and *you.* You may want to bless whoever insisted the word *the* did not have to change to *le/la* or *el/la* before nouns were sorted out as masculine or feminine. But who has not leveled curses at French with its illogical endings *of incidentally/evidently* or *moment/remnant.*

With the advent of movable type in the late 1400s, writers spelling the same word in two or more ways didn't bother printers, but it certainly did decades of schoolmasters—naturally. Once the first purely English dictionary with its 1,400 words was published in 1596 by Edmund Coote (a schoolmaster, of course), the "spelling problem" was presumed to have been resolved. In fact, it only started. As the English themselves turned world conqueror, they brought home a melting pot of unpronounceable or "unspellable" words such as today's *anonymity, blitzkrieg, chutzpah, Des Moines, pneumonia,* and *squirrel.*

Five centuries of "absorbing" terms from around the globe (plus the ever-changing teenage jargon) means that current estimates are probably correct about English containing nearly a million words. Today's largest dictionary (Oxford English Dictionary, 2nd Ed.) has 616,500 words. It's no wonder, therefore, that spelling bee winners are considered curiosities because they have extraordinary multinational linguistic skills, a photographic memory—and, too often, lonely arrogance, as a film about them revealed (*Spellbound*).

Despite this history and the fact that new words are being coined as you read this sentence, the reality you face in school and the outside world is that you still are expected to have flawless spelling. Unfair or not, teachers, college admission officers and employers who encounter misspellings consider the erring to be a dunce, lazy, or poorly educated. They're not interested in our language's history or illogic. Many don't even give the dyslexic a break if it's not mandated by law. You'll be treated just like those Anglo-Saxon serfs if you fail the frustrating, lifetime tussle of spelling in the most prevalent language on Earth.

Now, you can either give up and, like the unlettered of old, pay a scribe (i.e., ghostwriter, ghost editor) to do your formal writing. Or you can cower forever when asked to write in class or at work. Or you can rise up and look at spelling in a far different light than in the past. You may come to see that other methods of mastery offer you gifts unavailable to spelling champs or strict teachers.

Three chief gifts are teachability, curiosity, and a love of adventure in raiding the lost ark at your fingertips (the dictionary). Another gift is the fun of needling hidebound teachers about the illogical spellings *commit* or *infer* or *incur* or *begin* when they're expanded (*committed, committing, commitment; inferred, inferring; incurred, incurring; beginning, beginner*).

Teasing the teacher involves battlefield courage because those who hold the grade book—and almost never write—may counterattack with the reminder that even the world's greatest authors are subject to a publisher's corps of merciless and objective copy editors. Most editors don't write either, but are willing to lay down their souls for love of our vast and magnificent language. Writers saved from terrible gaffes, disorganization, and padding usually are grateful for those eagle-eyed protectors. However, none have urged that Pulitzer prizes be awarded to this unsung fraternity of underpaid and underappreciated: the copy editors. Equally, how many students render a thank-you to teachers devoting evenings and entire weekends laboring over their writing?—and for far less pay than copy editors earn.

It's easy to argue that when composition is written in class under deadline pressure, creativity's white heat surges past spelling, grammar, and mechanical errors. Students argue that those areas must be overlooked in favor of content. They fail to realize that classroom writing is an examination of their mastery of composition. Where spelling is concerned, what English classroom is without a dictionary? You can always circle questionable words and then check them before leaving class. The same creativity process goes on at home, whether a draft is written in longhand or composed on the computer. In classroom or at home, "parental" love is blind in composition, whether the work pouring out of a printer is an assignment, an article, novel, poetry, or a play.

Other anti-misspelling devices are rarely taught in the English class, but are well-known in the writing profession. Even though you're unlikely to make writing your career, these self-editing "gifts" from the profession should prove helpful to you not only in addressing spelling, but in all other areas involving composition.

For example, the wise let a piece "cool" for a few hours or days for detached objectivity. Spelling is usually the last area to be checked for those meeting deadlines. Authors are also well aware of patterns of error that seem hard-wired into their minds and which emerge regularly in typographical mistakes. If they know their individual "spelling demons" and catch them, you can do the same. Many writers read their work aloud, an instant and surefire method to detect mistakes of *all* sorts—and to add polish to the final draft. Yet how many students take the time to do this on homework compositions? Many were silenced by ridicule when they were first learning to read, but carrying that fear into high school and college is something that needs to be remedied.

Last, a new wrinkle, thanks to the computer, is editing by enlarging type to at least 14 point—used in first-grade reading books—and then returning it to default size. Misspellings leap off the screen at 18 point. For that matter, so do extra spaces and commas posing as periods.

So much for the gifts of working on spelling mastery. Let's now look at three other systems that may help your spelling: foreign derivatives, mnemonics (word associations), and the highly unorthodox "looks-wrong" method. The ultimate remedy is setting up a chapter of Spellers Anonymous after class, something explained later in this chapter.

Foreign Derivatives

The foreign-derivative method doesn't require you to be fluent in *any* language, but it does require a dictionary, preferably an unabridged version. The word's entry provides the country of origin and growth and variations of the word as it has moved through history.

Let's look at a few "demon" words to show how knowing even *part* of the foreign derivation can help your spelling:

> *kindergarten* (German. *kinder* = children; *garten* = garden)
> *mortgage* (French. *mort* = death; *gage* = pledge)
> *disastrous* (French-Latin. *dis* = apart; *astro* = star)
> *cigarette* (Spanish-French. *cigarro* = cigar; *ette* – little)
> *lieutenant* (French. *lieu* = place; *tenant* = tenant: an officer who holds a superior's place in his absence)
> *vaccine* (French. *vacca* = cow: the first vaccinations were gathered by tapping into a cow's vesicles)
> *manual* (French. manus = hand)

Mnemonic Devices

Memory techniques have been cited several times in previous chapters as a mastery method of problem words. Educators and psychologists call them *"mnemonic devices,"* the root of which comes from the Greek word *"mnemonikos"* (mindful).

In solving spelling problems, mnemonic devices are almost mandatory. And this word-association system is open to anyone with an imagination and a willingness to share their devices.

For example, one education major even spelled *"mnemonic"* correctly by associating it with *"demonic,"* led by an *"m"* and *"n"* in alphabetical order. The word *"cemetery,"* a killer for thousands, was solved by a high school sophomore who noticed its three *"e's"* might be uttered by visitors after dark. Another demon was *"separate"* until it was noticed that it has two *"e's"* on the "outside part" and two *"a's"* on the inside. One sharp-eyed student pointed out the "i-before-e-except-after-c" jingle didn't work for *"seige"* and *"seize"* (neither sounded like *"neighbor"* and *"weigh"* either). And a classmate got cheers when she was a "nice" niece (both begin with *"ni"*). The arch-demon *"receive"* was solved by the realization that in the slogan "it's better to *give* than rece*ive*," both key words ended in *"ive."* "Sophomore" was worked into a cheer, ending in *"oooooooooh,* no *more."*

As for the insufferable suffix problems bequeathed by the French in the adverbs *"accidentally,"* *"incidentally,"* and *"evidently,"* three words with *"ent"* in midsection: It was a police reporter who noted both *accidents* and *incidents* have to be *tall*-ied, but not *evidence.*

You might just be the one to find a device to spell the three demons of *"possibly,"* *"presumably,"* and *"probably"*—or those listed in the next section. If so, thousands of misspellers hope you'll share it.

Appearance of Words

Another spelling-mastery method is either unknown or unacknowledged outside the journalism profession. Yet to proofreaders, editors, and voracious readers, this device has been a quick and useful one to conquer misspellings. Few admit to using it perhaps because it seems bizarre and, as one copy editor admitted, the fear that her old English teacher would be shocked at such a device.

It's called the "looks-wrong" technique and requires a background of constant reading. That's because such a reader has seen so many words spelled *correctly* in hundreds of books and publications that misspellings *do* leap off a page. Some words, such as *"miniscule"* instead of *"minuscule,"* are such trip wires to teachers—as are British imports—that they leap off a page.

Those who make their living with words are rarely too proud to resort to a dictionary. Newspaper copy editors have the AP Stylebook at their elbows to check demon words. So why not follow suit? The alibi of "how can I find it in the dictionary if I don't know how to spell it?" is old; and you face the same thing with a computer's spelling-checker feature because it lacks a dictionary's capacity and passes most two-letter words. Either consult a dictionary or invent a mnemonic device for your demons and enjoy liberation.

Below is a list of words—illogical, baffling in spellings or not—that trip even editors. See if your demon is among them.

Incorrect	*Correct*
acommodate	**accommodate**
acknowledgement	**acknowledgment**
aid (noun-a person who helps)	**aide**
alright	**all right**
alot	**a lot**
anihilate	**annihilate**
billionnaire	**billionaire**
cancell	**cancel**
congradulations	**congratulations**
cooly	**coolly**
comradery	**camaraderie**
defence	**defense**
develope	**develop**
disc (computer)	**disk**
disatisfied	**dissatisfied**
dutchess	**duchess**
envelop	**envelope**
exillaration/exhileration	**exhilaration**
expell	**expel**
fulfil	**fulfill**
flourescent/flooresent	**fluorescent**
glamour	**glamor**
halleluja	**hallelujah**
hemmorahge	**hemorrhage**
honour	**honor**
humour	**humor**
innundate	**inundate**
judgement	**judgment**
likeable	**likable**
millionnaire	**millionaire**
miniscule	**minuscule**
pasttime	**pastime**
penence	**penance**
potatoe	**potato**
perjorative	**pejorative**
predjudice	**prejudice**
questionaire	**questionnaire**
quizz	**quiz**
sacriligious	**sacrilegious**
saleable	**salable**
saviour	**savior**
sargent	**sergeant**

skilfull/skillfull	**skillful**
sophmore	**sophomore**
tee-shirt/t-shirt	**T-shirt**
tenent (renter)	**tenant**
tenent (principle)	**tenet**
tenemant/tenamant	**tenement**
thru	**through**
theatre	**theater**
tomatoe	**tomato**
tradgedy	**tragedy**
vaccuum/vaccum	**vacuum**
vengence	**vengeance**
unecessary	**unnecessary**

Review Past Writing for Error Patterns

Yet another highly successful method to catch troublesome words is to check your past writing to monitor the errors. Most are repetitive because that's how they're recorded in your brain's hard drive the first time they were stored. Most errors stem from our earliest reading days. You'll suddenly discover an interesting and distinct pattern of misspelled words that are as unique as typing errors.

You may be comforted to know that everyone, even teachers and professional writers, have "blind spots," too. But their jobs and pride dictates that they usually force them into a "search-and-destroy" mission in that dictionary at the ready. Writers usually have posted a list of demon words because a dictionary hunt and dreaming up a mnemonic device take time.

For example, some people have trouble with word endings (suffixes), particularly the French imports that make no sense to no-nonsense Americans. Is it "*ent*," "*ant*," or "*int*"? Is it "*ence*," or "*ance*"? "*able*," or "*ible*"? Others have problems with prefixes ("*pre*" or "*per*"?).

Find your pattern. As has been said, awareness is the *first* step of action. Because you probably use them often, either put them on a card above your desk at home or post them on the inside of your notebook cover for quick consulting on classroom compositions.

The next step is to circle words you're unsure of if you're writing in longhand and spend the last five minutes of class checking them in a pocket dictionary or the classroom version (most English classrooms have one).

If you're writing a homework assignment, use the spelling checker as well as the FIND key on your "known" demons. Most professionals have an unabridged dictionary at their elbow even though their word-processing program may have a dictionary with more than the standard 50,000 words. Like it or not, if you have problems with spelling, the dictionary is *still* your best friend.

All these methods should help, especially if you combine some of them. Some may be more helpful than others. You may discover a new one. But when you realize that *one* method can't solve *all* spelling problems, you will have come a long way in conquering this major, age-old weakness in writing.

If none of these work, consider the system of Spellers Anonymous, a loose-knit organization started in a Maine high school. It required no dues nor meetings, bylaws or officers—just the recognition by members that they had a monumental problem that would dog them throughout their working lives. They finally were willing to go to great lengths to conquer those spelling problems. If your case seems to be hopeless and you *do* want to conquer spelling, read the next section to learn about the Spellers Anonymous method.

The Spellers Anonymous Method

The Spellers Anonymous method was born in this author's high school English classes in Maine when she ruled out double grades (content/mechanics and spelling) and deducted one letter grade for each misspelled word. She had long been aware that students paid little attention in double grades to anything but that given content. Misspellings were usually ignored or paraded around as idiosyncrasies. Draconian problems needed Draconian solutions—and a pocket dictionary at every desk on "theme day."

The results were instantaneous and astounding once the complaints died down in both high school and college classes. Desperate students averaging 15 to 25 misspellings per composition quickly dropped to few errors—even *no* errors.

The system combined the checking techniques used by researchers and reporters on TIME, Inc. publications (*TIME*, *People*, *Sports Illustrated*, *Discover*, *Money*, etc.) and those used by freelance writers unable to pay for copy-editing services.

This is the method:

Start checking spelling with the *last* word of the composition. Working *backward* word by word, put a dot over each word you're *certain* is spelled correctly. Look up doubtful words in the dictionary as you proceed rather than a check-later list. Reason: A list looks formidable and frustrating. Checking one word at a time gives you a sense of accomplishment and offers a brief physical break.

Below is an example of how a "checked" sentence should look. Remember, you *also* work from the last word to the first—like this:

> ·   ·   ·   ·   ·   ·   ·   ·   ·   ·   ·   ·   ·
> There are ways in which every police officer can fulfill duties without relying on force.

This method sounds peculiar at first, but several sound psychological principles support it, aside from the fear factor of getting an F on a composition.

By working backward, you detach yourself from the forward flow of a composition. You'll focus on each word and beyond spelling, you'll make startling discoveries about your writing patterns.

All those students did—and quickly. They caught errors in pronoun references, verb agreement, and failure to close parentheses or sentences. They also arrested chronic cases of comma-itis and the "howevers," and did surgery on overlong sentences. Best of all, even those who had struggled for years and hated writing began to view their work like professional writers.

The first two times students use the Spellers Anonymous method, they usually stun themselves by seeing they've eliminated almost *all* errors. That's because they *do* take time and great care in processing a composition. They may have made a list of demon words to flag. But then overconfidence usually sets in within the next two assignments and they again misspell even common words.

The lesson is that *each* composition must be treated as a separate challenge. It is also well to know that when you're working on a topic that's either interesting or familiar, you'll get sloppy. Errors escape you because familiarity *does* breed contempt or because psychologically your "child" seems flawless.

Professionals check a draft from the last page to the first so they *won't* get caught up in the content. They work by pages, not by words, but the good results are the same. At TIME, Inc., all magazine staffers use the dot method to ensure each word is spelled correctly, is grammatically correct, and is factually correct. Their editors put a premium on accuracy in both content and mechanics and it has earned them a reputation in the business of producing the best and most error-free string of publications. It all starts with dots over words.

Nothing is easy about the Spellers Anonymous checking method. It's an onerous and time-consuming process, despite its fascinating discoveries. But if you want to master spelling our complex and confusing language, you'll find it's well worth the effort.

SECTION

WRITING ABOUT COMPLEX SUBJECTS

CHAPTER **12**

OVERALL PRINCIPLES

This section will help you write about five of the most common fields for complex topics: science, technology, statistics, business, and government. This chapter is intended as an easy "warm-up" to the overall principles for these advanced compositions.

If you decide to do an assignment about, say, the Josephson switch, the U.S. Navy's sonar buoys, Wall Street's program trading, or flaws in polling the public, this chapter and the previous ones should help. You'll have mastered one of the most difficult aspects of writing, yet one that is perhaps the most satisfying and which is the most needed, especially in certain fields like math or the sciences.

You also have the possibility of earning an A+ if you turn in an assignment that's on target, says something, and translates material far better than the original research. And, as you'll see, that's not all that difficult to do considering how poorly most of it is written.

What makes a composition on complex subjects stand out? The secret is as close as a newspaper, the television or Internet screen: The ability to "translate" material from the *known* to the *unknown*.

Consider the genius of television writers who by the six o'clock news furnish clear explanations of a new discovery about Mars or, as happened, the collapse of the twin towers of New York's World Trade Center in the September 11, 2001 terrorist attack. The same thing is true for newspaper/magazine writers although they are aided by "infographic" illustrations which readers usually study *before* reading the stories.

Media writers were just like you in their high school days. Most were baffled by how things were taught and thought they were stupid until they noticed they weren't alone. Somewhere, between high school and just after college, they took the opportunity to remedy the gaps. Today, they write and provide guidance to infographic illustrators about complex things: ventricular-assist devices; public-utility district operations; construction of highways, bridges, and tunnels; Spaceship One's solo journey; a basketball team's defense tactic; a state legislature's proposed budget.

Their aim is not to impress intellectuals or to please experts in all these fields. Rather, it's to translate the unknown to vast audiences, including those reading at the six-year-old level and, especially with television, the millions of functionally illiterate adults. They are courted and well paid because media owners *must* reach a wide audience. The more readers and viewers, the greater the "head-count" and the higher advertising rates they can demand for reaching them.

To explain complex things like space shots or black days on Wall Street, media writers must keep stories *simple*. Simple words. Simple sentences. Simple examples or analogies. And because newspapers have tight space limits and broadcasters only brief bytes, writers can't dawdle or pad stories.

Most important, they must know the subject—and how to present it successfully to an audience with short attention spans and busy schedules. People read *Consumer Reports* magazine, for instance, perhaps without realizing or appreciating the depth of the testing procedures required to tell them which car is difficult to drive or which toothpaste is the best at fighting plaque. A staff writer had to take all the statistical data from those tests and translate it so that readers could weigh which product to buy.

Most readers and viewers don't have college degrees or extensive vocabularies. Too many don't even have high school diplomas. Add to this their nanosecond reaction time with remote control buttons based solely on interesting presentations. The teacher who will grade your assignment is little different and may read it after a dozen others, especially complex material. You need to make it interesting as well as something of substance and accuracy.

Writers with the knack of explaining the complex will always attract not only large audiences but the high salaries that accompany that gift, as the late science writer Carl Sagan discovered in articles, books, and the lecture circuit. You may have encountered a teacher who could "translate" something difficult so that you had no trouble understanding it—or made it so fascinating that you explored it further.

Most in the media or the Sagans admit an enormous sense of satisfaction and pleasure in such successful communication. It's the same kind of thrill teachers get when their classes understand, say, one key part of geometry or the Louisiana Purchase.

Those who disdain reaching people in that manner as "popularizers" or who level charges of "dumbing down" material are usually elitists who know well that "in knowledge there is power"—over others. They don't want the doors of knowledge flung open to a wide audience, lest their power and status vanish. They're little different from the breed of clerks in electronic stores who use technical jargon and thinly disguised contempt to feel superior to customers befuddled by yet another generational change in an expensive product.

Doing the Research

To explain something complex, get out those reference books or journals, or get on the Internet—or talk to experts in the subject field. You can choose to use the same tired examples or analogies and wording, of course, but why not come up with something far better that's original—yours?

Students usually know little about their subjects when beginning the advanced composition. The key to real mastery is to *admit* you know little about it. Nobody expects you to be a Junior Aristotle, an expert on all knowledge. One physician in the family practice specialty once admitted that although he was chief of surgery at a major Washington, D.C. hospital, it was a challenge to stay current in just that specialty. It required continuing-education courses, convention short courses and seminars, and reading the many journals dealing with his specialty. If *he* could admit he was ignorant about other areas and not feel shame, permit yourself the same admission. The teacher's perception certainly is that students know little and their purpose in such assignments is to learn something.

This sort of writing requires effort and fighting off the onus of "looking dumb." Everyone is ignorant about things, but only at the outset. It takes great courage to raise a hand in class to ask for a repeat of what's just been said by the instructor. But if you're puzzled, you can be certain most in class are, too. The classroom heroes and heroines are those who withstand a withering stare or a caustic remark ("You might try listening") to ask for repetition or amplification.

So take heart at being a blank page (tabula rasa). Play it for all it's worth.

Scrutinize and Weigh Sources

The Internet and your local or college library are major resources although you may have to read several books and spend hours surfing the Web for credible information. However, you might make the startling discovery that many authors have repeated misinformation or are biased. Doubt that? One highly credible encyclopedia repeated—edition after edition—what the major history textbooks said about England's King Richard III (1452–1485): That he was a hunchback who killed two boy princes and other family members to seize the throne. Yet such "facts" were based on those dictated by a usurper, Henry Tudor, whose army defeated and killed Richard on Bosworth Field. As Henry VII, Tudor mandated a slander campaign under pain of death to retain his line on the throne (Henry VIII, Elizabeth I, et al.). Shakespeare took his cue when he wrote *Richard III*. In creating one of the greatest villains in the history of theater, he perpetuated the Tudor lies that lasted for more than 400 years—until recent scholarship overturned them.

In short, that major fabrications go unchallenged demonstrates that you need more than one or two sources about a subject to avoid bias.

Once you do a swift run through available research, you'll understand why scholars are ordered to take a narrow focus on *one* thing. Instead of writing about *all* aspects of the Civil War, for example—easily a 10-book series—take just a small *slice* of it: a skirmish, a single mission, a small part of its logistical challenges. If you decide to write about electricity, four or five pages will never do; take one *small* part of the subject. If it's a paper on poets Emily Dickinson or John Keats, focus on just *one* aspect of their lives or poetry. That will keep you from emptying library shelves or ruining your eyesight scanning the Web's abundant sites and thousands of links.

After you've narrowed the scope, the composition will become manageable and perhaps engrossing. At least you won't feel overwhelmed to the point of procrastination or panic.

Understand the Material

As you pore over data on that narrowed-down subject, you'll discover the next step is *understanding* what you're reading.

Use the experience of one student teacher assigned to present a unit on gerunds and possessive pronouns. She had never mastered this use of pronouns. She feared asking fellow majors or professors lest she'd be labeled incompetent. But she was determined to do the first explanation of possessive pronouns used with gerunds that would be understood by restless and easily distracted high school sophomores.

She checked out a dozen grammar books about gerund usage. The first two textbooks were like reading Sanskrit, she said. By the fourth book, she began to understand the subject from the examples because the explanations were so poor and the writing was beyond her reading levels. But by the sixth book, she not only understood that use of gerunds with possessive pronouns, but had figured out a fresh and clear way to explain it.

It might take you a week of study to master your material as it did that future English teacher. But the fun is in creating a presentation understandable to a resistive, even hostile, audience. That's what needs to be done, whether explanations are about cancer, DNA, booster rockets, political caucuses, or the war against and occupation of Iraq.

Use Unorthodox Techniques

Another way to understand complex material employs methods that may strike you at first as strange. But that's just because you haven't done them in years and your friends might think of them as goofy. They don't have the writing assignment; you do.

Many who have "cracked the codes" of the complex have done some highly unorthodox things. Successful people do what unsuccessful people are too image-conscious to do, like drawing pictures. Or reading source materials aloud. Or acting them out with a skit. Notes just won't do. One maxim governing learning is: "Tell Me Something and I Might Forget It. Show Me Something and I Might Remember It. But Involve Me and I'll Master It." That's the aim of what is to follow in this chapter.

For instance, you may not have drawn pictures since first grade. Perhaps someone sneered at your artistic efforts. Maybe someone snickered when you read aloud (also in first grade), so you've avoided it since then. Equally, you might have been so shy that charades with friends still paralyzes you. But that was then and this is now. Most techniques that follow can be done in the privacy of your room. And little by little, your inhibitions will drop away and you'll discover a learning style that suits you.

Be Dramatic

Nobody is going to laugh at you if you dramatize explanations of such things as lasers all by yourself. Or the latest wrinkle in wave research or what can cause the corporate bond market to decline. Great teachers do this all the time.

One was a world-famous physics professor who taught adhesion by having students rub spoons on their foreheads until they stuck. A high school English teacher teaches nominative-case pronouns by bringing in cheerleaders to do the "Nominative-Case Locomotive" ("I, you, he, rah, rah!! I, you, he, rah, rah!! We, you, they, hey!! We, you, they, hey, hurray" etc.). To teach flight's key principles of lift, thrust, and drag, a professor gave each student a dime-store kite to master those three precepts by flying kites on the university quad.

Another teacher, faced with students hostile to science in general and learning about cancer metastasis in particular, combined dramatics with a "read-aloud" approach; she would read and they would use theater-improvisation methods to illustrate the subject. One challenge was to show what happened when a cancerous tumor birthed "baby" tumors that then rushed along hungrily searching for new sites. She read aloud—twice—a medical source's complex explanation to a suddenly super-attentive class of note-takers and doodlers.

The result was a cops-and-robbers classroom chase of "T-Cells" to destroy "Cancer Cells" through lines of students playing the blood and lymphatic circulatory systems ("Blood-and-Lymph Boulevard"). The "improv" was performed *twice* because the first time students were caught up in the excitement of creative fun; an immediate repeat brought mastery to *every* student about how cancer spreads.

Sketching

If you shrink from being dramatic, try drawing or reading aloud—or both.

The drawing recommended is not too different from that in television when cartoonists or writers have to translate something for viewers. They don't worry about looking dumb or past art "critics." Instead, they charge straight into understanding something that will be presented to millions on the evening news or a special.

You can use big sheets of butcher paper—large because that forces *overemphasis* of something unknown and lets you see the *small* elements. Use a wide felt-tip pen or a big crayon.

These are the basic tools whether you're explaining clear-cutting forests or program trading. You may come up with *several* sketches until the light goes on about your topic. If you're trying to understand a space disaster, the puffs of smoke may be enormous and the rocket's seams may be equally exaggerated. A coed's drawing of wind shear used a hose spraying a driveway. Because a volcanic lahar looked like an avalanche to another student, he used that *extended* analogy all the way through a composition explaining the eruption of Mount St. Helens.

The rough sketch below shows what a student did to teach herself how the video-cassette industry once recorded things on a single tape. Her source was a high-technology magazine that used jargon many "high-tekkies" use on "turkeys" (unenlightened and frightened customers).

She was more interested in being accurate, complete, and clear than worrying about her "look-good."

She sketched as she read the text. Her sketch, shown below, will mean nothing to you, but it *did* to her. Like hers, your sketches are intended to teach you something about a topic.

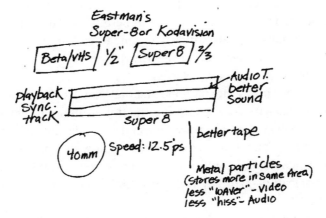

The point is that by drawing a process or precept, you'll free up your mind to see the basics "writ large." The trick then is to recast these images into an analogy.

Read Aloud

Remember learning to read in first grade? You may have been scarred for life by mispronouncing words and enduring smirks or a teacher's sigh of frustration. You vowed "never again!" and became an escape artist. Or perhaps you feel *above* reading aloud, regarding it suited only for parental bedtime sessions or for those who do Talking Books for the blind.

If you blench at drawing, why not try reading *and* drawing? The combination really works!

One teacher overcame student reluctance to read by dividing a class into three-member teams to master material almost in the same way as the college student translating the video system. One of three slowly read the step-by-step explanation of the Topic of the Day as the other two took notes or sketched information. They stopped the reader at confusion points for re-reading and discussion in what became known as the "R&G" system (Read-and-Grill). Nobody snickered at pronunciation because the focus was on *understanding* what was read, not *how* it was read.

You don't need a team. Read the material and stop when it becomes confusing. Reread it. It may take *several* rereadings. When you've mastered a section, draw a sketch that explains it—to you. Do it *slowly*. Are you trying to explain how a bill gets through Congress? Draw boxes that stand for each stopping point of a bill.

Consider that in many sources—encyclopedias, Web pages, books, journals—space is limited. Authors know they must be economical with words. So they pack one sentence with so many ideas or facts that the reader is overwhelmed and unable to sort them out. Reading aloud—slowly—reveals that shortcoming.

It also is a strong warning to apply to your writing style and organization.

Just for fun, try an exercise mentioned in a previous chapter: Circle a textbook sentence that you have difficulty understanding. Chances are you'll find they are long and so packed that they require lots of commas to separate clauses and phrases. Such sentences are difficult to comprehend because of psychological reasons.

Research by Nobel laureate Herbert Simon indicated that most people can't concentrate on more than one thing at a time.

The point is that long sentences equal information overload, and the meaning is revealed only if the sentence is read aloud. The big benefit is in being able to break that sentence apart. The "read-aloud" system permits you to stop in mid-sentence to absorb the information. It also gives you time to look up words in a dictionary.

A side benefit is that when *you* now write a composition, you'll know simple words and shorter sentences equal clarity.

Another discovery in reading aloud is that material is often poorly organized in terms of how ordinary readers absorb information. Authors forget to lead readers from the known to the unknown. They inform them at the outset that they're going to present, say, the "Pearson R" statistical test. Below that paragraph, in 18-point type, is the formidable Pearson formula. Most readers would never have fled— mentally or physically—had they been eased into that statistical test with something familiar *first*.

Another turnoff are authors who become enmeshed with details unnecessary for the length of the article or book.

In *your* composition or report, fix the translation so it sticks to presenting the *known* to the unknown and doesn't overwhelm readers with nonessential details. It should be organized along the lines suggested in the chapter on that facet of writing.

In any event, when you're reading aloud, drawing, or acting out a subject, let yourself go. Double-check yourself when you finish a phase to make sure you're accurate.

Talk to the Experts

To backstop whether you have understood your materials through these foregoing techniques, talk to at least two experts on the subject—after you've done the research and made considerable efforts to understand it. Too many students fail to do this because of concerns about their image or great fear they can't absorb information from authority figures.

You may be overcome with those same emotions, but think of the experts as people interested in the same topic who have nuggets of additional, must-have information. Talk to an instructor specializing in your subject, whether it's business ethics, water purification, or zoning. Or talk to those in the field. Librarians are superb sources also. These experts are nearby and will provide leads and advice saving you errors and trips down blind alleys. Most experts are flattered to be consulted *if you've done your homework on the basics*.

Many teachers arrive in the faculty lounge brandishing a student's paper and making that marvelous announcement, "Listen to this, people!" Make that your goal.

First Step in Writing: Translating the Material

Once you understand your subject, you're ready to write the composition. The first step is to decide *how* to translate the material for your reader.

One of the great teaching principles, repeated in this section, is to lead from the *known* to the unknown. Most people don't want to be pioneers. Minds shut down when confronted with a new idea or piece of information. After all, when a mass of unknown material comes our way without a user-friendly warm-up, we become overwhelmed. Fear enters the picture—of intellectual, financial or physical survival—and the mind shuts off. But dress new information in something *familiar*, and the mind remains open. Small wonder that food is the user-friendly analogy used to teach a host of material to both average students and plodders. Not for nothing were apples, oranges, and pies used to ease us into our first brush with arithmetic.

Apt and sound analogies are crucial to any translation or teaching process. The masters of analogies were people such as Plato and Jesus. No matter how complex the philosophic or theological subject was, their analogies were easily grasped by most people because they used familiar images still understood to this day. That's high art.

Jesus used lilies, sparrows, an unreasonable creditor, a house built on sand, a prodigal son, and a good Samaritan to convey lessons about morals and spirituality. He was not worried about other religious leaders' fears he was "popularizing" or "dumbing down" material, or their jealousy about the sizable audiences.

Socrates taught life's paradoxes by taunting students about why they blew on hot soup to cool it, yet blew on hands to warm them.

Students like you, however, have an overflowing storehouse of analogies, too—particularly food, the old reliable. To explain what solid fuel looks like, one student likened it to chocolate pudding left too long in a refrigerator. Popping corn was likened to brain cancer's snuffing out the vitals.

It's generally not long before they use other familiar imagery. A student writing about nuclear fission used a room packed with mousetraps, each rigged with ping pong balls. When one trap was sprung, he wrote, it flung a ping pong ball to another trap. That triggered the new trap to fling its ping pong ball to yet another trap, and so on, until these explosions released tremendous energy.

Romance is an attention-getter, too. A coed's composition explaining DNA used the boy-next-door analogy to place her couple (Sweet Adenine and Thyamine) on Nitrogen Street. No science textbook and almost no teacher would explain DNA that way, despite its quick, fresh, highly memorable effectiveness with students.

In all instances, these student writers grasped the idea that "translating" or "transmitting" knowledge requires leading readers from the *known* to the *unknown* lest eyes glaze over out of disinterest or fear of that unknown.

Some caveats exist about analogies.

One student pointed out that food is one image that *any* reader understands—especially chocolate. However, those who design IQ tests found out a few years ago that oranges were *not* common to the tables of poor people so using oranges in problems screened them out.

Attention also should be paid to the reader's age, sex, race, interests, and experiences, to name just a few factors. For example, when most word problems in mathematics use familiar situations of interest only to *boys*, it's been pointed out that girls recognize they're excluded. If word problems had ever involved a girl buying fabric or items at a thrift shop, perhaps gender-specifics might have been addressed years ago.

Second Step: Writing for Readability

Writing for a 10-year-old reading level guarantees reaching the average American—a factor most newspaper editors try to keep in mind. By contrast, the *National Geographic* magazine is said to be aimed at the 13-year-old reading level, *Scientific American* at university levels.

Check your writing's readability levels with a computer's word-processing program that includes a spelling- and grammar-checking feature. You'll find the readability scoring system in the grammar portion. Professional writers use it. So do teachers sleuthing for plagiarism.

How those levels are determined is based on a 100-point system invented back in the late 1940s by a Dr. Rudolph Flesch. He measured the number of words writers used per sentence and averaged each word's number of syllables. Obviously, writers who used short sentences with words of only one or two syllables presented few reading difficulties. Those who wrote long and convoluted sentences with words of several syllables presented horrendous difficulties.

Under Flesch's scoring system, the *higher* the score in a scale of 100—say, 60 to 80—the *easier* the writing was to read and/or comprehend. Writing that scored a 20 presented great difficulties for most readers.

To pinpoint school-grade reading levels for textbook publishers meant applying another readability expert's scoring system. Thus, under the Flesch-Kincaid system, a score of 7 means that writing is at the seventh-grade level.

The insurance industry was among the first to use the Flesch Reading Ease test, lashed as it was by high-dollar lawsuits over contractual language policyowners couldn't understand. Today, even the federal government, including the military, requires that all writing pass the Flesch-Kincaid test.

How to access Flesch or Flesch-Kincaid scores for your writing requires going into the "OPTIONS" part of the spelling and grammar feature. The grammar checker's "Show Readability Statistics." When you check its box, the readability scoring page opens.

Return to the document to be measured: your composition. Tap the spelling/grammar feature. The grammar-checker is activated *after* the spelling check. The last part of *that* check will display a field with both the Flesch Reading Ease *and* the Flesch-Kincaid Reading Level scores. Some programs even include an extra called the Gunning Fog index, which scores writing for confusion and comprehension.

The Microsoft Word program also counts the percentage of passive-voice sentences, a structure regarded as weak writing by those in almost all fields except fiction. Instead of a noun starting a sentence (as in the active voice), the noun is acted *upon*, much like a victim. MS Word also provides "counts" (of words, letters, paragraphs, sentences). Then comes the payoff: It "averages" your writing by the sentences per *paragraph*, words per *sentence*, and letters per *word*.

For example, MS Word's content analysis of the previous paragraphs reveals the following:

Counts

Words:	166
Characters:	93.1
Paragraphs:	15
Sentences:	8

Averages

Sentences per Paragraph:	4.0
Words per Sentence:	17.7
Characters per word:	5.1

Readability

Passive Voice:	12%
Flesch Reading Ease:	57.1
Flesch-Kincaid Grade Level:	9.6

Readability is an important area not just for writing professionals, but for you as a composition student. For one thing, those correcting your writing have college educations. Yet when it comes to understanding all of today's complexities, they probably would relish topics presented in simple terms.

Students in a specialty reporting class at a major research university were quick at the start of the term to brand themselves as "science boneheads." They proudly confessed great weakness in understanding the other major and lucrative fields that begged for writers able to explain topics to external audiences.

Yet a term spent doing all of the foregoing yielded spectacular results. Two students founded a biweekly science/high-tech supplement for the student daily newspaper, with articles drawing applause from researchers in those fields. One student was hired to write a pamphlet of synopses of foreign agricultural reports from several research projects aimed at attracting more. Several had stories published in the science section of *The Oregonian*.

Two of the three students who wrote the openers below entered high-paying, high-powered careers two months after earning their degrees. They wrote openers like those below with ease and rich content, well organized and clear, that were a great pleasure for this author to read:

> Meet Rudy Root Cap, unflappable if tipped on his head or if he falls sideways and can't get up again. Talk about carefree!

> Imagine you are on a peanut-butter-and-jelly sandwich enjoying a ride into space. Then, you see little critters nibbling away the edges of the bread. That's what could happen to a spacecraft's skin if its designers long ago hadn't developed an antidote.

> A freeway and its exits are just like a fiber-optics system of telephone communications.

All were ordinary students just like you, but they had a drive to open the doors of knowledge to their fellows. They went to extraordinary lengths to master the foregoing lessons and, as a result, had the experience of knowing their "translations" had increased knowledge of an audience far wider than just one professor with a grade book.

The next chapters will show you how you can do the same things.

CHAPTER **13**

SCIENCE
AND
TECHNOLOGY

If you've ever explained something scientific or technological to a friend or family member, you usually don't have much trouble "translating" it. So you *can* do this kind of writing. If you can do that, the likelihood is strong that you probably could write an explanation about something complex as well or even better than a textbook author. What most students don't know is that those authors must have their manuscripts approved by colleagues rather than students reading the published version.

Much of the previous chapter was filled with examples of the creative way students explained complex subjects. If they could explain the basics about genome cancer projects, so can you. Indeed, you may surprise yourself at how inventive and clear you are in this kind of writing.

One of the most refreshing stories about *DISCOVER* magazine, a science publication for lay readers, is that its first chief copy editor refused to pass writing that was not clear to ordinary readers, its major market. Not even if the author won a Nobel prize in physics. A copy editor approves every word in a newspaper story or magazine article or an entire publication. *DISCOVER*'s contributors and sources were (and still are) well known for being intimidating, even bullying. That's attributable to a culture fearful of peers sneering about "popularizing" or "dumbing down" research material. That's especially true in *Scientific American* or medical/science peer-reviewed journals—as if the "unwashed" might somehow penetrate their "private club."

However, that copy editor was buttressed by the publisher (TIME, Inc.) and senior editors—and the existence since 1872 of *Popular Science* magazine. Its century of success was built on translating the complex to the simple for thousands of loyal and avid readers. *DISCOVER*'s circulation would be competing with that publication. So stories in *DISCOVER* had *better* be "popularized" if the publisher wanted to retain readers—and, thereby, advertisers. That both *DISCOVER* and *Popular Science* are still around attests to the wisdom of "popularizing" science and technology because millions of ordinary readers *are* interested in these subjects.

It's also refreshing to note that dozens of daily newspaper editors and publishers in the mid-1980s, seeing such success, launched science sections, many of which still exist. They, too, insisted their writers translate stories from the complex to the simple for ordinary readers.

Stories in these publications tend to fall into three major categories: *people*, *processes*, and *phenomenon*. Their authors do exactly what you'll learn to do in the next few pages, and that is to pore over research. They read voraciously: newspapers, magazines, journals, books, and the Internet. They also stay current with a host of sources around the globe about what might be interesting to the general public. They also contact "newsmakers," whether it's a medical team at Harvard University or a crew out on the *Alvin*, Oregon State University's oceanographic-research vessel.

You probably are unlikely to give such movers and shakers a call or an e-mail for a composition or term paper. Yet that doesn't mean you can't tackle some aspect of what's *already* published about people, processes, and phenomenon in these fields. If you're attending a major research university, don't rule out talking to project leaders or staffers—especially if projects are funded by taxpayers—to write a feature story for the local newspaper about what they're doing. That's what journalism students did at Oregon State University, as noted in the previous chapter.

Let's first look at writing about people in these fields.

Writing About People

When students decide to write about such people as Galileo or Marie Curie, Thomas Edison or Steve Jobs, they tend to get overwhelmed by all the source material in the library or on the Internet. The result is usually a "dry obituary" of birth, childhood, accomplishments, and death.

The problem is that there's no life in a chronological approach. The scientist does not seem to be human, an individual who had head colds and family problems, or was curt with lab assistants. Readers *know* these individuals must have had emotional pain, attacks of egotism and loneliness, and exasperation on the seventy-eighth test drive or clinical trial. Famous writers of the 1800s such as Nathaniel Hawthorne and Robert Louis Stevenson certainly portrayed this part of their lives in classic short stories such as "The Birth Mark," and "Strange Case of Dr. Jekyll and Mr. Hyde," respectively.

Nor is a drop of ink usually spent on the day-to-day single-minded drive that possesses most scientists or those in high technology. Not *everyone* wins a Nobel prize or lands a $35,000,000 research grant for a college of engineering. The writing contains no laboratory odors, or the discouragement of losing a grant, the petty jealousies between colleagues—all areas of possibility if the writer tackles a *segment* of an individual's life instead of that cradle-to-grave version.

So don't use the chronological approach.

Writing about inventors or scientists is exciting stuff. One of the DNA discoverers had no difficulty making it interesting to the ordinary reader in recounting what went on in the lab in the best-selling book *The Double Helix*. So did the screenwriter of *Tucker*, the film about a major automobile designer's contribution to the industry.

Focus on One Achievement

If you're going to write about such people, put meat on the bare bones as you recreate the repetitiousness of constant trial-and-error that led to some achievement. Include something about repeated experiments that went nowhere despite the cost, time, energy, and devotion; all eventually led to a success. Thomas Edison's struggle with perfecting the light bulb is an excellent example of such inspiration—and exasperation. If you've read one or two sources about key people, you'll uncover instances of difficulties surrounding a major effort. Ideas *do* consume such people, often making home life difficult or impossible.

Put yourself into an imaginary lab jacket and your composition suddenly will have life and reality. One help might be to return to the section on how to write profiles (pp. 41–42). Once again, it must be said that key quotations are excellent ways to reveal someone's personality.

Once in that lab jacket, you must understand the "discovery" you are writing about, whether it's radiation or jet propulsion. The source book might explain it, but if it offers little information, check the Internet's *reliable* sources, an encyclopedia, or a book in the field.

To understand the person's work, you also should do those unorthodox things strongly suggested in the previous chapter: drawing sketches, reading aloud, or dramatizing events.

Organizing the Personality Piece

For the composition's structure, re-read the chapter on organization. A quick-and-dirty outline is an essential tool in writing about complex subjects.

Open with an inviting lead, one that will make a reader want to continue. An anecdote or event usually serves as an excellent avenue into any science or technological piece.

The next paragraph can be devoted to *briefly* summarizing the person's achievements, but only the *major* ones because most have lengthy lists of attainments and awards. Did the achievement trigger a trend? Or was it a "one-shot"?

The rest of the composition is the exception to the rule on chronological organization, especially if one major attainment leads to another.

Give credit to the work done by others that leads to an achievement. Most outstanding people in these fields are quick to insist on this, in fact. They know that one discovery is built upon others' efforts and strings of failures. For example, Jonas Salk may have been given credit for the polio vaccine, but his work was built on the tireless, often unsuccessful and heartbreaking research of others. That's true, too, in technology, though perhaps the only sector to publicly acknowledge the names of contributors is in computer software, as is seen on diskette credits.

When you begin mentioning a singular attainment, take a historical approach that not only includes previous work, but also what got the scientist or engineer interested in the subject. For instance, the laser beam began on a park bench in Washington, D.C., when its inventor sat gazing at the nearby flowers. The popular and indispensable Post-its got started because a 3-M employee complained to adhesive designers that place markers kept falling out of his choir hymnal. These are fascinating and human starting points of interest to ordinary readers.

As you write about the person's work week, give the reader the flavor of lab life, whether it's midnight pizza or worrying about paying the bills for burning midnight oil.

Paragraphs on the significance of the person's work should be placed near the end of the composition. Has the achievement(s) set off a new industry, as has been the case with space exploration? Radar certainly did. So did the discovery that selenium was useful to television's infancy.

The close could involve such results or perhaps selecting a significant quote that sums up the person's life work.

The structure of a personality piece is shown in the quick-and-dirty outline on the next page.

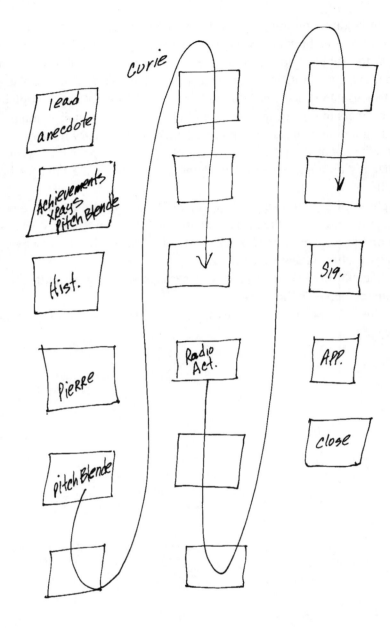

Writing About a Process

In writing about *processes* in technology or science, you'll discover they tend almost to organize themselves. ("This step leads to this. Then, that leads to this, etc.")

Whether you write about stem-cell research or the next generation of laser printers, once again you'll need to seize the reader's interest from the start. Why not begin with an action-filled anecdote tied to that process? One student did in explaining the genesis of an invention that radically changed the logging industry:

> As he sat eating, he noticed a colony of bugs making lunch of a tree trunk. Moving closer, he saw that their jaws moved a certain way. Out of this observation came the chain saw.

This lunch-time anecdote also has a human factor, another technique to catch a reader's attention.

An anecdotal opener needs to tell a reader what the process or product is. What will it do? When inventors excitedly explain their widget, the thrust is always what it will *do*. So follow their lead. And tell readers how it will fit into their lives. Will it keep death at bay? Will it create jobs? Will it open new vistas? If you're writing about stars, relate them to those who seldom look at the heavens except to see whether they need snow shovels or raincoats.

In short, link the reader to the process.

Organizing the Process Piece

Once you've established that reader's tie to a process, remember that what grabbed *your* attention about the subject probably will work here, too. In an assignment, you can include a brief paragraph early in the composition explaining how *you* became interested in the subject. If you were to rewrite it as a magazine article, you'd omit that bit of information, but your teacher probably will be interested in this factor.

Move next to the paragraphs about the historical development of the process or product. Bring in the pioneer efforts. After all, neither ethanol fuel nor cell phones suddenly arrived early one morning. Historical material also has the advantage of holding reader interest because it *begins* the process toward generational advancements; it doesn't overwhelm.

Once again, this approach employs the technique of moving an audience from the *known* to the unknown. History also is full of people, lending the human aspect to something that tends to be clinical or mechanical. Many might be interested to know, for instance, that the product began in someone's garage, the case with Tektronix's famed oscilloscope.

That done, now explain the process.

Processes almost always move in that one-two-three step order mentioned previously. Think of the amoeba's brief stages of birth to death. Or a star. The latest helicopter or gunship took to the air in stages, all involving the dangers of repeated test flights.

In short, organize the rest of the composition by those stages or steps.

One stage may be so extensive that it requires *several* paragraphs for clarity. Break down a stage by giving each element its own paragraph(s). You'll see that in the example below.

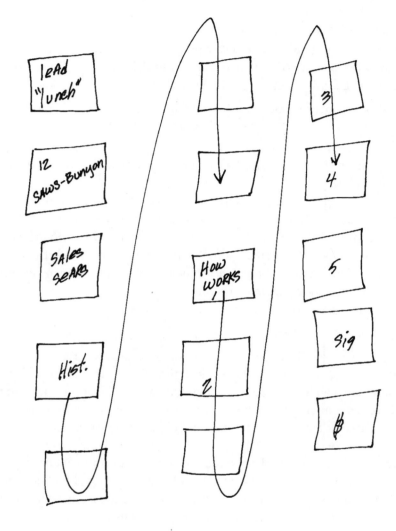

Breathers, Analogies, and Examples

Breathers *between* major steps or stages of a process are godsends to readers. They are described in the writing-style chapter and involve those short, one-sentence paragraphs that provide a place for readers to catch their breath after several data-filled paragraphs. Or their purpose is a typographic break for the eyes— as is the case with the next paragraph.

Two other godsends are vital to this writing area.

Two of the most welcome and beloved expressions of the English language, especially for scientific or technological compositions, are *"for instance"* and *"for example."* Use them liberally with complex stages or steps in your piece.

Both examples and analogies are essential in this category of writing, sometimes for *every* step/stage. Ensure that they are apt and part of the reader's world.

One student used a freeway's exits and entrances in an "extended" analogy throughout a composition explaining bypass procedures. An extended analogy is difficult to create, but is excellent to convey a reader through a process.

As was indicated in the previous chapter, complex subjects demand a presentation in simple words, simple sentences, and common examples. Emphasis has been laid on avoiding long sentences packed with too much information. But another danger is jargon from the field.

Writers fall into this trap because they either want to impress a source and forget the reader, or because they want to be scrupulously accurate in using the terminology of the field. Again, consider your audience which, right now, is the instructor who knows little about your subject.

Forget impressing sources. The challenge here is in translating what they've accomplished so ordinary readers may understand it and its significance to their lives.

The second and most prevalent danger is assuming readers already know the the subject and skipping a step. Omissions of steps in the world of computer users have led to near-apoplectic responses, as any technical service staffer can attest. That happens because the writers of instructions assume a step is self-evident; to a lay audience it usually isn't. The resulting rage is akin to a gourmet cook discovering too late that a step or ingredient was omitted in a cookbook or a magazine article.

The next paragraphs should be devoted to the significance of the process: why readers should care about this process or product. What are the results? The applications? The costs? Economic or employment benefits? Again, tie them to people's daily lives even though the benefit may be a long way down an expensive road.

The significance also might provide you with a close. One student's economical blend of significance and the composition's end was:

> The teletypesetter was the keystone that changed the newspaper backshop forever.

Writing About a Phenomenon

Suppose you decide to write about a phenomenon such as El Niño or, in space shuttles, gear rusting of actuators in rudder-speed brakes.

After researching the topic to understand these phenomena, you ought to be able to find some factor that will seize the reader's interest in your opening paragraph. Again, try the human element. For example, a composition on the greenhouse effect might open with a graphic description of what the earth will be like 100 or 1,000 years from now if the earth continues to warm. Readers want life to continue a healthy environment. Pointing out that the greenhouse effect ultimately will cause coastal floods and unending inland droughts, *will* get attention.

One book certainly did this decades ago. Rachel Carson's *The Silent Spring* caused readers to gasp in horror with an opening depicting a world in which no birds existed because the insecticide DDT had killed them.

Though she was a scientist, this book was not written in language of her peers or for the insecticide industry, a small, elite audience. It was intended to rivet the ordinary reader's attention with the message about what chemicals were doing to the food chain and life itself.

The book was a bombshell! President John F. Kennedy instantly ordered an end to using DDT on crops. The chemical industry was hard-pressed to stop the simple message Carson sent to the world—couched in simple words crafted around the dire results that even the slowest reader could understand.

You can do the same thing in your presentation if you use the Flesch Reading Ease test mentioned in the last chapter. Apply it not to the *finished* piece, but right after the composition's first two paragraphs to see if it's geared toward an eighth-grade reading level. If it is, you're off to a *clear* start.

Organizing the Phenomenon Piece

Once you've aroused reader interest, move into the paragraphs to describe what might *cause* the phenomenon. Many factors might be involved. For example, the Northern Lights are tied to light reflection, as well as metal particles, gravity, and the like. Each element you take up should get one paragraph at least.

Here, it's well to consider what is too often ignored in scientific and technological textbooks and even more often in classroom lectures: skimping on examples. One seems to be considered ample—and quickly or briefly presented. A single example may be adequate for bright students, but sadly that usually excludes perhaps 95% of those desperately trying to follow the textbook or instructor.

Students and readers deserve at least two analogies or examples. So provide more than one. Another welcome phrase is: "Put another way…" Pave the way for the comprehension of that struggling 95% who are left behind—among them, perhaps, your instructor.

Analogies may be even greater aids than examples to explain not only phenomena, but processes. Draw them from the kind of ordinary-life imagery that Socrates or Shakespeare favored, as suggested in the previous chapter. That may make creative juices work overtime, but you'll feel like Thomas Edison when an apt and familiar analogy suddenly arrives.

Some writers like to present the phenomenon itself and follow it with several paragraphs about the history of its observation and scientific theories and explanations. Other writers intersperse history with the phenomenon because they believe that a Benjamin Franklin flying a kite *does* spark up what otherwise would be a dull presentation. Again, remember that the human element always attracts readers.

The close could contain a paragraph on how a phenomenon is significant to the reader's life. Again, why should readers care? El Niño assuredly has changed our lives. So can the shifting of tectonic plates off the California coast. The Mount St. Helens volcanic eruption impacted people's lungs, the wood-products and shipping industries, tourism, and flora and fauna.

Among developments in technology, consider the impact of processes in one area alone: Speeding production and the use of ethanol to replace fossil fuels at the service station; it will impact automobile engine design, corn growers, the petrochemical industry, the environment, American foreign policy, car dealers, advertising agencies—and many more. Developments in the computer industry have the same kind of significance. Or light-rail, aircraft, and utilities. The topics are fascinating and endless.

A quick-and-dirty outline of a composition on phenomena might look like the one below.

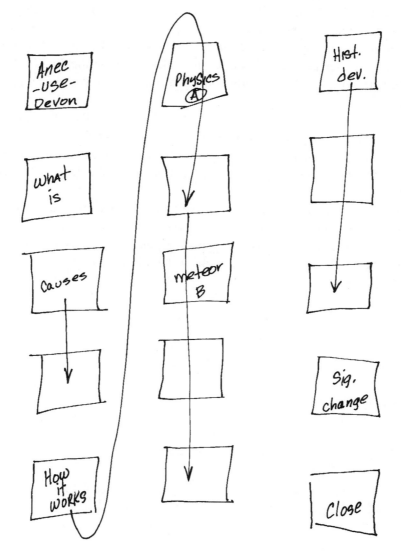

One spin-off of writing about technological or scientific subjects is that you can make a career in either field. Practitioners capable of writing for external publics—consumers to federal agencies—are so rare that most command high salaries reflecting such a sellers' market. They are always looking for freelance writers to put instructions or sales materials into "plain English" for customers or to furnish printed materials for state or federal regulatory agencies to demonstrate compliance with regulations. Foreign manufacturers have writers who speak and write English, but most have little mastery of American idiomatic expressions; they, too, need writers to "translate" marketing and regulatory messages.

If you have contacted experts in these two professions for your assignment, you have already begun networking that may be *translated* into a future job. Keep the connections going with a thank-you card for expertise and periodic notes about your continued interest in those fields.

One writer's postscript to this benefit was: "I get a high—maybe revenge— from telling engineers who thought writing was only for secretaries and speak only high-tek-ese, 'if you want to keep your job, you better spell out in plain English what this puppy does so I can get a sales piece out the door.' " They may grumble, she says, but they usually comply because a good "translator" is worth diamonds in the world of technology.

The same thing is true in the sciences because eventually either in public or financial relations, they need "wordsmiths," as one researcher admitted. He cited the parade of television advertisements from the pharmaceutical industry as a prime example of a field needing writers with a talent of selling its products and defending its prices.

Beyond these inducements are the excitement and elation of being on the ground floor of trends and discoveries. If you decide to become a writer in these fields, you'll experience that as you explain an array of never-ending topics that fascinate. You'll discover that writing about them is a labor of love.

CHAPTER 14

STATISTICS

Americans have had a first-class love affair with statistics for decades, judging from their prevalence in the media—print and broadcast. No survey has provided statistics to show that surveys entertain millions of viewers and readers, it would appear. But most daily newspapers, wise to reader interests, may include one every day from the large stock furnished by wire services and syndicates. One late-night comedian always uses at least one study in his monologue for a guaranteed laugh.

You hardly need to be told *you* are a statistic. Much data about you has been in data banks perhaps even *before* you were born. Businesses, industries, institutions, politicians, and the like pay small fortunes to survey firms to learn how many people own a car, buy fast-food, get suits off the rack, stay in high school, work at minimum wage, went to the dentist last year, or approve the new Crackerjack packaging.

Other things are counted statistically: rainy days in June, drug-related fatal accidents, remaining covered bridges, housing starts, healthy oak trees, garage sales, gas prices. And gifted writers can make all of the above so interesting that those studies are read, quoted, and saved around the globe—to say nothing of selling billions of goods and services.

Even life insurance statistics can become fascinating in the hands of, say, a Metropolitan Life writer who once reported that the men who live the longest seem to be symphony conductors. Why? Because actuarial statistics "show" their lifestyles were composed of doing what they felt passionate about while stressed-out underlings take care of the creature comforts—meals and travel, entertainment and finances.

Consider that writer. He's among those able to "translate" results from studies and probably never will lack projects or well-paid employment, whether in public relations for pharmaceutical companies or a myriad of other marketing firms. It could be a government agency such as the one determining periodic cost-of-living increases in Social Security checks; that's based on the Consumer Price Index, which tracks prices of essential goods.

Students exploring careers at one university were astounded to learn that "stats" majors spent a month in Hawaii's lush mountainous islands counting birds facing extinction. Or that they got to go abroad for at least one term to help one impoverished "dryland" country determine how many seeds of a new variety of wheat should be "broadcast" per hectare. They began to view math in a different light. You may, too, and even find a calling in the world of statistical writing.

An Overview

Statistics essentially counts ("quantifies") things: people, events, even the weather. That count stems from surveys, the results of which are subjected to special formulas for validity, reliability, and whether they're applicable outside the laboratory ("generalized").

But studies are confined to research firms or institutions. *Consumer Reports* magazine has survived and prospered as a non-profit organization for decades on product testing and publication of results. It tots up, say, the best buys in big-ticket items such as cars or laptop computers, as well as small ones (toothpaste, frozen pizza, cheap watches). It also reveals safety and repair records, durability, noisiness, and other factors.

Why do things need to be counted? Mostly to assess some need or interest in goods or services, but also determining population trends, even what kind of people collect Chevrolets built before 1939. Some cynics say they're spawned by graduate schools that have to keep doctoral candidates busy. One wag insists studies spring from Americans' desperate need to believe they have a lot of company in their physical, emotional, financial, political, and spiritual lives. Whatever the reason, the amount of money spent on statistical research is colossal.

Designing and Conducting a Statistical Project

The only way you'll understand statistics is to design a small project involving at least 30 people. It's not difficult to do, even for those with life-long mathophobia. Be assured, too, that your instructor won't expect you to apply a validity test to your findings such as chi-square or determine the f statistic. That requires taking a statistics class or two. Yet, novice as you are, you'll be expected to report your numbers and to draw conclusions—and to make all that information clear.

For such a writing project, trips abroad or being entrusted with clinical trial results on heart disease are unlikely. What *is* likely is a "straw" poll, rather than the tightly controlled quantitative analysis of the research world.

The benefits will be literally beyond count. You'll learn what goes into a major research project involving hundreds of people ("subjects" in clinical trials; "respondents" in polls) responding to a questionnaire (an "instrument") with several carefully designed questions ("items"). This kind of undertaking is called an "empirical" study or, more generally, what is known as "quantitative" research—counting the "quantity" of something (people, things, events, etc.). When you're doing a term paper on a historical event or the work of an artist, you're not "quantifying" (counting) or doing *quantitative* research; you're doing "*qualitative*" research.

In addition, designing and conducting a project will teach you why statistics are not an exact science, but nevertheless an absolutely absorbing and interesting one—especially in marketing research. You'll learn about "dangerous stats," particularly when the results involve medical and pharmaceutical fields. You'll not be fooled by advertisements that *used* to employ the band-wagon approach of "Nine out of ten doctors prescribe/recommend…" which eventually spurred the "truth-in-advertising" laws and watchdogs. The "doctors" might have earned a weekend degree from a diploma mill.

But that changed little. The latest slogan, undergirded by statistics, in media ads—print/broadcast/Internet ("Ask your doctor about..," "clinical tests show…") so alarmed the American Medical Association that it's lobbying for a law requiring drug companies to submit *all* research results to a federal database. Despite revenues from those ads, one major newspaper finally issued an editorial warning that should govern anyone involved in statistical writing—such as you:

> The public needs to know more about the studies that are halted because of troubling side effects, or that get shelved because the drug in question proved to be no more effective than a sugar pill. And the federal government needs to invest more in basic scientific research through universities and independent research laboratories, and not rely so heavily on profit-driven companies to decide the public's best interest. [7]

Results depend on *many* factors, as you'll learn, not the least of which is the *truthfulness* or condition of those polled (they're not under oath) or the care in which testing conditions are strung. The dryland study on wheat was confounded, for example, when the local help dumped them in one spot rather than hike around a hectare.

The first step in designing a questionnaire is to decide on the *subject* of a straw poll, perhaps the easiest part of the assignment. Traditionally, subjects stem from a researcher's theory ("hypothesis") about something being true or false. That this drug will make people live longer. That breaking up a large high school into small academies will create a better learning environment. That titanium is the best metal for aircraft. Or it could be a "null hypothesis" that tests a hypothesis to see if should be kept or discarded for another hypothesis.

Consumer Reports magazine's research is based on frequencies, however, not hypotheses that a product is poor or great. They test generally for quality and are largely focused on product advantages/disadvantages, prices, safety and noise factors, repair records and other vital information on big-ticket items or small items sold in significant volume.

Don't select a trivial topic or one in which you have little interest because your instructor may grade it accordingly. As long as you're going to invest effort and time on this kind of writing project, make a contribution of value. For instance, if

---

[7] Editorial, *The Oregonian*, June 24, 2004.

the school board faces a major issue and you poll decision makers (e.g., voters) about it, you'll have furnished valuable information to the board, the schools, and community.

Next, decide on whom you'll poll (the "population") as well as the where and when of conducting the study. In statistical codes, the number of respondents/subjects are reduced to the letter "N" (as in, N=274).

To have a validity, you don't have to poll hundreds. TV's audience surveys select only 1,500 out of millions, but the choices purportedly are made with such care designers insist that sample represents *all* viewers; programs live or die based on N=1,500. A major study involving high school English teachers winnowed the 1,500 "population" of a state to a third chosen at random (every third name). Most experts believe *at least* 30 people must be in a sample and no matter what the "N," the researcher must have a 70% response rate for the study to be credible.

So narrow your "sample" to a *representative* number of your population.

The time of day makes a difference in responses. So does the day of the week, the month or the seasons. Or weather (sunny days are different from snowy or rainy ones).

Where you poll is just as important. Professionals know that busy streets yield different people from near-empty ones. So do slums and affluent neighborhoods. In your situation, the factors might be: school bus stop at 8 or 3 o'clock? Halls *before* first class or *between* classes? Cafeteria at the start or end of lunch hour? Before the game or half-time at the concessions stand?

When respondents are in a hurry, incidentally, you'll get a far different response than when they have time on their hands; some pollsters have deliberately used this factor to be able to produce a certain result. A classic example was a poll staged by unthinking sociology majors at a major intersection in downtown Portland, Oregon—at rush hour! Until the police came to disperse them, it can be imagined that the N of furious "no response" was significant (or the open-ended one of "are you kids crazy?").

What follows is perhaps the most challenging part of statistics: designing the instrument and its item(s).

Determine which items are "musts." Stick to one or two items rather than five because studies and polling experience suggests a higher probability of participation. You may want to include as a last item space for comment (called an "open-ended" item). Those are generally welcomed in surveys concerning controversial subjects. For the opinionated, responses of "yes/no/no opinion" are inadequate.

Items must be crafted carefully. They can't be loaded such as the classic: "Do you still beat your wife?" Or biased by a preface as in: "Several studies indicate that boys are called on far more frequently in class than girls—grade school to college. Do you disagree or agree?"

Bias is usually in the eye of the beholder, true, but an item such as "Would you—or wouldn't you—drive without a seat belt?" might be faulted because "*wouldn't*" is placed in a secondary position.

Some items are unclear, compounded by length, and sometimes as cleverly crafted as ballot measures designed to be defeated:

> Would you support a program that creates a health-care finance plan for medically necessary services to all residents of this state, creates additional income and payroll taxes, under a governing board elected by the state legislature and/or the governor?

In short, make items short, unadorned, clear, and unbiased. Incidentally, if your range of responses is the equivalent of a "yes" or "no," add a third variation: "no opinion" or "don't know." If you receive a sizable number of "no opinions," that result may be *more* important than the others.

The other element that *must* be in your instrument are factors such as gender, age, and the like; statisticians call them "demographics."

Demographics play a large role in how people respond and what you write. Several variations are possible, depending on the topic. If it's academic, include indicators about respondents by class rank (freshman, sophomore, etc.), by major, or by faculty vs. student. If it's sports, use indicators for spectators and participants—perhaps breakouts for individual sports. If the instrument is work related, sort by those who hold jobs (breakouts on types, hours, etc.) and those who don't.

To ensure that an "instrument" is sound and research dollars and time won't be wasted, those in the statistical fields always do a dry run to screen out bugs and misunderstood words, catch spelling/grammatical errors, and, above all, monitor for bias.

The items also need to be asked in the *same* way each time. Respondents often are prone to provide an answer that pleases the researcher, as you'll learn; several will study your face intently. Be on guard if you want honest answers. Use the same tone of voice and emphasis each time you give the item—and maintain the same facial expression. Telephone polling may eliminate facial giveaways, but not tone and emphasis. Of course, if you use a written instrument, you'll eliminate all three of these elements that could invalidate your study.

You'll learn the same things about respondents that professionals do. Men and women don't always respond the same way. Age makes a difference. So do experience and background. Ethnic heritage may be a factor. A detail-oriented person will respond differently from a creative type or a chronic "agin-er."

The circumstances under which you polled also have a bearing on results. Was it during the excitement of a football game? The height of mall shopping at Christmas? Did you spring at people or wait until they looked curious?

Tallying the Results

Once you've contacted your last respondent, you'll sort and tally results into categories and breakouts within those categories.

Consumer Reports sorts by categories of effectiveness, cost, ease, and safety as well as factors fitting the goods or services. Your study is different, but your instrument still contains demographic categories.

Sort by categories and determine which one's results merits the greatest emphasis. That determination is essential in organizing the paper.

Then, get out the calculator and work the numbers into percentages by categories and breakouts.

Space does not permit an explanation either of tests that can be applied to determine the study's "tightness" or how to calculate the margin of error. Those you'll learn in a statistics course. But in toting responses, you'll see patterns leading to conclusions.

Writing the Results

The next step is to decide the thrust of the composition: What was the most important finding of the results, perhaps including the breakouts? That decision will determine the paper's organization in perhaps the quickest and easiest quick-and-dirty outline you'll ever do.

Organization

When you designed your instrument, you took care of organization: main questions, and demographics for the breakouts of responses.

Statistical pieces are among the easiest to organize just because of initial project design. For instance, the major finding is contained in the opening paragraph. The second paragraph traditionally adds particulars about the study and the five W's (who—and how many, what, when, where). It certainly must contain data about the sample size so readers judge the study's overall worth. They are critical.

Just how critical was shown with the first study about fetal alcohol syndrome; the sample group involved *less* than a dozen women. However, despite that tiny sample, the conclusions received national attention and terrified thousands of pregnant women and mothers even to this day.

That study has been cited repeatedly as a hallmark example of generalizing from a study of few subjects. But it also illustrates that many other factors can make statistical research worthless or highly dangerous if all the methods and circumstances are *not* revealed by the writer. Until recently, heart ailments of women were diagnosed using research concerning men. Clinical trials involving derelicts as subjects are flawed for generalizing principally because street survival makes them tougher than most populations.

As to lesser categories, devote separate paragraphs for results from *each*. Rank them: second most important finding, next; the third, after that, and so on down to the *least* important result.

The quick-and-dirty outline below may help your organization. This study involved a poll about setting up a smoking area.

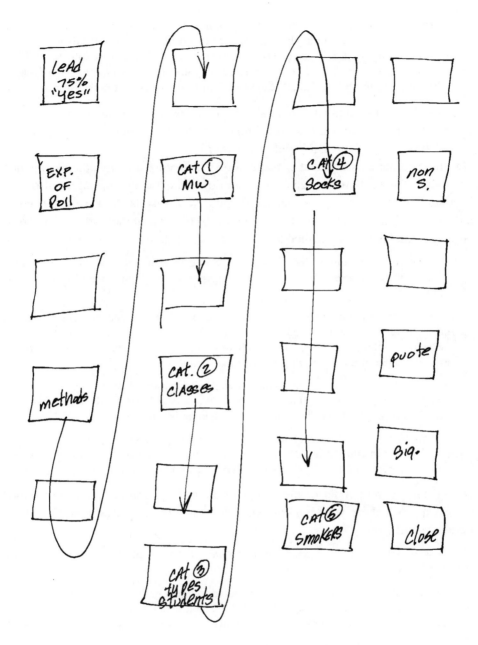

Writing Style

Writing a statistics piece may be the easiest you've ever done because you're weaving your numbers into results. However, this is the sticking place because readers won't suffer through paragraphs overloaded with numbers or endless percentages.

Consumer Reports and thousands of other quantifiers both show how to translate numerical data into something lively and interesting. Its articles are undergirded by illustrations, but most readers go straight to the text and read to the end. That's because the presentation has zip, sparkle—and meat. For instance, a piece on electronic keyboards lured readers in with this opener:

Today's hills are alive with the sound of computerized music. More than 25 million people now play electronic keyboards. You can find little under-$50 keyboards with miniature keys in toy stores; you can find more elaborate keyboards, costing up to $500, next to the stereo rigs in department stores; and you can pay anywhere from $500 to $10,000 or more for "professional" keyboards and synthesizers at music stores.

An article's words reporting data about a dishwasher hovered around a Flesch readability score of 8; such super-simple diction and sentences included the bounce of "*snazzy*," "*boosted*," and "*swaddled*."

Opening paragraphs of statistics pieces are no different from any others contained in this book. They still must seize reader attention. Here, though, they must also contain a study's main findings. Consider framing your results the way you'd tell a friend and you'll have the gist of the first half-dozen words of the lead for your composition. It can be just as polished and informative as these lively openers:

Sales of compact cameras have boomed….Some are trim enough to slip into a shirt pocket….You can squeeze more people into a group shot without having to back up too far…

When more than half a class flunks a required class like College Algebra each term, perhaps changes in how it's taught are overdue. That's the view of 73% of the nearly 80 who are retaking it this term, though most thought a spirited demonstration to remove it as a required course might spur those changes.

San Francisco fans might want to reconsider their position, according to Jerry Reiter, a Duke assistant professor of statistics, whose numbers indicate the Giants are likelier to score when [Barry] Bonds is walked than when he is pitched to.

Although most single young men aspire to marriage, about one-fifth are deeply skeptical of the institution and their prospects of making it work, according to a new national survey that closely links men's marital outlook to their upbringing.

In writing the remainder of the composition, perhaps the best and most unobtrusive way to include your numbers and their impact is by wrapping figures in parentheses, like this:

Most boys (41%) had dropped out at the end of their junior year while most girls (42%) dropped out as sophomores.

Nine out of 10 Standard employees appeared to crave praise when asked if they got enough from their bosses. When 56% of the home office's personnel (897) thought about praise, they seemed to echo one employee's lament: "If they can't give a raise, how about some praise?"

Quotes do spark up statistical writing because respondents' unvarnished remarks often are blunt, on target, or humorous. Quotes are drawn from items with "open ends" or statements made to researchers (names are never used because surveys should be anonymous.) Don't select dull ones or those that aren't germane or don't reflect the tenor of responses. Never use quotes to pad a thin piece of research. The instructor will be the first to notice.

One element that will affect your assignment is the perishability of the statistics, sometimes barely outliving the interview hour. That's why conclusions need the customary scientific hedges of "*it would seem*," or "*it appears*," *or "the evidence suggests that…*" Scientists use such qualifiers because even if tests show

100% of something happens nearly 100% of the time, the possibility still exists that an outside factor might not have been included or a flawed "inside" factor might have confounded the results.

For example, even though the link between smoking and lung cancer seems to be an undeniable example of cause and effect, the tobacco industry has fought multimillion dollar lawsuits with findings about the pre-existing poor health of smokers. It's also well to remember that back in 1492, 99.9 out of 100 explorers seemed to conclude the world was flat.

So never write "the results showed that this attitude *is* prevalent." Instead, make it "the results showed this attitude *seems* to be prevalent."

Above all, be accurate, fair, and honest—even if the results seemed to suggest your hypothesis was dead wrong. Double-check the math in converting numbers to percentages. Your readers might catch an error.

If statistical writing appeals to you, examine those studies reported in the media. Most are "reader-friendly" models. You might drop the authors an e-mail of admiration, something they rarely receive. The contact might well lead to a future in numbers.

CHAPTER **15**

BUSINESS

If you're looking for an exciting topic for a composition or paper, master's thesis or doctoral dissertation, why not select business? It's one area that will fascinate you *and* your instructor. After all, anything involving money and power is *never* dull. Business keeps roofs over heads, food on the table, and provides enormous outlets for energy or just moving ideas into goods or services. Even if you believe *love* of money is the root of all evil, even that kind of passion might be an excellent subject. Real-life people have been models for fictional characters such as Scrooge and Silas Marner, Horatio Alger and George, the hero of *A Wonderful Life*, for years.

One major company, TIME, Inc., began in 1922 as an idea for a new kind of magazine from a talented (but broke) college senior named Britton Hadden. Boiling with an entrepreneur's energy, he talked a classmate (Henry Luce) with business smarts and contacts into the venture. They wooed venture capitalists into a $90,000 grubstake. The result was *TIME* magazine, which soon financed *FORTUNE* magazine despite the Great Depression; next, *LIFE* magazine and, in the mid-1950s, *SPORTS ILLUSTRATED*, followed by *PEOPLE, MONEY, DISCOVER,* and the Time-Warner conglomerate.

What's boring about a multimillion-dollar shoe company (Nike) that started by another vigorous entrepreneur using a waffle iron on soles? Phil Knight sold the first Nike running shoes from a truck on a Los Angeles street corner. Or how about the three whipsmart young men who launched a global high-technology company (Tektronix) in a garage? Or thousands of their counterparts in places as diverse as Hong Kong, Hamburg, and Honduras?

Or you may be concerned about the stock-market scandals involving huge conglomerates such as Enron or WorldCom that have stolen millions in pension and retirement funds. Or rigged electrical sales in the West and chortled at the powerless ("Grandma Minnies") yet pay only $10 in business taxes. A meaty paper may deal with why robbers of convenience stores and tax cheats get speedy trials and long jail terms, but robber barons may stave off trials for years and, if ever found guilty, get only a few months of house arrest or minimum-security prisons with golfing privileges.

Whether you write about the honest and hard-working entrepreneurs, those guilty of "high crimes and misdemeanors," or a new product, you still need to understand the fundamentals of how business operates. No better device exists than an imaginary business—a lemonade stand. This chapter's aim is to provide those basics and then show you how to write about it.

Overview

You know more about business than you think because you're surrounded by it whenever you spend money. Or work. Movies about Wall Street or classics such as *Glengarry Glen Ross* or *A Wonderful Life* may have given you a glimpse of what life is like in what once was called the "counting room" where owners toted up the day's profits and decided on tomorrow's direction. You may hold an over-the-counter job and call the accountants "bean counters," but you still may be curious about the internal workings that keep that business "growing or going."

You certainly can understand a "pyramid scheme," the illegal multilevel selling scheme by which one greedy person lures another to invest in an enterprise with promises that if that individual can lure another (and each recruits still more), they will make thousands on a growing pyramid of investors. When they run out of investors at the bottom, the entrepreneur usually disappears with the cash.

But legitimate startups make good topics too, such as the founding of TIME magazine. Like that venture, people borrow money (capital) for starting a business from every Tom, Dick, and Mary—and gimlet-eyed bankers who deny loans if 95% of what the founders are using as security ("*collateral*") for the loan is mostly borrowed capital. You certainly can follow the plot if the venture is successful *initially*, but when things go sour, the owners' frantic efforts to avoid bankruptcy involve pressuring bookkeepers (or outside auditors) to claim profits. The pattern then is usually borrowing from *both* "Peter and Paul" to meet dividend or interest payments. It's an ancient scenario.

That even *small* daily newspapers contain business sections demonstrates reader interest is as keen about this subject as it is about sports. You may shudder at pages of fine print concerning stock market results, but not if you own a share or two of some company. You'll rejoice in its rise even by one-eighth of a cent or agonize about selling if its value drops by the same amount.

Those business pages teem with an array of ideas for a composition or paper beyond the mega-topic of sending ("*outsourcing*") jobs to Asia or the rise of billionaire landowner Donald Trump. They are just around the corner and include such topics as school vendor trends, second-hand clothes shops, online shopping, car-repair services, apartment price drops and availability ("A Dollar Moves You In") fed by tenants finding low-interest rates to buy houses—and, always, new hand-held electronic devices.

Think about the firms your family and friends patronize; if they're just opening, folding, or long-timers, you have grist for an assignment in your backyard. An insurance agent in a small Oregon town attributed his Million Dollar Round Table success to strolling around a business and then asking the owner how it started. "That's a sure-fire opener," he said. "I've never met one yet who didn't talk my arm off about the startup."

The Lemonade Stand—Business Simplified

The lemonade stand is an excellent, non-threatening route to understanding business structures and operations. In fact, whenever warfare or upheaval pauses for a moment in ancient or modern times, the first people venturing forth tend to be either seeking or selling food.

So the forerunner of the lemonade stand undoubtedly dates back 10,000 years to Western civilization's origins in that famous valley of the Tigris and Euphrates rivers. Most civilizations start along riverbanks, wells, or other crossroads where people gather. Then came the vendors selling fancier drinks such as lemonade, food, clothing, and services. Behind them came the vendors' suppliers. Some enterprising fellow (or his wife) saw a good living in ferrying people across those rivers—which meant the first marketplace now had a competitor. Thus were born the thriving towns of Babylon, Ur and others. When towns extended to the Mediterranean, the silk route to and from China was born.

Every civilization has had much the same origin. We need only look at how our country was settled—and continues to be settled—to see what is owed to traders selling supplies and food to trailblazing colonists, "sodbusters," and subdivision builders. Hold a parade or festival and vendors gather to sell refreshments and food.

So a lemonade stand is a familiar and excellent vehicle for learning enough to write credibly about business basics: money is made off goods or services people *need*, but location also is essential.

Now, a lemonade stand may start with two or three kids, generally a buddy support system (an informal "*corporation*"), but someone always quickly emerges as the mover-and-shaker (the "*chief executive officer*," or "CEO"). That individual generally is so bossy that soon only a best friend or sibling sticks around: a "*partnership*." If the partnership ends in squabbles about operations and "*profit sharing*," the stand becomes a "*sole proprietorship*." The bossy CEO gets every cent in the coffee can.

That's basically how business ownerships evolve.

Like that buddy-run lemonade stand, a CEO's big idea and enthusiasm needs funds ("*operating capital*") to buy equipment and supplies and pay the help, rent, and light and water bills. That's done by selling shares ("*stock*"), usually to a network of family or friends. They'll receive the "*earnings*" from profits after operational expenses ("*overhead*") are deducted.

The CEO signs paperwork with the state to "*incorporate*." If it's a family operation, it'll probably be a "*closely held*" corporation; with others, it could be a "*Subchapter S*" corporation—a tax-code nickname—with the *advantages* of a sole proprietorship and few of the disadvantages of a corporation.

In any case, every four months (called a "*quarter*") these stockholders receive earnings when sales are good (a "*boom*"), and none when they're bad ("*flat*"). If the company fails, they lose their investment money. Yet one advantage of forming a corporation is that if it gets sued or goes broke with a mountain of debts to settle with "*creditors*," no stockholder's personal property (houses, cars, etc.) can be seized ("*attached*") and sold to pay off the creditors.

Let's return to the lemonade-stand start-up. The CEO's investors (the parents) have paid for lemons, sugar, cups, swizzle sticks and napkins ("*inventory*") and a prime operating expense (the water bill). They've also contributed the property rent-free, and additional inventory of property and equipment (two card tables, chairs, juice squeezer, cutting knife, measuring spoons).

If a heat wave strikes and the location attracts many customers dropping by ("*high traffic*"), the corporation stands to make a killing. If the weather holds and the kids' sidewalk promotional skills are effective, they'll have to hunt more capital to finance more supplies.

However, like many business owners, they refuse to plow their hard-earned profits into the purchase. They try to sell more stock to the principal stockholders (by now, a "*board of directors*"). But the board sees high risk in cooler weather and refuses. Let's say the kids are the spunky types. They inform the stockholders they're going to run around the neighborhood and sell *more* shares at a *fraction* of the price the original investors paid; instead of $5 per share, new stockholders will only have to pay 25¢.

These charter stockholders howl "unfair." They were the original risktakers; newcomers shouldn't get the same earnings for a far cheaper stock price. They threaten to shut down operations unless they get preferential treatment. Faced with a stockholder's revolt, the kids cave in. They make their stocks "*preferred*" and pacify them with 95% of the earnings from profits. They'll sell neighborhood investors "*common*" stock for the remaining 5% of earnings.

In the real world, if a company fails, preferred stockholders are paid off *before* creditors with cash from the sale of inventory and property and collecting customer's bills ("*accounts receivable*"). Those holding common stock usually get nothing but exciting memories.

Interpreting an Annual Report

Because you know what debts and profits are ("*liabilities*" and "*assets*"), you now have the ability to paint that key portrait of operations—the annual report—when the kids' counterparts seek new investors and work to retain current ones.

When those kids cruise the neighborhood for new investors, they are unlikely to have a printed report. But what they tell prospects echo what's in an annual report. Some are prohibitively expensive—fat, 16-color glossy booklets with handsome photography and charts and graphs on every page. Some are bare-boned—especially in a bad year or if stockholders oppose profits spent on printing.

Overdressed or underdressed, an annual report's *meat* is the "*balance sheet*" (aka the "*financial statement*"). Generally, it's the centerfold. The company's assets are listed on the *left* side, the debits on the *right*. The bottom-line totals from each do *balance* each other, but that does *not* mean they are *equal*. If you look at each entry (the "*line item*"), you'll see that earnings may be stupendous and the debts all but nil. Or the reverse.

Veteran investors go straight to the balance sheet to check the company's health. Only the novice investor is taken in by a pretentious or parsimonious presentation or perhaps the most artful text this side of a politician's spin doctors or advertising copywriters. Because the report is the potential stockholder's major piece of information, a dishonest company may spin text to conceal losses or exaggerate gains.

Let's say that our imaginary lemonade stand survives and thrives longer than the usual two or three days because of continued hot weather. But we'll change one crucial element: the CEO's parents are hard-headed types who decide to make this venture a "learning experience."

Mom advances a $35 loan at an *annual* interest rate of 5% to capitalize this venture until the kids can round up 10 other people willing to invest $5 each in the business.

The parents don't provide anything except Mom's loan. The kids will have to buy property (card table, chairs) and equipment (juicer) and work out a payment plan with Acme Grocery for their supplies. But the kids promote the stand so well that they woo and win 10 preferred stockholders (@ $5 per share) and 30 who buy common stock (@ 25¢ per share).

The Balance Sheet

As another part of this "learning experience," Dad says he's got a half-dozen co-workers who *might* buy preferred stock if they could see a balance sheet to prove the stand is a prosperous outfit. Because they have no idea how to do one—and are more interested in quarters dropping into the coffee can—they appoint Dad chief financial officer ("CFO").

Dad draws a microcosm of the "real thing," containing only the basics about understanding balance sheets:

MAIN STREET LEMONADE STAND BALANCE SHEET

Assets		Liabilities & Shareholder Equity	
Current Assets		Current Liabilities	
Cash on Hand	$16.50	Mom's Loan ($35 @ 5%)	$36.75
Accounts Receivable	00.00	Acme Grocery	21.99
		Utilities	2.00
Inventory			
Sugar	6.35		
Cups	4.15		
Swizzle Sticks	2.87		
Napkins	2.64		
Lemons	5.98		
Total Current Assets	**$38.49**	**Total Current Liabilities**	**$60.74**
Long-Term Assets		Long-Term Liabilities	
Property, Plant, Equip.		Equity, Preferred Stockholders	
Card Table	12.86	10 Shares Outstanding (@ $5)	50.00
Juice Squeezer	2.98	Equity, Common Stockholders	
Garden Hose	7.34	30 Shares Outstanding (@ 25¢)	7.50
Plastic Pitchers	6.13		
Total Long-Term Assets	**$29.31**		**57.50**
Total Assets	**$67.80**	**Total Liabilities & Equity**	**$83.24**

You already know *some* terms used in a balance sheet from the extended analogy of the lemonade stand—*inventory, accounts receivable, assets, liabilities, property/plant/equipment.*

A balance sheet divides assets and liabilities into *subcategories.*

Ideally, the balance sheet is accurate, thanks to outside auditing firms whose accountants comb documents and grill officials to ensure honesty. If the company sells stock to the general public, the balance sheet also is inspected by a federal regulatory agency, the Securities and Exchange Commission (SEC); the commission can blackball firms from selling stock on the major stock exchanges if it suspects honesty is not its policy. If the company is private, buyers don't have that extra safeguard.

So let's check the lemonade stand's balance sheet, beginning with the assets.

Assets

The assets side indicates what cash would be available if the company suddenly went broke.

Assets are split into the two subcategories of cash on hand ("*current assets*") and what could be *converted* into cash down the road ("*long-term assets*") if needed.

Current assets includes cash in the till and what's due from accounts receivable—plus income-tax refunds. Inventory is considered a *current* asset because it could be sold *instantly* by brokers, auction houses, or on the Internet. However, the inventory's cash value may have dropped ("depreciated") to garage-sale levels because buyers know sellers would be grateful for a couple of pennies, even on an unopened box of swizzle sticks.

The long-term assets are what can't be sold instantly. For example, reselling "*property, plant, and equipment*" might take months or a year or more. But this category also includes investment profits from stocks and bonds as well as interest paid on the company's bank account(s).

If you also know the difference between a block of ice and running water, you'll understand why assets that can be cashed in *immediately* are called "*liquid*" and why those sharp-eyed investors take hard looks at a company's "*liquidity.*" If the firm fails, they want to recoup every invested dollar.

Those looking for long-term, steady earnings check other key assets. The giveaways about a moribund or dying company are too much inventory, too much property/plant/equipment, or too much cash tied up in investments—or all three. They can see little is left for research to develop new products (R&D), any company's lifeblood. Or expanding operations, or enough employees to handle growth.

Liabilities

The liability side of the balance sheet is even more revealing. Sometimes such a page is called "*liabilities and shareholders' equity*" or "*capitalization and liabilities.*" Both are still fancy expressions for "*debts,*" an ancient word synonymous with imprisonment and/or shame for all except business owners; they regard debts as much a normal part of doing business as the rest of us do eating and sleeping. Only a fraction of businesses over the centuries have started and operated on a debt-free, cash-on-the-barrelhead basis.

Some debts *must* be paid immediately: bank loans, back taxes, interest on bonds, and the big-ticket IOUs floated to trusting investors. People failing to meet payments on bank loans or taxes will have their houses, property, and possessions attached and sold by lenders and tax collectors. It's no different with businesses.

The "Peter/Paul" borrowing pattern was mentioned previously, with the debt-ridden scrambling to find another lender for the equivalent of debt consolidation. The problem is that those kind of lenders know the borrowers who resort to them are in terrible shape; that the risk is high in recovering the money if the firm goes under. So they charge horrendously high interest rates.

For the borrower, that means even greater debt piled atop the debt it covers. But at least operations continue, creditors are held at bay, and credit hasn't been damaged. Their fervent hope always is that by some miracle, profits will suddenly increase so they can pay off the entire debt.

The long-term liabilities are the dollars that preferred or common stockholders have invested in the company. On the balance sheet, these funds are called "*equity.*" If you were to buy a $5 common stock from that lemonade stand, you'd have $5 worth of equity in it. You get earnings from its profits, but that $5 is the *least* amount of what you'd expect to get if you sell that stock while the kids are doing a roaring business. That equity is akin to a sacred trust for the kids (or any company)—a financial resource that must be paid back *eventually*.

Stock Options

One missing factor on too many balance sheets has set off an explosive, ongoing war between stockholders and companies. That's the practice of issuing new stock as part of a salary package to recruit, motivate, and retain top talent. The stock is worthless paper *until* it reaches a price *preset* by the company in the hiring contract. When that happens, the "*key person*" has the options of: 1) buying the stock at a discounted price; or 2) waiting until the price climbs even higher and then returning the "paper" to the company's "stockpile." In exchange for that "return," the company pays cash for the difference between its "goal" price and the price when it was returned to the company.[8]

Giving "stock options" began in 1945 by startups to recruit talent because they couldn't pay competitive wages. Stockholders grumbled about an expanding circle of investors diluting their earnings off profits, but recognized such talent could make the company rich and increase their take. The SEC didn't ban the practice. And so the stock-option bonus hardened into an unquestioned given.

At the lemonade-stand level, the practice would go like this: The kids discover a fireball likely to expand their stand to a chain on seven streets—and boost profits accordingly. To hire and motivate Ms. Fireball, they sweeten the salary offer with a $5 share of preferred stock. But she can't exercise her option to buy it until the share is worth $10. The discount rate will be 15%—a loss of $1.50 in profit to the kids ($10 × .15= $1.50), but Fireball's skills and energies may make the company so rich, the loss will be only another drop in the coffee can.

If Fireball can't afford that share, even with a 15% discount ($10 − $1.50= $8.50), and holds it until its worth reaches $15 and then returns it to the stockpile, the kids will give her $5; that's the difference between *their* goal price and *Fireball*'s "turnback" price.

Let's now say the kids have fought off stockholder muttering about stock options from the time they first learned about the courting of Ms. Fireball. Aside from the risk they might be stuck with a dud, they're miffed about: 1) issuing an extra share, worthless at issue or not; 2) knocking 15% off the $5 price *they* paid. Mom raises the what-if points of Fireball buying the stock at option time: 1) she gets a vote about company direction that could let in a raider investor; 2) even if she "grows the company," adding another stockholder means subtracting earnings from them.

Meantime, Dad takes the kids aside and asks *where* to enter stock options on the balance sheet. Assets side to explain why this expense lowered profits? Or liabilities side as part of labor expenses, or R&D? The kids declare it's *not* an expense *this* year. And if Fireball exercises the option to buy the stock when it reaches $10, it's out of her pocket, not the lemonade stand's. When Dad argues a turnback even of a nickel is an expense, they tell him to bury it with "creative bookkeeping," instead of a line-item deduction from profits. Dad reluctantly agrees to bury the turnback in labor costs, but declares honesty demands he enter stock-option expenses as a footnote on the balance sheet.

Jump from the lemonade stand to a real-world company.

---

8 Ted Sickinger (business reporter, *The Oregonian*), in interview with the author, June 29, 2004.

You can imagine the impact on stockholders earnings and voting rights if Fireball buys 1,000 or 10,000 of those bonus shares at option time. But think of the impact on company profits—and stockholder earnings—if Fireball turns them back and receives a $5 differential on *each* stock (1,000 × $5 = *$5,000*; 10,000 × $5 = *$50,000*)!

That's what happens to profits if a company not only offers stock options to CEOs and key executives, but far smaller blocks to talented "hourly" employees (called "*overhang*"). Not all will buy the stocks at the option price, but whether turnback sums are $5 or $500,000, they *still* come out of earnings and, hence, profits. And the sums are not small. Some dwarf profits. Minuscule or megabuck, stock-options are an *expense* item that investors have a right to know about.[9]

The stock-options war erupted not over stockholder votes, but stockholders' discovery in the midst of the scandals that creative bookkeeping also buried millions of dollars in stock-option expenses. A company celebrating, say, $25,000,000 in net income in the opening text of an annual report and, again, on the balance sheet, concealed spending $20,000,000 on stock options because actual net income would be exposed as $5,000,000. A corporation might report $7,000,000 in net income, but not $8,000,000 in stock options because it would reveal a $1,000,000 deficit. In both instances, such information would cause a tidal-wave departure of present and prospective stockholders unwilling to listen to a CEO plea that the fireballs would grow them thousands in future earnings.

In fairness, many companies have been mindful of crackdowns by the SEC and IRS and have dutifully reported such expenses and taken their lumps on lower profits. Others, mindful of investors as well as the SEC/IRS, reported them in footnotes— perhaps hopeful the small type would be overlooked.

An exciting composition or term paper is ahead for any student who chooses this war as a topic. On one side are the stockholders and friends (regulatory agencies, consumer advocates). On the other side are startups firms and giants both ferociously opposed to new laws or regulations. They've been sidestepping the "creative" profit issue by insisting a startup can't match salaries offered by giants to fireballs so they *have* to offer stock options; giants declare that to *remain* giants, they must do the same. Amid the shot and shell are Congressional backers of *both* sides waving suggested laws. One would exempt companies making an annual $25,000,000 profit, that issued such stock to the CEO and the next four top executives. Other proposed laws undoubtedly will mandate either a line-item expense listed in assets or liabilities or at least in a footnote in a size readable to investors.[10]

Five Factors of Business Success or Failure

Let's return to the lemonade-stand chain (which now has *two* fireballs holding stock options). Dad announces he's been contacted by several prospective investors, but warns they are sharp-eyed and stingy. They'll be checking five factors in the kids' balance sheet for the first lemonade stand before opening their checkbooks to invest in this fast-growing chain:

---

[9] Ted Sickinger, "Oregon firms weigh options," *The Oregonian*, July 1, 2004, B-1,3.

[10] Jeff Koseff, "Options debate framed outside party lines," *The Oregonian*, June 29, 2004, C-1, 3.

- solvency
- liquidity
- inventory
- property/buildings/equipment
- price-earnings ratio

Dad explains that their first stand has to be relatively debt free ("*solvent*"). To determine its solvency, look at the balance statement. Divide the total *current* assets by the total *current* liabilities. If the kids owe twice or more than twice what they've got in assets, the stand is *not* solvent.

That balance sheet shows current liabilities on that first stand were $60.74 and current assets were $38.49. You don't need a calculator to see that the kids were then dangerously close to insolvency—mostly because of the need to repay Mom's loan.

Next, check the stand's liquidity. Add the cash and accounts receivable. Then *divide* that sum by the total *current* liabilities. If the ratio is *equal* (1•1), a firm can quickly convert the assets to pay off the debts. You don't have to divide the kids' $16.50 in assets by the $60.74 indebtedness to see the ratio is nearly 4•1. Not good, Dad says.

The third factor, inventory, doesn't appear to be excessive with that total of $21.99, with the exception of lemons, a perishable item. Yet if the company had folded, would you have paid $21.99 for the kids' inventory?

The property/plant/equipment factor of the assets comes to $29.31. Would you have paid *full* price on those items? Chances are, the goods would go for ten cents on the dollar at a garage sale.

Seasoned investors look to see if equipment is new or the plant has been upgraded (roofing, wiring, plumbing, seismic protection). In real life, they may look at five past annual reports to determine if this year's line-item is significantly large. If it is, the investor knows repairs will be negligible for the years ahead. But if the plant/buildings/equipment figure is a *fraction* of the last five years, the warning is out that repairs and replacements are due and will involve major costs.

Which brings us to the price-earnings ratio, something easy to calculate despite its complex-sounding label. Those who intend to buy and sell stocks quickly aren't concerned with the company's health. All they want to know is how much they're likely to make in earnings if they buy a company's stock. That's the "*price-earnings ratio*" (the "*p/e*"),the fifth factor revealing the stand's health.

Remember that the kids are selling common stock at 25¢ per share, its "*market*" price. A "p/e" isn't on Dad's balance sheet, but *is* contained elsewhere in an annual report. You'll need to know how it's calculated to write about businesses.

Obviously, the kids won't be running that lemonade stand for a year so the investor won't see sales for *four* quarters. Because of the stand's seasonal nature, Dad tells the kids four days of sales—Thursday to Sunday—will represent those four quarters. Common shares of 25¢ aren't going to fetch profits enjoyed by preferred stockholders' $5 shares, but Dad decides more investors are likely to be buying common stock. The daily earnings after deducting expenses were:

Thursday	.01
Friday	.02
Saturday	.03
Sunday	<u>.04</u>
Total Earnings (common stock)	**.10**

Calculate the p/e ratio by dividing the stock price (25¢) by total earnings (10¢).

The result (2.5) is the p/e ratio. In short, each share will have earned almost half what it originally cost in that four-day period. No holder of common stock made a "killing," but it's ten cents they didn't have four days previously.

In the business world, investors in a public company would just check the p/e ratio by reading stock-exchange numbers for that firm in the newspaper. Those are from the previous day's trading, however; investors can't wait that long. They call their brokers or go to the Web for closing figures seconds after the markets have closed.

But the smart investors know that a "quick read" doesn't reveal much history about a company. They would get the p/e for the last four *quarters*. The numbers would come from a Web site called "Free Edgar" which provides data filed by the firm with the SEC.

Investors check out the line item called *"continuing operations"* for each of the last four quarters. They add up those quarterly p/e sums and, just as you just did, divide the stock's market price to get the p/e ratio.

But on almost every business topic involving a company's structure and what's reflected in its performance via the annual report, you now can apply those facts to operating that lemonade stand. This is true even for companies not listed on the stock exchanges because they are not big enough to be among the Standard & Poor list of 500 publicly offered stocks with a high-paid manager advising investors. Today, the computer has launched a system which offers far *more* stocks to investors at far *lower* fees for buying and selling. These are called *"index funds."*

Unfortunately, stocks for the kids' lemonade stand won't qualify because it's a private, closely held corporation. Moreover, companies have to be sizable to have their stocks traded on the exchanges.

Nevertheless, once you understand the precepts about the lemonade stand's operation and balance sheets, you're capable of writing a composition on a basic business topic. It's a good springboard to the dizzying complexities of yet another topic that's been prevalent in the last three decades and shows no signs of stopping.

Imagine the kids seeing a startup rival selling apple and cranberry juice and seeing profits by adding that competitor's business to their own (an *"acquisition"*)—whether the target is willing or not. To do this, the kids will woo the rival's stockholders with promises of greater p/e ratios (a *"takeover"*). If they succeed in such pirate tactics in the business world, they would be called *"raiders."*

You may find topics about raiders, acquisitions, mergers, and divestitures far more exciting and topical than one on a traditional business subject.

Raiders, Poison Pills, Takeovers, and Divestitures

Because of the wild and lightning pace of this side of business, the easiest way to learn about it is with the career of one of the most successful corporate "raiders" in history.

T. Boone Pickens was not much different from Britton Hadden in using spectacular salesmanship and financial contacts to make millions from an idea. He was living in his car and shaving in service stations when he got wind of a landowner looking for someone to drill for oil. Pickens knew an independent driller and matched him with that landowner. When two small gas wells resulted, he earned a $2,500 fee and quickly sought other matchmaking deals with far greater agent commissions. Soon, financiers were earning fortunes off lending him capital and he was making millions. Eventually, he bought the huge Gulf Oil Corporation to use its profits and reputation with lenders to finance a series of million-dollar "takeovers."

In short, buccaneers such as Pickens generally target firms holding a lot of cash reserves and other assets, or those with greedy or lazy management unwilling to push a firm to its fullest potential. A raider may want to take over a thriving business to "share" the profits without putting in energy or ideas. Some merely buy a significant block of shares (*"tidal wave purchases"*) and then threaten (*"greenmail"*) to take over a company just to drive up the stock's value. If they succeed, they'll sell the stock when they estimate it's at its highest level and make a sizable profit. If they don't, a threatened management may bestir itself to drive up profits so raiders still benefit.

A raider will put together a significant package of money—usually by borrowing most of it because lenders profit even off five seconds on the interest they charge. Some financial institutions do nothing *but* set up loans for raiders; many major banks have mergers-and-acquisition departments staffed by legions of high-priced lawyers and financial experts to help engineer a takeover. A lender might get from 5 to 10 percent of the sale price of a targeted company. Imagine the 10% commission on the $20 billion sale years ago for the RJR Nabisco company or on the $13.1 billion for Kraft Foods (Wall Streeters call these commissions *"feemail."*)

Then, a raider goes to work on the stockholders, knowing major ones always sell when stocks rise or fall past a certain figure. Loyalty is fatal in a stockholder's world where smart investors operate on the slogan of "Bears make money; bulls make money; pigs lose money." They usually tell stockholders to sell them the company by claiming (often correctly) that management is lazy or overpaid or that stock is undervalued.

When a raider offers to make changes that will increase stockholder profits (*"dividends"*), most will back the raider. An especially attractive pitch is declaring that the raider's new board will decide to issue, say, six new stocks for one old one they intend to devalue. That inducement is called a *"stock split."*

After stockholders vote to sell, a raider siphons off the millions in assets (*"leveraging"*) to repay the loans. They rarely reinvest them in research and development (R&D) for new goods and services or in marketing current product lines. Energies are on quick profits by cutting costs through massive layoffs (especially R&D) and charging higher prices.

If it's a manufacturing company, quality often loses. If it's a service company, service disintegrates; if it's a utility, service not only disintegrates, but maintenance goes down while rates go up. Generally, within a half-dozen years or less, the raiders sell the well-plucked firm (*"divestiture"*) or fold it all together. The process could take two years if profits plummet, or if a customer revolt earns a bad press, threats of expensive litigation or federal intervention.

However, takeovers aren't limited to raiders. A healthy company may see high future profits in offering a sick one a "blood transfusion" and some executive talent in a friendly takeover. Sad to say, the results are not much different from a raider's takeover because to borrow capital for the purchase, the leveraging lender *directs* operations at the target firm *and* the "mother company." Costs will be sharply curtailed and the "mother" will spend so much time and effort paying off the debt that they'll become super-cautious about growth. Morbidity and death lie ahead.

Pickens finally went too far when he attempted to buy Boeing Aircraft, Washington state's major industry, in a "hostile" takeover. The state legislature called an emergency meeting and passed a law instituting a weapon called a *"poison pill."* A poison pill's strings are attached to employee benefits (increasing pension benefits, big severance-salary and deferred-salary payments, offering big blocks of stock as gifts). That's a Damoclean defensive tactic that *does* scare off raiders because it could bankrupt them. But the targeted firm may have unleashed employee demands that management keep such contractual pledges.

Targets rarely go down without a spirited and expensive fight with imaginative weapons—which is why raiding is such a lively and absorbing topic for *any* kind of writing project.

If management of a targeted company sees stockholders responding favorably to a raider, it may rush around and use other *"shark repellents."* One weapon is to to lure a friendly company (*"a white knight"*) that will not touch operations to make an offer. Or management might threaten or actually sell its most profitable product line or subsidiary (the *"crown-jewel defense"*).

Another counterproductive tactic for a publicly traded company is to threaten or to "go private." To do that means buying out all stockholders, a potentially suicidal route because of the prohibitive expense and because it nearly always leads to virtual ownership and direction by a lender.

Another excellent and *current* topic lies in the public sector where no poison pill exists for, say, a utility company operating in the red and eager *for* a takeover. The consumers' only protection from rate increases and poor service is the weak reed of an elected public utility commission.

Yet another subject that's current and exciting is voters overthrowing a utility company's death grip on rate payers by forming a public utility district (PUD). A PUD usually means far lower rates and better service because of no executive salaries and trimming fat from other operations. The effort to establish a PUD is mind-boggling because the sitting utility spends millions on media ads to defeat any vote. Their major point is always falsely claiming a PUD requires heavy initial investments to buy out the utility, and though employees remain the same, that a PUD staff is inexperienced.

If you're taken with this fast-paced, dramatic area of the world of high finance—moviemakers are—you may find several topics in comments of two outraged financial columnists in the same newspaper, though different years.

Both advocated government protection of the public and company employees suffering from the excesses of takeover pirates and outright fraud and grand theft at stock-market brokerages. One column (1988) concerned takeovers; the other (2004), quoting an investment expert, expressed dismay about the seemingly unstoppable, monumental crimes perpetrated even at reputable brokerages and cohorts in auditing and banking. The first columnist wrote:

> These (takeover-protection tactics) are complicated, taking squads of lawyers and investment bankers just to put them together. (The law firm representing Kraft reportedly submitted a bill for $20 million.) But they are not all that hard to understand. What happens is this: A publicly owned corporation is taken private. The stock is bought with borrowed money. Then the new owners of the firm sell off various pieces of it to pay for the buyout and trim the costs of what's left. What's created is debt—not new products or new jobs. Stockholders make a killing, but the real killing is made by those who put the deal together....Corporate debt is [thus] subsidized by the taxpayer.... [because] Interest payments are deductible—a cost of doing business.[11]

The second columnist first quoted an angry financial expert and added her view:

> "To me, the real scandal of the brokerage industry and of the mutual fund industry is not late trading and it's not pump-and-dump [stocks] and it's not conflict of interest....The real scandal is that the Securities and Exchange Commission still doesn't give a damn about investor expenses." While New York Attorney General Eliot Spitzer has been successful in getting mutual fund company settlements that call for reduced expenses, the SEC does not regard [broker] fees as its mandate. The SEC has not called for expense reductions in its settlements with companies involved in the current trading scandal.[12]

Or you may want to write about famous raiders such as Pickens or "Irv the Liquidator." The business pages, business data bases, and the Internet are full of their deeds and the implications.

Stocks

You already know a lot about stocks through the ventures of the lemonade-stand kids, as well as raiders' claims to stockholders. You can see why the stock market attracts gamblers and also understand why veteran traders and ethical account executives urge people never to "play the market with the grocery money."

One of the riskiest market "games" is gambling on whether stocks are going to rise or fall by a certain date ("*options buying*"). A deal to sell by a certain date is called a "*put*"; to buy by a certain date is a "*call*." Because the market is so volatile and unpredictable, puts and calls have made a few millionaires and many paupers.

---

11 Richard Cohen, Washington Post News Service, reprinted in *The Oregonian*, November 6, 1988.

12 Julie Tripp, "Dr. Know: A Coos Bay neurologist's passion for investment wisdom produces highly rated books full of clear and informative advice," Business, *The Oregonian*, E-8, March 21, 2004.

Insider and Program Trading

If gamblers have always gravitated to "playing" the market, so have clever cheats who figure ways to manipulate it. That aspect of business offers an engrossing topic because recent years have been filled with scandals involving dishonest brokerages and "outside" auditing firms falsifying records.

One subject may be "*insider trading*" whereby someone *inside* a lemonade stand discovers expansion is planned or that the books have been falsified ("cooked") to reflect imaginary profits and company officials are going to bail out with "*golden parachutes*" of huge pensions, severance pay, and gifts of large blocks of company stock.

If an insider either buys/sells stock because of that secret information or tips outsiders about what's happening inside a company, that insider has committed a federal crime. That's what happened to household style maven Martha Stewart, whose rags-to-riches-to-rags journey ended in a guilty verdict for conspiracy, obstructing justice, and lying about an "inside" trading tip.

Another topic might be buying and selling large blocks of stocks by computer; those actions have shut down an overwhelmed stock exchange. That's "*program trading*."

In the infamous Black Monday of October 19, 1987, part of the market's fall was blamed on investors deciding to dump those blocks of stock when their computer programs recommended they "get out." The plug was pulled and the subsequent market drop so vast and so quick that communication systems were overwhelmed and blocked. Small investors found they couldn't contact their local brokers. After these major transactions locked up the market, bandwagon panic drove down the worth of many other key stocks.

One stock-market scandal involves market manipulation of mutual funds to the detriment of large groups of nickel-and-dime investors. Mutual funds have been considered for years the safest avenue for these conservative investors. They pool their money and invest in several stocks suggested by brokers specializing in this trader niche. Investors get broker expertise on the cheap and more safeguards and earnings collectively than they would in traditional trading.

What investors didn't know was that several mutual fund brokers were secretly buying and selling stocks *after* the exchanges had closed for the day ("*late trading*") and pocketing the difference without clients suspecting it had been accomplished off their holdings.

Another topic along this specialty market might be hidden fees investors pay to their account executives. You'll need to draw diagrams to understand fees hidden in "*expense ratios*" whereby a ratio of, say, 2% means that investors are paying $20 to the mutual-fund company for each $1,000 it manages—plus trading costs.[13]

Bonds

If you've ever received a U.S. Savings Bond as a present, you already know the principle of bond buying and selling. A bond is a long-term IOU with interest. Or

13 ———————————————— "Computer Associates executives admit fraud," The Oregonian, April 9, 2004.

like a passbook savings account with such costly penalties for gutting your account that you leave your money in the bank for 10 to 30 years.

Most bonds cost much more than a $25 U.S. Savings Bond. They usually start at about $1,000 each and are bought in blocks. Thus, bonds are not for the small investor. They are issued by companies, institutions, and governments—villages to the U.S. Treasury Department—to buy something costly like bridges, schools, companies, and the like.

But if they're so costly and don't pay off for years, why buy them?

First, even 30 years later, investors will get back every penny they once invested in them—unlike stocks which might strip you of your life savings with a sudden market downturn.

Second, because bonds are expensive, the interest is equally high. It's paid at regular intervals (quarterly, semiannually, annually, etc.) when you clip the interest coupon and present it to the bond issuer's representative for cash. Many people live well on the interest alone.

The only risk is that inflation (price increases) or deflation can change what you'll get when the bond finally "matures" 10 to 30 years later. Also, if the issuer sets a stipulation in the original purchase agreement that the bond can be "called" at any time, the owner might not get those years of living off interest and have to face current inflation or deflation rates as well.

The only major risk—an infrequent one—is that the bond issuer goes broke at the time of maturity and can't pay it off.

The most attractive type is the *municipal* bond. It is issued by governments to get cash so that major projects or programs can be funded immediately. A city may need money to repair hundreds of potholes. A county may need to replace a bridge. A state may need to finance a university building or a highway. The federal government may need to float bonds to pay for anything from weapons or disaster relief to rescuing farmers.

The *"muni"* generally is a highly attractive investment vehicle because, unlike the bonds floated by private companies, the profits (interest) are tax free. Stockholders must pay income tax on their dividends (though they get tax relief if they *lose* money on stocks). But "muni" owners enjoy the best and safest investments—provided they investigate the background and credit ratings of bond issuers. Because it's possible to buy "bond insurance" to boost a poor credit rating from, say, a B to an A, that means the debt load is increased; insurers charge premiums for policies.

For instance, if a local government has relatively few people or businesses to tax for operational revenues, it probably has difficulty meeting payroll or maintaining everything from vehicles to sewer lines. Because taxes meet payroll and other major expenses, it's not likely that a municipal bond can pay much interest. So its credit rating will not be high and most bond buyers will not invest in that entity. Knowing all this, would you be likely to buy those bonds?

An Act of God or a major error in the bond issuer's judgment also can cause a loss to bondholders. The largest default in the history of munis happened in the 1980s when the state of Washington's Public Power Supply System voted not to go ahead on two nuclear-power plants they had floated bonds to build. The 25,000 bondholders, who had invested $2.25 billion for the plants, filed a class-action suit and spent years in the courts to recover only $700 million (a third went to their lawyers).

Junk Bonds

Let's go back to the lemonade stand to understand *junk bonds*. Imagine that the kids have gone broke three summers in a row for one reason or another. Yet they believe this summer somehow is going to be different because an apartment complex has just opened a block away, guaranteeing high traffic on hot afternoons. The kids are experienced—no more getting stuck with inventory. They also have an excellent and patient staff.

But when they try to sell stock to buy supplies, former investors shake their heads sadly and bring up the track record of "bankruptcies" and the "bad credit" accompanying them.

How will they get capitalized? Probably not by a first-class bank because its loan officers take a dim view of risking depositors' money on the lemonade stand's history. The kids know better than to go to a payday-loan firm asking interest of 65¢ on each borrowed dollar.

Mom suggests the kids issue a "junk" bond paying investors an incredible 30% interest *by the week* instead of the regular bond's 8% interest paid quarterly or annually. She's a high-roller who believes nothing ventured, nothing gained. She likes junk bonds.

A "*junk*" bond's colorful and apt name was coined in the mid-1970s when raiding began. A junk bond is a speculator's favorite tool for quick-buck deals. It's also a high-risk lender's favorite instrument because if a venture fails, the high interest covers a good portion of the loan.

If sales soar, the kids can pay off the bond instantly and don't have to share profits with anyone. Like a skilled gambler, they'll have made a killing without spending a nickel of their profits. However, the expended stress and energy output to sell those bonds and produce something can be considerable.

Unlike regular bonds paying, say, 8% interest that mature in 10 or 20 years, junk bonds mature well within a year. Buyers know the kids will *have* to pay interest every week *plus* return the original loan sum (the principle) that can be "called" on short notice.

The higher the interest rate, the more interested buyers are, but Mom's high-flying 30% frightens them into setting the price at 15%. Instantly, they have dozens of buyers.

Bond buyers also know the kids aren't going to be in business longer than summer, nor likely to build a chain circling the globe with the staying power of a McDonald's. If they were, they'd be offering long-term bonds (investment-grade) with low interest rates, but with great credit ratings of AAA and AA or a least a BBB. What the kids are offering are high-risk, short-term bonds worth a Standard & Poor rating of BB, CCC or a least a C (a default earns a D rating).

Unfortunately, stress about paying the weekly 15% interest to bond buyers and lack of energy sets in even before the kids buy their supplies. Mom says they at least ought to give this fourth startup a chance. Dad says life's too short for that kind of fretting and to cut their losses now.

They elect to shut down, return the investors' capital, and offer their services as lemonade-consultants to kids setting up a stand by the apartment complex.

If you chose a topic on stocks or bonds, your best research sources will be found in business databases on the Internet, or in the *Readers' Guide to Periodical Literature* for magazine articles—or the daily newspaper's business section. You also can pay a visit to a local brokerage, but only *after* the stock markets have closed for the day (3 p.m. EST). Staffs are looking for future clients, one reason they're eager to reach students today either with school visits or literature and information about buying and selling stocks.

Overall Precepts on Writing About Business

The overall precepts on writing about business are no different from others mentioned throughout this book.

The language should be simple, but lively. Use analogies as homespun as that lemonade stand. After you put time and energy trying to comprehend most original sources, you'll realize that you probably can do a far better job of "translating." Too often, the original source resorts to jargon familiar only to experienced investors. Authors may have had to seek approval of experts or decided to use that diction to impress them. Instead, write for ordinary readers so they can understand business topics.

The complexity of your sentences probably will be directly tied to how many commas you have to use; "sentence surgery" on long ones is highly recommended.

Don't forget the breather between sizable sections or paragraphs. And paragraph between *sections* of something particularly complex.

Another reminder is to *humanize* situations. Readers stay interested if you start with anecdotes about people caught in a bind or earning a fortune in day trading.

Be *scrupulously accurate* when you cite figures, operations, or the names of people involved, whether you are writing a composition or a term paper. Name your source(s), if any, in the same manner. Your instructor knows you couldn't possibly master all that you include in an assignment unless you've read about it or talked to a primary source. Besides, the more sources cited, the more thorough and academically sound your work will be regarded by that instructor.

Organization

What about the structure of a composition or term paper?

The first paragraph must lure the reader into the composition. It has been said previously that business topics can be as lively as anything on the sports page. A fine composition on a major southwestern bank failure began with nearly two dozen Cadillacs tooling into the parking lot of that bank's main branch. Subsequent paragraphs revealed the cars were not full of the Mafia bound for a major holdup, but U.S. bank examiners pouncing on the bank's books.

Another composition led off with a Vietnamese storeowner repeatedly shaken down by a gang of teenage Asian thugs. That anecdote then led the reader into the lives of several storekeepers too terrified and too prideful to call the police.

What comes after that opener depends on the subject.

A profile of a business personality should be handled like the structure explained in the chapter on descriptive compositions (pp. 37–47).

On products, the opener should show a product being used. Follow it with information about its manufacturer and its significance to the marketplace. Then, get into its history. How did the product come into being? Include the trials—and early failures—because readers are fascinated and inspired to know about tribulations that eventually create something.

After this, describe the product, starting with its overall look; then, spell out its functions. Close with information about who's likely to buy it, the competition, suggested price, and where it's going to be sold.

A quick-and-dirty outline used by a student for a hand-held calculator looked like the one below.

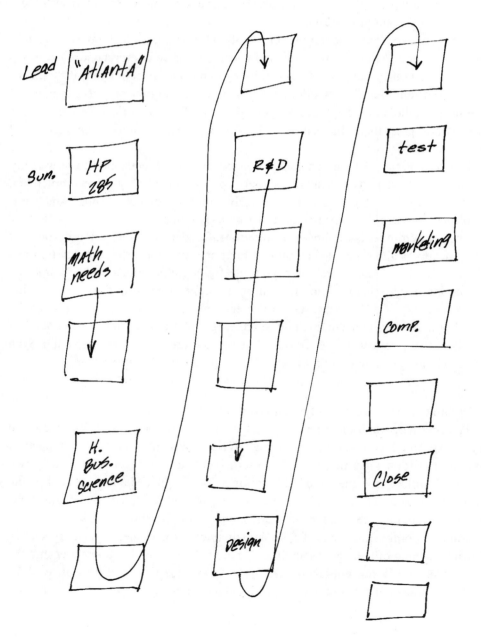

Another student compared four companies as investment possibilities. She set up the composition with an opening that had her turning on an electric light because that's easier for readers to relate to than nuclear reactors, kilowattage, and p/e ratios. Her outline looked like this:

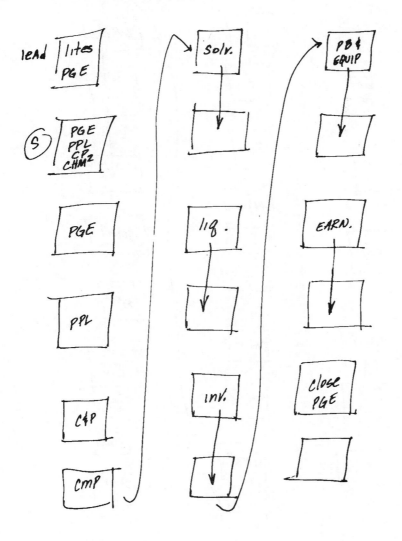

Yet another student used a wave of takeovers as the peg for an assignment about methods to stop raiders. He started with Bluebeard the Pirate and his high-seas forays. His outline is below.

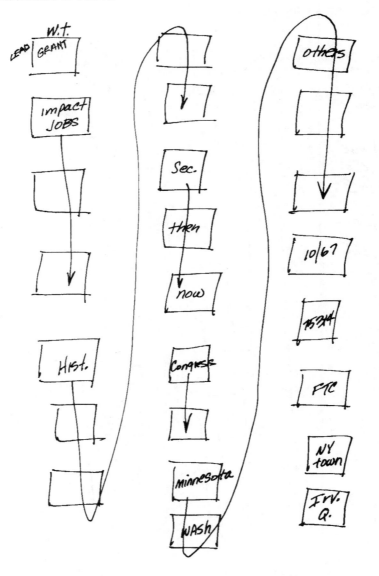

You were told at the start of this chapter that anything involving money and power is *never* dull. And that the business world offered a myriad of exciting topics for a composition or a paper for undergraduate or graduate work. The chapter has provided you with the basics about business structures and operations, as well as touched upon several areas as potential topics. Business stories in the media will furnish hundreds of other ideas. At any rate, you should be able to sally forth and do a commendable job on business stories.

Ultimately, however, it is the *clear* presentation of those topics that counts—because what businesses do impacts ordinary people, whether it concerns new products or old stocks, pensions or electrical rates.

CHAPTER 16

PUBLIC FINANCE

If you study New York City's history in the 1870s and learn a political leader named Boss (William Marcy) Tweed stole $100,000,000 from New York City's treasury, it may mean nothing—even if you know the sum would be worth $129,900,000,000 today. But if you're earning minimum wage and read that Tweed put a plasterer on the city's books at $50,000 *per day* (2002 value: $649,500), the enormity of this graft-driven crime might show you that public finance is far from boring.

That's because you just read that a "little guy" supposedly earned thousands of dollars more than you do well over a hundred years ago. He didn't *actually* get that money, of course. Tweed and his Tammany Hall gang did.

If you can't identify with *him*, you probably can with a struggling single mother of four. She was forced to sell her home at auction for about $71,000 to a pair of housing inspectors who resold it for $173,000 seven months later. Their pattern, according to court documents, seemed to be piling on overwhelming violation penalties to obtain such "force-outs," then buying and remodeling the houses for quick resales. They were suspended, but their deeds set off the woman's $5,000,000 lawsuit against the city. Yet the *real* victims are the taxpayers and those who depend on city revenues because if the city loses—and that looks likely—other victims are sure to mount a class-action suit. Millions of tax dollars thus will have to be shifted from the general fund to cover the court settlements.

So public finance is anything but boring.

Now, because newspapers have always humanized this kind of complex topic to arouse reader interest and comprehension about the "city kitty," use that technique in writing about public finance.

Topics are endless because governments—White House to state house to city halls—use taxes deducted from your paycheck (and businesses' profits and people's properties) to pay for a myriad of services you may take for granted: street and sidewalk repairs, keeping water systems and the environment pure, ensuring sewers and drainage systems function, providing police and fire protection, spraying for mosquitoes and other pests, and the like.

On the state and national level, those taxes pay the bills for the Department of Defense and others like Agriculture and Interior, public schools, the Veterans Administration, and Air Force One. Taxes are also spent on highways, prisons, rivers and harbors, airports, and regulatory agencies of all descriptions: air traffic, broadcast media, foods and medicines, slaughterhouses, utilities, and stock market, to name a few.

Budgets: Gold Mines for Writing Topics

The accounting books and even projected budgets of each of these governmental offices are legally *required* to be open to the public whether the records involve schools or the sheriff's office—and dozens of other departments. Budgets are gold mines for topics, particularly for term papers. They can provide the basis of an exposé about some misuse of public money. A topic might warn about the need to raise taxes. Or pursue new revenue sources *beyond* courting the usual: a sizable industry or a population increase. Budgets are open to you and as near as the clerk's offices at city hall, a county courthouse, their Web sites or the public library.

If you're in high school, you might encounter a clerk who initially may refuse your constitutional right to public documents. But a note about your purpose from a teacher or a telephone call prior to visiting should ensure cooperation. If you still have difficulty getting access to budgets, you'll begin to identify with journalists who often have to get the newspaper's lawyer to draft a "Freedom of Information" petition to pry open public documents from such clerks. Journalists persist. So should you.

"Checking the books" was how one appalled college student reacted to the electric bill for field lights at the local high school. She not only wrote a composition about it, but went on to reveal that officials hid varsity-sports expenditures in the budget's line-items of band, speech, and other programs to prevent their being axed in any financial crisis. Another student, in checking a sheriff's budget, discovered he'd hired an interior decorator—his wife's company—to repaint and refurnish his office. Tracking favored vendors sometimes *does* open a Pandora's box of public officials' "gifts"—from mowing lawns and building decks to playing chauffeur for a wife's shopping expeditions—to relatives or backers of elected officials.

A knack for reading budgets has uncovered many scandals such as the federal government's overpayments for plumbing supplies and basic tools. Equally, it doesn't take an accountant's degree to see that a major drop in tax revenues means school closures, staff downsizings, and boosting grade-school class sizes to 45 pupils. Or that cutting health care to the poor—those most unable to complain—means the insane wandering the streets, an upward spiral in indigent deaths, and turning emergency rooms into charity hospitals. Too, you'll develop admiration and appreciation for a farsighted decision of a county commission in setting up a rainy-day fund that pays for repairing bridges and roads without the need to tap the infrastructure or general funds—or to float bonds.

Translating Financial Jargon

Public finance *does* have a formidable jargon until you discover it's easily decoded into "bricklayer's English." "*Public finance*," for example, is nothing more than spending taxpayer money on *public services* such as those police/fire departments, schools, and water/sewer agencies.

You certainly know what a budget is even though you may hate that term. If you have a job or get an allowance, you have income ("*revenue*"). When you spend that revenue or withdraw it from a savings account, you're into "*expenditures*." If you overspend and get an advance on next week's salary or allowance, you're doing "*deficit spending*." If a certain sum *must* be paid monthly such as car insurance, that's a "*dedicated fund*." When you amass a sizable sum, you've got "*reserves*" and if they're set aside for a rainy day (i.e., an unexpected large expense), you have a "*sinking fund*."

Capital Expenditures and Bonds

Most of a government department or agency's funding comes from the "catchall" part of the budget called the "*general fund*." The general fund is like a general household expense system that pays cash on a monthly or yearly basis for regularly occurring expense items; instead of paying for groceries or car insurance or rent, of course, it's earmarked for salaries of public employees, gas for public vehicles, water and lights at public buildings such as libraries, and motor vehicle facilities.

A big, one-time-only expense for, say, building a sewage plant or light-rail system is listed in the budget as a "*capital expenditure*." Even a *small* capital expenditure probably would gobble up the *entire* general fund, perhaps for a year or more. It's like your wanting to buy something major and expensive that your paycheck or allowance won't cover—used car, computer, Disneyland.

If you charge it on a credit card, you might reach your credit limit; if not, you'd still be paying at least 19¢ interest on every dollar you owe on that must-have big-ticket purchase. It's far cheaper and more effective to go the IOU route. Instead of targeting Mom and Dad for the *entire* amount (they may say "no"), you decide to expand your base of lenders and offer an interest rate so attractive—let's say 10%—that you'll have no trouble getting lenders. To protect yourself, you set a long, long "maturity" date (10 years) for the lump-sum payoff of the loan (the "*principal*"). By then, you'll be earning a big paycheck and have a sizable bank account. The only drawback for you, say, is that your track record of prompt payment of debts is spotty. Perhaps only 15 hand over the money out of the 25 friends and family you contact—even though you've vowed to change your ways. The lenders have weighed that vow against your present (and possible future) "creditworthiness" and the IOU's enticing 10% interest rate.

A public entity's IOU is called a "*municipal bond*." ("Munis" were explained in the previous chapter on business writing.)

Though public officials tout IOUs in ads and at brokerages selling bonds, their efforts to get money for building a courthouse or 20 acres for a park are essentially the same as yours. If the government entity "floating" the bonds has an excellent credit rating and sufficient taxes coming in to guarantee payment of interest and principal, bond buyers will snap them up.

However, some differences exist. Your IOUs are from a private corporation so buyers will have to pay taxes on the interest. One of the great attractions of munis is that because they're issued by a public entity, their interest is not taxable.

Secondly, your 15 IOU holders aren't going to demand you pay them the 10% interest every week or month until the maturity date of paying off the principal in a lump sum. But bondholders are paid *interest all during the loan period*, sometimes monthly, sometimes quarterly, twice a year, or annually. Because bonds are sold in large blocks, many bond buyers live well by clipping those interest coupons.

Third, private IOUs and private company bonds rely *solely* on the borrower's income. By contrast, a public entity has *four* sources of income and bond types to match, offering far safer guarantees to buyers that they'll get every cent of interest and principal they're due by the time the bond matures.

General obligation bonds ("*GOs*") are paid from property and business taxes.

Revenue bonds are paid from "turnstile" income off a project's use (turnpikes, stadiums, transportation systems, airports, etc.).

Special assessment bonds are paid from a tax on property owners benefiting from an improvement to their neighborhood (sidewalk, sewer and street repairs/replacements, etc.).

Special general bonds are paid from a one-time tax assessment levied on *all* property and business owners.

All sorts of interesting writing topics are available if you explore the kind of munis a community has financed (or is lobbying to finance), such as a baseball stadium in a basketball-mad city or a light-rail system leveling a low-cost housing project. A lengthy and ferocious battle in one city pitted an aroused neighborhood against state plans to build a cable railway over rooftops running day and night to link a state medical school on a hill with its facility in a valley.

Such projects reveal whether residents believe in setting aside money for capital improvements or in living from hand to mouth—only to learn some long-neglected major repairs to a bridge, for example, will require floating either a "GO" or special-assessment bond—payments of which all will share in November's tax bill.

Because it's taxes that fund a state or municipality, let's turn now to them, the principal thrust of this chapter.

Taxes

Taxes furnish the main portion of any public entity's revenues and have been doing that since ancient times. Whether it was the "*publican*" (tax collector) in the Bible or today's counterparts—the *assessor* or the IRS—those who set values on income or property have endured hatred and bared teeth. They persevere, often cheerfully, because they know even greater howls and violence would come if these complainers were for a day living like citizens of a third-world nation—without water, cleared sewers, fire and police protection, decent roads, postal services, and other essentials provided by governments. On a federal level, the same complainers expect to be protected by an army, and to have interstate highways, dams, and national parks kept in good repair, dollars and coins to be printed and minted, and the like.

Services usually taken for granted are funded mostly from taxes levied with considerable efforts, toward fairness especially in small towns. Citizens have recourse to oppose assessments, liens, and collections—petitions to lawsuits; whether they resort to them is often questionable.

The clout forcing people to pay for their share of federal services comes from IRS threats of prison or seizing bank accounts and property. Locally, people either pay taxes or lose their property. Other avenues are fines, high interest on overdue taxes, eviction, condemnation of property and/or sale at auction. When sheriff's deputies evict a homeowner and cart possessions—even a Christmas tree—to the curb, it's not just a scene in a film. Nor is a courtroom filled with the nation's best legal talent fighting high values on a company's newest equipment set by a lone, unyielding assessor; she's made brave by price knowledge, a strong sense of fairness, and the cost of county services to that company.

If you choose to write about taxes, taxpayers, or assessors, you'll find human drama in almost every topic, as well as an unusually receptive audience.

Property Taxes

As indicated, all taxes are figured by an assessor who inspects property, equipment, and improvements and then estimates values—but not market values; the result is a bill that must be paid in November. The taxes are arrived at by a *rate* per assessed valuation; that sum generally is determined by how much money it'll take to pay a government's bills for the coming year.

Let's say you own a house and yard that the assessor last year valued at $100,000 (though market value was $80,000). The tax rate was $20 per $1,000 so you paid a tax bill of $2,000 ($20 × 100). However, this year's tax bill shows that the assessor has valued your property at $150,000 which is bad enough, but with inflation and all those seemingly minuscule "mills" voted in during the year (library, parks, bike paths, etc.), the tax rate has jumped to $25 per $1000. So you owe $3,750 ($25 × 150).

You are outraged enough to join furious property owners packing the assessor's office. The assessor listens patiently and attentively until the final tirade ends. You are then informed that people and businesses are moving away which means less tax revenue has to be made up. The county can't endure more draconian cuts.

The assessor has the right of reply and uses it fully: The county has combined five departments and eliminated 150 jobs. Repairs have been postponed on two bridges and the water system. Twelve health/welfare agencies have been closed. Libraries, parks, and recreation centers will be open only on Saturday and Sunday until 4 o'clock. Weed control and drainage will be limited to two weeks per year. Perpetual care at cemeteries is up to families of the dead. And damaged or dimming streetlights won't be replaced. The only *unaffected* services will be fire, police, water, sewage, and jails—all hard hit by increased and expensive labor and equipment. When the crowd is asked which one of these five services should be cut to resurrect any of the above, not even the least angry speaks up.

That tableau is not far-fetched these days, particularly in schools, as you can attest. It's a frightening result of what happens when public needs outrun public funds; or when tax sources are either squeezed dry or discover loopholes to evade paying their share of the tax load. Government officials wring their hands at a multimillion-dollar utility paying only $10 in property taxes. Or court a major industry by providing thousands of taxpayer dollars spent on gifts of free water, sewer, electrical hookups, roads—and significant tax incentives—only to see them depart two or three years later.

Worse, the taxpayer revolts that began in the 1990s show no signs of slowing, reflected most acutely in schools. Some have 40 students per class, worn textbooks with missing chapters, faculty working two weeks without pay, custodians hired off the streets, and even month-long closures. By contrast, taxpayers with no children gleefully vote down school levies and "sub-tax" measures when they face property tax bills of $5,000 with $2,000 earmarked for schools.

You'll now begin to understand why state, county, and city officials bend every effort to attract new residents and large and small businesses to their tax rolls; the agonizing irony is, of course, that they'll want all the public services that the public treasury can't fund anymore.

You'll also have to admit that public entities are not heartless when the budget cuts forced on them force them in turn to evict the jobless from their homes from tax foreclosures, to deny health and mental care to the poor, and to raise transit fees until only a few can afford to ride buses or streetcars.

Yet writers have been among the legions who have affected positive outcomes for *both* assessors and the assessed. A Corvallis, Or., reporter covering street improvements got wind of an elderly resident, living on $8,000 a year, who was about to be evicted because he couldn't pay the special assessment of $49,000 for his frontage. The story broke just before the sheriff arrived to put him on the street; the council voted to make an exception to residents in the same situation.

Business Taxes

The owners of a lemonade stand have yet to be visited by any assessor. Or be told to register for a federal tax identification number. Or pay $35 to a state for incorporation documents. But that day may come in an era when owners of a funky store were threatened with fines for violating sign codes in their crude, if colorful, mural on the shop's façade. Defiance meant the city would paint over it and tack labor and costs to this penny-ante form of taxation. Such is the frantic search for *any* revenues that some cities tax businesses more than $100 per sign on outside walls.

If those lemonade stand owners used that experience to open a burger outlet when they became teenagers, they would learn about the assessor's and the IRS' long reach. They would be subject to all kinds of taxes—city, county, state, federal.

For example, taxes must be paid on property and equipment. Owners must send in withholding deductions and Social Security payments on employee wages. Add to this contributions to the government's unemployment insurance fund and payments to the state workmen's compensation fund for job-related accidents. On top of this, the federal government demands regular reports on operations, including forecasts of future profits. Submission days for reports, payments, and filings are on paydays, monthly, quarterly, and annually. Paperwork is time-consuming and backbreaking for small businesses such as a burger stand.

If owners let any of this slide or refuse to cooperate, the penalties are daunting. Bank accounts are seized, liens put on personal property and real estate, and the IRS padlock is affixed to front and back doors. If they refused to pay, their bank accounts would be seized, liens would be put on personal property such as a car or mountain bike, and an IRS padlock would close the front door.

Using the Human Element

That both property and business taxes impact people means a rich source of topics for writing projects. The tax situations may be complex, but confusion lessens if you include the human element, because readers can identify with other people.

Reality shows are tame when compared to people's emotional investment in public-finance situations where the assessor is an entity dependent upon taxes or taxpayers and service users. For instance, write about a business owner short of cash one month who uses withholding sums to fill the gap. Letting payments and reports slide are the usual route to bankruptcy.

Or a topic might trace the number of bankruptcies caused by taxes raised to the breaking point. Considering businesses located in malls must pay rent and a percentage of their profits, it's no wonder so many are in physical, emotional, and financial distress.

Talk to a business owner, perhaps where you work. Ask how a public entity impacts the business. Point out you're not asking for their "numbers" (profit figures), but what their tax headaches are, right down to the number and variety of forms they must submit. Or ask for their suggestions on how the various taxing entities could streamline the tax system. You'll get many meaty and colorful quotations to liven the assignment.

Or talk to the assessor or the assessment office staff to find out the challenges they face, not the least of which is outright hatred from some individuals. A major paper or book could contain how they survive the daily "reality shows" confronting them when the doors open until the last unhappy citizen departs.

Topics are plentiful also when shortfalls become monumental, beginning with the idea that suffering by the wealthy and influential is scarcely equal to that of the poor and helpless. If services are to be cut, it's rarely the disadvantaged who have the energy, smarts, and loquacity to storm a city council meeting, or to organize a demonstration, or mount a class-action lawsuit. If police patrols must be cut or potholes left unfilled, it's unlikely to be in affluent neighborhoods. If schools slide into failure, the poverty-stricken slide with them; the children of the well-to-do enroll in expensive private academies.

Topics abound concerning the public employee aspect as well, especially those dedicated to service. What about a composition on maintenance crews trying to cover expanded areas with fewer employees and aging equipment and trucks? If repairs and replacements must be delayed or cancelled, a gigantic capital-improvement expenditure better be on the drawing board, along with an attractive bond proposal. You could explore how trimming air-quality services can trigger respiratory ailments. Or cuts at the libraries, the coroner's office, or parks and recreation centers. A sudden bustle at the surveyor's office may provide the first inklings of an annexation that is bound to increase taxing sources.

Some of the most worthwhile topics to save or earn money for the public could trigger action from public officials—county commissions to school boards—if students are willing to write advocate pieces for local media outlets.

One student's suggestion for an express bus to campus at slightly higher fares drew high interest from potential riders and city officials. Unfortunately, it was blocked by the transit authority's director because it required removing a bus for two hours per day from a route with low ridership. The student still was thrilled just to have an idea almost become reality. You may come up with one, too.

Organization

You can't organize a piece of any kind unless you first understand *all* of its facets, as has been pointed out repeatedly in this section on writing about complex subjects.

Again, break down all your research to sort out *all* of the topic's aspects. That may mean resorting to drawings, rechecking data with sources, or reading information aloud until you're clear about it. Or eliminating data that, while fascinating, isn't germane to your composition's thrust.

In constructing a quick-and-dirty outline, remember that the opener must seize the reader's attention. In public finance writing assignments, you have the great advantage of writing about one of the most controversial, yet fascinating subjects: taxes.

Material for an anecdotal opening is plentiful as the topics above suggest. One student's opener described what a new city council member saw when he climbed under a heavily used bridge to check for signs of metal fatigue in the girders (he found them). Another student, using a "what-if" premise to jolt the reader, wrote:

> What if your house caught fire and burned to the ground because fire services were farmed out to a county unit which took longer to arrive than if the city hadn't had to shut down Fire Station No. 242 a block away?

In the second paragraph, deal with the point you're making, plus the significance of implications shown in the opening paragraph. Is the city going to have to cut its court system? Does the failure of a levy mean that a women's shelter will be closed? Will the community college be able to raise enough in bonds to cover a $700,000 repair on a chiller and meet other major maintenance costs? Will the county begin releasing non-violent prisoners or increase home arrests if overcrowding continues at the jail? Subsequent paragraphs should fill in the reader about the topic's financial history, including past impact.

Move next to the future.

What's ahead if things continue? Sprinkle in meaty quotes from sources where they pertain to the point you're emphasizing. Either quote the source exactly or paraphrase with great care that what you write reflects the overall views. If you're using items from the media or the budget, ensure that those sources are credited. Your instructor knows there's no way you could be the source of all the information you include in the assignment.

A student describing the cuts a school superintendent had to make to get the district budget passed, set up the quick-and-dirty outline below:

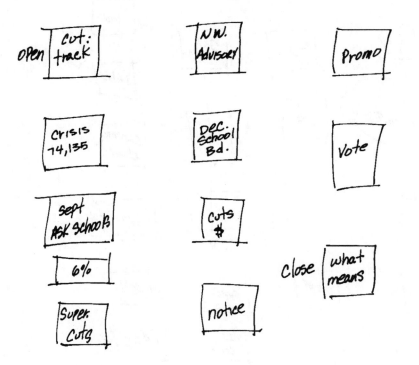

When another student traced the various methods used by a town to increase its tax base over a 10-year period, his outline looked like the one below:

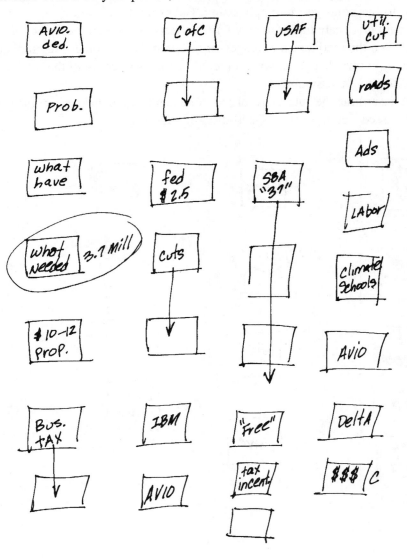

As you move from outline to writing, remember to use a simple vocabulary and uncluttered sentences. Public finance writing projects must reduce dollar figures to meaningful terms. For example, when you're writing about how much is being spent on the police department, add how much it takes to keep one patrol car on the road per day or the kind of daily duties an officer performs—along with the high risks—for the salary paid (it's in the budget). If you're trying to explain costs in the water department budget, include how much it costs to fix just one household pipe. Or mention the amount of water the average family uses in a day.

Use breathers for major breaks. And start a new paragraph each time you move to something new or complex. Segue smoothly into each new paragraph with a transitional phrase so the reader knows it's a new facet of the topic.

> Bentley and Harris thought they'd seen everything with snout houses until builders began submitting blueprints with houses designed for 20-foot lots.

> The city's Neanderthal action raises a more troubling issue: Will the sign police now move out in force? We've noticed plenty of other murals that have appeared on commercial buildings around the city since 1998 when the new regulation went into effect. Is more of the city's wonderful outdoor art about to be whitewashed in the name of conformity?

> The zoo's budget is something else again.

Analogies are essential in converting data to levels an ordinary reader can comprehend:

> If the $400,000 estimated to cover the reservoir were converted to nickels, it would fill ten just like it.

> The Lorenzo family said that if all the paperwork they had to submit to the INS was laid end to end, it probably would have reached Paraguay.

> The money spent for last year's football season could have easily built four Habitat houses.

> Stock-option overhang is like a group project. Two girls do all the work. Four boys just hang around. But all six get an "A" and the girls get a big resentment.

Summary on Writing About Complex Subjects

In writing about complex topics, the first step is getting up the courage to deal with something difficult. The second step requires focusing on *one* key aspect of the subject. Then, concentration on understanding *everything* about that aspect. The suggestion is made again to draw pictures. Read aloud. Or pore over *several* source materials dealing with that same aspect. The next step is to boil down the subject to its fundamentals and to work up analogies or find examples that will lead the average reader from the known to the unknown.

Once you complete that kind of groundwork on the subject fields in this section, always do a quick-and-dirty outline, whether on scratch paper or Post-its. You'll know exactly what to include in each paragraph—essential to avoid procrastination on the project—and where to put them.

From that point on, take a breath and in your simplest words and sentences, begin to write. Forget the well-turned line, but not the homespun analogies and examples explaining complex points. And remember to use that opening paragraph to attract and hold the reader's attention; write it *last* if perfecting it consumes too much writing time.

When you finish the first draft, edit ruthlessly for sentences so packed with ideas or facts that they overwhelm readers; do some surgery and cut them into two or more sentences. Prune complex words and deathless prose as well as paragraphs that are repetitive or don't contribute to the topic. Stay on track and focus on teaching the reader something complicated through basic English. Last, read your writing aloud to spot the clinkers and unclear information.

When all of that is completed, pat yourself on the back. No greater thrill exists than taking a complex topic and turning it into something clear and absorbing to those who initially would have fled from it. That's what Plato and all other great teachers accomplished in opening the doors of knowledge to ordinary people. The reward has always been that wonderful moment when a reader's eyes widen and you hear, "I get it!"

SECTION

THE TERM PAPER

CHAPTER 17

THE PREPARATORY WORK

When a sizable portion of your grade in a class depends upon a term or research paper, the effort you put into it certainly might save that grade. But the purpose of this ancient requirement is the opportunity to do some in-depth investigatory work, rounding out a course beyond lectures, reading assignments, and tests.

You also get to experience the essence of an education: using coursework and curiosity as springboards to develop expertise in a subject and perhaps even make research contributions to a field; some students *have* made discoveries. Even if you aren't interested in being a pathfinder, you're still going to learn a lot about people, places, and things.

You're also following the path of students after the tenth century. Many were only 12 or 13 when they went to Europe's great universities in the centuries before high schools existed. Armed only with Latin learned at a church school or monastery as an entrance requirement, they knew that to get their baccalaureate degree, they would be spending three or four years to produce and defend some theory (a thesis).

However, instead of writing a document—paper was beyond price—students *orally* presented and defended their findings for hours before a brilliant, rigid, and demanding faculty. In medieval times, the process was called "disputation." But by the time students stood trembling before those "inquisitors," they usually knew their stuff from lectures and debates, extensive preparation in logic and how the "bac" process worked. Today's equivalent is in a doctoral program in which candidates choose a topic, research it, write a dissertation and then defend it ("orals") to a faculty committee.[14]

---

[14] "Medieval Science, the Church and Universities," *Bede's Library*, http://www.bede.org.uk/university.htm (accessed March 31, 2004).

At the start of classes, all these students—past and present—felt just like you at the start of producing a term paper (fear and perhaps loathing). But if they chose a topic they found absorbing—an essential ingredient then as now—and dug into it, the interest and even enthusiasm grew apace. Your counterparts ten centuries ago became detectives and devil's advocates, moving carefully through an investigation, weighing the evidence piece by piece to support their thesis. They became authorities on a subject and usually came to know more than their professors about it.

After answering the last grueling question, their elation was just as yours will be when you finally hand in the "major opus." Whether it's preparing for a disputation or writing a term paper, students throughout history usually have found these labors a wonderful capstone to a course. For many, it's a writing project remembered for a lifetime—and perhaps tucked in among their keepsakes.

You have the advantage of a library, computer, the Internet, and photocopier as "tools" for *your* project. Most medieval teenagers had no access to the expensive and hand-copied books from which they would "defend" a thesis. That data came from lectures given by professors who *could* afford to own such books or had access to them.

Nor were those students permitted to range beyond the handful of stipulated research sources: the Bible and the writings of Aristotle, Euclid, Galen, Porphyry, Sacrobosco, Peckam, and Ptolemy. Sound dull? Not when the great and controversial Abélard was teaching those books to a thousand enraptured students shivering on straw piles along the banks of the Seine in 12th century Paris. He goaded them to question those authoritative sources as sacrosanct and, thereby, to do some thinking "outside the box" of preconceived notions. Perhaps you'll have the same experience as you probe a controversial or brand-new topic and present your views.[15]

Finally, to offer some comfort and to ease your aggravation about footnotes ("endnotes" if placed at the paper's end), be grateful you weren't a student at a medieval university. In disputation, they were expected to defend *every* sentence uttered by citing its source(s)—Aristotle and Euclid to the Bible and Ptolemy. Thorough understanding of their writings was mandated and if they misunderstood the material or muffed too many citations, a "retake" might be a year away.

As for Aristotle, the one thing those professors and *your* teachers recognized was that this famous Greek philosopher/writer perhaps was the last person on earth who knew *everything* in the world during his lifetime (384–322 B.C.)—the sciences and math to the arts. After that, things became complicated and stratified. So your teachers are well aware that *you* are *not* the source for *anything* you include in your term paper; you're not Aristotle. Medieval students had to credit their sources orally. You *must* credit sources with footnotes and bibliography.

---

[15] Ibid.; Burns, E.M., Lerner, R., & Meacham, S., *Western Civilizations: Their History and Their Culture,* Vol. 1 (New York: W. W. Norton & Company, 1980), 353-57; *Encyclopaedia Britannca*, 15th ed., s.v., "Abelard, Peter."

So push aside the dread and get at the term paper—or major writing project—early in the term when class work is fairly light, when library resources and equipment have few users, and when your social calendar is wide open. You're about to embark on a wonderful, satisfying, and challenging piece of detective work that for over a millennium is *still* considered the epitome of scholarly endeavor and experience. You're about to become an authority on something.

Picking a Topic

Select a topic with a view toward interesting both yourself and the instructor (called "the reader" or "audience" throughout this book). A prize-winning feature writer on a major daily said that the key to her success (i.e., many loyal readers) was to always ask questions she knew interested the ordinary reader.

In graduate school, students know topics for theses or dissertations must be approved initially by their advisory committee. But the chair will rule on almost every step of its production from focus and view to research, organization, and writing. So a reader is in charge.

That means ruling out obscure topics, or too-easy topics, extremist topics, or topics bound to irritate or outrage. If you decide to needle or infuriate your instructor, you also must be willing to "pick up the tab" for that satisfaction. The price may range from a low grade or an Incomplete, to rewrite it according to "suggestions," or to replace it with another topic.

Choose a topic that will benefit your own store of knowledge and one that will not bore you. If you're going to put in time and effort, why not select a subject that will enrich or enhance your education and your life?

Research paper topics usually are assigned or the blue-sky type of "U-Pick."

Assigned topics are given from a list related to a course, as determined by its instructors. If this is your situation, don't waste time and energy trying to budge a teacher beyond that list. The choices *are* germane to the course and designed to enhance material presented in lectures, the textbook, or audio/visual materials. Select a subject you perceive as interesting or challenging because you'll be living with it for weeks. Something new and different will get you out of a rut.

Blue-sky topics also are expected to relate to the *course*, so don't attempt to argue a history teacher into letting you do a paper on wind sailing. Or Michael Moore's films for a geography class. Or kinetic processes for a literature course. Not if you're aiming for a high grade on a writing project. Students trying to "turn a topic" instantly raise red flags that they're planning to turn in a paper from another course ("doubledipping") or one from a term-paper factory.

That means knowing the scope of that course, one of the reasons blue-sky papers are the hardest to produce. However, because students plow untilled soil, they usually are the most exciting research projects to author and teacher. Faculty rejoice at seeing "originals" because they've read papers on ground plowed too many times. To them, something new means they have first-rate scholarship at hand from a student who may one day provide a major contribution to a field—the mark of candidates for advanced degrees.

Avoid a "sweep," a too-broad approach to a topic. Narrow it to comfortable size so that it represents a complete take on a topic. If the paper is for a history course, it's tempting to choose, say, World War I. It's far better to limit it to smaller chunks of this conflict as, for example, *one* French mutiny. Or *one* logistical problem at Verdun for the British. Or *one* demonstration of Erich Ludendorff's use of infantry on the Eastern front.

Even with a biographical topic, take only *one* phase of the person's life—especially the famous. It would be wiser to write a paper on "Vlaminck's Return to Landscapes" or "Bush and the 9/11 Commission" than cradle-to-grave "sweeps" on these individuals.

Narrowing a topic makes it easier for you to do research. You'll be able to weed out thousands of words and dozens of pages in books, encyclopedias, magazines, or Internet searches, and limit interviews. Your paper will have focus and perhaps deal with an aspect about the subject your instructor knows little. Too, you'll avoid that tempting tendency to copy everything word-for-word from source materials.

If your paper is to be a critical study of something or someone, make it *critical*. This includes criticism in favor of and against the subject. If it's a *comparison* of two or more things, fill it with both *similarities* and *differences*. If you're contrasting, ensure that the *differences* are pronounced and are used *throughout* the paper. A project that presumes to deal with the *effects* of something has to include *causes* and certainly the *effects*. In short, stick with the topic and aspect you've chosen. That's the way an A+ is born.

Before you commit yourself to a topic, ensure *enough* material is available. Surf the Internet at the outset.

A trip to the library is next and essential—or at least a call to the reference department to outline the subject to pick up research leads. Librarians are highly trained researchers, experts on many fields, and love a challenge; but they won't do your research for you. Branch libraries or high school libraries rarely offer enough resources because they're designed for neighborhood "reach" only.

Their handful of computers or microfilm readers are often so tied up that users are often limited to an hour per day.

Community college budgets may provide a library that has more acquisitions than a high school, but far less than most small colleges. Unless they have a large enrollment of evening students, the college may not be open after five o'clock on weekdays, and not at all on weekends.

For a credible paper, you need a dozen to two dozen *solid* sources. Check the library's computerized card catalogue. Comb encyclopedias and the *Reader's Guide to Periodical Literature* for magazines and journals. If you're doing a paper on special fields—medicine, home economics, engineering, entomology, sociology, drama, etc.—they have their own special reference works.

If you learn that resources are slim, select another subject. You can only stretch one or two sources so far in a definitive term paper.

Other students may be working on topics in the same general area of your subject. If so, consider changing your topic because that discovery means books, journals, etc., you'll need probably will be checked out continuously. Even if the reference materials are on reserve, someone may be quicker than you to retrieve them and hold them until the library shuts down for the evening. If you need materials ordered off the Interlibrary Loan service and you are in Los Angeles and they are in Columbiana, Alabama, expect their arrival in six weeks or more; that can impact a deadline, and few instructors will permit that as an excuse for missing the due date.

Once you've learned materials are available for your topic, consult the teacher about your choice, its thrust, and organization. Few students do this. Most have the mistaken belief they've no right to bother a busy teacher or it looks like bootlicking. To get the high grade you deserve on a major writing project, rid yourself of that foolish and self-defeating attitude. Behave like a graduate student and set up a conference with your teacher. Remember that students getting F's and I's on papers fail to meet content standards, something that wouldn't have happened if *they'd* bothered to talk to the teacher at the outset.

Go armed. Come to a conference with a *written* plan on how you intend to develop a subject instead of expecting the teacher to do your work. Giveaways are showing up without pen, paper, plan and asking a lead-in, pick-the-brain question such as: "How should I do a paper on the homeless?" That student has done no thinking, no research, no planning—and deserves a curt response of, "Come see me after you've done some thinking, some research, and have some kind of plan."

You'll be treated far differently if you turn up with a written plan—and *specific*, instead of vague, questions. And get straight to the point. It's not a social call. The teacher has something tangible to work with and can put you on track for an A.

You may be advised to skip one aspect of the topic. Or to shorten another. The thrust might need adjusting if it's too shrill or too wishy-washy. Seeing that you have not come empty-handed with source leads, the teacher might add one or two.

Once the teacher has given you time and the advantage of advice, follow the suggestions to the letter. Just like a doctoral candidate, you'll have received *pre-approval* on topic, thrust, and development of content from the person who will be reading the paper and grading it. To avoid subsequent visits or calls to the instructor, take careful notes and ask for repeats or clarifications at that interview. Make it a productive meeting.

Getting the Information

Material for a high school term paper is usually either in the library or on the Internet. University students depend on those two resources, too, but some may involve contacting governmental units such as the National Archives or, say, the Environmental Protection Agency, or the U.S. Senate, or a governor's office. Students may seek genealogical data or letters, or conduct interviews, or design questionnaires, and the like.

Unfortunately, this book's scope does not include how to do masters' theses, doctoral dissertations, use of questionnaires, or original scientific studies. Many other books specialize in complex projects requiring months or years for research and writing.

Nevertheless, to start a high school or college paper, it's wise to locate your information source and estimate how much time you have to locate data. If you're going to use data from governmental agencies or letters and the like, contact them within a day or two after the project is assigned. If you're relying upon the Freedom of Information act to secure documents, be aware it may take months—and then may be classified. The Inter-library loan system may be answering hundreds of other requests. Materials may not be available. Too, mail deliveries may be slowed by holidays such as Christmas, run-ups to elections, or just unexpected heavy use.

No matter *what* source you're relying upon, get busy on that project as soon as possible. Each week, set aside an hour or two to do *some* phase of research or writing. This section will emphasize that work habit repeatedly.

If you follow that regimen, your stress level will drop dramatically. For one thing, the project will not be hanging over your head every day and be thrown together at the last minute to earn a C or D or F instead of an A. Materials will be available. Study tables and carrels will be virtually empty and the area quiet. Computers will be available for longer periods, a real problem at colleges where fistfights over printers during finals week are common. Best of all, you'll be finished with that project long before term's end and can put your energy into other activities.

Libraries

Most term papers are based on what's available in school libraries, particularly if that's your only access to the Internet. If your school has only a small library, you'll have difficulties getting material that goes beyond one set of encyclopedias and other basic reference works—especially books and/or magazines and journals. Don't fault your library in these days of monumental cuts in school budgets. Even if unlimited funds were available, it's unfair to expect a high school or small college to buy, say, the *Almanach de Gotha* or a *Universal Jewish Encyclopedia* because few patrons would demand such a specialized reference tool.

Nor will you find specialty fields such as political science, medicine, music, the sciences, engineering, law, etc., in the branch libraries. For those reference works, you'll need to go to a large public library or major university. Even then, you may be told that materials have been moved to a nearby university or other repository.

If you're attending that nearby university, you may discover that certain documents are reserved in special collections or in archives requiring the red tape of applications and waiting. You may also be told to store your possessions, even a laptop computer, in a locker. Access to priceless documents, especially at state libraries, may well involve weeks for the approval process and your passing through annoying security checks and donning gloves to examine documents.

Instead of showing temper at staffs and regulations, respect them. Major scholars and professional writers certainly do. They plan ahead for those regulations as well as library hours and days of operation. They also know better than to annoy the gatekeepers to needed materials.

No matter how small the library, it usually has the three basic reference tools adequate for most term papers. Most have a set of *Encyclopaedia Britannicas*, a computerized card catalogue—or a hard-copy card file—listing every book and periodical in stock. You'll also find the *Readers' Guide to Periodical Literature* with its indexes of articles from the early 1900s to the present. Don't use the *World Book* or the *Collier's* encyclopedias, however. Most teachers rightly regard them as suitable references only for grade and middle school pupils, not high school or university students.

If you're a "super sleuth," you may discover that even sources with almost impeccable records of reliability are only as good as their contributors' expertise—which might be limited—or their biases. For example, one reputable encyclopedia's lengthy entry on the history of the chocolate industry failed to note that it is *still* based on slave labor and brutalization of thousands of African children. But, then, the entry's author wrote a book on chocolate and was president of a major chocolate company benefiting from such conditions. He seemed unaware its popularity is steadily destroying Earth's ecosystems.[16]

Science journal bibliographies are among those professional publications listing the most current studies *first*. However, what if the first or other studies were flawed? If so, subsequent research will be equally flawed.

The same thing is true for whoever heads a research team producing erroneous results. In medical topics where life and death is involved, it's well to look first at the number of people (30 are better than 3) and types involved because many are derelicts whose street life toughens them against diseases or students whose diets are scarcely average; check-backs ("longevity results") should be at least five years. Note especially *who* paid for the study if a medication they manufacture is involved.

Other disciplines have similar areas to be checked. In history, for example, early chroniclers of an event or someone's life may have based findings on myth or bias. Subsequent scholars may harden a myth or prejudice into the cement of "indisputable facts." Mention was made earlier in this book about the Tudor kings blackening the name of Richard III for centuries until two modern biographers of Richard learned the truth.[17]

The Internet

The Internet has opened vast storehouses of information ranging from a virtual tour of the original Olympic grounds and baton-twirling's origins to the history of chocolate. Or the startling discovery that 14 years *before* the *Titanic* sinking in 1912, a novel prophetically chronicled the *same* fateful voyage of a great ocean liner named *Titan*.

The ship was nearly the same size, had the same kind and numbers of passengers (and survivors), same overconfident crew, and the same lack of lifeboats. Operating at the same speed as the *Titanic*, this fictional vessel sank at almost the

[16] L. Russell Cook, "Cocoa Production," *Encyclopedia Britannica*, Macropaedia, 15th ed.; Caroline Polgarand and Cathy White, "Chocolate," Colby Environmental Coalition (Waterville, ME.: Colby College, August 1, 2003), http://www.colby.edu/env.council/food/foodissues/chocolate.htm (December 18, 2003); Roxanne Khamsi, "GREEN LIVING: EATING RIGHT: Enlightened Indulgence; Organic Chocolate Companies Help Make Calories Count Toward Conservation," *emagazine*, July/August 2001, 4:Vol. XII, http://www.emagazine.com/july-august_2001/0701gl_eating.html (April 9, 2004).

[17] Josephine Tey, *The Daughter of Time* (New York: The MacMillan Company, 1951); Charles Ross, *Richard III* (Berkeley: University of California Press, 1981).

same time and position after colliding with an iceberg that also sheared open its starboard side.[18]

All it takes to open the vaults to millions of other topics is your typing the code-like letters of: *http://www.google.com* or *http://www.yahoo.com* into a narrow strip at the top of the page (the "URL" or "uniform resource locator"). Then, a tap of the "ENTER" key brings the world of information to your screen as these search engines come up to help you find material in their storehouses.

Currently, more than a dozen search-engine companies exist, but many piggy-back offerings off those of the two major firms of Google and Yahoo. Other once-popular engines have merged or disappeared altogether—sometimes within a year or less—because expenses have to be met either by advertisements on Web pages or by institutional sponsors. They need staffs with encyclopedic and technological knowledge to be sure, but survival requires high traffic on those engines' Web sites; if advertisers have few sales from user visits ("hits") on *their* Web sites off search-engine ads, they'll switch to another company. So no search-engine firm is immune to death by disuse or merger.

Overall, select an engine that has the greatest access either to *most* that appears on the Internet or to *most* that pertains to your term paper topic.

Not long ago, people narrowed searches with "subject-tree directories" containing lists of fields such as environment or fine arts. Each had breakouts of, say, water or Picasso, respectively, and more breakouts within *those* links. But because engines like Google or Yahoo began collecting information on a vast scale, people began skipping those stratified and limited directories as time wasters.

However, that's not altogether true. Much depends upon your topic. For instance, neither Google nor Yahoo or the smaller search engines bother stocking their shelves with major classics such as the Bible or Shakespeare's complete works. But Bartleby does (http://www.bartleby.com). Indeed, its wares include standard reference books—regularly updated—such as *The Columbia Gazetteer, The Fact Book, Roget's Thesaurus*, the latest American Heritage dictionary, *Gray's Anatomy, Bartlett's Familiar Quotations*, and the like. You don't have to buy or store these expensive and necessary references.

Bartleby also has major anthologies of poetry, plus the complete works of major poets (Virgil, Dante, Shelley, Keats, *et al.*). If your eyesight is up to it, its fiction ranges from ancient classics (Aeschylus' plays) to modern ones (F. Scott Fitzgerald's *This Side of Paradise*). The site also contains non-fiction standards

---

18 _____ "Welcome to the tour of Olympia!", Quick TimePerseus Project, Tufts University, http://www.perseus.tufts.edu/Olympics/site.html (July 18, 2001); Ralph Pippey, "Now, Where Did The Twirling Part Come From?" *No-Mystery Majorette History*:2 of 5, 2004.

http://www.majorettes.ca/hist2.html (April 9, 2004); Justin Kerr, "All About Chocolate: History of Chocolate," (Chicago: The Field Museum, 2001).

http://www.fmnh.org/chocolate/history.html (December 18, 2003).

"Titanic-A Voyage of Discovery," Sail on Titanic, http://www.euronet.nl/users/keesree/intro.htm (April 5, 2004); Jacqueline Simpson, "The Wreck of the *Titanic* Foretold?" *Folklore Society*,

http://www.findarticles.com/cf_dls/m2386/2_111/69202920/p1/article.jhtml, 2001 (April 5, 2004); Fred Donnelly, "The Titanic's Humanist Paradox.," *Humanist*, July 2000, http://www.findarticles.com/cf_dls/m1374/4_60/63257727/p1/article.jhtml (April 5, 2004); Arthur and Rosalind Eedle, "The Loss of the *Titanic*," *Recognising the Hand of Judgment*, nd, http://www.oxleigh.freeserve.co.uk/rhj19.htm (April 5, 2004).

such as the autobiographies of Benjamin Franklin and Ulysses S Grant, Adam Smith's *Wealth of Nations* and Thomas Paine's *Common Sense*.

Neither Google nor Yahoo stores your ancestor's service records from the Revolutionary War or Vietnam, but the National Archives site does. Nor do these search engines provide the U.S. Census or the Library of Congress. They also lack the capacity to provide detailed histories of, say, Britain, as does the incomparable "Bubble" engine (*http://bubl.ac.uk.*).

To show you how to conduct a search, let's pretend you've decided to do a term paper on some aspect about the *Titanic* that's relatively unknown (particularly to your teacher).

The cardinal rule about *any* research project, whether your resource is the library or the Internet, is first to find out if someone else has covered the subject. If you don't, you may wind up re-inventing the wheel or possibly raise suspicions about plagiarism. Professional researchers in all fields always start with a "literature search," an overall surfing of *everything* ever published about a topic—including masters' theses and doctoral dissertations.

You don't need to go that far, but to show you how the process works, let's follow it on a smaller scale. We'll surf the Internet for the *Titanic*.

When the search-engine comes up, type "Titanic" in the locator line and, then, tap the "ENTER" key. Google once had 2,410,000 documents mentioning the *Titanic* in its storehouse, but continuous interest and research about the ship has added more entries each year. The time will come for you to narrow your topic. That's when you'll "go Boolean," the name of the system helping you to use two or more key words to limit a subject's range. When the engine brings up the first page, you'll see a list of 10 links, each with one-sentence descriptive blurbs. The most current data always is the first entry on a list. Aside from three sponsored links, the rest of the *Titanic* links might offer exhibits of banners, paintings, photographs of relics dredged from the wreck, a model of the ship, and data from the *Titanic Encyclopedia*, the Titanic Historical Society, and the 1997 film.

At the bottom of the page is a line of numbers signifying the *next* 10 pages, starting with "1." To go to page two, put the cursor on "2" and click. At the right of those numbers is the word "NEXT," the gateway to dozens of subsequent pages with links for those 2,410,000 results. At the left of the numbers is the word "PREVIOUS" which permits you to return to the last page. Many develop what is known as the "Addiction to Next Syndrome" plowing relentlessly through all the pages either because they fear overlooking data or are curious about a link's alluring descriptives. The line of 1-10 soon becomes 11-24 and on up to dozens of pages. The *Titanic* once may have had only 10 pages on Google, but will probably climb well beyond 100 in the next five years.

Yet a fair-to-middling term paper *should* involve examining at least 20 pages of links.

Yahoo offers 20 links per page and recently claimed 3,930,000 results for "Titanic." Their first page has included three sponsored links (the film's DVDs). The rest may be repeats of Google's links, but have included the musical, 1913 phonograph records, a game, the Halifax cemetery section for unknown victims, and an entry in German, the first of foreign-language links.

Let's say you want an A on the paper. You know that 10 pages of links will just scratch the surface of research. Let's also say that because the links become increasingly fascinating, you comb through 88 pages of Google and, then, discover a link to the Library of Congress archives (*http://www.loc.gov*). You know thoroughness is the route to high grades. You surf those links and spot "ADVANCED SEARCH." You click it open to a page of links to "140 results." Uncharted waters perhaps with unsalvaged gold at the bottom. The link called "OVERVIEW" is always good place to start.

You click on it. Up comes an article written by a Copyright Office staffer about the library's collection of all *Titanic* documents. You skim to its bottom and find a "stopper": He writes about the novel *Futility* which predicted the *Titanic's* sinking with eerie accuracy more than a dozen years before it happened. The author is Morgan Robertson, a maritime expert and prolific writer of sea stories before the twentieth century.[19]

Term paper topic in hand—an exciting one with narrow focus—you return either to Google or Yahoo's main page to play detective. You now "go Boolean" and type in the key words of "Morgan Robertson AND Futility" or "Titanic NOT genealogy." (The shorter form is "Morgan Robertson + Futility."). Those restrictives keep you off the shoals of genealogy websites as happens when you enter only a name.

Let's also say Google offers 1,520 results and Yahoo, 2,690, and you are stunned to see sponsored links for the book's recent reprinting. You may be initially disheartened to realize you've not blazed a new trail for *Titanic* scholars or hobbyists, Yet you'll be cheered to know your work will fascinate your teacher.

Most of all, you'll know that if you'd confined yourself to library books and periodicals, it might have taken a year to strike this vein of pure gold. True, professional researchers would use both resources as well as other primary documents found in courthouse basements, maritime data, or documents found in family attics. But Internet resources are adequate for a term paper. You stand before a gold mine of information—and misinformation—that now awaits your pick-and-shovel and siftings.

Working With the Data

You've got your topic and have now reached the pick-and-shovel stage of the term paper: working with the data. For some students, it's the readings that take the most time; for others, it's writing the results. Whichever category you fall into, the next tips should help you do both far more efficiently and successfully.

Approach this topic well rested, your curiosity and teachability at the ready, and armed with pen and two inches of index cards, preferably the 3×5-inch size that force you to be brief in summing up the document's content or gist. Buy white cards because colored ones make re-readings difficult.

---

[19] Mark F. Hall, "*Titanic* Treasure Trove: Reference Bonanza on Ill-Fated 'Unsinkable' Ship," *LC INFORMATION BULLETIN*, May 1998, http://lcweb.loc.gov/loc/lcib/9805/titanic.html (December 22, 2003).

Let's look at the preliminaries *before* entering your gold mine of information.

Buy a library photocopier card to download data so you won't have to bother with coins. Before you download Internet material, create a word-processing file for copying/pasting its data. In either situation, use the index cards to record the data's gist and its citations *immediately* after you print or download a batch of materials. Putting that task off until the last document is in hard copy will look like an overwhelming "carding project"—and you might get writer's cramp besides.

Be sure you know which citation format your teacher wants for footnotes/end-notes and the bibliography. The three most prevalent styles are nicknamed "MLA," "APA," and "Chicago," but others exist. If you are told to select your own, it's in your later interest to try one of these three.

How to use the cards, how to create an efficient reference file, and how to insert citations quickly into the first draft will be explained in subsequent sections of this chapter. For now, let's take a brief overall view of the steps ahead *before* getting into sections on *how* to do all of the above, as well as a rapid "read" with comprehension and how to detect "fools' gold" from the real thing.

What's ahead are ten tasks. In brief, they are:

1. Return to the source materials you spotted in your general surfing of library or Internet holdings.
2. Skim the document to decide if it's vital for the term paper.
3. For Internet materials, create a word-processing file for references. Copy and paste them into that file—including citation information (online citations now require the URL, set inside "angle brackets" (< >) and the date you accessed them).
4. Photocopy or download the materials. Hard copies also are vital in case of computer malfunction or a virus or worm destroying your files or hard drive.
5. Record the document's gist on one side of the card. Leave room for a boiled quotation.
6. Record the citation on the other side, *first* as a footnote/endnote and, *second*, as a bibliography entry.
7. Sort the cards into three piles: "Vital," "Maybe," "Bib Only." The "Bib Only" materials tell your teacher they were scanned and added to your knowledge about the subject. (Writers of non-fiction generally put those citations in a bibliographic section called "Works *Consulted*" rather than "Works *Cited*.")
8. Sort hard copies into three piles with the same labels of "Vital," "Maybe," "Bib Only" for easy retrieval when you write the first draft of the term paper.
9. Organize the paper by spreading the cards on a table.
10. Take the extra step of boiling even the card gists to small Post-it notes because they're easily shifted. Tape them to sheets of typing paper and hang near the computer.

Citations

Irksome though including footnotes and bibliographic citations might seem at first—and stumbling blocks in books and journal articles—they serve several purposes, all ultimately beneficial.

The first is obviously to credit the source of the data you're using. Some students enter the world of term papers *still* believing the teacher will regard them as "F" students if they give *anyone* credit for information. Or they fail to put quotation marks around direct quotes, or indent and single space data lifted from a source. But the reverse is true. Teachers assign term papers because they *want* students to learn what they *don't* know; besides, considering the students' heavy schedules and interests, how could they be the *original* fount of all that information? The "A" student knows that the *greater* number of citations (including quotes, indentations), the *higher* the grade because teachers themselves have been held to these rules for term papers, theses, or dissertations.

The second purpose of citations is an act of generosity to readers who become fascinated and want to learn more about a subject. That's why dates and page numbers in footnotes are so important. And that's why online material now includes the URL (and why this chapter provided them for those interested in cheerleading, chocolate, or the *Titanic*).

The third purpose indicates the accuracy of data or what's called *"reliability."* The Information Age's famous slogan of "Garbage In, Garbage Out" sums up reliability for *both* Internet and library materials. For example, who's likely to be the most reliable source concerning the views of the 1800's radical leader Emma Goldman: a conservative historian in a book about labor leaders, an actress playing her in a film, or Goldman herself in her writings?

The fourth purpose of citations is that it reveals *when* the information was published so readers can see if it's when something happened or someone lived or years later after all the "extrapolators" might have muddied the evidence. Equally, a paper on something current should have material that's current.

Citation Format Styles

Before beginning an in-depth reading of the source materials, you'll need to know how to do citations and, too, how to use the card system. Then, when you're poring over the data, you'll be working faster and smarter instead of slower and harder.

Your teacher may have designed a citation format or borrowed one not in general use, but, as mentioned, the three most popular styles are: MLA (Modern Language Association of America), used in humanities subjects; APA (American Psychological Association) for the physical/social sciences; and Chicago (*University of Chicago Manual of Style*) for all fields *except* the sciences. Other formats exist that tend to be a blend of these three styles, but all are designed to fulfill the purposes listed above.

A major irritant for students with more than one term paper to write is one teacher demanding MLA style, another insisting on APA or Chicago or a blend of several. Term-paper veterans have learned to accept the reality of "different disciplines, different footnotes" because a standardized form seems unlikely in our lifetime. In the world of writers, editors, and researchers, when these formats are updated, howls go up about having to relearn format and to pay more than $50 for an upgraded stylebook to do it.

Once the teacher stipulates the style, write an example of the footnote and the bibliography entry in super-large letters on a durable notebook divider so that it's instantly accessible as a model when you're recording citations on those index cards. You'll be using these two constantly. Circle *all* punctuation in red because at the university level, some professors deduct a half-grade for omissions or misplaced commas, semicolons, and periods. For style points about the paper's text—quotations, indenting, etc.—check the style sheet or those format books.

Incidentally, most people have difficulty seeing punctuation errors—including double and single quotation marks—in *any* publications. After all, the marks are tiny and/or taken for granted.

Three remedies prevent punctuation errors in the finished paper. First, when you record the citation on the card, read it *aloud*—especially punctuation. Check it against the model on the notebook divider page. Second, when you're transferring the card's citation to the keyboarded version, read it aloud again off the screen with an eye to the model. Third, highlight and enlarge the type size to 18-point so you can see the punctuation. Then, check it against the model citation. If it passes, highlight the citation and reduce it to footnote size. By "getting it right the first time," you'll not have to worry about that citation no matter how many drafts you write.

It's even easier if you've set up that separate file for the copy/pasted data lifted from the Internet. After you record the citations on the card, type them just above the start of the source material. Include the URL, the Web site name, the copyright date, and the date you accessed the material in the reference file. You'll have a ready-made footnote to be copied and pasted into your draft. Also, if you have to return to the Web site, it takes only a moment to copy and paste the URL onto the Internet locator strip.

Some professional researchers and writers save even more time by then constructing a separate bibliography file off what's been copied into the source document. They alphabetize as they paste. When the project is finished, so are the bibliography pages.

No matter what the format is, you can't go wrong if you card the following citation data:

Author(s) last name first, first name and middle initial
Title of article and subhead or book
Book's publisher in *full*, first city of publication, date of edition
Name of periodical or Web site
Periodical article's first and last pages, date and volume
Online material's URL, author, Web site name, copyright date
Encyclopedia's name, edition number, entry heading (s.v.; "*sub verbo*")

Reputable and long-established encyclopedia companies such as the *Britannica* list author's initials at an entry's end. The full name and credentials applicable to the entry is in the contributors' list, generally in the first volume. Some citation formats just require the encyclopedia's name and edition date, but the credentials could reveal bias or cast doubt on expertise.

The 15th edition of the Chicago stylebook (2003) has several changes. One excludes encyclopedia entries in bibliographies, though its editor told the author that "you are free to devise your own style." Chicago's new style for *footnotes* involving online material is:

[1] A. E. Weed. *At the Foot of the Flatiron* (American Mutoscope and Biograph Co., 1903), 2 min., 19 sec.; 35 mm; from Library of Congress, *The Life of a City: Early Films*

of New York, 1898-1906. MPEG http://lcweb2.loc.gov/ammem/papr/nychome.html (August 14, 2001).[20]

As a bibliography entry, it should be:

Weed, A.E. *At the Foot of the Flatiron*. American Mutoscope and Biograph Co., 1903; 2 min., 19 sec.; 35 mm. From Library of Congress, *The Life of a City: Early Films of New York, 1898-1906*. MPEG http://lcweb2.loc.gov/ammem/papr/nychome.html (August 14, 2001).[21]

Photocopying and Downloading Data

Even *after* the typewriter's invention, students copied material by hand—which at least meant they read and made notes about it as they copied and then carded the gist, quotes, and citations. The photocopier's invention meant students could reprint periodical articles and sizable chunks of books and reference works. However, that still means spending money per page, long lines if you wait until term's end to do a term paper, resentments about those duplicating mounds of materials, and breakdowns from overtaxed printers.

The Internet hasn't ended fights with "printer hogs" or duplication costs because many libraries charge for paper. Even if you work at home, the Internet charges subscriber fees and you'll still have to buy ink cartridges, refills, and paper.

Yet whether you're photocopying or downloading, it's imperative that you have hard copies of your material. In this, you're just like students prior to the Age of the Typewriter. Trying to read material with comprehension even for a half-hour on a computer screen is hard on the eyes, neck, shoulders and back—let alone comprehending the content. The mind still doesn't assimilate information well when it's scrolled 20 lines at a time, especially if set in a sans-serif fonts in 12-point or less. Hard copies are far easier to read, digest and comprehend. They're portable and can include your notations.

Indeed, the marriage of Internet with word-processing programs can create the *best* hard copies ever printed, ones that make comprehension extraordinarily easy.

To save time, paper and especially ink, don't print data straight from the Web site because the hard copy will include advertisements, home-page headings, and other extraneous material. Instead, highlight and copy/paste only data you need into the reference file.

Once the data is in the file, you can manipulate it any fashion that not only helps comprehension, but finds that document in the stack of hard copies. You can save ink by setting the entire document in 9-point type. Annotation devices abound. You can enlarge key sections. Put them in different colors. Underline. Use bold-face or italics or your favorite font. Insert your comments *inside* sentences or paragraphs.

---

[20] CMOS Web site Q&A Staff, e-mail to author, 5 April 2004; *The Chicago Manual of Style*, 15th ed., 726.
[21] Ibid.

Taking Notes: Carding the Data

Before you lift that pick and shovel and begin a thorough read of all the documents in the reference file, you need to know *how* to record ("card") that data.

That's where the index cards come in.

They got their name and function from publishing houses of non-fiction and reference works and are still an essential tool for any professional indexer. They're *still* an essential tool for term paper work because they contain the gist of a document's important passages, quotes, and citations for footnotes and bibliography. Cards are handier, sturdier, and quicker retrieval tools than shuffling through stacks of copied materials or scrolling through 300 pages on a file—even with the "FIND" tool.

"Carding" forces you to boil content to its bare bones and then to decide if it "flies or dies" in a project. That's determined by sorting the finished cards into three piles: "Vital," "Maybe," and "Bib Only." If you're using cards *larger* than the 3×5-inch size, beware of overpacking the space or you might as well be hand-copying material from a library book or periodicals as in bygone years.

Here's how it's done:

After you pore over one document, you'll mull its overall content and then put its gist on a card. You'll then sort both card and corresponding document into two separate sets of those three categories, the card in one and the corresponding document in its mate. This is how you'll read and sort all the materials you've reprinted.

This means careful scrutiny of every document and weighing its inclusion into the term paper. Be discriminating and tough. Some data will be fascinating, but way off the subject. Some may be boring, but so important or so relevant to the topic that you'll be grateful to have found it. Carding prevents duplication and also reveals glaring gaps that must be filled.

Determining worth is not easy. Researchers and writers of non-fiction often go to great lengths and expense to obtain material. They're just as crestfallen as you are in relegating data to the "cutting-room floor." "Material Magpies" file it away for later writing projects.

Most "A" students rarely pad a term paper with irrelevant data, perhaps because they know most teachers reading 20 to 30 papers *per class* near the end of the term can distinguish a steak dinner from a "snow job". Teachers are little different from book editors who discard "style" for substance every day. At the university level, some professors *do* resist awarding a "D" or "F" and scrawling a comment so searing that it's memorable for years. Instead, they may give an Incomplete for a rewrite without the fat. But don't count on such charity.

It's important to be scrupulously accurate about the data the *first* time you enter its gist, quotes, or citation on a card. The information—and your handwriting—also should be understandable when you write that first draft. Legibility alone may save you a trip to the library or having to return to the Internet page.

Some minor points on carding: For direct quotes—use the exact words and put quotation marks around them. Change nothing! If the quote is lengthy, enter a one-word summation on the card. Then, circle it in the document with a felt-tip pen so you can find it with ease when you're writing the first draft. If you're omitting *part* of a quote, use ellipses (p. 107). Carding's byproduct on quotes is that it will force you to see you might *not* need the full quote to make a point. If a quote is too long, too complex, or too confusing, resort to paraphrasing. The only danger involves your interpretation of a quotation's gist. Be careful not to twist it or to use it out of context. The best method for crafting a paraphrase is obvious: Read the quote aloud to determine its core.

Cards serve another vital function.

They're a godsend for pre-organizing a paper. That stack of "Vital" cards will be your guideposts. The key words will enable you to pull the corresponding document from the source stack and weave its information into the paper—along with footnote and bibliography entries.

All it takes is laying out the cards on a table—or Post-its with one or two words off the cards. You'll quickly see what order to use ("these three sources go here, those five go there, and I'll end with this one"). The author tapes the Post-it arrangement to typing paper and hangs it near the computer to stay on track.

Some instructors demand students turn in cards *and* documents with the term paper. Aggravating practice or not, swallow your reaction. They may want to help you fine-tune carding. Or to take notes more efficiently. Or to be more discriminating in your selection of documents. But it also could be to determine whether a term paper has been duplicated or purchased from ghostwriters or the "term paper companies." Whatever their reasons, your cards should not be in such disarray nor so illegible that it takes a cryptographer to decipher them.

Some Sample Cards

The examples of cards shown below demonstrate notes with substance. Everyone makes notes in different ways, but these should give you an idea of how to card information that will help write the paper.

Even if you've read only six sources, you should be able to see certain trends of key points that will serve as the foundation of your paper. In a biographical study, you may spot a half-dozen or a dozen turning points in the person's life. The paper on an event can use key occurrences that brought on the final situation. If your project is an analytical one, your readings should reveal the most important items. If you're writing about a process (how-to-do-something), you should be able to single out the major steps to be described if you're thorough in reading source materials.

What you're doing as you *separate* items is a form of basic quick-and-dirty outlining. You'll be able to see also what materials you won't need. Out will go the cards with the irrelevant, though fascinating, notes. Perhaps it's taken you hours to read the material you're discarding. That's the woeful experience of professional writers; but they put it in a cutting-room-floor file because it may be useful in another article or book. If something digresses from the subject, enter the source in the bibliography. If a "bib" grows large, writers set up a "Works Consulted" category for this situation. Put the data itself in your own cutting-room-floor file. Be ruthless in sticking to the subject.

"IRA's: Costs, Benefits, Problems,"
Consumer Reports, Vol. 45, January
January 1980, pp. 40-46

    Why buy — pros and cons —
front end loading

3 × 5 size card

    Judith S. Wallerstein and Joan B. Kelly,   "
"California's Children of Divorce," Vol. 13,
January 1980, pp. 66-76.

    fathers — pp. 71-76
    how they are as adults — pp. 74-75
    money/support — p. 68
    statistical sources — p. 70
    parental adjustment p. 72

4 × 6 size card

Alexy Tolstoy, *Peter the First*, translated by Tatiana Shebunina, New York, New American Library, 1961, possim.

Agov victory was a Pyrrhic one. Russia not prepared. Had to find allies, improve the army and get money. One of the reasons of Peter's interest in the West.

3 × 5 size card

Marc Slonim, *An Outline of Russian Literature*, New York, New American Library, 1959, p. 90.

"Nekrassov's social poetry, as well as his poems of self-recrimination, continued the moral trend so typical of Russian literature... Nekrassov questioned man's behavior in man's society and explored the twists of conscience resulting from social environment or practical responsibility."

4 × 6 size card

Reliability of Sources

What about the accuracy ("reliability") of your sources? How could you as a high school or college student be able to detect "Tudor lies" or bias? Or "why should I want to?" you may say.

Certainly many teachers have urged you not to accept everything in life as gospel, though admittedly believing everything you're told or read or see in films seems the easier, softer way to go. For research on a major paper, you'll *begin* to develop a skeptical attitude, something essential in research. If Christopher Columbus and Galileo had not questioned previous beliefs, the discovery of America and the magnificent photographs of Saturn's rings may have been delayed for centuries.

Nobody is totally objective. We all have truths we "hold to be self-evident"—and wield them whenever someone attempts to widen our body of knowledge. Many authors you'll be reading are adept at using a set of facts—statistics, quotations, dates, events, etc.—to support their views. If you recognize the truth in the axiom "it's easy to lie with statistics," you'll begin to see that bias and blind spots occur in almost all fields—not just on the Internet where anyone can build a Web site. The day will come when you detect significant omissions such as the one concerning child/slave labor and chocolate—because the piece was written by an executive of a chocolate factory.

Learn about reliability by starting with your magazine sources. Scan the table of contents because article titles alone usually reveal what kind of people buy the publication. If you can tell the difference between *People* and *Better Homes and Gardens*, use this kind of "study" to determine if a publication is ultraliberal or ultraconservative, or somewhere in between.

Expand that skill by selecting one controversial person or small event likely to be cited on the Internet, encyclopedias, or publications. See how each author presents the "facts." A half-dozen presentations will be an eye-opener. You'll see many authors also base their views on something another author has stated as fact. Some authors dealing in half-truths, outright lies or innocent misconceptions have stunning credentials, dynamic writing style, and millions of readers. But in the last 10 years, at least three such writers on well-regarded publications (*The New Republic*, *The New York Times*, *USA Today*) were unmasked as having made up much of their work.

The route to an "A" may well be your pointing out that source A says this, but source B disagrees. To a teacher hoping students develop inquiring minds, such a paragraph makes all the years in a classroom worthwhile.

Lessons From the Internet

Too many people have a tendency to believe anything set in type is holy writ. That belief may have originated because the first writings were literally "set in stone" and handed down as sacrosanct by tribal rulers. The processes also were expensive whether on stone, papyrus, parchment, or handmade paper. Opponents lacked the means, courage or time to issue rebuttals to a largely illiterate public. Not even the advent of the printing press or television changed views that if it's in writing, it must be true.

What is changing that view is the Internet where *anyone* can send e-mails or snapshots anywhere in the world. We know Aunt Matilda is no more an authority about politics than Cousin Charlie is an expert on Tunisian wheat diseases—though they *have* learned something about them off the "Net." Spam has taught millions that anyone able to buy a site can peddle acne cures or sell the Brooklyn bridge at auction. If Richard III had been living now, he and his friends and family would have a blog-clogged Web site attacking the lies of the Tudors and Shakespeare.

Yet is an Internet source any less reliable than library books and reference works? If you wanted information about heart-attack treatments, wouldn't you seek the expertise of editors and contributors from the venerable *New England Journal of Medicine* in the periodical room rather than the Web site of *Uncle Jim's Remedies*? But the NEJM is online and we can access it in the comfort of home. Most teachers know that the *Britannicas* are the most reliable encyclopedias in a library, but they also can be accessed online. That's true for the Library of Congress or the Louvre.

It's also true, of course, that much online information comes from "secondary sources" with no footnotes so reliability can be verified. But any researcher familiar with primary data (official records, diaries, letters, interviews) knows that footnotes can be built on omission of critical documents or diaries edited by their owners for publication. So can medical trials funded and staffed by a pharmaceutical company.

So both library and the Internet have reliability shortcomings. Yet to use the *most* reliable sources from either place, follow the suggestion above of collecting as wide a variety of source materials as possible. Unlike library materials, online materials can be verified for authority or quackery within nanoseconds. If you have suspicions about library sources, you also can check them out online just as quickly and easily.

The Appendix contains a list of current and fairly trustworthy Internet sites for several fields. It was based on one built for the American Society of Copy Editors, the professionals requiring reliability on an hourly basis at the nation's daily newspapers. The Appendix also contains a list of "red-check" sources used for books and reference materials by all the TIME, Inc. publications.

How do you check?

One axiom is that if *no* author or organization is listed on the title page or included in the online material, don't use the data no matter how intriguing or essential it seems to be. If the organization seems suspect, "google" the official title. That is to say, ask Google or Yahoo for the homepage. When it comes up, look for the "About Us" link and click it open. Check the mission statement. Google the names of its board of directors or staff.

Weigh their expertise for authoring the document you want to use in your term paper. Someone purporting authority about Montana who's never lived there has questionable validity. Equally, an organization creating a dozen successful public utility districts would seem to have significant credibility.

Though misspellings and grammatical errors are common and irksome, the Internet constantly proves that flawless writing is not necessarily a hallmark of reliability. That's true in library resources as well because of bias or flawed research even though articles are reviewed by a battery of editors before publication. Again, google the source whether the material is from the library or off the Internet.

A Sample Search: The Titanic

To show you how to test for reliability on the Internet, the author has set up a sample concerning the 1898 novel *Futility* which seemingly predicted the *Titanic*'s sinking in 1912. No online documents about this eerie coincidence had footnotes, the hallmark not only of a credible investigation, but the springboard for future research. But two sources quoted a recent book that apparently was well documented, although readers were expected to trust their judgment. In fairness to you, however, that's the kind of faith your teacher is going to put in you on a term paper.

The first small challenge encountered was the nationality of *Futility*'s author, Morgan Robertson. Two sources said he was British; but four others insisted he was American. Two of the four had him born in Oswego, New York. All four stressed identical things, suggesting that repetition was changing myth to fact: that Robertson was the son of a sea captain; a sailor for a half-dozen years; then, a jeweler; wrote sea stories for a living after reading a Rudyard Kipling story and because of failing eyesight ended work with gems.

So which source would *you* believe about Robertson's nationality? The two authors with no specifics about British origins or the four providing American data from secondary sources? Should the verdict be based upon four authors versus two? To find the answer, you'd have to google the six.

Now, one of the four included birth and death dates, parental names, bride's name and marriage date (May 27, 1894). He also claimed the father captained a steamer on the Great Lakes and Robertson spent from 1877–1886 in the Merchant Marine and rose to become a first mate. He added that the author learned the jeweler's craft at New York's Cooper Union trade school and opened a shop setting diamonds. Here was data none of the other five had so shouldn't it be considered gospel? Not without footnotes.[22]

But no credible researcher would write Robertson was an American without footnoting data such as a birth certificate or marriage license. None of the six protected themselves with the scholarly "hedge" of: "Evidence *suggests* that Robertson was an American." Other hedges of "it would appear" and "it seems that..." even show up in research in the sciences.

Another warning from this investigation could help you: Never speculate off raw data, a danger called "extrapolation" in research circles. To their credit, all six authors resisted extrapolating about *why* Robertson quit his father's calling despite a rapid rise in rank and higher pay than an ordinary seaman. A quarrel with the father? A sweetheart begging for a less risky job—or her father bankrolling the jewelry shop? Or was it a sea tragedy caused by his (or his father's) dereliction on the bridge?

An online search yielded secondary materials, undocumented, about Great Lakes steamers that *did* open questions about wrecks. Sources revealed that over a million immigrants from Montreal and Boston came to the Midwest and West in the 1800s. That more than 700 wrecks occurred on the routes of Lake Michigan and Superior alone. That high death tolls were attributable to few lifeboats, burst boilers from overloading, collisions from high traffic or fog, and capsizings from sudden storms.[23]

---

22 E.D. Howard, "Morgan Andrew Robertson, September 30, 1861-March 24, 1915." http://members. tripod.com/~rhazz/frobertson.html (April 8, 2004).

23 Jim and Robin Halladay, "Shipwrecks in Lake Erie," *Aquatic World*, September 22, 2003, http://www.aquatic-world.com/ErieWrecks.htm (April 8, 2004); David D. Swayze, "The Great Lakes Shipwreck File: Total Losses of Great Lakes Ships 1679–1999," Lake Isabella, MI: June 2001. http://www.boatnerd.com/ swayze/shipwreck (April 8, 2004).

So much for Robertson's nationality. What about the stunning *Titanic-Titan* coincidences?

The author found dozens of links focused on the supernatural. These were countered by two links—all undocumented—reporting that modern "ghostbusters" had destroyed the premonition aspect. The author knew that ships aren't built in a day, especially not one of the *Titanic*'s size. Years could elapse between idea to blueprints to financing to launch. Both sources confirmed that fact. They stated that six years *before* Robertson's book was published, the White Star owners announced plans to build a huge liner.

One link noted that the dimensions, fittings, and customer base had been published that year and that ship-iceberg mishaps in the North Atlantic route were common. They both hinted that any writer of sea stories with a maritime background certainly would be alert to those plans.[24]

But the most definitive blow to the paranormal theories was that link's revelation that a few weeks *after* the *Titanic* sank in April 1912, Robertson's publisher reissued the book under a new title (*The Wreck of the Titan*) with some revised tonnage and horsepower data that *nearly* matched those of the White Star liner. That was verified with online bookstores, as was the fact that the 1912 edition has been republished in the wake of the most recent movie version. The author left the opportunity open for some dedicated student to get both the 1898 and the 1912 versions and to do a term paper comprising a comparative study of both editions. It might earn an "A," as would a paper tracking the Robertsons' seafaring lives.[25]

Reading and Understanding the Material

All of the foregoing material—particularly getting the information, carding, reliability—has been designed to help you *before* you begin reading all the material you've collected for the term paper. The most challenging chore now is to read that data and apply what's been suggested. No one can do it for you, but this portion of the chapter offers a few ideas on how to read it with efficiency.

For one thing, you will have already skimmed library and/or Internet materials. For another, the carding section will force you to read with greater care and with greater comprehension than in the past. And you're not in a timed test. Allow yourself to read the data a second time or more. New things often turn up in subsequent readings. You'll also probably read with a gimlet eye to reliability about the source, knowing that what's printed is not holy writ.

Moreover, don't worry about changing your mind if "Vital" data suddenly duplicates other material or needs to be reclassified into "Bio Only"—or vice-versa. A term paper is designed to introduce a subject and spur you to think and weigh what you're reading. And when you've finished, you'll become somewhat of an expert on the topic you've chosen. At bottom, that's what education is all about.

So let's begin the "read."

---

[24] Simpson; Donnelly; Simpson.
[25] Howard.

The sensible way to understand your topic is first to read a source that puts it in the *briefest* way possible—a capsule wrap-up. That's why encyclopedias or works such as *Facts on File* are so useful as starting points. They provide the *overall* view that puts the topic in a nutshell. The rest of your readings will flesh out the details.

The details will consume most of your efforts. But shortcuts exist through the dozens of leads you've found in source materials. One method is to first *skim* the source and catch the key facts. Then do a thorough study of those facts.

If the sources involve books, scan the table of contents and/or the index to see if data you want is included in a few pages. If you were doing a paper on Napoleon at Marengo, for example, the table of contents/index of the hundreds of books on this emperor would single out that battle.

Magazine articles have telling titles and sub-headlines to indicate the various aspects in the piece. Another device for a quick read is to look at the first sentence of a paragraph. Many writers use it as a key sentence for a contention, followed by supportive examples or quotations.

Encyclopedias offer no table of contents/indexes, but if the entry is a long one, editors use sub-headlines.

What to do about the Internet's billions of Web sites and search engines fetching up 30–70 pages of URLs that have dozens of links to investigate? How does one *skim* those links? At the outset, the most *recent* material leads the first page of a search's find. If your hunt involves something less current—two decades ago—tap the "NEXT PAGE" bottom leader for however many pages you want to check, 2–80.

Whether you're checking page 1 or 80, the key to content and slant in each URL is contained in those half-sentence blurbs. The entry also includes how many kilobytes the site has—8K is brief, 1024 isn't.

Once your research is completed and the highlights carded, you're ready to organize the term paper and begin the rough draft. The next chapter will help you with those two components.

CHAPTER 18

THE MECHANICS OF THE PAPER

Before you begin writing the paper, you need to know the academic "form" that makes this kind of writing project so different from ordinary compositions. This side of producing a paper involves the mechanics such as margins, spacing, footnotes and endnotes, indenting quotations, bibliography, and the like.

This may be your first experience with what some students call "fussy form" while foaming with fury at getting an A- on an A paper (no double grades on term papers) for misplacing a comma in a footnote or bibliography. Or a "markdown" for fudging on margins or increasing spacing half a notch, or raising (or lowering) the type size—all to either pad or get around a teacher's rule on minimum number of pages.

Form of the Paper

A lowered grade because of "format" bobbles is not unusual in college. At the graduate school level, "form" for theses and dissertations extends to ensuring that a printer's toner is the same at the *last* page as it is on the *first*.

In college, the presumption is that students learned form rules from writing papers in high school. If you're in high school, the presumption is you know the days of middle-school rules are over when a teacher insisted form wouldn't count. But it obviously did or far fewer "papers" would have had wood-carved covers, elaborate art, and yarn for staples. Those with beautiful handwriting and no substance clearly had the edge over the student with outstanding research presented in handwriting suited to a doctor's prescription. Those with access to a computer at home fared better than those without.

Form removes such obvious unfairness and levels the playing field for you. It's content and following a standardized form that counts, not style. No student gets an edge because of graphics skills or ability to disguise "thin" research abilities (or verbose ones). Form, even at the medieval university, has always guaranteed you equality. The added plus is that if you discover something, you get credit for it from scholars following after you. The patent and copyright offices protect people's work so they get royalties and residuals for all their time and effort.

Form does all of the above, but one of its practical benefits is that the student listing the greatest number of sources usually gets the higher grade.

Form "fussiness" isn't confined to school. It extends to *other* corners of the writing world as well. Screenwriting, for example, has form rules so rigid that breaking even one means a script five years in the making gets "tossed" in the first five seconds by a reader. Rules involve margins on dialogue and "action lines," but also that scripts be done in 12-point Courier and no longer than 120 pages—and that page numbers have a period.

In short, instead of grumbling about form, follow the rules for academic papers.

When the teacher announces a term paper is part of the course, the general procedure is to provide rules about a paper's mechanics either orally or in writing. Once that's been done, a contract is set in stone for the class.

Forms *do* differ, especially in high school. But most are governed by the half-dozen academic styles now in use in the United States. The traditional form is emphasized heavily in this book. If your teacher veers from it, you'll still need a form for citing your sources and the "look" (margins, indentations, etc.) of the paper.

High school teachers usually reprint style sheets to save parents from having to buy these expensive term-paper format books. Professors don't give that service in an era where use of a department's photocopier is rationed out to faculty. If the rules involve a special format not contained in the traditional stylebooks, professors usually provide them.

Because many students and writers can't afford the stylebooks (*The Chicago Manual of Style* is over $50), most photocopy pertinent formats or share the rules.

This section's first chapter explained the reasons for citations and showed examples of how to construct footnotes and bibliography citations. So you have an inkling about form style.

Three of the most prevalent stylebooks of form used in documentation for academic papers are published by the Modern Language Association of America (MLA), the American Psychological Association (APA), and the University of Chicago's Manual of Style ("Chicago"). You'll discover in college that courses in English and languages usually require papers be done in "MLA" style. Papers for the sciences and social sciences use "APA" style. Courses in art, history, political science, music and philosophy use "Chicago"; so do most publishers of non-fiction books.

Each has a little different style, frustrating university students taking three classes, each with a different citation and bibliography style. APA and MLA styles have virtually eliminated footnoting/endnoting by referencing sources and pages in the text that allude to a full citation in the bibliography. Chicago style retains footnotes/endnotes.

One book publisher came to their rescue with a small handbook still being sold that contains all three styles on the most frequently used factors in documentation.[26] However, if one of the forms is radically revised, as is the case with Chicago not long ago, students must shift with the upgrade.

Below are examples of the three styles when used in *text*:

> **APA style:** Eddings (1987) notes Hawthorne took meticulous care to underscore his artistic agonies to craft *The Scarlet Letter* (p.106). His economy of words was pointed up by Aldington (1981, p. 302).

> **MLA style:** Eddings notes Hawthorne took meticulous care to underscore his artistic agonies to craft *The Scarlet Letter* (106). His economy of words was pointed up by Aldington (302).

> **Chicago style:** Eddings notes Hawthorne took meticulous care to underscore his artistic agonies to craft *The Scarlet Letter*. His economy of words was pointed up by Aldington.[5]

In examining these three styles, you'll probably fault APA and MLA styles of interrupting sentences with parentheses enclosing citations and applaud Chicago style for its straight-shot presentation, ganging citations in a note at the end of the paragraph. But faculty and scholars learn to leapfrog over the parentheses. Most of all, writers (especially students) have rejoiced because they don't have to do notes; the burden is on readers to use the bibliography.

Note well, however, the differences in APA and MLA styles in placement of *parentheses* and use of *commas*. Your instructor will if your paper uses either of these styles.

Because some book and periodical publishers have listened to readers' complaints about footnotes being a distraction in text, recent style changes insert a footnote at the *end* of a paragraph. That "gangs" all the paragraph's citations in one note. Each citation must be separated by semicolons.

That notes can be ganged at the end of a paragraph has been perceived as a blessing by readers and writers, though a mixed one for the latter.

You may undergo challenges if you delete material *within* a paragraph or change the order of material because the note also has to be fixed. If it's lengthy, the search may take time and there's risk in deleting part of *another* citation. A ganged citation looks like this:

[1]Quintus C. Wilson, "Confederate Press Association: A Pioneer News Agency, *Journalism Quarterly*, 28 (June 1949), 165; Montgomery *Daily Mail*, Oct. 14, 1864; National Archives, Confederate Record Group 1055, Co. H., 154th Senior Regiment of the Tennessee Infantry, Card Nos. 50195544, 5626, 5962, for Pvt. John Magevney, Company Muster Roll, May 6, 1863 at Shelbyville, Tenn.; OR, ser. I, vol. 10, pt. 1, pp.441-57, 574, 446-49, 571; Frank Luther Mott, *American Journalism* (New York: Macmillan, 1941), 364.

---

[26] *The Holt Guide to Documentation and Writing in the Disciplines* (Fort Worth, 1986).

Those grinding teeth while grinding out notes Chicago style are grateful that it's no longer required to insert the footnote where the citation is made, too often in mid-sentence. That made for interrupted reading, too, albeit with tiny numbers. Many see only one rather significant advantage, aside from far easier reading. They can add vital information to the note, as is shown below:

> [8] Commanding generals such as Ulysses S. Grant and William T. Sherman were constant readers of the *Appeal*. Sherman had a pathological hatred of the press, but he read that paper with avidity. Subordinates like General George Thomas rushed him copies in the field (OR, ser. I, vol. 24, pt. 3, 175; vol. 38, pt. 5, p.185). Grant perused the *Appeal* to size up the South's morale and broad civilian and military indicators even in November 1861 when he was a brigadier general posted at Cairo IL. He signaled one St. Louis captain that "There seems to be great effort making [sic] throughout the South to make Columbus [MO] impregnable. I get this information from the *Memphis Appeal…*" (OR, ser. I, vol. 7, p. 1038).

Before you conclude the trend is against footnotes and learning how to do them is pointless, the fact that word-processing programs have actually enhanced them indicates they're alive and well. In the major revision of the Chicago stylebook, there they are even with examples of citations for source materials from the Internet. Thousands of faculty still mandate them. So learning how to do footnotes and endnotes is still essential for your future.

So is mastering the different styles of *bibliographies*, as you'll see in consulting one of these style reference books.

If you're in high school and the teacher gives you the luxury of choosing a form, mull the major you might choose in college and select one of these three accordingly. You'll be getting advance practice for your future.

If you have *no* access to a computer and are using a typewriter, you still will have to follow term-paper formatting rules. One is that ribbons must be blue or black. You'll have no problem with margin stipulations or making minor changes with the aid of correction fluid. But you will have considerable retyping ahead if you need to add or delete or rearrange anything beyond a sentence.

Footnotes also will be a challenge because space must be left at the page bottom for their inclusion. One solution is to use *endnotes* because they are placed the text and before the bibliography. You'll learn to do what decades of students and researchers did *before* computers: Make faint pencil markings (so they can be erased) to reserve space at the bottom of a page for the notes.

Computer users take the "footnote/endnote" feature for granted, but when you finally use one, you'll consider it one of the greatest benefits of a word-processing program.

If this is your first brush with footnote formatting on the computer, know that after you insert your first three or four, they'll come with ease.

Here's how to do it.

Essentially, pressing two keys simultaneously (on the Macintosh: the "Apple" and "e") automatically inserts a footnote in the text at the bottom of the page. You can then tailor it to any size and type font you've chosen by highlighting it and making the change. Also, if you or the instructor decide that footnotes interrupt the

THE MECHANICS OF THE PAPER | 221

flow and ease of reading, they can be shifted to the document's end as "endnotes," or at the end of a section or chapter.

If you've never done a footnote, it just takes practice, but don't attempt it for the first time on the term paper's manuscript. Practice first.

Start by learning how to open the footnote feature—usually in "INSERT" up on the menu. Pull it down to "FOOTNOTE" either with tutoring, self-tutoring, or the word-processing program's directions.

Write a sentence.

Tap the two keys simultaneously that insert the footnote and open the citation area. The program will have inserted a footnote number after the period like this.[27] It's also inserted a corresponding footnote number at the *bottom* of the page (or end of the section/paper). Write a sample citation.

Generally, most form styles have footnotes appearing either at the *end* of the *sentence* or the *paragraph* where the source material appears. But some forms still mandate footnotes appear exactly where the *source material* ends, mid-sentence or not.

Space doesn't permit showing all three styles for other elements of the paper, but if you've received no instructions about form from your teacher, what's offered in the next pages are examples of such essentials as a title page, table of contents, list of tables, list of figures, and the paper's first and fifth pages.

The style is a combination of formats from APA, MLA, and Chicago.

---

[27] The footnote number from your text is repeated in the footnote itself, as it is here.

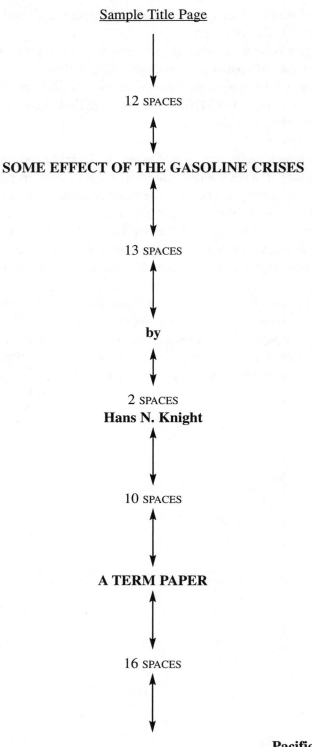

Sample Title Page

12 SPACES

SOME EFFECT OF THE GASOLINE CRISES

13 SPACES

by

2 SPACES

Hans N. Knight

10 SPACES

A TERM PAPER

16 SPACES

History 202
Dr. Charles J. Evans

Pacific University
May 30, 2005

Sample Title Page

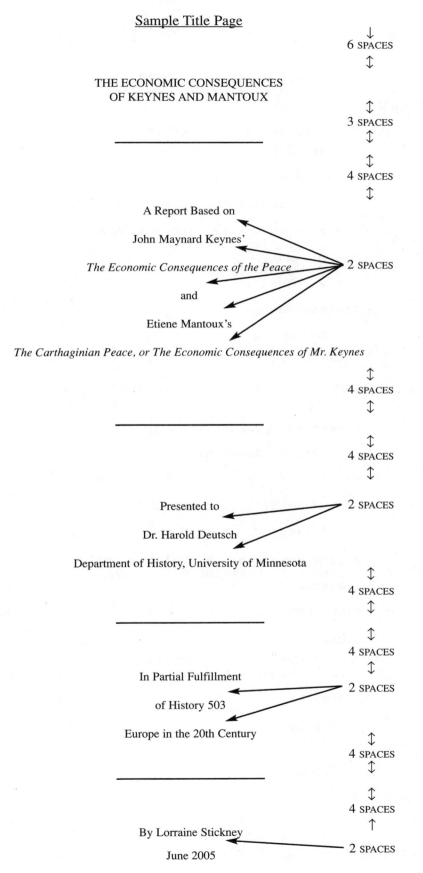

↓
6 SPACES
↕

THE ECONOMIC CONSEQUENCES
OF KEYNES AND MANTOUX

↕
3 SPACES
↕

—————————————

↕
4 SPACES
↕

A Report Based on

John Maynard Keynes'

The Economic Consequences of the Peace

and

Etiene Mantoux's

The Carthaginian Peace, or The Economic Consequences of Mr. Keynes

2 SPACES

↕
4 SPACES
↕

—————————————

↕
4 SPACES
↕

Presented to

Dr. Harold Deutsch

Department of History, University of Minnesota

2 SPACES

↕
4 SPACES
↕

—————————————

↕
4 SPACES
↕

In Partial Fulfillment

of History 503

Europe in the 20th Century

2 SPACES

↕
4 SPACES
↕

—————————————

↕
4 SPACES
↑

By Lorraine Stickney

June 2005

2 SPACES

Sample Table of Contents

TABLE OF CONTENTS

Sample List of Tables

7 SPACES

LIST OF TABLES

4 SPACES

TABLE   **PAGE**

2 SPACES

Sample List of Figures

LIST OF FIGURES

7 SPACES

4 SPACES

2 SPACES

Sample First Page

8 SPACES

HOW ONE CONFEDERATE SHIP EQUALLED TWO YANKEE FLEETS

2 SPACES

In mid-July 1862 a spectacular 23-day ship saga off Vicksburg lifted spirits of beleaguered Vicksburgers and the Confederacy and terrified Washington and two Yankee fleets. It was the story of a Southern Goliath, the *CS Gunboat Arkansas*, that attacked 50 ships of Admiral Farragut's and Davis's fleets besieging the river city.[1]

It was eight in the morning when the *Arkansas* sailed into the Mississippi river, the moment Captain Brown and his jubilant crew had awaited for six weeks: confrontation with the Federal fleet lining both sides of the river—military craft on one side, steamers on the other. One Yankee sailor's letter described the scene from the *Richmond*'s decks:

> .... we lay at anchor as careless and unprepared for an emergency as we would be in New York harbor. . . . The first words I heard were "the rebel ram Arkansas is coming down upon us......Around us lay the combined power of flag officer Farragut's and Davis fleets. Frigates, gunboats, iron-plated boats, wooden rams and iron-cased rams were anchored along the bank for a mile and a half. And slowly steaming along the hollow of a bend in the river just above us was a long, low, dull, red, floating object. She showed neither flag nor sign of life.[2]

Yankee gunners opened up on the *Arkansas* as soon as she started her famous and destructive 20-minute run straight through the two fleets. A crewman aboard the *Richmond* wrote that the *Arkansas*'s armor flattened and shattered shells thrown by each ship it passed. "Each hit looked like a 'flash of fire,'" he said as the eight-inch sheath of iron deflected the U.S. Navy's best gunnery. The only damage the Yankees could see was that it careened a bit from the 32- to 100 pound cannons roaring all at once.[3]

Despite two rams attempting to hole the *Arkansas*, its 10 guns belched shells toward *both* sides of the river, aiming fire through the heavy gunsmoke from answering flashes. As soon as the *Arkansas* passed out of range, Yankee gunners fired at their own ships across the river, inflicting terrible damage and casualties. The *Lancaster* then took a shell in the boiler from the *Arkansas* ("The scalded wretches threw themselves into the water. Some of them never rose to the surface again.") The last ship in the line was Farragut's flagship, the *Benton*. The Rebels let her have a "starboard broadside," which surprisingly was not returned. As the *Arkansas* plodded toward Vicksburg's docks, the skipper of a mortar schooner dead ahead saw she was about to run him down. He

---

[1] Richard Wheeler, *The Siege of Vicksburg* (New York: Harper Perennial, 1991), 51-57; Shelby Foote, *The Civil War: A Narrative, Fort Sumter to Perryville* (New York: Random House, 1986), 387, 549-556, 580-581; *The Memphis Daily Appeal*, July 15, 1862.
[2] *Appeal*, July 29, 1862.
[3] *Appeal*, July 29, 1862; Wheeler, 58; *Appeal*, July 16, 1862; Wheeler, 51-57; Foote, 553-554; *Appeal*, July 30, 1862.

Sample Fifth Page

When Hawthorne turned up at the *Salem Gazette* office in 1835 with a story featuring two women as the principals,[4] the editor probably gave more scrutiny to this submission than the offerings of "regulars" to the newspaper's popular literary column. What must have caught his attention was that "The Hollow of the Three Hills" was a well-written Gothic story with appeal for local readers, given Salem's witch trials.[5]

The storyline about a runaway wife's torment over the turmoil left back at home carried a message on three levels. On the surface, the lesson was that the price of a wife's abandoning her duties is death and chaos. This was the kind of fare Henrik Ibsen's Torvald Helmer might quote to his wife to keep her in line.[6]

But his second and secret message seemed to ridicule the idea that abandoned husbands and children go mad with grief and could die. That was hardly true in a era when women's death in childbirth was so widespread that the Episcopal church's *Book of Common Prayer* contained a sacrament for their surviving.[7] Few men at, then or now, go mad. Depression lifts by remarrying a combination babysitter, cook, and housekeeper. In my experience and observation, a runaway or dead wife may be an ego-smasher, but is usually a major inconvenience.

The third message seemed to be pointing out in the safety of allegory that women had little refuge if a marriage was loveless, cheerless, or abusive on top of their unending dawn-to-dark duties.[8]

Two years later, Hawthorne had several sales behind him—*many* involving women as victims and "volunteers" to misery.[9] Roy Male points out that he apparently was testing "just about every possible alternative to the union between man and woman,"[10] and editors knew women readers represented a major source of sales.[11]

The woods are the setting for "Young Goodman Brown."[12] Up to when Leo B. Levy devoted an entire article on Brown's good wife Faith,

---

[4] *The Salem Gazette*, October 19, 1835.

[5] Arlin Turner, *Nathaniel Hawthorne: A Biography* (New York: Oxford University Press, 1980), 356.

[6] Henrik Ibsen, *A Doll's House*, London, Nelson & Sons, 1879), act 1, sc. 2, lines 27-53.

[7] "The Service of Churching of Women": *The Book of Common Prayer* (New York: Oxford University Press, 1944), 305-07.

[8] Nathaniel Hawthorne, "The Hollow of the Three Hills," *Hawthorne's Women* (Chicago: Hickory Press, 2003), 98-173.

[9] *Passim.*

[10] Roy R. Male, *Hawthorne's Tragic Vision* (New York: W.W. Norton & Co., Inc. 1957), 4-5.

[11] Jean Folkerts and Dwight L. Teeter, *Voices of a Nation: A History of the Media in the United States*, 2nd Ed. (New York: Macmillan Publishing Company, 1989), 77-79.

[12] Nathaniel Hawthorne, "Young Goodman Brown," *Hawthorne's Women* (Chicago: Hickory Press, 2003), 42-68.

The title page examples show what letters must be capitalized and the spacing between lines. On most word-processing programs an inch equals six single-spaced lines. In the second example, the divider rule lines also are counted out for you.

To set margins, page numbers, and the like, open the "FORMAT" menu and scroll down to "DOCUMENT." It will have a field for margin selections for all sides of a page and one for numbering.

For margins, set the left margins for 1.5". You'll need room on that side to hole punch for a binder or staples. Set the other three margins for 1". Enter this format as a "DEFAULT" so that every page will have those margins.

The page numbering classically does not include the number "1" on the first page, but some programs don't have a feature that omits that number in a document. The solution is just to white out that number after downloading. Numbers should be in the upper right corner, as shown in the examples.

The rest of the formatting is done from the menu at the top of the screen. For line spacing, the document should be double-spaced. The text should be flushed left and open on the right. The paper is not a book or a newspaper which classically has had right-hand lines butting against the right column rule ("justified"). Moreover, readership studies have always revealed the easiest reading is with what is called in the printing business "flush left, ragged right."

As to font selection, never choose a sans-serif face for text because its slender starkness makes reading difficult. If beginning readers cannot see the letter "O" because they stare right through it, you'll begin to understand printer's wisdom: The *wider* the letters and the more adornments (serifs) a font has, the more *surface* a reader is given. Those reading primers are not set in sans-serif type.

You'll see it below in the comparison between the computer's workhorse, Helvetica, and one of the oldest fonts, Caslon, or one of the most beautiful, Palatino.

Helvetica is difficult to read as a text type because it's a sans-serif font with narrow strokes and no adornments. This sample is set in 10 point.

Caslon is easy to read as a text type because it's a serif font with wide strokes and adornments. This sample is set in 12 point.

Palatino is easy to read as a text type because it's also a serif font with wide strokes and adornments—and is considered one of the most beautiful type faces ever designed. This sample is set in 12 point.

If you use more italic than for a word or two, it is a challenge to read as this line in 12-point set in Times demonstrates.

Type size also has everything to do with readability, as the previous examples demonstrate. If a teacher has 30 term papers to grade, the wise student opts for 12 point on text.

Don't use boldface in text and use italics sparingly. More than two words or one long one in italic, as shown above, are difficult to read because of the tipped characters.

In text, setting the format to flush left will eliminate those annoying hyphenated syllabication breaks from line to line. But it's breaking paragraphs from page to page that will cause comprehension problems for the reader. Professional writers avoid them because readers have difficulty retaining the previous material even in the brief act of turning a page. They and you do have some control. If you elect to break paragraphs, have at least two sentences for the second page.

The cover binder may be prescribed by the instructor. If it isn't, don't believe a better grade will result from the most expensive ring binder at the store or those in neon-bright colors. That's an instinct from grade school when those arty covers might have impressed the teacher. At the high school and college level, novelty says "style over substance" and red flags go up. Buy an inexpensive cover at the supermarket or drugstore—preferably in dark colors because they don't show wear and tear or fingerprints.

Quotations and Excerpts

Direct quotations and excerpts should never be too long, surely no longer than two paragraphs or it might appear you either don't have much judgment in selecting the important portion from sources or you're padding the paper.

In quoting directly, copy the material *exactly* from its source. Don't doctor it up or twist words and sentences because they don't quite illustrate the point you're making. If the source sounds highly intelligent or ungrammatical, quote with accuracy.

Tips for the traditional use of quotations and excerpts will be found in the next section.

Omitting Part of a Quotation

You might want to omit words or entire passages from a direct quotation. Perhaps the entire portion of the quote is unnecessary to convey a point. Use ellipsis periods. The word "*ellipsis*" is Greek for "to fall short" or to omit something. To omit part of a sentence, use three spaced periods (. . .). It works like this:

> Four score and seven years ago, our fathers brought forth . . . a new nation, conceived in Liberty, and dedicated to the proposition that all . . . are created equal.

To omit *whole sentences*, use four ellipses (. . . .) as in the next example:

> Now we are engaged in a great civil war . . . . The world will little note, nor long remember what we say here, but it can never forget what they did here.

To omit *entire paragraphs*, use a centered line of three periods *between* paragraphs:

> He had never once looked at me. He stood with his back to the fire, which set off the herculean breadth of his shoulders. His face was dark and expressive, his underjaw squarely formed, and remarkably heavy. I was struck with his remarkable likeness to a Gorilla.
>
> . . .
>
> I looked up; he had already forgotten my presence, and was engaged in pulling off his boots and coat. This done, he sank down in an arm-chair before the fire, and ran the poker wearily through his hair. I could not help pitying him.

Quotation Marks, Long and Short Excerpts

Suppose the excerpt involves only a half-dozen words. Put them *in the paragraph* and include quotation marks around the excerpt. A short quote looks like this:

> Who can forget his reminder that "going home is pain."[5]

If the quotation is longer than a half-dozen words, use a colon *before* the quote and include it in the paragraph:

> One can see this with Voltaire's famous remark: "I do not agree with what you say, but I will defend to the death your right to say it."[7]

To format lengthy quotes, indent the passage on *both* sides to set it off from the text. A lengthy quote, without quotation marks (because indentations show it's an excerpt), is single-spaced and can be justified or flush left/ragged right. Set it in 10 point either in boldface or regular weight. Handle it this way:

Lyman remarked:

> To American audiences who first saw him in the late 40's, what was most apparent about Mr. Brando was that compared with other actors of the period, he was brooding, muscular and intense. Detractors called him a slob. He appeared in tight blue jeans and torn T-shirts, grimy with sweat, alternately slack jawed with stupidity and alive with feral cunning. And he was more openly sexual—in an animal way—than the actors who immediately preceded him. Often, Mr. Brando was accused of mumbling his lines, but audiences watching those early performances today would notice none of that, so completely has the Brando school of antiglamour taken root in American acting.[3]

Poetry Excerpts

Poetry requires special care and faithfulness to the original work. Quote *exactly* to retain the poet's metrical foot. So don't change *"n'er"* to *"never,"* and *"o' "* to *"of"* or omit the apostrophes for the missing letters. Indent lines and make the same line breaks as the poet.

Many modern poets aim for visual and/or aural impact via typographical devices (e.g., indentations, non-capitalized letters, no punctuation, etc.). So it's essential their challenging patterns be followed.

If the selection has only one or two lines, use quotes and a virgule (slash mark) at the line break, like this:

> The poet forecast it when he wrote that "I have a rendezvous with Death/At some . . . barricade."[2]

Two or more lines need an introductory lead-in line. Set it up like this:

Donne showed the same defiant spirit in "Death":

> Death, be not proud, though some have called thee
> Mighty and dreadful, for thou art not so;
> For those whom thou think'st thou dost overthrow
> Die not, poor Death; nor yet canst thou kill me.[4]

What if the line is far *longer* than the margins? Obviously, you'll have to break lines unintended by the poet, something that requires explaining in the text. Indent at least 10 spaces to indicate it's your line break, not the poet's use of stylistic indentation:

> Now as I was young and easy under
>> the apple boughs
> About the lilting house and happy as
>> The grass was green,

A great deal of poetry includes a capitalized letter on the first word of the line, largely to indicate a *separate* line, but most modern poets have discarded this traditional typographic device. Break that lengthy line like this:

> With floods of the yellow gold of the
>> Gorgeous, indolent, sinking
>> Sun, burning, expanding
>> The air
> With the fresh sweet herbage underfoot,
>> And the pale green leaves
>> Of the trees prolific,

Yet yesteryear poets like William Blake (1757-1827) gave printers fits. His breaks on long lines are aided by those capital letters, especially helpful for students, confronted by space limits in a term paper, who must break long lines. In his famous attack against poet John Milton's intellectual elitism, he unleashed not only capitalization on words starting a line (and mid-line), but punctuation starting each line, ampersands (&), colons and semicolons— plus 18th century spelling:

> 'Who creeps into State Government like a catterpiller
>> to destroy;
> 'To cast off the idiot Questioner who is
>> always questioning
> 'But never capable of answering, who sits
>> with a sly grin
> 'Silent plotting when to question, like a thief
>> in a cave,
> 'Who publishes doubt & calls it knowledge,
>> whose Science is Despair,
> 'Whose pretence to knowledge is envy,
>> whose whole Science is
> 'To destroy the wisdom of ages to gratify
>> ravenous Envy
> 'That rages round him like a Wolf day & night
>> without rest:

If you're omitting stanzas, insert four asterisks between stanzas.

> Come, fill the Cup, and in the fire of Spring
> Your Winter-Garment of Repentance fling;
>> The Bird of Time has but a little way
> To flutter—and the Bird is on the Wing.
>> * * * *
> Some for the Glories of This World; and some
> Sigh for the Prophet's Paradise to come;
>> Ah, take the Cash, and let the Credit go,
> Nor heed the rumble of a distant Drum.[2]

The two previous examples show how important it is to use the poet's capital letters, often used to personify words. Equally, indented lines sometimes indicate suspended thoughts. If the poet uses underlinings, follow suit. If the stanzas are handled with peculiar indentations, stick to the presentation, even one such as this:

see
the fiery windmills
                turning,
                        churning,
                                whirling,
                                        shriek-
ing,
creak-
ing
                        on
the hill.[3]

Dialogue From Plays and Films

Quoting dialogue or other material from plays and films also requires scrupulous attention to exactness. A short quote would look like this within a paragraph of textual material:

> Hamlet shows this attitude with his remark that "there's a special providence in the fall of a sparrow."[6]

A longer quotation drawn from a play would have the introductory line and resemble the next example:

> Gertrude is shown to be afraid not for Hamlet's sanity, but for her life in the scene at the end of the third act:
>
> QUEEN: What wilt thou do? Thou wilt not murder me? Help, help, ho!
>
> * * *
> * HAMLET: How now! Rat? Dead, for a ducat, dead!
> * POLONIUS: O, I am slain!
> * QUEEN: O me, what hast thou done?
> * HAMLET: Nay, I know not: Is it the king?
> * QUEEN: O, what a rash and bloody deed is this?
> * HAMLET: A bloody deed! Almost as bad, good mother, as kill a king, and marry with his brother.
> * QUEEN: As kill a king![10]

Film and television formats differ from plays, perhaps because, aside from theatrical tradition, a play's left-handed structure for cues suits a cast and crew needing no script after initial rehearsals.

Neither film nor TV productions are done in sequence. Rehearsal times involve only a few days, rather than the weeks for plays or musicals. So cast and crews have to be able to find their cues quickly.

This is how to set out dialogue with a lead-in line:

The 10-year-old Dead End Kid gets caught in another tall tale when the designer's daughter gives him a ride in the prototype:

FLETCHER

Hey!! This is the *Cornet*!!

The vapor pickup!! Ommigosh!!

You gotta be Patti Heflin!!

(eyes the gauge)

What this baby gettin'?

(no response)

C'mon. Ever'body'll know by tonight!

PATTI

Listen up, you little track rat:

I'll get you into the trials.

But here's the deal: You agree to show for

class, beginning Monday,

or I'll call Children's Services!![18]

Blocking (action) instructions for dramatic works often are as vital as dialogue and must be detailed accurately in a paper. Format for plays are in parentheses *within* the dialogue. Screenwriting format requires that "action lines" be separate from dialogue and flushed left with single-spacing. Note the difference between the first example (a play) and the second (screenplay) that follow a lead-in sentence:

The playwright couples important action with dialogue in many places such as this important scene:

JOHNSON: I cannot do it. (He slams his right fist into the wall in futility. Raina comes toward him, but halts at the table and grips the chair.)
RAINA: You will have to do it.
JOHNSON: I . . . . All right. (He moves behind her, his hands gripping her neck. She struggles briefly but slumps against him. He lets her fall to the floor. She is quite dead.)[2]

The typical approach would have been the usual exterior scenes of Triangle employees jumping from the 8th and 9th floors. Instead, we're inside and among the doomed:

DOZENS rush back to the Washington Place side of the room to the forbidden elevators and locked stairway door.

Flames surround the outside windows on all sides of the room, waiting for them to pop from heat, to attack the ninth floor.
The first windows to explode are by the cloakroom.

Francesca sees the terrified gaze from FIVE waiting to get on the fire escape—and hears the result.

VOICES

Ladder break!!

They fall!![4]

'Sic'

The word "*sic*" is Latin and means something has been copied exactly from the original with all the mistakes. It's placed in brackets *after* an expression that may be misspelled, ungrammatical, or incorrect. It's used like this:

> When I am going hoame [sic] tomorrow.[1]

Brackets

Many authors use parentheses in the source materials you may be quoting. For you to do this would only confuse the reader of your paper. Use brackets around *your* comments or clarifying points. This may clear up a misunderstanding that the original author might have created, as in this example:

> They [the Ministry of Agriculture] considered it necessary to issue a warning of the hazard of going into [arsenic] sprayed fields, but the warning was not understood by them [livestock, wild animals, and birds], and reports of poisoned cattle were received with monotonous regularity.

If the original document is being reviewed or commented upon by *someone else* who has inserted bracketed corrections, scholarly honesty comes into play. It's not *your* comment. Handle it this way:

> Spitzer suggested reading the July 4 file of Robert Fisk of Britain's *The Independent*, in particular his biased account that:

> America's occupation continues in many other ways. Its 146,000 soldiers [officially put at 138,000—Nathan Spitzer] are still all too much in evidence in Iraq, its tanks guarding the walls of the US "embassy," its armour littered throughout Baghdad, its convoys humming—and sometimes exploding—along the highways outside the city. The "new" and "sovereign" government cannot order it to leave. Mr. Bremer's raft of reconstruction contracts to US companies ensures that American firms continue to cream off Iraq's money, described quite accurately by Naomi Klein in *The Nation* as "multibillion robbery." And Mr. Bremer managed to institute a set of laws that the "new" and "sovereign" government is not permitted to change.[24]

Footnotes/Endnotes

You already know from the previous chapter that the *purpose* of footnotes and endnotes is to credit sources and to add clarifying data.

Examples from previous pages have shown how to set up footnote and endnote citations—including online materials—for books, magazines, encyclopedias, newspapers, plays, pamphlets and the like. They even included special sources such as the "OR" (*The Official Records of the War of the Rebellion*), a key reference for the Civil War.

You've also seen the differences among APA, Chicago, and MLA formats. The font size is always *smaller* to distinguish it from the text. If the text is set in 12 point, you may choose to set notes in 9 or 10 point. Before you set it in anything smaller, do a test run and consider your instructor's eyesight—particularly if dozens of papers were turned in. Some students set notes in boldface weight for greater readability.

If you're unsure about *any* aspect of typography—font, point size, weight—ask the instructor for guidelines.

Your *main* challenge is to use correct and *complete* citations following the style format (APA, MLA, Chicago, etc.) mandated by the instructor.

Wise students who are term-paper veterans usually set footnote and bibliography samples—including Internet materials—from the stipulated format and tape it above the computer for ready reference. That saves them from having to check stylebooks each time they use a note. Follow suit.

After doing three or four citations, you'll be experienced with the form mandated for the paper. Yet it's still smart to recheck each when it's completed (particularly punctuation) to ensure it follows the format. If you do that each time, you won't have the onerous chore of doing the same job when the first draft is finished.

The best way for rechecking citation—especially punctuation because it's small—is to highlight citations and enlarge them to 18-point type. Errors in spacing, punctuation, misspellings, and failure to italicize *do* leap from the screen. Once you've approved what's on the screen, highlight and return the note to its original point size.

If you have to repeat a citation, an abbreviation system exists that's acceptable to almost all faculty, especially in high schools. Today's students owe gratitude to 18th century scholars who finally threw down their pens and declared that common sense dictated having to repeat the *same* note wasted paper, ink, and led to writer's cramp. We can imagine they argued for using "*do*," the 18th century abbreviation for "*ditto*" (quotation marks were 19th century inventions).

They won half a battle because the result was abbreviations, but in *Latin*, the language of scholars for 2,000 years. So today's students save paper, ink, and avoid "keyboard cramp" with four of the most frequently used abbreviations: "*ibid.*," "*loc. cit.*," "*op. cit.*," and "*passim.*" In recent years, even these terms have undergone a change whereby a keyword and page number(s) are permitted for subsequent citations off the original one, as the following examples show:

[1]Frank Luther Mott, *American Journalism* (New York: Macmillan, 1941). 364; Robert Talley, *The Commercial Appeal 1840-1965: The Story of a Great Institution Dedicated to the Peoples' Right to Know* (Memphis: The Commercial Appeal, 1965), 19.
[2]Mott, *American Journalism*, 329-59, 343, 443-49, 358-59; Talley, *Commercial Appeal*, 40.

However, because thousands of teachers prefer the traditional Latin abbreviations, the next pages explain how to apply them. Before you begin work, ask your instructor which system is preferred.

Ibid.

The expression "*ibid.*" is the abbreviation for "*ibidem*" which means "in the same place." It's used for subsequent citations of the same source—but that original source must be *directly* above it. In a ganged citation it only can be applied on the *first* source of that above, not others following after it.

Follow *ibid.* spelling and punctuation exactly; then add the page number and period. The term is capitalized *if it leads the note line* and/or italicized because it often stands for the title of a magazine, book, encyclopedia, etc. This is how the previous footnote would appear with an *ibidem*:

[1]Frank Luther Mott, *American Journalism* (New York: Macmillan, 1941). 364.
[2]*Ibid.*, 329-59, 343, 443-49, 358-59.

Loc. Cit.

Loc. Cit. stands for "*loco citato*" and means "in the *place* referred to." Use it to repeat a citation when others *separate* it from the original. It must be drawn, however, from the *same page* as the original citation. Common sense and common practice dictate that the name of the original citation be included. It looks like this:

[1]Frank Luther Mott, *American Journalism* (New York: Macmillan, 1941), 364.
[2]Robert Talley, *The Commercial Appeal 1840-1965: The Story of a Great Institution Dedicated to the Peoples' Right to Know* (Memphis: The Commercial Appeal, 1965), 40.
[3]Mott, *loc. cit.*

Op. Cit.

Op. Cit. is the abbreviation for "*opere citato*" and means in the *work* cited." This expression performs much the same function as *loc. cit.*—except that it refers to a *different page* from the original citation. It looks like this:

[1]Frank Luther Mott, *American Journalism* (New York: Macmillan, 1941), 364.
[2]Robert Talley, *The Commercial Appeal 1840-1965: The Story of a Great Institution Dedicated to the Peoples' Right to Know* (Memphis: The Commercial Appeal, 1965), 40.
[3]Mott, *op. cit.*, 291-94.

Passim

This expression means "everywhere" or "throughout." It isn't used often—almost never in high school term papers, but when it is, it means the *entire* source is being cited to demonstrate an overall *flavor* of the material.

University professors tend to frown on students using *passim* as an escape from citations, by the way, and may reject the paper until they are included.

The notation instructions apply to most citations. However, it is your source material and the format style that direct *how* you lay out that note or bibliography entry, as was shown earlier in this chapter. The style book will show you how to do citations for everything from books, magazines, and speeches to pamphlets, interviews, government bulletins, and law cases. They'll also solve quandaries about books with translators, articles with several authors, newspaper editorials, and the like.

An overall caveat about notes is to ensure that from the original citation to the last *op. cit.*, all page and volume numbers are *correct*. Many teachers, especially if they believe a paper is suspect or sloppy, will hunt up the source material to verify accuracy.

The Bibliography

A bibliography (or "References") is the alphabetical listing of *every* source cited or consulted that you'll use in this project. This book's bibliography provides a model for contents, though it may not conform to the format style mandated by your instructor. Yet like all bibliographies, it is placed at the end of a work.

When the author is unknown, as is often the case, alphabetizing is done according to the *first letter of the title*. Articles (*a, an, the*) don't count.

Each format—APA, MLA, Chicago, etc.—has a slightly different style, but do share some common characteristics. None include entry page numbers, for example. All stipulate that when one author has been cited for more than one book or article, the name may be omitted, but the source material must be set up as usual. All entries differ in style for footnotes/endnotes.

Generally, publishers, publishing dates and sites are placed *inside* parentheses in footnotes, but left "open" in a bibliography. The date of publication appears in parentheses—right *after* the author's name. *Periods* are used as item separaters instead of commas.

Sometimes, stylebooks are drastically revised—usually because of common sense or greater clarity for scholars trying to find a work in the bibliography. For instance, in the latest edition of Chicago format, encyclopedia entries have been stripped down to name and edition date rather than including the publisher's name and address and volume numbers.

Follow the indentation style of the format. Indentations are designed so that readers can see where one source ends and another begins—aided by spacing: single-spacing *within* each citation, double-spacing *between* each entry. Some styles stipulate the first line be flush left and subsequent lines indented five spaces. Others prefer the reverse.

As noted, experienced researchers create a bibliography file as they lift materials, alphabetizing as they go so that it's complete when the paper is.

If you've created a file listing *both* footnote and bibliography citations when you began gathering material from the library or Internet, you'll have a readymade item to highlight, copy, and paste (HCP) on a bibliography page. Most term papers are not lengthy enough to require more than a one- or two-page bibliography.

If they are more than two pages, sort them out by categories (e.g., books, periodicals, newspapers, encyclopedias and the like). Yet no teacher is likely to fault you if you categorize even with only one page of references, as is shown in the following illustration of a bibliography:

Sample Bibliography

REFERENCES

Books and Pamphlets

Battles and Leaders of the Civil War. (1884–87). Vols. I–IV, (Ed. Robert Underwood Johnson and Clarence Cloug Buel). New York: Century Co.

Bierce, Ambrose. (1956 [1912]). *Ambrose Bierce's Civil War*, (Ed. William McCann). Washington, D.C.: Regnery Gateway.

Catton, Bruce. (1956). *This Hallowed Ground.* Boston: Little, Brown and Company.

Chesnut, Mary. (1981 [1880s]). *Mary Chesnut's Civil War.* (Ed. C. Vann Woodward). New Haven: Yale University Press.

Gordon, George (Lord Byron). (ND). *Poems by Lord Byron.* London: George Routledge and Sons.

The Literature of England: An Anthology and a History. (1941). (Eds: George B. Woods, Homer A. Watt, and George K. Anderson), Vol. 1, Chicago: Scott, Foresman and Company.

The Papers of Ulysses S. Grant (1973). Vol. 5, (Ed. John Y. Simon). Carbondale, Ill.: Southern Illinois University Press.

The Tennessee Civil War Veterans Questionnaires. (1985). (Eds. Colleen Morse Elliott and Louise Armstrong Moxley; Compiled by Gustavus W. Dyer and John Trotwood Moore). Easley, S.C.: Southern Historical Press.

The War of the Rebellion: A Compilation of the Official Records of the Union and Confederate Armies. (1897). (Eds. Daniel S. Lamont, Daniel, Maj. George W. Davis, Leslie J. Perry, Joseph W. Kirkley). Washington, D.C.: U.S. Government Printing Office.

Xenophon. (1947 [BC 399]). *The March Up Country.* (Trans. W. H. D. Rouse). Ann Arbor, Mich.: The University of Michigan Press.

Young, David N. (1968). *The Mississippi Whigs*, 1834–1860. Unpublished doctoral dissertation, University of Alabama, Tuscaloosa, Ala.

Encyclopedias, Censuses

Encyclopedia Britannica, 15th ed.
Census of 1820, South Carolina

Newspapers

Larabee, Mark, "Audubon offers $1,000 reward for information in eagle death," Metro/Northwest, *The Oregonian*, B7, April 13, 2004.
The Rebel, Chattanooga, Tenn.

Periodicals

Baker, Thomas Harrison III (August 1963). Refugee Newspaper: *The Memphis Daily Appeal*, 1862-1865. *Journal of Southern History*, 29, 326–44.

—Forrest's Raid on Memphis. (1864, September 10). *Harper's Weekly*. 4, No. 402, p. 588.

O'Connor, Flannery. (1960). The Comforts of Home. *Kenyon Review*, 22, 523–46.

CHAPTER 19

ORGANIZING
AND WRITING
THE ROUGH DRAFT

The writing of their findings is a job that seems to many students to be the hardest part of doing a term paper. Actually, it's not. The most difficult part—research—is behind you. Because you know what the focus is to be, the writing will be the easiest part of the project.

The first step in organizing the paper is to sort the note cards into main areas or aspects. Most subjects can be categorized, as you'll see when you begin this part of term-paper work. Here's how three students organized their term papers:

> *Some effects of life in a Housing Development*
>
>   A. *financial angle*
>   B. *social   "   for parents*
>   C.   "   "   for kids to 18*
>   D. *aesthetic "   for family*
>   E. *community spirit angle*

Topic "Why Dunkirk?"
failure Fr. holding effort
* miscal. by Brit.
* efforts of Ger. high command
   (air)
logistical snarls for Allies
communications = failure by "

"Some Comparisons Between Gogol & Dostoyevsky"
 - use of trivia - great messages
 -   "   " humor (D- little)
 - revelations of Russian life
 - use of char. as types
 - philos. themes (religion, esp.)
 - use of dialogue (G a playwright)
 - use of description
 - use of settings
 - points of view used
 - use of history, social structures

The next step involves clearing a table large enough to hold all your cards—either stacked or lined up with each other for categorization. Get the Post-its and a felt-tip pen and write one for each category. Give each a spot on the table room enough to line up or to stack the cards and any supplementary data.

Then sort the cards and other data into those categories, as shown above. You'll have to make some hard decisions for cards that *initially* seem to belong in *two* or more categories. Set them aside until you've done the main sort. Try them in each possible category and follow your instincts on where they belong.

Cards and/or supplementary materials that don't seem to have a "home" probably don't. Put them in a pile with a name such as "orphans" or "cutting-room floor," and set them aside. Never discard them because one or two might fill a gap you overlooked.

After you've done the sort, decide which category goes first in the paper. The author organizes by making a duplicate set of Post-its for ease in moving them around in "try-out" positions. Once the sequence order has been decided, she pastes them onto a sheet of paper, and runs a piece of Scotch tape across them all to hold them in place. That paper will be pasted beside the computer screen. The cards will be stacked in the same order on the desk for handy reaching as the paper is put together.

But you may decide to gather up all the cards/data in each category, put the Post-its atop each pile and move them around to test the sequence order for the paper.

Whatever organizational system you use, decide which category gets first play in your paper. Move it to the lead position at the head of the table.

Follow it up with the second most important category. Then, the third, fourth, and so on to the last category—the close.

Unorthodox as this system may seem, it's fast, easy, and you're physically "into it," unlike the two traditional systems of "playing it by ear" or the formal outline of Roman numerals, capital letters, numbering and the like.

That's how easy it is to organize a paper. And if you're organized, you'll know exactly what goes where. That spells an end to procrastination and its weighty and disabling result: stress.

Writing the Text

Make the writing style formal and scholarly. Rule out whimsy, chattiness, and especially false modesty ("Though I didn't understand all that I read…"). They have no place in a term paper. Neither does overenthusiasm ("What a poet Heine is!!!!!" "The grasp of regimental action here is magnificent!"). Scholars use a quiet dignity.

Gear vocabulary to the level used by your instructor in class. One instructor may use an elevated style; another may stick to basic English. Before you go beyond two pages of writing, measure the level by the content-analysis option of the grammar-check feature in your word-processing program.

Avoid mentioning yourself. If you believe you must, use the third person as in "This student noticed that…" or "This researcher concluded that…"

As recommended in the last chapter, use the "scientific hedge" (qualifier) about your findings if you want to be considered an A student. Those key expressions are: "Evidence suggests that…" or variations on "it seems" or "it appears." Mathematics and the sciences are among many fields in which *several* conclusions are possible from data. Even if scientists have a experiment turn out the same way 99 times out of 100, they still are careful to report findings with those all-important qualifiers because later research may disprove their results or their methods or choice of subjects. Or equipment may have been flawed.

By the way, most researchers in the medical and other scientific fields *never* like to use terms like "*breakthrough*" or "*discovery*." That's because results *always* are built on the foundations laid by efforts of previous researchers. It took Thomas Edison years to develop the light bulb from the failures of other inventors; and the Wright Brothers' airplane took centuries of trials and deaths.

The Introduction

Limit your introduction to one page; more is padding. *Briefly* summarize the scope and your major findings—with those qualifiers. Graduate students are taught to mention areas they excluded ("delimitations") as well.

Instead of struggling over an introduction, do what many professional writers do: write it last. If you do it first, knowing it must be impressive, you may stall in writer's block and anguish. Those drawbacks rob you of production time and bring on frustration or a poor opening.

The advantage of writing the introduction last is that you'll know exactly what's in the paper. That enables you to encapsulate what the reader is going to learn from reading it, its scope and thrust.

The opening paragraph needs to be diagrammed in the following way with the most important contention or point placed first:

```
┌─────────────────────────────────────────────────────┐
│ OPENING SENTENCE (reveal topic)                      │
├──────────────────────────────────────────┐          │
│ Point No. 1 (most important point)        │          │
├──────────┐                                │          │
│ Point No. 2                               │          │
│ Point No. 3                               │          │
│                     ┌─────────────────────┘          │
│ Point No. 4         │                                │
├─────────┐           │                                │
│ Point No. 5         │                                │
│                              ┌───────────────────────┘
│ Point No. 6                  │
│                         ┌────┘
│ Point No. 7             │
└─────────────────────────┘
```

What such an opening paragraph looks like when it's filled with words is:

Nearly 23,000,000[23] Americans are now living in modern housing developments and most are not really happy about it. They have found that buying such a home might have had a good reason originally, but it is far more expensive than they planned. Americans also have found that a development seems to stifle aesthetic values because there are only four or five architectural styles available. Parents object to the rigid social life they must carry on with the neighbors. Children are seemingly affected in that they know other children only of the same economic and social levels. Even the community spirit, so high in small towns, undergoes a remarkable adverse transition—it would appear for the worse—in a housing development.

If you don't like to waste words, your brisk and short introductory paragraph could look like this:

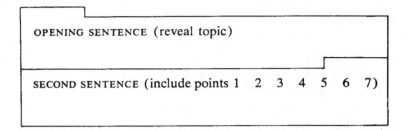

Nearly 23,000,000[23] Americans are now living unhappily in housing developments. They find those complexes have more than a dozen important drawbacks in such things as finances, aesthetic values, social life, and do nothing to create community life.

The introduction could be only one paragraph, or it could involve three or four paragraphs. Perhaps you feel uneasy if your introduction doesn't fill up the first page. But restraint is encouraged, as is the surgery of tight editing lest it be viewed as padding by the instructor who wants you to get into the subject.

The Body of the Paper

When you begin writing the rest of the text, you'll see the value of a sheet of those Post-its above the computer, a ready reference to cards and corresponding source materials. You'll know which category follows that introduction and line up your cards and supplementary data accordingly.

So you don't feel overwhelmed, take only that first category from the pile and leave the rest on a nearby table. That will enable you to sort cards *within* that first category in the order you'll use their data and put them at your elbow for ready reference in 1-2-3 order.

The construction of each category or section is much the same structure that has been recommended for writing compositions in the previous section: Start with a key sentence. Then, underpin it with your specific example(s) to support what's contained in that key sentence. This is what the structure will look like:

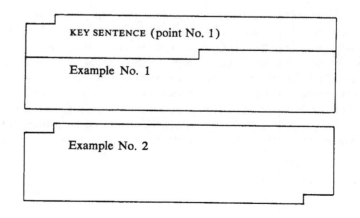

> Example No. 3

The text for that outline would resemble this:

> It seems that many readers do not feel Salinger's confused teenager, Holden Caufield, is worthy of sympathy. Critic Nancy Roboz said that because Holden has plenty of money and opportunities, he should not be pitied. ⎫ **key sentence**
>
> "It seems to me," she wrote, "that teenagers who are plagued with poverty, perhaps only one parent in the home, acne, poor grades and other attendant difficulties will wonder just what troubles Holden. Worrying about phonies will seem a very small problem to them."[1] ⎫ **example No. 1**
>
> This observer has known many poor people, and they have none of the questions that Salinger gives Caufield. One of the boys from the Upward Bound program said he felt Salinger's hero had things pretty nice. ⎫ **example No. 2**
>
> What he said is echoed by Prof. Francis Karam in a comparison of Salinger and Charles Maturin. He wrote: "A boy who has been facing life in its cruelest terms knows that life is made up of phonies by the million. But so what?"[2] ⎫ **example No. 3**

You can use more than one paragraph for each example, of course. Don't limit yourself. You might even need to write two or four paragraphs to do justice to your examples. But as is shown above, offer commentary or some observations as you work in the examples.

Using the same structure as shown in the previous diagram, an analytical term paper would look much the same as the next example:

Another important difference between Shaw and Ibsen is humor. Shaw had far more of it and a greater variety than did the Norwegian. When Ibsen used humor, it was was with the heavyhanded approach of the North European. There is nothing subtle about it. — key sentence

In *An Enemy of the People*, Ibsen thunders almost without letup on the venality and mendacity of mankind. Near the end of the play, Ibsen sees fit to employ some comic relief of the earthy variety so dear to the Germanic races. Dr. Stockmann enters, trousers damaged, from his street orations about the water pipes and certain individuals of the town. At one point he says: "You should never wear your best trousers when you go out to fight for freedom and truth."[1] This is hardly even Wildean humor. — example No. 1

By contrast, Shaw's many-sided humor turns up constantly. It is as if he cannot help himself. Even his prefaces to his plays are full of it. The preface to *Pygmalian* cannot help making the reader smile. Says Shaw: "The English have no respect for their language, and will not teach their children to speak it. They cannot spell it because they have nothing to spell it with but an old foreign alphabet of which only the consonants—and not all of them—have any agreed speech value."[2] — example No. 2

Where can Ibsen match such wit as that give Cusins by Shaw in *Major Barbara* when explaining why he [Cusins] will not join her for prayers: "Well, you would have to say before all the servants that we have done things we ought not to have done, and left undone things we ought to have done, and that there is no health in us. I cannot bear to hear you doing yourself such an injustice."[3] Ibsen would never make humor out of the *Book of Common Prayer*, but Shaw dares and tastefully so. — example No. 3

If one of your contentions or points has *many* aspects to it, use the key sentence to touch upon the *overall* contention. Then, give substance to each additional paragraph with an aspect of the main point. Follow it up with the example or fact. The diagram below shows you how to do it:

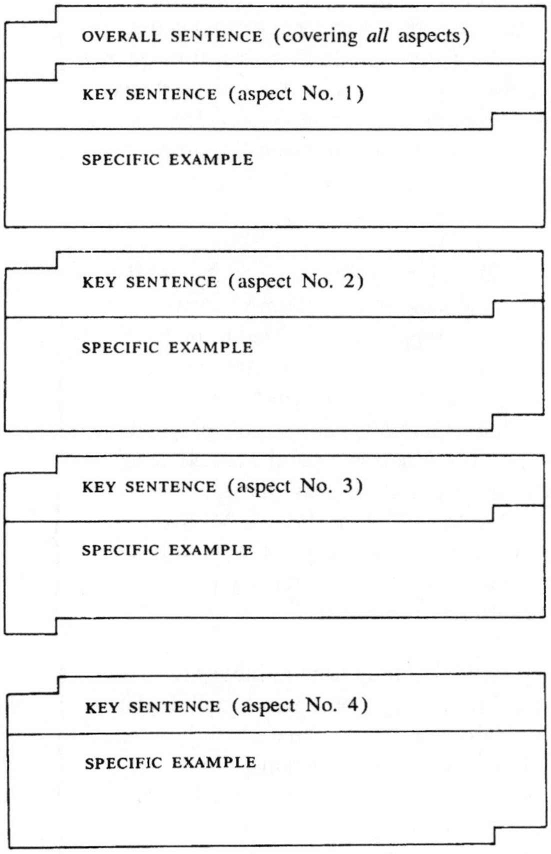

OVERALL SENTENCE (covering *all* aspects)

KEY SENTENCE (aspect No. 1)

SPECIFIC EXAMPLE

KEY SENTENCE (aspect No. 2)

SPECIFIC EXAMPLE

KEY SENTENCE (aspect No. 3)

SPECIFIC EXAMPLE

KEY SENTENCE (aspect No. 4)

SPECIFIC EXAMPLE

The example below shows how the paragraph's structure works out in text:

The press of this country, in the main, still refuses to meet its responsibilities to the public when it interferes with the publishers' pocketbooks. When it became clear that there were a lot of meat processing plants—nearly 9000[1]— that cut meat products under appalling conditions, the posture of many papers was that it was happening somewhere else, if it were happening at all. One liberal magazine was moved to say: "Here we have meat processing plants that work amid flies, vermin, rodents and who stoop also to adulterating old meat or meat from diseased livestock. Yet only seven daily newspapers really pursued the matter relentlessly."[2]

> overall
> key sentence
>
> key sentence
> (aspect No. 1)
>
> example No. 1

Many newspapers also shirked their duty to the public, especially the elderly and sick, in the matter of overpriced drug scandals. Profits on drugs were admitted to be based on what the traffic would bear. This was sometimes a 1000 percent mark-up, according to the findings of the late Senator Estes Kefauver's famous drug investigation more than two decades ago.[3] If the nation's publishers covered the drug hearings at all, they put the play in back pages or editorialized to the effect, as did one Midwestern paper, that "when the millions spent for research on just one medicine are considered, the drug industry is only getting its fair return on its investments."[4]

> key sentence
> (aspect No. 2)
>
> example No. 1
>
> example No. 2

Too many newspapers also fought child labor laws, knowing their carrier boys would come under such legislation. One California daily argued that "there is little wrong in helping train a child to meet adult responsibilities. He has an opportunity to earn his own money and to contribute to the family income. Perhaps he will be too tired at the end of the work day to engage in mischief or crime."[5]

> key sentence
> (aspect No. 3)
>
> example No. 1

When advertising revenues were jeopardized if newspapers reported too fully the recent housewives' strikes for lower grocery prices, the stories were played down if they were covered at all in most papers. Checking 47 dailies from areas affected by the lady pickets, I found that only four really covered the story at all. Of these four, only one followed the event until the end of the strike. This is a shocking but fairly regular happening where the seemingly public-minded newspaper business is concerned.

> key sentence
> (aspect No. 4)
>
> example No. 1

If your paper is a biographical study, it would use the same structure as is shown in the next example:

	His temperament proved to be irresponsible also in many ordinary things. Take his regard	key sentence for overall section
aspect No. 1	for editor's deadlines. One editor told him over lunch that he'd like two paragraphs changed by the end of the week. Two years later, the changes were still not made. His publisher had at least six editors quit because of his carelessness with deadlines.[1]	example No. 1

Other irresponsibilities had to do with his family life. He was divorced from six wives. All but one declared in court that once he had shown up for the wedding, he considered his marital duties as over.[2] He was an affectionate father to his 15 children, but even his favorite, Sean, admitted to one magazine reporter that his father felt devotion to irresponsibility was a kind of responsibility in itself.[3]

    key sentence (aspect No. 2)
    example No. 1

    example No. 2

Financial responsibilities put him in poor shape through most of his life. He seems to have the perpetual beer pocketbook and champagne tastes as well as a generous heart that could be taken advantage of. When times were good as with that important first novel, he spread around most of the royalties to his friends. His parents received a new house in Shreveport.[4] Two down-on-their-luck poets he met in an uptown bar were startled to learn they were to join him for an opulent midnight supper at the very expensive Four Seasons.[5]

    key sentence (aspect No. 3)

    example No. 1

    example No. 2

Each category of your paper should follow the same pattern as has been shown for the first one in these diagrams and examples.

Endings

Your ending section should not be difficult to write once the rest of the paper is finished. The maximum length is two paragraphs. Sum up the main points of the paper. Don't ramble. Don't gush ("This paper has changed my whole outlook on life" or "I have learned so much, thanks to this great opportunity to…"). One student wrapped up his paper *without* such flourishes this way:

> It has been seen that the Empire ruled the Emperor rather than the other way around. Militarily, he was forced to accede to his generals rather than the Senate. Even in the Senate, he was at the mercy of the five chief politicians. The populace even had his services which he was afraid to curtail. His family was so insistent in its demands that he continually pacified them with his influence and extensive holdings. Nations crushed by his armies made vociferous demands; and he believed it was far less costly to negotiate than to crush uprisings like his predecessors. Little wonder his contributions to the Empire were so minimal.

Fine-Tuning

What you have is only a rough draft of the finished paper. When you complete the rough, resist the temptation to turn it in, no matter how exhausted you may be. That's the path taken by 85% of students despite all the research effort and writing that first draft. Only rank amateurs turn in a first draft. The psychological reason for "letting it rest" is that, having given birth, you're too exhausted to see mechanical errors (typos, misspellings), let alone gaffes in writing and organization.

Second, resist the temptation of editing the moment the printer churns out the last page. Again, exhaustion will make you miss errors of commission (mechanical, substance) and, worse, omission. As they say in the writing profession, "you're too close to it." Let the paper cool for at least a day.

If you want an A, when you reread the paper, you'll get out a red pen. You'll then pretend you're the gimlet-eyed instructor and edit—ruthlessly. You'll discover another writing truth: Beyond the niggling typos, misspellings and grammatical errors (that you'll catch with relief), the substance always needs fine-tuning. Maybe not a lot, but certainly a little.

If the writing flows easily from one area to another from start to finish, that's a tribute to your organization. However, that's rarely the case. Perhaps the flow has meandered from the mainstream into a tributary or two that go nowhere. Or a better example exists in the cutting-room floor file than the one used.

You may have a moment of shock as you notice one category/section should be placed elsewhere until you realize it can be shifted within a minute or two. The method is to "highlight/copy/paste" (HCP). Or that a terrible gap is apparent that the instructor assuredly will detect, jot a tart margin note, and drop the grade accordingly.

Again, don't let all the time and effort invested in the paper go to waste because you're either tired of the project or because you're on deadline. Go for the A. Fine tune.

The errors of commission can be fixed quickly and easily. Those of omission and reorganization may take a few hours more.

Adding New Material

Adding new material requires either new research or rescuing data from the cutting-room file. Go to the screen and leave a two-inch space so you'll be able to find the spot to insert the new material.

When you have that data at hand, set up a *new* file. That will give you a feeling you're not cramped for space so you can give the addition adequate coverage. Look at the hard copy for the paragraph immediately above it so you can determine the transitional lead-in phrase for the new material. The insertion must fit smoothly.

Then, write the addition. Use the same writing structure in the other sections of the paper: Key statement followed by example(s).

Download, edit—ruthlessly—and make any changes.

HCP the addition into the hole you left in the paper for its inclusion. Close up the spaces fore and aft.

Repairing Organization

Reorganization looks easy, but don't be fooled by the swiftness of the HCP system. If professional writers make mistakes when they move chunks of text from one place to another, you are five times as likely to fall into the HCP trap because of your inexperience.

The principal problem is that the HCP "switching-and-stitching" often results in a pasted section referring to something *above* that's been deleted or to something that once appeared *below* it. That's because of the visual and psychological drawbacks of being able to view material only 20 lines at a time on a screen.

A better repair method exists that requires only scissors, Scotch tape and the hard copy.

Cut out the misplaced section from the hard copy. Tape it to its new spot.

Beginning at the point where you made the cut, reread all the way through and up to where it's been pasted. Then, read what goes immediately *before* and *after* the insertion(s) to check the flow *and* references. Fix any flaws you spot on those references. The change should flow seamlessly into the text above and below.

Next, return to the screen. Put two inches of space before and after the section you're going to move so you can make those changes without being distracted by the surrounding text. Then, HCP the section into its new position.

A Final Word

A strong suggestion to ensure an A paper is to do at least three or four drafts. The second draft will carry most of the major changes. The third and fourth are easily and quickly done because only minor touch-ups are needed for a polished final draft.

Put each draft aside for an hour or two before rereading and editing because "you're too close to it." Check for missing periods, failure to close parentheses or quotation marks, and the like.

Then pat yourself on the back. The paper should merit an A, as well as laudatory comments from the instructor that will put that paper among your keepsakes.

TABLES, GRAPHS, AND OTHER ILLUSTRATIONS

Illustrations have accompanied written material ever since recorded history began. As our prehistoric forebears talked about danger or the weather, they either made descriptive gestures or drew pictures with a stick in the dirt. Whole civilizations have been revealed by pictographs on pottery, jewelry, walls, and other artifacts. Symbols such as the cross, swastika, and hammer and sickle say volumes.

Some fields such as technology, the sciences, education, government, and advertising rely heavily on illustrations to tell their stories. Stockholders may not read every word of an expensive, glossy annual report, but they *will* pore over all the tables, graphs, pie charts, or diagrams to see how their earnings are doing.

Illustrations also give vital information in seconds for certain research papers in high schools and universities. Computer software has eliminated a lot of the hard work in doing tables and graphs and other illustrations. Decades ago meticulous care was required to draw by hand a bar graph with crosshatched and solid lines. Today, students simply have to dump numerical data into a computer program and out come illustrations—professional looking and in a dazzling array of designs: a pie chart, bar graph, or polygraph of extraordinary creative skill. And in color.

However, before you spend nearly $100 or more on a charts-and-graphs software program or try to master one on the school's computer, ask yourself five major questions:

1) Is the expense, time, and frustration/stress invested in program mastery worth one or two illustrations that can be done by pen and ink?
2) Does the software control *how* the research is presented or can it be manipulated so that the *research* controls the software?

3) Do you have the time to master a charts-and-graphs program? It could take several days and several more to execute the precision work required for illustrations. For instance, just setting the date/time/year/month on one "axis" and frequencies on the other takes time. So does changing defaults, fonts, point sizes or colors. Or shifting headlines and illustrations. Or repairing errors seen only when the first (or last) proof pours out of the printer.

4) Do teachers put less value on a pen-and-ink illustration than a computer-produced illustration? Most recognize the thought and laborious effort expended in each.

5) Do term papers need the showstoppers found in annual reports? Many failing companies use stunning 16-color charts and graphs to divert investors' attention from losses or dangers revealed in the plain-vanilla balance sheets. Many teachers view computerized illustrations in a similar light and little different from those dressy book-report covers of grade school days. They're looking for "more matter, less art."

Remember, too, that those software programs are designed for graphics customers, not students needing just a couple of charts or graphs for a term paper. Most word-processing programs include a basic tables-and-form feature adequate to your needs. Even the earliest Microsoft Word version had three icons up in its "dashboard" so that ordinary users could make basic spreadsheets, tables, charts, and graphs.

Your school's computers may contain pagination/illustration programs capable of producing the most complex or basic designs you can create. For example, this chapter's illustrations were produced by a Quark program. The author mastered most of its features—and limits. It provided total flexibility in design so that the program was the *servant*, not the master, in dispensing original work.

All of the foregoing is not intended to discourage illustrations for your paper. The fundamental rule is to use common sense about money, time, and energy expended on them.

You may be taking a course in which the instructor *requires* illustrations in a writing project. That's always the case in fields where surveys must be presented in tables. Or those in which fieldwork mandates maps, charts, schematics, or graphs.

Moreover, it's entirely possible that producing one or two illustrations becomes so enjoyable and absorbing you'll decide to develop this skill. The byproduct could well lead to a career in business, the media, or cartography where a picture has always been worth a thousand words—and high salaries.

Once you've answered the questions above and decided to use illustrations, move to the dos and don'ts and brief explanations about the purposes of the most common types. This chapter's last portion includes a portfolio of sample illustrations for each of them.

Getting Started

The cardinal rule of graphics for honest annual reports and newspapers is still: "Keep it simple" and avoid "chart junk" because it detracts, rather than enhances, the points being made. Follow that rule.

Second, allow sufficient time to execute an illustration. Learning how to make a pie chart via software in four hours before a paper's deadline is a recipe for high-order stress and disaster. Each illustration for this chapter (except for the map) required *at least* three hours, not counting the time spent in conception and design.

Annual report designers know that one large illustration makes a stronger point than several small ones. They also know the illustration must be *appropriate* to the material. If you're illustrating trends, for example, bar graphs traditionally are the best means to convey the point. Pie charts show how something is *divided*. Tables use lists of names, numbers, and percentages. Flow charts and continuums depict the sequence of actions or events. Line graphs compare at least two things. The use of each type will be explained later in this chapter.

A few words about overall design principles:

The computer's word-processing programs have provided users with the widest choices of type fonts and sizes, but few except graphic designers know much about readability. White print on a color field (a "reverse") not only is difficult to read in 12-point type or less, but colored ink fills in the white lettering; use 14-point or more.

As has been emphasized in the chapter about the paper's mechanics, typography experts point out that fonts with serifs (those decorative bits and "beaks" at the end of letter stems) are the best for readability in *text* and *numbers* in tables. The stripped-down "sans-serif" fonts are best for *titles*. Script or gothic fonts are not recommended for academic papers because the former is frilly and the latter is unreadable.

All-capital titles are also difficult to read if the line of type is lengthy. Too, borders for term papers should not be decorative, no matter how tempting the typographic choices. Incidentally, the trend for borders is .35% of a 1-point rule. The trend for space around text set inside boxes is at *least* 6 points.

Some colors such as yellow or orange should never be used because they're "hard to look at" and often fade into the white background. By the way, anyone who recognizes black can be "faded" into degrees of gray—100%-10%—can come up with "color" even with a black-and-white illustration. The portfolio demonstrates that point.

Whichever kind of illustration you're going to do, clarity to the ordinary reader should be the overriding rule in its design. One of the greatest flaws of charts, for instance, is that they attract "junk," perhaps because designers operate *outside* the rigid rules of, say, tables or maps.

Chart junk is defined as any non-essential element that clutters the thrust of the illustration. The antidote is to ask yourself if you're trying to cram more than *one* point into the piece. If you are, make a *second* illustration. Fancy borders are also distracting from the content; there's nothing wrong with a 1-point border.

Last, before proceeding, ask your instructor what's wanted. For example, fields such as mathematics and education have specific guidelines for graphic presentations of ordinates and abscissas. Other disciplines may rule out more than four lines in a graph or even color. Many instructors have seen so many distracting charts and misleading diagrams that they dictate the styles.

Materials

Even if you're producing computerized illustrations, the instructor may require a different paper stock from that used for the text. Blue-gridded graphing stock, for example. If you're using pen and ink, ensure the illustration can be photocopied because some graphing paper doesn't produce lines in black and white.

In hand-drawn illustrations, tips abound from decades of bitter experience. For instance, pencil in preliminary sketches *before* applying ink. Erase the penciling with an art gum after the ink has dried. Black India ink and a set of mapping pens provide an array of line widths. Felt-tip pens are good only for *filling in* large areas within boundaries set by a mapping pen. Circular illustrations for chain-of-command and flow charts need a compass for diametric consistency. Metal rulers work best for straight-edge drawing, providing the inked line has dried.

Whether hand-drawn or computerized, fold-out illustrations should be 8.5 inches from top to bottom, but can be of *any* width so long as the paper can be folded into the rest of the project. Thesis and dissertation writers should be aware that the bookbindery's trimmer knives could slice illustrations in two at the right-hand side of the manuscript if the foldout is not tucked well inside the text pages.

Placement

Put each illustration as close as possible to its text reference, a luxury that books don't always have. The reference must be clear and allude either to a variation on "*above*" or "*below*." If it's several pages behind the illustration or several ahead, use the page or "*figure*" number. The assumption is that you've done a few drafts of the paper so you know on which page the illustration appears.

If the illustration is small, put it on the same page where it's cited. If it's large, give it full-page treatment on the next page. Reference it this way:

> The usual cycle of turnover (Figure 10, page 18) is begun when the employee decides the job has no future.

If you reference the illustration elsewhere, use the same form of citation. Help the reader find the material with ease.

At a few schools, students are allowed to place illustrations directly *across* from the page where they are mentioned. Because term papers and other scholarly papers are printed on only one side of the paper and this treatment means a reader will be confronted by a blank page (with the illustration on the back), indicate what's afoot by placing a centered message in the middle of the blank page, like this:

Figure 20
Comparison of Annual Returns
For S & P 500 Stocks and Real Estate Properties
(Facing Page)

Numbering

Number illustrations *consecutively*. Tables require Roman numerals, but *all other* illustrations are marked "*Figure 1*," and so on. Capitalize the *F* in *Figure*. If you use more than six illustrations, set up a page for a "List of Tables" or a "List of Illustrations" to follow the title page or table of contents. (See pp. 225–26.)

Page numbering follows a common-sense rule: Put it where you've numbered the rest of the pages in the report.

If you've grouped the illustrations in an appendix, the pages should be numbered with *small* Roman numerals, centered, at the bottom.

Titles

An illustration's title must explain clearly and briefly, like a newspaper headline, what the material covers. It's placed *above* a table, but *below* any other illustration.

Titles for tables generally are centered and in all capital letters. If you're using both capital and small letters, however, capitalize the *first* letter of each word except the articles (*a, an, the*) and short prepositions and conjunctions.

Titles for all other kinds of illustrations also are centered and capitals and small letters are used, again with no capitalization for the types of words listed above.

Neither tables nor figures use periods at the ends of titles, but they do follow punctuation usage elsewhere. A period *follows* the figure or table number:

Figure 10. Performance of "Seminar Fund," 1934-76,
Initial Investment $250, Adding $100 per Month

TABLE XII. PERCENTAGE YIELD NEEDED
TO MAINTAIN PURCHASING POWER

As shown, all titles are single-spaced and centered. If you're using fold-out illustrations, titles still must be centered with regard to the total width of the page.

Avoid long titles because they detract from illustrations. If headline writers can boil long stories into a few pithy words, so can you. Don't repeat material word for word from the text of the report. And don't use obvious expressions such as "This table shows ..." or "This is a drawing of ..." Readers recognize the obvious.

Spacing and Margins

Spacing is shown in the sample pages (pp. 227–28). Margins must leave room for binding on the left-hand side of any paper. If you plan to use a vertical illustration, leave room at the *top* for the binding area. Don't run the risk of a missing title. In tabulations, space once between *every five or ten* figures. The result is easier for a reader to follow and looks inviting.

Footnotes, Figures, Asterisks, and Daggers

It's academically honest to credit sources if the illustrated material has been based on other people's work. However, if *you've* taken a poll, or originated the work, you'll not need footnotes for the citations.

Basically, the rules for footnotes in term papers apply with illustrations. Put the original citation at the *end* of the title, and the matching footnote at the *bottom* of the page (see pp. 227–28). If the illustration is full of numbers and numbered footnotes prove confusing, use asterisks or daggers (doubling or tripling them, as needed).

Figures

The word "*Figure*" and its abbreviation "*Fig.*" are essential reference designators for illustrations in a term paper or graduate writing project. That's because they either might *not* be on the same page as the text reference or because they distinguish one illustration from another if *more than one* appears on a page. Preferred use is to spell out "*Figure.*"

Asterisks, daggers, and other seemingly odd symbols are "rank" markers generally found in tables of numbers that must be distinguished from each other. The classic rank order is: 1) asterisk (*); 2) dagger (‡); 3) double dagger (‡‡); section mark (§); parallels (ll); and number sign (#).

Types of Illustrations

This section of the chapter has been arranged so that the major type of illustration is *first* described—along with design dos and don'ts—all followed by a portfolio of examples.

Let's begin with charts—and their chief varieties.

On the whole, charts provide the most creative and numerous illustration designs, as is shown in the portfolio. They contain the major geometrical figures—rectangles, squares, diamonds, circles—as well as thin or thick lines with patterns and shadings ("gradients"). Or arrows, as in the "fishbone." Or three-dimensional figures. Plus a wide array of fonts. Yet such creative freedom also has made this kind of illustration the worst offender in design because of chart junk, unreadable fonts, confusing arrangements, and using more than one point.

Charts: Flow and Organization

Flow charts show a series of steps, phases, cycles—or bottlenecks. Arrows move the reader's eye to and from those geometrical shapes to grasp the flow at a glance.

The flow chart in the portfolio (p. 265) was designed to show supporters of a night-school program what optional actions to take for a school board's "yes" or "no" decisions about each step of their plan. One option involved funding; another, a tryout at a Catholic school. For optimal clarity to readers, the chart also included a key explaining that ovals represented the project's start and finish; diamonds, the board's decisions; and rectangles, the actions to either "yes" or "no" responses.

Perhaps the most familiar kind of flow chart depicts an organization's chain of command (p. 266). Resembling a family tree, the structure shows who reports to whom and the responsibilities of each officer. Given the trend away from looking like autocratic rulers, many leaders prefer the new design. It tips the structure on its side: The boss is positioned at the left with connective links to secondary and tertiary leaders flowing to the right.

Another flow chart, hugely popular at conferences, shows cause-and-effect via a circular structure. Arrows direct readers around a series of smaller circles containing the text. However, a major challenge to designers is boiling text to fit each circle while retaining readability. The major challenge to readers is dealing with small type and trying to remember each circle's content at the finish.

Aside from the point made above about elements to avoid in creating *any* kind of flow chart, whether the movement is vertical or horizontal, clarity must be the first priority in design.

Charts: Continuum

A first-cousin to a "timeline" or schedule, the continuum chart generally marks *progressive* steps of a process—ecological damage and solving crime to product development and military tactics. Filmmaking is depicted on p. 265. In the sciences, for example, continuum markers start with observation, then asking questions, followed by naming and classifying natural objects, using resources, recording the data, rational conclusions, and writing the results. A continuum also can show intangibles such as political, social, and economic values and attitudes, all ranging from the left side of the spectrum to the right.

A continuum chart almost demands a horizontal line with hash marks at significant points between left and right sides. Some lines have a single arrowhead pointing right if it's a journey. Others have arrowheads on both ends of the spectrum if something is being measured that's static. To design a continuum means first listing the main points to be hung on that line. Color gradients on wide lines depict stages by dark-to-light routes.

Charts: Fishbone

A look at the illustration on p. 266 shows why this chart is called a "fishbone." Some designers even trim it with fish head and tail. Its origins come from industry's "quality-circle" (QC) system of the 1980s whereby each employee unit targeted and eliminated production glitches. The design is an offshoot of flow charts and depicts cause and effect. The layout indicates sticking points to be solved and specifics to keep the focus from being global or vague.

The challenge of a fishbone is determining those specifics. Many fields with QC histories have predetermined categories so that their subsets can be ranked for remedial action. For example, manufacturing bottlenecks are sorted by categories of machines, employees, materials, measurements, and methods. Service industry categories are split into customers, employees, environment, and supplies. The fishbone illustration concerning a major overhaul of how a required math course should be taught included problems within categories of class size, curriculum, labs, students, teaching, and textbooks.

Once the chief categories are determined, the design challenge is to resist packing the "spine" with *minor* factors lest it look overwhelming to a viewer. The clue that condensing is necessary generally comes when the subsets have to be set in type below 10-point size if all factors are to be squeezed in.

Charts: Bars and Double Bars

Bar charts are considered to be the simplest and the most easily understood illustration and, thus perhaps the most effective of them all in instantly translating complex data to readers. Horizontal or vertical lines are used to make comparisons, as is shown on p. 266 with examples of single, three-dimensional bar and double bar charts.

The bars are of equal width and positioned as close as possible to numerical levels reported in data. Bars can be distinguished by making one wider than the other or by using color gradients or crosshatching. Footnotes should be within the unobtrusive 6-to-8-point range. To save space on numbers, the traditional practice is to boil them to four or less digits with a parentheses stating that figures are set in "ooo's" (or thousands, millions, billions, trillions).

A major caveat is not to have *too many* bars lest readers have difficulties sorting out, say, which schools have the highest math scores, which car requires the fewest repairs, or which gender earns the highest annual income. Another is to ensure the bar ends at the *exact spot* if it's between interval numbers.

Charts: Histogram

The histogram's distinguishing visual feature—aside from resembling a city skyline—is that it places bars in *close* proximity, unless an interval is a statistical blank. The bar heights match frequency numbers at the left side of the illustration (the "*y-axis*"). Their bases are placed on a horizontal line (the "*x-axis*") which marks key intervals, as is shown on p. 268 with the six kinds of imagery that poet John Milton used in "Paradise Lost."

Graphically, the frequency numbers are set a tad higher than the bar's maximum height on the vertical scale at the left. Again, the design challenge is to ensure the bar ends at the exact spot stipulated by the data when it falls between interval numbers.

Charts: Gantt

One chart is named for the time-motion pioneer Henry L. Gantt whose studies of textile workers' performances in the early 1900s led to a still-popular measurement of task performances. A Gantt software program is a best-seller. As the illustration on p. 268 shows, today's version of his "stop-watch" system enables firms to plot timelines of estimated and actual project completion times and, thereby, the ability to calculate costs of each step.[28]

The temptation is to make a "Gantt" so full of arrows and symbols for starting, stopping, and continuing that interpretation of results may require more than one look. The solution is to keep it unadorned as you devise timelines for estimating steps either for a quick task or of a long-term project—fund raisers and beach cleanups to staging conventions. Color helps, but gradients of black are just as effective in showing the start-stop patterns of staff members.

Charts: Pie

Pie charts are familiar to anyone who's learned how to divide and knows the total value of the pie is 100%. Today, they're often three-dimensional figures and sometimes a large slice is pulled just outside the pie. Size is critical and requires precision. If a slice is labeled 43%, it can't equal the 50% slice.

---

[28] Robert Kanigel, "Taylor-Made. (19th-Century Efficiency Expert Frederick Taylor)," The Sciences, May 1997, v. 37,i 3, pl 8(1), 4, http://216.239.53.104/search?q=cache:uaC2LfOL1XEJ:www.ams.sunysb.edu/~weinig/Taylor-made.pdf+Gantt+%2B+Gilbreth+%2B+%22driver%22&hl=en&ie=UTF-8 (April 21, 2004); David Warburton, "Beyond the Gantt Chart: New Methods for Measuring Product Development." *Medical Device & Diagnostic Industry,* January 2003, http://www.devicelink.com/mddi/archive/03/01/014.html (April 21, 2004).

The designer rule is *never to use more than eight slices* because that causes difficulties in labeling and reader comprehension. This problem is still solved either by enlarging the pie or running lines ("rules") from the minuscule pieces to "outside" space for the percentages.

Pies can have white letters on a colored field (a "reverse"), as is shown on p. 269). Or they can be designed with gradient shadings or crosshatches. However, labels should be in at least 14-point boldface to prevent ink "fill-in."

Graphs: Line

A graph's function is to show the comparison of at least *two* things. Unlike a bar chart, the lines may cross. In this respect, they are far easier for readers to understand than a histogram.

Graphs predict trends or one factor's impact (or none) on another, as is shown in an election-campaign graph on p. 270. That line travels along the x-axis at heights pegged at numerical frequencies on the y-axis. Other line graphs may have lines crossing *each other* as, for example, when the designer wants to show annual comparisons of figures or the ups and downs of a politician's career.

The singular danger again is that the line(s) may not be "true" to the numbers *between* intervals that aren't shown on the y-axis. To correct that flaw, download a draft and use a ruler to pencil in a line from the y-axis to check the height of the line (or dot if you're "capping" the line).

To distinguish one line from another without using color involves thickening a "rule" from 1 to 2-point weight. The example's comparison of supporters for 2004's four presidential candidates used a 2-point rule, dots, and broken lines.

Graphs: Frequency

The "cumulative frequency" graph is closely related to the line graph in rises and falls. But its function is to show numbers of people, views, events, or objects that are measured against *how frequently* they fit categories listed on the x-axis.

Unlike line drawings, frequency graphs represent only *one* measurement with (or without) dots marking the frequencies. (See example on p. 270.) Because frequency graphs are uncluttered illustrations, most people instantly grasp their results. You certainly should with that example and may appreciate the great amount of overtime that composition instructors devote to helping students write—particularly the 27% who spent at least 16 to 25 extra hours per month correcting compositions. Few other disciplines outside of athletics and drama involve such investment of time.[29]

However, the frequency graph has that same drawback of pegging numbers between intervals. Use a ruler to be precise with the line.

Tables

A sample page for a list of tables is shown on page 225.

A table should present only one fact or a series of *related* facts so that it's easy to understand.

---

[29] Barbara G. Ellis, "Major Inhibitory Factors in the Assessment of Themes by Oregon High School English Teachers," (doctoral dissertation, Oregon State University, 1990), 293.

Put the title in capital letters and *above* the table. The number should be in *Roman numerals*.

Once you move into tabulated material, you'll need to use capital and small letters for columnar titles. Such titles should include only *one* word (two if they're small) per line. Use either boldface or regular weights.

Single-space them and either *center* each line or *align* all lines at the *left-hand side* of the column. Capitalize the *first* letter of the *first* word, but don't use any other capitalization. If you're numbering the columns, center the numbers and enclose them in parentheses, like this:

Number	**Number**
of	**of**
positive	**negative**
responses	**responses**
(3)	**(4)**

Tabulated numbers must be aligned at the *right*. Put decimal points or commas directly *under* each other so readers can keep track of the statistics.

If you're using a dollar sign, put it only *before* the *first* figure at the *top* of the column and then *before* the *last* figure when you give the totals. Temperature-degree and percentage marks are used only *after* the *first* figure:

MDRT Amount	**% to last year**	**Temperature for July 9**
$3,330.00	138%	103°
2,935.00	172	98
300.00	29	88
928.00	75	110
1,148.00	100	49
$8,641.00		

Suppose a figure is unknown in one of the tabulated columns? A source may not include one for a certain period. Use either a blank space or dots, *never zeros*; they will confuse. Sometimes many unknowns are involved. Use horizontal lines to prevent misunderstanding.

Generally, horizontal lines are limited to the *top* of a column for headings and the *bottom* for conclusions or totals. Horizontal or vertical lines within columns make the formidable appearance of tables even more forbidding. White space—called "*air*" by designers—makes a table look inviting.

Double horizontal lines are a graphic device for fencing off data. Single lines distinguish headings and statistics. The table above illustrates one of the various possibilities.

If you're working with a lot of digits—millions, billions, etc.—and they can be rounded off, save time and wear on the "0" key by indicating under the table's title that the figures are given in millions, billions, etc.:

TABLE V. SALES BY AGENCY
INDIVIDUAL LIFE INSURANCE TOTALS
(in billions)

If you need more than one page to complete a table, use the "continued" format. On subsequent pages, repeat column titles on top of the table, using the same form for single and double horizontal lines. If data requires a repetition of subtitles from a left-hand column, they'll have to be repeated too. This technique avoids the inconvenience of having to turn back to the first page of a table to find the subtitles.

Use either the short or long form for continuing a title on subsequent pages:

**TABLE III. SOME EFFECTS OF THE TELETYPESETTER
ON THE NEWSPAPER (Continued)**

TABLE III. (Continued)

A warning on both figures and tables: Ensure that data is accurate. Use a calculator to check math totals. Your instructor just might see if the figures are correct. Proofread statistics to catch any omissions or transpositions as you move data from your notes to the finished term-paper page. Sometimes students have worked with data for so long they can't see errors. Check and double-check. Your instructor might find your paper flawless—except for a single careless error in data entry or illustrations.

Maps

Maps should be confined to the *essentials,* whether hand-drawn or copied from the Internet—either by HCP or a pasted download. Make sure, therefore, you don't take up space with a map of the United States if you are making a point about an Arkansas village.

Some of the mapping offerings by Yahoo or MapQuest or Topographic target a specific street address and even offer aerial photographs of it. Thanks to zoom lenses, cities such as Portland, Oregon have aerial maps that seem to be only a few feet above rooftops and bushes.

On hand-drawn maps, don't add places *not* mentioned in your term paper. That's the equivalent of chart junk and will confuse your teacher. Again, mark maps with solid or dotted lines and arrows to convey the point(s) you're making, particularly if they involve military or naval operations such as is shown on p. 271.

Unless you've done some original mapping, all of those you've used must include a footnote and bibliographic entry about sources.

A Final Word About Term Papers

Getting a grade of "A" on a term paper requires substantial content that displays your research abilities and the ability to report the results. But the writing that presents that material—bare-boned or expansive—should be clear, cogent, and polished. The best way to determine whether it is, still requires *reading the text aloud*—punctuation and all.

True, it takes time for this final touch, but considering the thought, time and effort you'll have invested in the paper, it's well worth doing. You'll pick off grammatical and punctuation errors, incomplete sentences, misspellings, as well as confusion, repetition, perhaps a bad case of the "howevers," plus citation bobbles and more.

When you finish reading and doing damage control—possibly a fifth or sixth draft—give yourself permission to say: "That's the *best* thing I've ever written." It probably will be. As someone once said: "You must learn how to give yourself applause, because your audience never goes away." When your final draft emerges from the printer, know that completing a term paper is well worth applause. Lots of it.

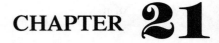

A PORTFOLIO
OF
SAMPLE ILLUSTRATIONS

Charts

Flow

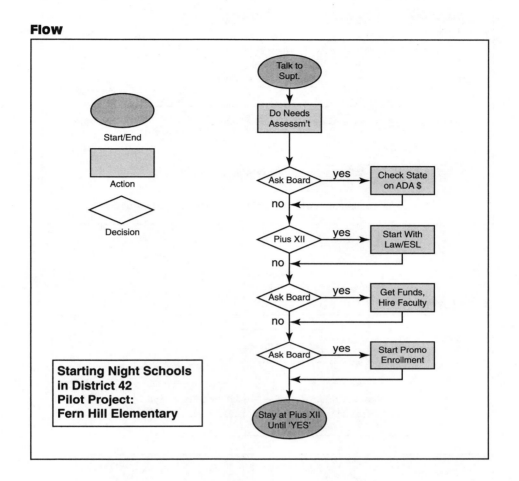

Continuum Chart

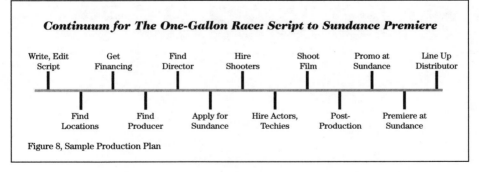

Fishbone

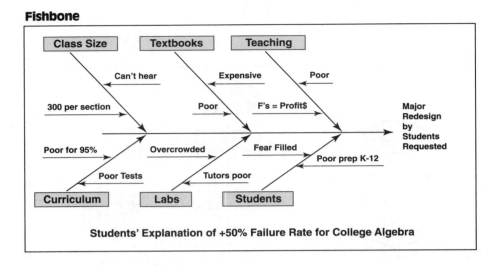

Students' Explanation of +50% Failure Rate for College Algebra

Organization

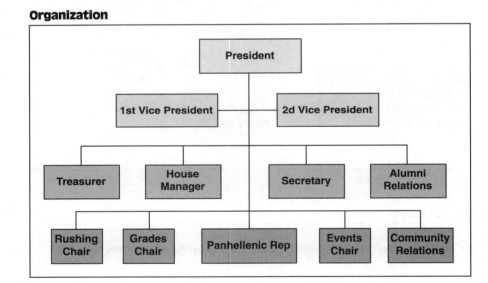

Double Bar

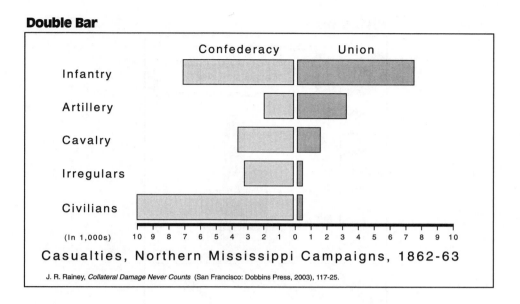

Confederacy   Union

Infantry

Artillery

Cavalry

Irregulars

Civilians

(In 1,000s) 10 9 8 7 6 5 4 3 2 1 0 1 2 3 4 5 6 7 8 9 10

Casualties, Northern Mississippi Campaigns, 1862-63

J. R. Rainey, *Collateral Damage Never Counts* (San Francisco: Dobbins Press, 2003), 117-25.

3-Dimensional Bar

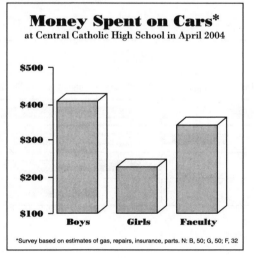

Money Spent on Cars*
at Central Catholic High School in April 2004

$500

$400

$300

$200

$100

Boys   Girls   Faculty

*Survey based on estimates of gas, repairs, insurance, parts. N: B, 50; G, 50; F, 32

Histogram

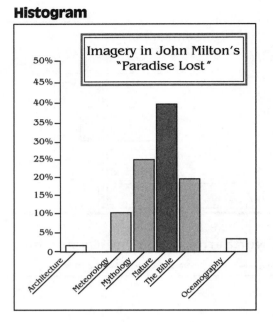

Imagery in John Milton's
"Paradise Lost"

Gantt

DISTRICTS	TIME					
	Sept./Oct.	January	March-May	June-August	September	October
DIST. 49						
DIST. 42						
DIST. 44						
DIST. 45						

Legend

 Canvassing

Idle

Pie

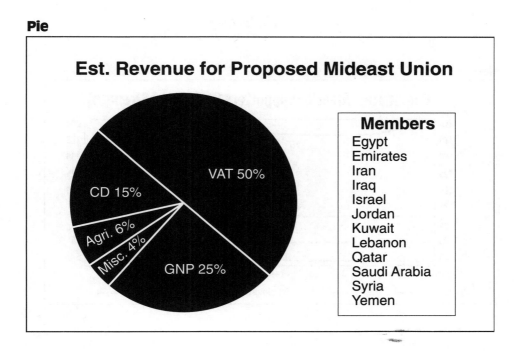

Graphs

Line

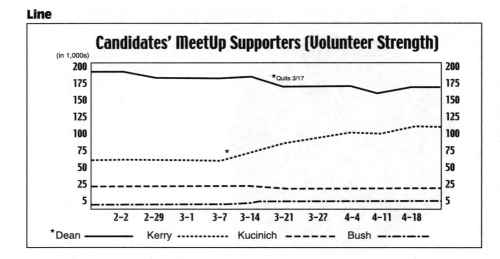

Frequency

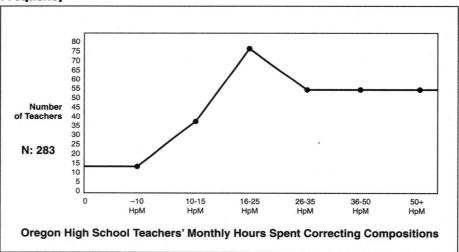

Maps

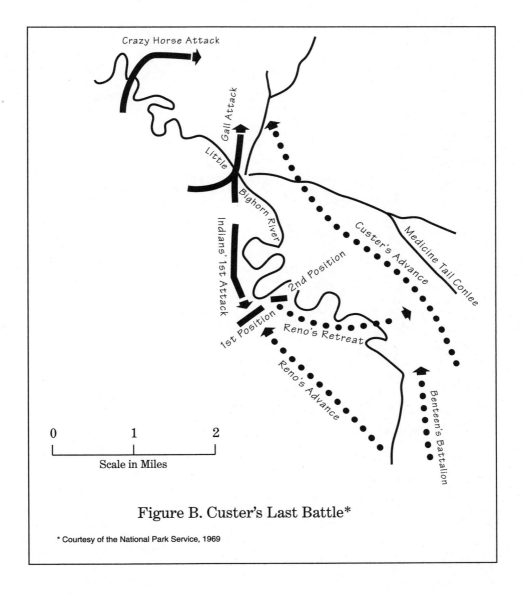

Figure B. Custer's Last Battle*

* Courtesy of the National Park Service, 1969

COLLEGE ADMISSION ESSAYS

CHAPTER 22

THE COLLEGE ADMISSION ESSAY

No matter what college admissions officials call them—personal essays, personal statements, insight résumés™—most except open-enrollment schools demand a personality sketch behind the documents submitted for entrance.

No one has to tell you how crucial this essay is to enter the 193 prestigious private institutions now sharing a common application and five choices of essay topics (250–500 words). But essays are just as critical at all other private *and* public colleges and universities. All but the most endowed face colossal budget shortfalls, so they're looking for students with drive and discipline who will stick with a school until graduation.[30]

If you're a transfer student, you're *still* going to have to write another admissions essay. You're probably well aware that today's admission staffs are separating out "stickers" from what are called "institutional tramps." The "stickers" are serious students who buckle down to college life and "make satisfactory progress to a degree,"often in four years. The latter are trying to "find themselves" or are majoring in social life and taking up classroom space and a professor's time.

A college has your transcripts and test scores in both cases. If you're a late bloomer or a vagabond, the admissions essay gives you the opportunity to show you've changed your attitudes in the last few months; you're ready to "stick" and develop the discipline to earn that degree.

---

[30]Common Application to 193 Private U.S. Colleges and Universities. 2003-2004. Harvard University, Cambridge, MA; http://www.admissions.college.harvard.edu/prospective/tools/download/HarvTsfrSupp.pdf (April 25, 2004).

Preliminaries

Whether you're a transfer student or high school junior or senior, the first rule of essay writing is to use the Internet to go *beyond* the college's home page with its glowing promotion, mission statement, and catalog data. Most high school applicants are unaware that the site *also* carries the schedule of classes, perhaps the most revealing portrait about an institution.

Another benefit of booting up the class schedule is getting instructors' names so you can begin networking that will lead to a campus visit. Investing a day attending classes will furnish you with specific examples of why you do (or don't) want to attend the school. Faculty welcome visits. Also your writing later that "Dr. Anna Berliner advised me to..." sets you apart from competitors as one who's gone to some lengths to investigate not just a college, but a major. It says "retention" to admission officials and to department chairs who see you're serious about being a major. They'll support your admission enthusiastically because departmental survival depends upon numbers of majors and graduation rates.

The admissions essay is terrifying only if you're not ready to go *immediately* from high school to college. If you *are* ready, you'll have done plenty of research and be applying at schools fitting your interests and personality—not because family or friends want you to or because it's a "name" school. If you have the passion and ability to be an engineer, don't waste your time (and an admissions officer's) applying to a college with no pathway to the limited spaces at an engineering school. That's true for *any* field—environmental sciences and graphics to teaching and computer programming. You'll also be able to use *any* experience tied to your interests in that essay. If you're aiming for law or medicine and have worked for a law firm or at a clinic, you'll have a store of anecdotes for a meaty and authentic essay about your goals and abilities in those professions.

You don't have to be a great writer to write a solid admissions essay. In fact, those focused on style and verbosity instead of substance may go down on "thinness." The University of Florida's essay instructions say: "The best personal statements are not necessarily the longest ones."[31]

Substance also means *honesty*—about your abilities, attitudes, interests, experience, strengths and weaknesses. Those afraid to be honest who *are* accepted usually are doomed to a bad fit and probably washing out.

It may ease your anxieties to know that colleges are as desperate to enroll a good fit as you are to find one. Most want "stickers" even more than diversity these days. That's why so many essay topics focus on curiosity, study habits, follow-through on efforts, why you've picked their school, or "why you believe that your unique cultural, educational and life experiences will enhance the educational experience of the freshman class."[32]

Remember, too, that most college graduates become community activists and leaders. That explains topics about leadership, problem solving, discrimination,

---

[31]Application for Admission, University of Florida. 2004. Gainesville FL,; http://www.reg.ufl.edu/pdf/freshmen-undergrad-app.pdf, p. 6 (April 28, 2004).

[32]Application for Admission, Auburn University. 2004. Auburn AL. http://www.auburn.edu/student_info/student_affairs/admissio/admissform.pdf (April 28, 2004).

and resourcefulness. Subjects about health issues and arrests are designed to test your honesty and prove positive changes are being made. (Records about both are easily obtained.) Officials want to know if these roadblocks to a bachelor's degree have been resolved.

If you've been deeply involved in only *one* activity or job or have attained significant achievements, be comforted that a straight-A average and high test scores are *not* necessarily expected. Schools want sociable, high-performing "finishers." As alumni, they usually reflect credit on their fields and colleges. Many are also far more loyal and generous to their alma maters than most "A" students, a vital factor for any college's financial survival.

What if you're a late bloomer? Your grades are marginal and you *weren't* involved in extracurricular activities? Admissions staffs take those things into consideration. They know that some students' gratitude in squeezing through closing doors can pay off in hard work, retention, and successful careers leading to million-dollar gifts to a college.

The University of Tennessee, for example, advises frantic applicants with core GPAs of less than 3.05 or SAT scores below 1040 to take advantage of the personal-statement option as an avenue of redemption:

> If your credentials fall below this range, we highly recommend that you write a Personal Statement. This statement is **optional,** but you can increase your chances of being considered for admission by writing it.[33]

One major benefit of the essay has nothing to do with getting into college. It forces you to discover your "calling" as an adult and thus removes doubts and panic. The outcome is rising self-worth, confidence and direction. One young woman told the author that whenever she wanted to cheer herself up or "get some insight on my hectic life," she wrote a résumé just to *see* her attainments and contributions.

Pre-Writing Resolutions

What if you're a "non-writer?" Don't worry. With 100 to 300-word limits, essays are not being judged for literary prizes, but for the kind of substance used in job résumés. Those require plain English, straight-shot sentences, no misspellings, and basic skills in grammar and punctuation. Computers come equipped with checking tools for the latter three essentials. This book should help you master the rest. But you have to supply the data for that writing. Right now, it's probably locked in your "memory cache" and needs some prodding to be released. That's the purpose of this section, as well as laying the groundwork for responding to the essay topics from *any* college.

We'll start with the "Pre-Writing Resolutions" on the following pages.

These resolutions are easy and fast to do and a quick orientation to an admissions essay. Make two copies for later use, but for now, just check the items.

---

[33]Application for Admission 2004, University of Tennessee, Knoxville TN, http://admissions.utk.edu/undergraduate/AdmissApp04.pdf, 4 (April 27, 2004).

Once you've done that, you'll know a lot about the essay's purpose, content, and organization even *before* you start. That's half the battle.

You'll then be ready for the next section on organizing the content and writing any kind of admissions essay, whether it's the new insight résumé or the traditional "blue-sky" instruction: "Please write and attach an essay of your personal goals and educational objectives and why you have elected to continue your studies at...."[34]

Checklist of Pre-Writing Resolutions

> **Before you begin to write the admissions essay, make two copies of this checklist. Check the boxes *right now* on these pages. The resolutions will make you aware of content requirements and dos/don'ts, as well as prepare you for the writing helps in the pages that follow.**
>
> **Check the second copy *after* your first draft. Check the third copy just before the *final* draft.**
>
> **Just in doing the first run-through, you'll sharpen your self-perceptions, attitudes, and goals. You'll find a college that's an excellent fit for you and/or whether you'd like to take some time off between high school before tackling the demands of 12 to 16 credits per term for four or five years.**

Preliminaries

- I will not put out effort on an essay for a college I don't want to attend. ☐

- I will use the Internet to surf the "Schedule of Classes" of a college I like and cross off every major I've no interest in until I find two fields I like. ☐

- I will check out the department of those two fields to see: a) how many credits are required for a major; b) required minors and credits; c) use that data in showing genuine interest in that school. ☐

- I will *call* (not e-mail) the chair of my department choice to: a) introduce myself as a prospective major; and b) ask about the range of internships and job placements so that my essay will reference both the chair's name and a specific career resulting from that major. ☐

- I will be willing to pour everything into the first draft—oversights, errors, and all—so that I have something to work with. ☐

- I will download each draft, read it aloud, and "hard-edit" as if I were a weary Admissions reader tackling the fiftieth essay of the day. ☐

---

[34]Application, 2004, Augsburg College, Minneapolis MN, 1; http://www.augsburg.edu/irb/forms.html (April 29, 2004).

Tone

- I will resist the temptation to be: a comedian, contemptuous, contentious, defiant, dogmatic, fawning, grandoise, maudlin, officious, snide, snobbish, unrealistic—or excessively modest. ☐

- I will be positive and avoid being critical, cynical, or gloomy. ☐

Diction

- I will not waste word limits on terms such as *"however/moreover,"* *"also,"* *"very,"* *"really"* or expressions such as *"I think/believe/feel."* ☐

- I will not waste words: a) repeating the topic, or b) repeating most achievements and data included in records I submitted to the college. ☐

- I will limit the number of *"I/me/my's"* and *"when's"* by recasting sentences. ☐

- I will find smoother and less obvious transitional words than *"meanwhile"* and *"next"* as I segue from one area to another. ☐

- I will not use teen jargon/slang, nor fad or tired expressions and current buzz words such as *"communication strengths,"* *"building trusting relationships,"* *"family of origin,"* *"identify with,"* *"absent the…,"* *"uptick,"* *"spike,"* etc. ☐

- I will remember that some readers despise one-word sentences or those starting with *"And,"* *"Yet,"* and *"But."* ☐

- I will re-read this book's section on clichés, bromides, and sweeping generalities (pp. 74–80) to ensure I don't use them. ☐

Content

- I will remember that the Admissions staff wants to know about my: a) retention until graduation; b) study discipline; c) intellectual curiosity; d) researching potential; e) problem-solving abilities; f) leadership/teamwork abilities; g) attitudes; h) community involvement; and i) away-from-home behavior. ☐

- I will download the application's section on essay topics to make sure I understand them *all*—from directions and word limits to the subject's thrust (what they want to know about me). ☐

- I will spot the telltale words *"or"* and *"and"* in topics with suggested approaches to avoid writing about six instead of one. ☐

- I will not be so overawed by the author of a quotation that I fail to understand the quote. ☐

- I will remember that quotes are open to several viewpoints. ☐

- I will fill the essay with *specific* examples for all topics. ☐

- I will do a one-word list of factors to be covered and match each with a one-word example to jog my memory. ☐

- I will resist the temptation to do a laundry list of accomplishments in and outside school and, instead, use only one or two exemplifying the topic. ☐

- I will not lay out false or unrealistic goals, but use those based on what I've learned about the department's career services. ☐

- I will be able to give three reasons for wanting to enroll at that particular school because I will have researched a major and minors, classes, faculty, and job placements. And I will be honest about preferences for large or small schools, location, and finances. ☐

- I will remember that sticking to an after-school job demonstrates, persistence, maturity, responsibility, and retention. ☐

- I will remember that in-depth effort in one or two extracurricular activities speaks far louder than a thin membership in two dozen. ☐

- I will point out examples of my being a team member as well as a leader. ☐

- I will remember to include an example of my efforts to correct a weakness that can hobble me in college. ☐

- I will remember that family or health crises or a job may have kept me from extracurricular activities. ☐

- I will read a current book(s) tied to my probable major to enable me to respond to topics about reading interests. ☐

- I will resist the temptation to waffle responses on controversial topics by stating my position and indicating respect for opposite views. ☐

- I will remember in topics asking about things, events, or people inspiring me that the major ones have been done to death. I can include simple things, unspectacular events, and ordinary people. ☐

Structure

- I will resist the temptation to do a chronological "lifeline," and instead, start with a major attainment and follow it with key events feeding into it. ☐

- I will write each factor and each example of Post-its and then lay them out in logical order—a simple and easy organizational method. ☐

- I will remember that Admissions readers, like those at publishing houses, pay attention only to the first three to five words. So my first words must be a "stopper" example, illustrating the topic's goal, value, or attitude. ☐

- I will present an example first and then point up its purpose throughout. ☐

- I will start sentences with a *subject* instead of the object of that subject. ☐

- I will close with a brief sentence alluding to how all the foregoing material has ended the K-12 phase of my life and will underpin the college phase. ☐

Polishing the Next-to-Final Draft

- I will enlarge the type to 18 point to pick off errors in spacing, commas and periods, paragraphs, and in copying/pasting shifts. Return the type size to 12 point. ☐

- I will read the essay aloud from the screen. ☐

- I will use both the spelling- and grammar-check tools, remembering that two-letter words are passed over, but that grammatical errors and passive-voice sentence structure will be pointed out. ☐

- I will run the Flesch reading ease test off the grammar-check (see pp. 138–39) to ensure that the scores meet the levels of the Admissions readers. ☐

- I will download and circle *all* sentences to ensure a variety of lengths. ☐

- I will read the essay aloud for the last time. ☐

The Changing Essay

Three decades ago, applicants were usually instructed to "tell us something about yourself." The applicant had no guidelines and no word limits in what was a "blue-sky" essay. Colleges got personal statements as lengthy as a *New Yorker* magazine profile. Yet a Wesleyan University admissions dean defended this essay form. He said it told more about applicants than "we can gather from all the scores, recommendations, and references put forward in their behalf."[35]

Nevertheless, with an acceptance rate of around 30% and, say, room for only 600 freshmen in that sought-after Connecticut school, many readers had to be hired to process hundreds of such hefty tomes. Thousand of colleges faced the same situation. Even when admissions offices began setting word limits, bleary-eyed staffers often may have read nearly 100 essays per day. Worse, some schools quietly stopped reading the essays. Open-enrollment institutions then and now rarely require them.

Readers' complaints mounted about essay content. They detected ghostwriters, plagiarists, shy students passing themselves off as movers and shakers, party types posing as Trappist monks. The selfish became the selfless serving Thanksgiving dinners to the homeless or vowed they planned to join the Peace Corps in Gambia after graduation.[36]

---

[35]John C. Hoy, "The Candidate Speaks for Himself," *The Journal of the Association of College Admissions Counselors*. 12, No. 3.

[36]Maleah Harrids (public service officer, Admissions Office, Oregon State University), in discussion with author, October 14, 2003: Michele Sandlin (director of admissions, Oregon State University), in discussion with author, October 14, 2003.

The mounting payroll for readers, the reading volume, and unreliability as predictors of graduation all began to change the essay.

Some admissions directors set 500-word limits. Others ended puffery and vagueness by specifying applicants write about goals, values, influential people or events, strengths/weaknesses, qualities such as leadership, creativity, reasons for selecting a school, sociability, possible contribution to the institution or communities. Even then, a read still was so daunting that readers became as exacting as their tough counterparts at publishing houses. If the first five words had no substance or sparkle, the application was rejected.

Something drastic had to be done, particularly at large public universities where budget shortfalls were bringing suggestions of "capping" enrollments. Schools with open enrollments soon may be forced to toughen standards and institute an essay.

The solution might well be an assessment study developed by Dr. William Sedlacek at the University of Maryland. His research showed that eight questions cut the reader payroll and reading time and are now proving to be excellent predictors of student success and retention until graduation.

Dr. Sedlacek's approach is now used at Maryland, the State University of New York, The Ohio State University, Oregon State University, the University of Washington, and the University of Wisconsin. The list is expected to grow rapidly while hundreds of other schools still may continue using traditional and costly essay forms for the remainder of this decade.[37]

To write *any* kind of essay, read the next section on the "Sedlacek Approach" as it is used at Oregon State University because it will furnish you with help on the longer essay. You'll discover its lessons—particularly brevity—can be applied either to a specific or "blue-sky" essay, a scholarship application, or, beginning March 2005, an SAT essay.[38]

Both the Sedlacek Approach and other essays share basic dos and don'ts that are hinted at in both the Resolutions section and other parts of this book.

Basic Dos and Don'ts

The main "do" is to follow directions. If you're limited to 250–500 words or two inches of white space, don't fudge with 110 words or respond in eight-point type with tight tracking. Admissions readers will notice. If the space in the application form has seven lines and no suggestion about using a separate piece of paper, don't write "small."

Don't repeat the topic or load sentences with clutter singled out in the Resolutions section ("*I think*," "*very*," etc.)—or all those "*the's.*"

Quotations are clutter, too. The Sedlacek Approach permits no space for them, but others often are padded with them. Readers know that most quotes are lifted from Bartlett's *Familiar Quotations* or the *Oxford Dictionary of Quotations* or some "fad" sources. They're weary of Horace and Philip Massinger, Susan Sontag

---

[37]Michele Sandlin (director of admissions, Oregon State University), in discussion with author, October 14, 2003.

[38]Wendy Sleppin (project editor, Barron's Educational Series, Inc., Hauppauge, NY), in discussion with author, May 6, 2004.

and Michael Moore. As one reader said: "If I see another quote from Emerson or Bacon, I'm going to throw up."

Don't "turn" the topic from what is asked to an area in which you're more comfortable. For example, if the topic is how you responded to and learned from an incident of discrimination, don't turn it into a history of bias or a judgmental editorial. Stick to the topic.

Do understand that topic. When it's that perennial: "Please submit a personal statement regarding your academic goals and objectives," know that the difference between a goal and objective is so razor thin that footage is wasted trying to split them into *two* factors. But if you're asked to "define your *personal* goals and *educational* objectives," the difference is obvious. Split them.

Don't go blank because a topic contains a famed quotation such as:

> Mahatma Gandhi said, "We must become the change we want to see in the world." Reflect on your world and your place within it. Discuss how you have changed or plan to affect change within that world.[39]

But don't go "global" either in rolling out vast plans to fix the world in 100 words. Stick to *your* world. For instance, what if you'd like to get rid of school bullies? Or what if you'd like the school to focus on lifetime sports (tennis, golf, etc.). What steps might achieve those objectives?

Don't panic if you encounter this kind of lengthy and seemingly complex topic centering on the words "*rational*" or "*reasoning*":

> Explain a belief you accepted at some time in your life but have rejected on the basis of a rational process. Perhaps the change was initiated by something you heard or some experience you have had; but for this essay you must go beyond reporting what you heard or describing what happened to you. You must display the process of reasoning that carried you to your new belief. In your essay, be careful to explain the belief itself, reasons you had for holding it, and, most important, the rational process that led you to reject it.[40]

Even highly intelligent people often base lifetime decisions on *emotions* rather than the common sense of rational thinking, or fail to make a pro-and-con list. The topic is designed to see how *logical* you are. They've given you a "three-parter," of which only the *third* represents a challenge. All you have to do is write about a rigid belief you once held and explain how your vistas were widened by *thinking* it through rather than reacting *emotionally*. Or an experience that led to an "awakening." It could be the death penalty. Faith. Labor unions. Pre-emptive war. School uniforms. Discrimination. Cliques. Voting. Co-dependence. Workaholism. Siblings. Drafting women.

A simple test for a topic is to make a list of something that angered you. Then select one that forced you to change your thinking.

Do look for the word "*or*" in a list to avoid writing on *each* subject of the topic, as in: "Discuss some issue of personal, local, national, *or* international concern and its importance to you."[41]

---

[39]Application for Admission, University of Southern California. 2004. Los Angeles CA. http://afaweb.eds.usc.edu/USCAFA/upload•images/UGApplication0405.pdf (April 23, 2004).

[40]Application for Admission, University of Texas/Austin. 2004. http://bealonghorn.utexas.edu/bal/essays.WBX (April 28, 2004).

[41]*2003-04 Admissions Application,* Reed Collge, Portland OR., APP-4.

Don't be a showoff like this applicant:

I have consulted Aristotle and Lucretius on the true meaning of life. Is it a *sine qua non*? Nowhere have I found my own quest answered in the "Vision of God to his Universal Form" section of the *Bhagavad-Gita*. As Arjuna says at one point: "Universal Form, I see you without limit./Infinite of arms, eyes, mouths and bellies—See all the sages, and the holy serpents." This signalizes my feelings.

Equally, avoid foot-scrapings such as this:

Who am I to try to believe I might be the kind of top student your university strives to enroll? I know that the competition may well turn my efforts to molten dust. Your magnificent standards are known throughout this great land of ours. My own small intellect can only try to stay the pace expected.

Don't write in lists more suited to a yearbook's senior section. In weaving activities into prose, *two* activities are the maximum to illustrate interests and responsibility. Look at the "list" in this student's essay:

I have been in the following activities: Silver Tri my sophomore year; Blue Tri, senior; Red Cross Club, sophomore and junior, vice president my senior year; Unity Helpers, sophomore, junior and senior; the Echo newspaper, sophomore, junior and senior; the Echowan yearbook, senior; Poetry quarterly, sophomore, junior, senior; Web Designers, junior, senior; Leadership Club, junior; SAT Scholars Club, senior; National Honor Society, senior.

And the same credentials presented in readable fashion:

Because community service is important, I joined the Blue Tri organizations and Red Cross. My eventual career choice is journalism, one of the reasons I've been on the staffs of the school newspaper and yearbook for the past two years. What I learned in Leadership Club, especially about study habits, led to my being tapped for the National Honor Society this year.

Do start with a *specific* example followed by a sentence applying it to the point you're making. The idea is to seize the reader's interest in those critical first five words. Don't waste them by "backing in" or doing a lengthy run-up to the topic. In diagram form, it should look like this:

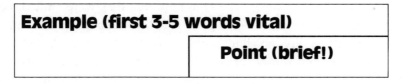

This is the reverse structure from that taught elsewhere in this book where length is *no* object. An essay can be shaped like this:

It's one thing when you're 16 to have your voice crack on a pop tune belted in the shower, but quite another on a high E in preliminaries to the Metropolitan Opera auditions. This happened despite weeks of rehearsals with a great teacher, a good voice, and cajoling the accompanist (my mother) to shift from schmaltz to Verdi. I had to accept that my minimum wage at Regal Cinema's candy counter wouldn't stretch to the expensive lessons to make the Met. This experience taught me a lot: 1) All performers have off nights; 2) fear comes when you're "carrying yourself and not the music"; 3) few 16-year-olds in Minneapolis were likely to solo on grand opera; 4) I had worked hard for something and had the courage to put my talent on the line; and 5) the ho-hum response of sister and parents was sad, but it neither discouraged nor humiliated me. Some of us have to be our own cheerleaders.

The Insight Résumé

Oregon State University is testing a new type of essay based on Dr. Sedlacek's research. Its Insight Résumé refashioned Dr. Sedlacek's eight topics into six, and set a 100-word limit for each. Their perception was that high school seniors might not be able to cope with eight subjects, especially with a 100-word limit.

Because the "IR" form is state-of-the-art and expected to be replicated around the nation—and, thus, useful for your writing any kind of admissions essay—it's used in this section. In other words, even if the school you've chosen *never* adopts this kind of form, your borrowing the IR's content-rich succinctness should impress any admissions reader struggling through stacks of wordy, vague, uninteresting, and disorganized essays.

The one element the IR forces an applicant to consider is that 100-word limit. A *visual* idea of how long a 100-word, double-spaced limit is shown below in Latin so you'll focus on the length, not the content:

Si meliora dies, ut vina, poemata reddit, scire velim, chartis pretium quotus arroget annus. Scriptor abhinc annos centum qui decidit, inter perfectos veteresque referri debet an inter vilis atque novos? Excludat iurgia finis, "Est vetus atque probus, centum qui perficit annos." Quid, qui deperiit minor uno mense vel anno, inter quos referendus erit? Veteresne poetas, an quos et praesens et postera respuat aetas? "Iste quidem veteres inter ponetur honeste, qui vel mense brevi vel toto est iunior anno." Utor permisso, caudaeque pilos ut equinae paulatim vello unum, demo etiam unum, dum cadat elusus ratione ruentis acervi, qui redit in fastos.

This is why examples must be boiled to the bone. So discard those favorite adverbs ("*really*," "*very*"), all the unnecessary "*the*'s," as well as the "*I think/feel/believe*." The foot-shuffling of "*There is/are*" into a sentence eats up words, too. But do this surgery *after*, not *before*, you've written this "mini-essay" because life-long habits take time to break. Then, hard-edit your work.

A careful reading of the topics attests to how well they were crafted, not only to a reader's rapid determination of a good match of school and student, but for flexibility and fairness through choices offered *within* the topics. Circle the word "*or*" and you'll see. The words "*examples*," "*interests*," "*things*," "*experiences*," "*projects*," "*goals*," and "*efforts*," are indicators you'll need more than *one* factor, but not more than *two*. The two must be your most *powerful* choices.

The structure of a response is to open with an example and *then* underscore the point it makes. It's the same storytelling arrangement as Aesop's fables: story first, followed by its moral in a *short* sentence. Authors of children's books and screenwriters first determine the point of the main plot. Perhaps it's redemption, revenge, conquering fear, or the seven deadly sins (pride, covetousness, lust, anger, gluttony, envy, sloth). They, then, search their imaginations for a plot illustrating that point, one that will hold the audience's attention. It should be easier for you because you *have* applicable events. The challenge is selecting choice anecdotal examples to rivet a reader's attention.

The six IR topics and their thrust are dissected below to show you how to respond. They are just as applicable to essays with 250-500 word limits. To get started, choose as your first topic one that seems to be the easiest.

Dissecting the Topics

Dissecting the IR topics will overcome your fear. Let's look at the first one:

1. Leadership/Group Contributions: Describe examples of your leadership experience in which you have significantly influenced others, helped resolve disputes, or contributed to group efforts over time. Consider responsibilities to initiatives taken in or out of school.

The IR designers recognized that if you're a gadfly or the "power behind the throne," you're probably *more* of a leader than the person elected to that position, as is seen historically with weak rulers. Equally, they knew many leaders don't need anyone in the wings.

The key word "*or*" tells you to choose *one* of three areas in or outside school in which you played either role in: 1) influencing others; 2) resolving disputes; and 3) contributing deeds or input to a group on a *long-term* basis.

The last sentence asks you to include duties of your choice. Stick to two.

This example is stripped of fanfare and descriptives:

Gadfly editorials of mine for the last two years about lowering obesity and raising interest in lifetime sports meant doing health research, selling it to the school board, the principal, and students. The result was vending machines trucked away last summer, and pizza, macaroni, fries, and pudding waddling off the lunch menu in fall. The kids forgave me because they now can choose either physical ed class or 35 documented hours of golf, tennis, bowling, jogging, swimming, skiing, or skating. Persistence, passion and graphics (showing lost revenues would be offset by buying high-carb food) all paid off.

Break the second topic in two also.

2. Knowledge in a field/creativity: Describe any of your special interests and how you have developed knowledge in these areas. Give examples of your creativity: the ability to see alternatives; take diverse perspectives; come up with many, varied, or original ideas; or willingness to try new things.

Once again, take the topic apart. Two factors lead into it: 1) describe your interests and 2) describe *how* you've learned *about* those interests. Reverse the order in your response because you'll have to describe those interests, too.

Use examples *first*. *Two* "*or*'s" in the statement tip you about *four* areas from which to draw those examples: 1) ability to see alternatives; 2) diverse perspectives; 3) at least two original ideas; and 4) trying something new.

On the critical points, sift through all your interests and select *two*.

How you learned about interests needs one example for each to lead into the subject. Pair the "how" to lead into *both* interests with an interesting anecdote. It'll conserve those 100 words and can be a variation on this kind of opening:

The doorstep tirade on the school levy was hard to take, but it was the first and best introduction to my interests in politics and taxes.

Each interest needs at least *one* example; two if you are concise.

The third topic can be dissected in the same way.

3. Dealing with adversity: Describe the most significant challenge you have faced and the steps you have taken to address this challenge. Include whether you turned to anyone in facing that challenge, the role that person played, and what you learned about yourself.

For starters, *significant* in the academic world means *huge*. Secondly, a reader scoring your response may have already read 30 essays that day on what are irreverently called "poor-pitiful-Pauline" examples. Adversities don't have to be limited to the five commonest adversities: family crises, accidents and physical disabilities, shame over not having the "right" clothes, getting fired, or police encounters.

Try the seven deadly sins. Or the four cardinal factors prompting fear and underpinning all anger: threats to pocketbook, self-esteem, ambition, and personal relationships.

On the fourth topic–community–one day at a soup kitchen won't count. Readers are looking for *months* of sustained altruism. So the sooner you get active in some outreach project, the better. That you've been too busy for community service or believe you're not wanted is understood and expected by most admissions committees, by the way. They know most teens are focused totally on survival, school, and perhaps a job.

Topic number five is a hot button for most applicants because they believe colleges will reject them if they've been guilty of *any* kind of discrimination: racial, gender, religious, sexual, physical attractiveness, or economic, artistic, and intellectual snobbery. The topic asks:

5. Handling systemic challenges: Describe your experiences facing or witnessing discrimination. Tell us how you responded and what you learned from those experiences and how they have prepared you to contribute to the OSU community.

If the college is significantly diverse, the admissions office is subtly warning applicants to understand that lack of respect for others won't be tolerated on campus. The richness of a college education comes from the discovery in class that those you fear are just as full of ideas and abilities that you bring to the classroom. However, the topic's designers knew fear of diversity and standing out from the "herd" requires monumental courage that few teenagers have yet. They're also aware of teens' narrow prism of judgmentalism and self-centeredness.

That's the reason for many colleges asking what you learned from bias experiences and how those may prepare you to deal with the *same* situation in college. So honesty about the deed *and* a show of willingness to shift attitudes *is* the best policy.

The IR designers have made this topic the easiest of the six in *both* structure and content. You're asked to describe *experiences* of bias. Limit it to two experiences, preferably on *different* forms of discrimination. Diversity, as indicated above, is *not* limited to race or gender. The first sentence requires the incidents and your role in both. Try pairing your reactions. The paired anecdotes below contain 45 words, including reaction and what was learned:

The "queens" hogged the sinks and laughed as I slunk from the lavatory. In my next class, a nerd drove me off the new computer ("G'wan to the mall!!"). I was a coward, but speaking up or standing up in high school means social death until graduation.

Don't waste the remaining words judging yourself or other participants, no matter how tempting or what relief it might bring. Admissions people are solution minded and know awareness usually leads to corrective action in those with consciences. Neither you nor they can predict your future reaction when confronted with the same situation in college. But the idea behind that topic seems to be for you to make an *unwritten* contract that your behavior, if courageous, will remain; if cowardly, that it will change.

The sixth topic may make you sigh with exasperation.

6. Goals/task commitment: Articulate the goals you have established for yourself and your efforts to accomplish these. Give at least one specific example that demonstrates your work ethic/diligence.

You've been subjected to variations of this question all your life from family, friends, teachers and preachers, employers or people at bus stops. It's the American culture's point that life is so short, it must have purpose. So teens declare they plan to go into law, medicine, or whatever they sense the audience wants to hear. Most fear failure so they drift through public schools "exploring" their options. But college will cost *someone* thousands of dollars and cost *you* time and effort. In an admissions essay, topics about goals and efforts are *not* idle questions. So if you are frightened into indecision, put off college for a year or two.

Because most people change career paths four or five times in life, declaring goals at age 18 *is* futile. But don't waste words pointing that out. Admissions staff want students to enter fields for which *they* feel passion and in which they've invested time, money, and energy. In bygone days, colleges admitted "drifters" who stayed a term or two, but today, classroom space is becoming limited to goal-oriented students. This is seen particularly in pre-enrollment for required undergraduate classes whereby, say, a chemistry class at a community college or university has a dozen sections fill up within a few minutes. Those quickest at the computer keyboard get in; the rest will have to wait for another term.

Even if you're in a quandary, boot up the school's schedule of classes and winnow out departments in which you have *no* interest for those you do. Chances are you'll probably have done *some* work in or reading about that field and *can* show evidence of interest.

Note that the topic asks for more than *one* goal and "*efforts*" toward attaining that goal. Give each goal one "effort" apiece. Again, start the sentence with an example showing efforts toward a pair of goals.

Other Essay Forms

Other essay forms can be divided into either the "blue-sky" variety ("tell us about yourself") or the specific type that may ask:

Please explain why you believe that your unique cultural, educational and life experiences will enhance the educational experience of the freshman class.[42]

Whichever essay type you encounter, substance steeped in brevity is what's wanted in today's admission essays, as noted in the IR section. Colleges now subtly demand brevity by those 250–500 word limits or small boxes asking you to write "in the space provided." Some boxes contain four to nine lines. Many have stopped offering that traditional luxury of "attach a separate sheet if necessary."

If brevity *is* a problem, re-read the IR section before beginning this one. It will help you to compress a lot of substance into a small space.

Whether you're a potential freshman or transfer student, the topics listed in personal statements are designed to determine evidence of eight factors—as well as your writing abilities:

- College Retention
- Study Habits
- Intellectual Curiosity
- Goals/Efforts
- Strengths/Weaknesses
- Community Service
- Handling Adversity
- Leadership

Transfer students usually must write an *extra* topic explaining why they're leaving one school for another, or how many applications they've submitted elsewhere—and where. Preference today is against "institutional tramps" taking classroom space that should go to freshmen. Such topics may make you angry, but they also may force you to either take a vacation from school or to get serious about earning a degree.

Much emphasis thus far has been laid on the importance of capturing the interest of admissions readers. If you don't within the first five words, other applicants certainly will. So *start* the essay with the *strongest* example of your inner drive or abilities or background to illustrate one of the eight factors. You might begin with a current situation and use flashbacks or key points about growth and interests from childhood to the present. Examples must show you as a *participant*, not a spectator.

Whether it's a "blue-sky" or specific essay, you'll still have to be organized. Leaping from aspect to aspect of your life with no connection can give readers the impression that's what you'll do in college. Stay on the subject. One essay specialist describes the organization as "Experience A demonstrates my commitment to B, which leads to experience C that drives me toward objective D."[43]

Moving from one factor to another requires the same finesse of a composer whose piece changes key (or beat) logically, effortlessly, and seamlessly.

---

[42]Application for Admission, Auburn University. 2004. Auburn AL. http://www.auburn.edu/student_info/student_affairs/admissio/admissform.pdf (April 28, 2004).

[43]EssayEdge.com. CyberEdit Network Site. 2004. http://www.essayedge.com. (April 26, 2004).

Here's that kind of organization and transit:

Being bitten by a "friendly" dog as a third grader and the rabies shots could have made me afraid of dogs. However, the veterinarian who had to put the dog down talked me into helping him do pet-safety talks in our school. I learned to love dogs and have worked as a tech for the last three years at her clinic which led to my decision to major in veterinary medicine and to open a small-animals practice when I graduate.

The Specific Essay

In the specific essay, you're usually asked to include information about goals and values, an influential person or creative work, strengths and weaknesses, accomplishments, community service, leadership, and teamwork. Whatever the topics are, the suggestions in the IR section will be of great help in writing the essay.

Other topics might be about the family or cultural impact or significant experiences. Transfers can expect to write about why they left their last college (with prompts about cost, numbers of students, location, distractions), or the difference between the last college and this one.

If the topic asks you to cover *five* points, do *five* no matter how you yearn to add a bonus point or find more than three to be painful.

The organizational example below shows how the student with veterinarian aspirations used the jot-outline (see pp. 2–6). She organized it by "book-end" structure, opening and closing with the most influential person in her life. She wove in the stipulated factors—example *first* and its point, second—on a framework of lifelong interest in veterinary medicine.

Paragraph No. 1	**Uncle Joe (prf. Boston U)—frogs—age 5**
	science start

Paragraph No. 2	**BU lab kid 8=12 Sat/Sundays**
	role mod. /infl

Paragraph No. 3	**Science fair-3 yrs.—prez Nobel Club, etc.**
	prep. BU/accomp.

Paragraph No. 4	**BU/AP (Bs)—h.s./GPA drop (2.43)**
	stren/weak

Paragraph No. 5	**NSF prize/church—GPA 3.64**
	fix/social, etc.

Paragraph No. 6	**Joe/Alzheim—neuro.med/Prof Eliott/BU**
	goals/why BU

One of the land mines most applicants perceive in specific essays—and skip if offered other options—is a topic about cultural maturity or curiosity. It asks them to explain *why* they've been inspired or "intrigued" by something in the fine arts or film, or literature, music, history, the sciences, technology, etc. You don't have to have spent a summer in Florence doing the galleries, or have studied the musical patterns of Gustav Mahler or know about stem cells or obscure writers or battles. It could be something threadbare with overuse or something simple. It's dangerous, by the way, to pretend knowledge or to select something impressive that *hasn't* inspired you.

Why not tackle that topic and honestly? What admissions officers want to know is *why* something ignited your interest, not necessarily what it was. It could be the mundane, banal, or simple. The song "Amazing Grace" or books such as *Diary of Anne Frank* can be made to carry the same impact as "in" tunes or best sellers. The next example still leads the paragraph(s), but it's the point of the anecdote that gets the most footage about a chance encounter with automotive design:

The 1935 news story about a Ford coupe said it got 130 miles per gallon (!!) in a round trip from Winnipeg to Vancouver in winter. It used a carburetor invented by Charles Pogue, a Ford engineer. That was the spark plug that sent me to Google and for the patent and to read 56 websites about how the oil business has kept car makers from using Pogue's vapor-power system. They may pay me and my friends a visit because we've been working on adapting Pogue's carburetor to the fuel-injection system in my car.

The "Blue-Sky" Essay

Essay directions without specific topics that permit a separate page may seem like freedom at last to write an open-ended, helter-skelter profile. Only fools should assume that. Instead, focus on those eight factors listed in this section—retention and intellectual curiosity to leadership and goals. The presentation also should open with a riveting anecdote such as the one below explaining strengths/weaknesses and handling adversity:

> I used to get out of shoveling snow, be the one who made my little sister cry, and do a half-baked job in every class. My dad deserting us changed all that. We moved to the projects. No snow to shovel, but plenty of rats-and-roach duty. To protect my sister after school, we camped in the library until an hour before our mom got off work. I started tutoring my sister, which led to doing my own homework. Which is how we both got on the honor roll and learned to cook.

The organization is the same as the specific essay. The illustration below has the eight factors. They can be switched and shifted as you please, though it's always wise to start with one you consider the most important. They'll furnish you with content for a fine essay. Space has been left open for you to insert those start-up anecdotes for each factor. Just make sure they seize a reader's attention.

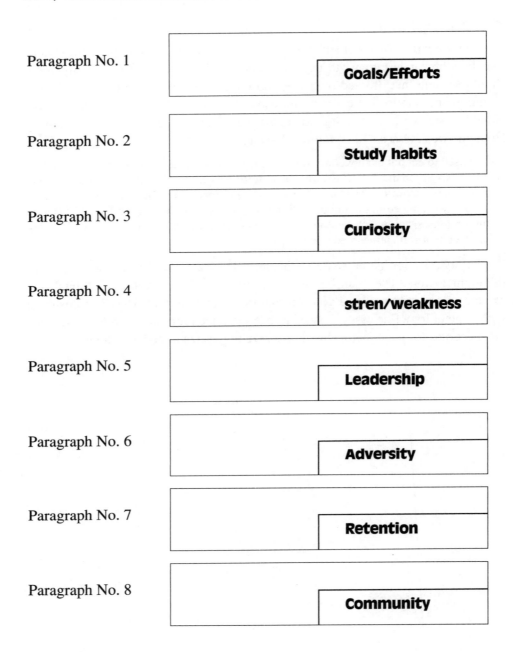

Paragraph No. 1 — **Goals/Efforts**

Paragraph No. 2 — **Study habits**

Paragraph No. 3 — **Curiosity**

Paragraph No. 4 — **stren/weakness**

Paragraph No. 5 — **Leadership**

Paragraph No. 6 — **Adversity**

Paragraph No. 7 — **Retention**

Paragraph No. 8 — **Community**

A Final Word About Essays

Much rides on the admissions essay, to be sure. It may be the deciding factor governing whether you are admitted to the college of your choice. However, don't let that frighten you from starting on the essay. Get at it now! You have everything going for you: the raw material (your life) to work with, the drive to be accepted, and, now, the knowledge about organization, tone, writing style, and moving smoothly from point to point.

In other words, if you've read this chapter carefully, you're well prepared to begin the first draft, to lay the clay on the table and pummel it into shape by editing, editing, and more editing on subsequent drafts. It's vital time and energy that will give your essay polish. Doing several drafts is not a sign of failure, but the polish given a piece of writing by professional writers. Improvement comes with each draft. Even if you believe the *last* draft is the best, edit once more and download. The essay you finally send to the college probably will be the best writing you've ever done.

APPENDICES

APPENDIX A

Internet Research Sources

All sources provide only links to *guide* you to references, books, periodicals, etc. about subjects.

WARNING: Some sources, such as the *Encyclopaedia Britannica*, require a subscriber's fee.

Search Engines

http://www.searchenginewatch.com
http://www.alltheweb.com
http://altavista.com
http://www.askjeeves.com
http://www.bartleby.com
http://bubl.ac.uk
http://dogpile.com
http://www.google.com
http://www.hotbot.com/tools
http://www.robertniles.com/data
http://whowhere.com
http://www.yahoo.com

Encyclopedias and Other References

http://www.britannica.com
http://www.xrefer.com
http://www.refdesk.com

http://www-sci.lib.uci.edu/HSG/Ref.html
http://www.ipl.org/ref/QUE/PF
http://www.economist.com/countries
http://www.cia.gov/cia/publications/factbook
http://www.mediabistro.com/resources
http://www.educationindex.com/education_resources.html
http://Columbiagazetteer.org/Main.asp?Acc=true

Conversions (weights, measures, densities, etc.)

http://www.onlineconversion.com
http://www.megaconverter.com/Mega2

Dollar Value Comparisons : 1800-2002

http://www.westegg.com/inflation

Subject Fields

Agriculture

http://usda.gov
http://www.lib.iastate.edu/collections/eresourc/agricu.html
http://www.educationindex.com/ag
http://www.lib.umich.edu/govdocs/stag.html

Arts: Dance

http://url.co.nz/arts/dance.html
http://wwar.com/categories/Dance
http://www.artslynx.org/dance

Arts: Film

http://infodome.sdsu.edu/research/guides/film.shtml
http://www.duke.edu/~kennethl/filmsite.html
http://www.artslynx.org/film
http://www.imdb.com

Arts: Fine Arts, History

http://www.culture.fr/louvre/louvrea.htm
http://thebritishmuseum.ac.uk/sitemap/sitemap.html
http://www.tate.org.uk/home/default.htm
http://www.arca.net/db/musei/uffizi.htm
http://www.metmuseum.org/collections/index.asp
http://moma.org/menu/collection.htm
http://wwar.com
http://wwar.com/categories/Artists/Masters
http://www.witcombe.sbc.edu/ARTHALinks.html
http://www.asu.edu/lib/hayden/ref/hum/art/arthist.html
http://www.artcyclopedia.com

Arts: Music

http://bubl.ac.uk/link/m/musicresearch.htm
http://bubl.ac.uk/link/c/classicalmusiclinks.htm
http://bubl.ac.uk/link/e/earlymusic.htm
http://bubl.ac.uk/link/f/folkmusic.htm
http://bubl.ac.uk/link/j/jazzmusic.htm
http://bubl.ac.uk/link/m/musicians.htm
http://bubl.ac.uk/link/w/worldmusic.htm
http://www.music.indiana.edu/music_resources/research.html
http://www.netsoundsresources.com/links/1/news/80's%20Modern%20Rock/1/
   80's%20Modern%20Rock_news.html
http://www.music.indiana.edu/music_resources/rock.html
http://bubl.ac.uk/link/r/rockmusic.htm
http://bubl.ac.uk/link/o/opera.htm

Arts: Photography

http://bubl.ac.uk/link/p/photography.htm
http://www.libraryoflinks.com
http://www.libraryofphotography.com/linkstop.html
http://harrysproshop.com/Links/Great_Photographers/great_photographers.html

Arts: Theater

http://bubl.ac.uk/link/t/theatrelinks.htm
http://www.rhodes.edu/public/2_0-Academics/2_5-
   Library/2_5_2SubjectGuides/2_5_2_29-Theater.shtml
http://wwar.com/categories/Theater
www.artslynx.org/theatre
http://www.ipl.org/div/subject/browse/ent85.00.00

Astronomy and Space Exploration

http://fits.cv.nrao.edu/www/astronomy.html
http://dir.yahoo.com/Science/astronomy
http://www.ralentz.com/old/space/homespace.html
http://spacelink.nasa.gov/Instructional.Materials/NASA.Educational.Products
http://spacelink.nasa.gov/xh/library.html

Business and Finance

http://finance.yahoo.com
http://www.corporateinformation.com
http://www.hoovers.com
http://www.10kwizard.com

Census and Statistical Abstracts of U.S. Populations

http://www.census.gov/prod/www/statistical-abstract-us.html

Criminology

http://www.utpb.edu/library/crim.html
http://sobek.colorado.edu/SOC/RES/crim.html
http://www.ncjrs.org

Engineering and Technology

http://link.bubl.ac.uk/engineering
http://dir.yahoo.com/Science/Engineering
http://www.motionnet.com
http://www.rspa.com/spi

Economics

http://sun3.lib.uci.edu/~dtsang/econ.htm
http://www.educationindex.com/econ/
http://rfe.org/
http://dismal.com
http://finance.yahoo.com

Education

http://www.educationindex.com/education_resources.html
http://www.eric.ed.gov/
http://ericeece.org/
http://ericps.ed.uiuc.edu/

Government: National, State, Local

http://www.nttc.edu/resources/government/govresources.asp
http://www.lib.umich.edu/govdocs/federal.html
http://www.loc.gov/global/state/stategov.html
http://www.statelocalgov.net/index.cfm
http://www.lib.umich.edu/govdocs/state.html
http://www.govspot.com/
http://www.sree.net/tips/government.html

Government: Public Records

http://www.searchsystems.net

Health

http://www.lib.berkeley.edu/PUBL/internet.html
http://dir.yahoo.com/Health
http://www.cdc.gov
http://www.mayoclinic.com/index.cfm?
http://www.merckhomeedition.com/home.html
http://www.intelihealth.com/IH/ihtIH/WSIHW000/408/408.html

History: African-American

blackquest.com/link.htm
web.uccs.edu/~history/index/afroam.html

History: American

http://thrall.org/history
http://www.rhodes.edu/public/2_0-Academics/2_5-
   Library/2_5_2SubjectGuides/2_5_2_17-History.shtm
http://historymatters.gmu.edu/browse/wwwhistory
http://www.us-history.com

History: Ancient (Babylonia-Greeks-Romans)

http://www.rhodes.edu/public/2_0-Academics/2_5-
Library/2_5_2SubjectGuides/2_5_2_17-History.shtm
http://www.geocities.com/Athens/4752/

History: Asian, Middle Eastern, African

http://www.rhodes.edu/public/2_0-Academics/2_5-
Library/2_5_2SubjectGuides/2_5_2_17-History.shtm

History: British

http://bubl.ac.uk/link/b/britishhistory1100-1800.htm
http://www.lib.msu.edu/widder/guides/subjects/history/british
http://www.britannia.com/history
http://vos.ucsb.edu/browse.asp?id=1017
http://www.spartacus.schoolnet.co.uk/Britain.html   *(1900-2000)*

History: European

http://www.rhodes.edu/public/2_0-Academics/2_5-
Library/2_5_2SubjectGuides/2_5_2_17-History.shtm
http://bubl.ac.uk/link/e/europeanhistory.htm
http://www.vlib.org/History.html

History: Holocaust

http://www.us-israel.org/jsource/holo.html
http://arginine.umdnj.edu/~swartz/holocaust.html
http://www.rhodes.edu/public/2_0-Academics/2_5-
Library/2_5_2SubjectGuides/2_5_2_17-History.shtm
http://www.nizkor.org

History: Latin American

http://users.snowcrest.net/jmike/latin.html
http://lanic.utexas.edu
http://www2.truman.edu/~marc/resources/internet.html

History: Military

http://www.rickard.kakoo.net/main.html
http://users.snowcrest.net/jmike/ancientmil.html
http://www.deremilitari.org/resources.htm
http://tigger.uic.edu/~rjensen/military.html
http://users.snowcrest.net/jmike/war2.html
http://bubl.ac.uk/link/m/militaryhistory.htm
http://www.wtj.com/wars/napoleonic
http://cdl.library.cornell.edu/moa/browse.monographs/waro.html
http://cdl.library.cornell.edu/moa/ browse.monographs/ofre.html
http://sunsite.utK.edu/Civil-war/warweb.html
http://www.emporia.edu/socsci/journal/military.htm
http://www.army.mil/cmh-pg/websites.htm
http//www.archives.gov/research_room/genealogy/research_topics/military.html

History: Native American

http://www.hanksville.org/NAresources/indices/NAhistory.html
http://www.cowboy.net/native
http://www.si.edu/resource/faq/nmai/start.htm

Law and Courts

http://www.law.harvard.edu/library/ref/ils_ref/annotated
http://www.lawsource.com/also
http://www.lawschool.cornell.edu/lawlibrary/guides/foreign2
http://www.un.org/law
http://www.findlaw.com
http://www.romingerlegal.com/supreme.htm
http://www.clubs.psu.edu/SCTSociety/links.htm
http://www.access.gpo.gov/su_docs/supcrt
http://supct.law.cornell.edu/supct

Libraries

http://www.nypl.org/branch/eresources.html
http://www.thebritishmuseum.ac.uk/compass
http://www-urbs.vatlib.it/urbs/index.asp?language=eng.

Literature: General

http://www.usd.edu/library/instruction/literature.html
http://library.scsu.ctstateu.edu/litbib.html -
http://www.lib.duke.edu/ias/latamer/lit.htm
http://riceinfo.rice.edu/Fondren/Virtual/Netguides/eng.html
http://www.columbia.edu/cu/lweb/indiv/butlref/frlit.html
http://www.classicalhomeeducation.com/ classic_literature_d.html
  www.bartleby.com

Literature: American

http://college.hmco.com/english/heath/lit_links.html
http://www.lang.nagoya-u.ac.jp/~matsuoka/AmeLit-G.html
http://www.nagasaki-gaigo.ac.jp/ishikawa/amlit
http://falcon.jmu.edu/~ramseyil/amlit.htm

Literature: Asian American

http://www.sjsu.edu/faculty/awilliams/AsianAmResources.html

Literature: British

http://www.wade.org/BritishLit.htm
http://www.library.adelaide.edu.au/guide/hum/english/E_major.html
http://www.usd.edu/library/instruction/literature.html
http://wwwshs1.bham.wednet.edu/curric/english/britlit.htm
http://education.yahoo.com/reference/shakespeare
http://www.bartleby.com

Literature: French

http://www.columbia.edu/cu/lweb/indiv/butlref/frlit.html

http://www.utoronto.ca/stmikes/library/research_guides/
rgfrenchliterature.htm

Literature: German

http://library.wustl.edu/subjects/germanlit/germanrefrev.html

Literature: Irish

http://www.questia.com/popularSearches/irish_literature.jsp

Literature: Mythology

http://www.bartleby.com/cgi-
bin/texis/webinator/sitesearch?FILTER=&query=mythology

http://www.spiritwheel.com/myth.htm

http://members.bellatlantic.net/~vze33gpz/myth.html

Literature: Latin American

http://wwwlibrary.csustan.edu/lboyer/modern_languages/mexican.htm

http://www.uky.edu/Subject/latinamlit.html

http://www.bu.edu/library/guides/spanish.html

Literature: Russian

http://www.slavweb.com/eng/Russia/literat-e.html

Maps: U.S., World, Street, Aerial, Topographic

http://www.mapquest.com

http://maps.yahoo.com

http://www.topozone.com

http://mappoint.msn.com

http://www.atlapedia.com

http://www.nationalgeographic.com

Maps: Historical

http://www.lib.utexas.edu/Libs/PCL/Map_collection/ Map_collection.html
Perry-Castañeda Library Map Collection.

http://www.rhodes.edu/public/2_0-Academics/2_5-
Library/2_5_2SubjectGuides/2_5_2_17-History.shtm

Philosophy

http://www.refdesk.com/philos.html

http://www.earlham.edu/rpeters/philinks.htm

www.epistemelinks.com

Political Science

http://www.polifs.com/tpg.index.html

http://www.lib.umich.edu/govdocs/poliscinew.html

http://www.potifos.com/tpg/index.html

http://www.psr.keele.ac.uk

http://sun3.lib.uci.edu/~dtsang/pol.htm

http://www.vanderbilt.edu/~rtucker/polisci/miscpol.html

Psychology

http://www.psywww.com/resource/bytopic.htm
http://psychcentral.com/resources
http://www.vanguard.edu/faculty/ddegelman/amoebaweb
www.earlham.edu/~peters/philinks.htm

Religion

http://www.lib.iastate.edu/collections/eresourc/religion.html
http://www.refdesk.com/factrel.html
http://www.cojoweb.com/ref-religous.html
http://www.newadvent.org
http://www.episcopalchurch.org
http://www.lcms.org
http://www.episcopalchurch.org

Science: Environment, Ecology

http://www.doi.gov
http://habitat.fws.gov
http://contaminants.fws.gov/http://www.lib.iastate.edu/collections/eresourc/
    aefawr.html
http://www.gwu.edu/~greenu/subject.html
http://epa.gov

Science: General, Organic and Physical

http://bubl.ac.uk/link/lif.html
http://bubl.ac.uk/link/sci.html
http://dir.yahoo.com/science
http://wdcrobcolp01.ed.gov/cfapps/free/displaysubject.cfm?sid=8
http://www.refdesk.com/factsci.html
http://enchantedlearning.com/science/dictionary

Science: Medicine

http://www.sciencekomm.at/index.html
http://dir.yahoo.com/Health/Medicine/
http://www.pslgroup.com/MEDRES.HTM
http://www.slackinc.com/idirectories/general.htm
http://www.healthsquare.com/medcare4.htm
http://www.rxlist.com
http://bartleby.com
http://www.webmd.com
http://nih.gov

Science: Oceanography

http://www.esdim.noaa.gov/ocean_page.html

Science: Wildlife

http://www.utyx.com/wildlife
http://www.projectwildlife.org/resources.htm

Sociology

http://vax.wcsu.edu/socialsci/socres.html
http://www.colapublib.org/services/ethnic
http://www.rootsweb.com/~wiwood/WLHN/cultural/ethnic.html
http://www.lib.vt.edu/subjects/soci
http://dir.yahoo.com/Social_Science/Sociology
http://www.sociolog.com/links/index.html

Speeches and Quotations

*http://douglassarchives.org/directory/General_Collections_of_Speeches_and_
Historical_Docs*
*http://www.library.vanderbilt.edu/central%5Cref%5Cguides%5CSpeech%20
Resources.htm*
http://www.bartleby.com/100/s0.html
http://www.bartleby.com//63

Sports

http://www.hickoksports.com/history/olympix.shtml
http://www.sportspedia.com/menu.html
http://www.ai-press.com/SENA.html
http://directory.google.com/Top/Sports/Resources/News_and_Media
http://www.el.com/elinks/sports
http://www.sportsci.org/encyc/indexalpha.html
http://www.perseus.tufts.edu

Women's Studies

http://www.library.wisc.edu/libraries/WomensStudies/hist.htm
http://research.umbc.edu/~korenman/wmst/links.html
http://bubl.ac.uk/link/w/women'sstudies.htm
http://www.mith2.umd.edu/WomensStudies/OtherWebSites/
http://www.columbia.edu/cu/lweb/indiv/mideast/cuvlm/women.html
http://www.unl.ac.uk/library/aishums/womenweb.shtml

APPENDIX B

Special Reference Works

The most commonly used special reference works are listed below. Some are for fields that may overlap and, as has been said, some entries are found only in major libraries.

OVERALL REFERENCES

Bibliographic Index
Guide to Reference Books
How and Where to Look It Up: A Guide to
  Standard Sources of Information
Index to Indexes
United States Government Publications
U.S. Catalog, with Cumulative Book Index
World Bibliography of Bibliographies

GENERAL ENCYCLOPEDIAS AND ALMANACS

American Year Book
Encyclopedia Americana
Americana Annual
Encyclopedia Britannica
The Britannica Book of the Year
Chambers' Encyclopaedia
Columbia Encyclopedia
Encyclopedia International
New International Encyclopedia
Facts on File
New International Year Book
The Statesman's Yearbook
Information Please Almanac
The World Almanac

PERIODICALS

International Index to Periodicals
The New York Times Index

Nineteenth Century Readers' Guide
Poole's Index to Periodical Literature
Reader's Guide to Periodical Literature
Ulrich's Periodical Directory

AGRICULTURE

Agricultural Index
Cyclopedia of American Agriculture

ART AND ARCHITECTURE

Art Index
Art Through the Ages
Bryan's Dictionary of Painters and
  Engravers
Harper's Encyclopedia of Art
History of Architecture
Index to Reproductions of American
  Paintings
Portrait Index

BIOGRAPHIES

Current Biography
Dictionary of American Biography
Dictionary of National Biography
International Who's Who
Webster's Biographical Dictionary
Who Was Who in America
Who's Who in America
World Biography

QUOTATIONS

Bartlett's Familiar Quotations
Oxford Dictionary of Quotations
Stevenson's Home Book of Quotations

BUSINESS

Business Information: How to Find and
Use It
Business Periodicals Index
Encyclopedia of Banking and Finance

DRAMA AND SPEECH

Dramatic Index
Index to Plays in Collections
University Debaters' Annual

ECONOMICS

Dictionary of Modern Economics

EDUCATION

Bibliographies and Summaries in
Education to July 1935
Cyclopedia of Education
Education Index
Encyclopedia of Educational Research
How to Locate Educational Information
and Data
Introduction to Educational Research

ENGINEERING

Engineering Index
Sources of Engineering Information

GEOGRAPHY

Columbia Gazetteer

HISTORY AND POLITICAL SCIENCE

Bibliography in American History
Cambridge Ancient History
Cambridge Medieval History
Cambridge Modern History
Cyclopedia of American Government
Dictionary of American History
Encyclopedia of World History
Guide to Historical Literature
Literature of American History
Guide to Materials in Political Science
Guide to the Study of the United States of
America
Public Affairs Information Service
Reference Shelf
Yearbook of the United Nations

INDUSTRIAL ARTS

Industrial Arts Index

LAW

Index to Legal Periodicals

LITERATURE

A.L.A. Index to General Literature
Articles on American Literature
Authors Today and Yesterday
Baker's Guide to Historical Fiction
Baker's Guide to the Best Fiction
Bibliographical Guide to English Studies
Bibliography of Writings on the English
Language
Book Review Digest
Cambridge Bibliography of English
Literature
Cambridge History of American Literature
Cambridge History of English Literature
Columbia Dictionary of Modern European
Literature
Concise Bibliography for Students of
English
Contemporary American Authors
Contemporary British Literature
Dictionary of World Literature
Essay and General Literature Index
Firkins' Index of Plays
Firkins' Index to Short Stories
Granger's Index to Poetry and Recitations
Literary History of the United States
Living Authors
Oxford Classical Dictionary
Oxford Companion to American Literature
Oxford Companion to Classical Literature
Oxford Companion to English Literature
Sonnenschein's Best Books
Twentieth Century Authors

MATHEMATICS

Guide to the Literature of Mathematics

MUSIC

Grove's Dictionary of Music and
Musicians
International Cyclopedia of Music and
Musicians
Song Index

PHILOSOPHY

Dictionary of Philosophy
Dictionary of Philosophy and Psychology
Guide to Readings in Philosophy

BIBLIOGRAPHY

Works Cited and Consulted

Books

Allen, Eliot D. and Colbrunn, Ethel B. *A Short Guide to Writing a Research Paper*. Everett Edwards, 1975.

Anderson, Jonathan. *Thesis and Assignment Writing*. Wiley, 1970.

Anderson, Kenneth E. and Haugh, Oscar M. *A Handbook for the Preparation of Research Reports and Theses*. University Press of America, 1978.

Astle, Cedric. *English at a Glance*. Arden Library, 1968.

Atteberry, James L. and Atteberry, Ruth D. *Guide to Research and Report Writing*. Tam's Books, 1974.

Avery, Thomas E. *A Student's Guide to Thesis Research*. Burgess, 1978.

Barzun, Jacques and Graff, Henry F. *The Modern Researcher*. Harcourt Brace Jovanovich, 1977.

Bazerman, Charles and David Russell, eds. *Landmark Essays on Writing Across the Curriculum*. Davis, CA: Hermagoras Press, 1994.

Behlins, John H. *Guidelines for Preparing the Research Proposal*. University Press of America, 1978.

Berry, R. *How to Write a Research Paper*. Pergamon, 1969.

Burns, E.M., R. Lerner, and S. Meacham. *Western Civilizations: Their History and Their Culture*, Vol. 1. New York: W. W. Norton & Company, 1980.

Cash, Phyllis. *How to Write a Research Paper Step by Step*. Monarch Press, 1975.

Cely, Jonathan. *Writing a Research Paper*. Indiana Scholastic Press, 1978.

Chase, Mary Ellen. *Constructive Theme Writing*. Holt, 1957.

The Chicago Manual of Style, 15th, Chicago: University of Chicago Press, 2003.

Christianson, Pauline. *From Inside Out: Writing From Subjective to Objective.* Winthrope, 1978.

Coggins, Gordon. *A Guide to Writing Essays and Research Papers.* Van Nostrand Reinhold, 1977.

——————————————"Computer Associates executives admit fraud." *The Oregonian*, April 9, 2004, D-1.

Cook, L. Russell. "Cocoa Production," *Encyclopedia Britannica*, Macropaedia, 15th ed.

Cooper, Charles W. and Robins, Edmund J. *The Term Paper: A Manual and Model.* Stanford Universitty Press. 1967.

Corbin, Richard and Corbin, Jonathan. *Research Papers: A Guided Writing Experience for Senior High Students.* English Council, 1978.

Cordasco, Francesco and Gatner, Elliot S. *Report and Research Writing.* Littlefield, 1974.

Coyle, William. *Research Papers.* Odyssey Press, 1976.

Cummings, Marsha Z. and Slade, Carole. *Writing the Research Paper.* Houghton Mifflin, 1978.

Deighton, Lee C. *Handbook of American English Spelling.* Harcourt Brace Jovanovich, 1978.

DeVillez, Randy. *Step by Step: College Writing.* Kendall-Hunt, 1977.

Doremus, Robert B. *Writing College Themes.* Oxford University Press, 1960.

Doubleday, Neal F. *Writing the Research Paper.* Heath, 1971.

Draper, Lowell A. *A Curse on Confusion: An Individualized Approach to Clear Writing.* Cambridge Book Co., 1976.

Ellis, Barbara G. *The Copy-Editing and Headline Handbook.* New Cambridge, MA: Perseus Publishing, 2001.

Ellis, Barbara G. "Major Inhibitory Factors in the Assessment of Themes by Oregon High School English Teachers." PhD diss., Oregon State University, 1990.

Emig, Janet. Writing as a Mode of Learning. *College Composition and Communication.* 28 (1997).

Encyclopaedia Britannica, 15th edition.

Encyclopedia Britannica, s.v. "Cocoa Production" (by "L. Russell Cook), 15th ed, Macropaedia.

Ewing, David W. *Writing for Results.* Wiley, 1974.

Fergus, Patricia M. *Spelling Improvement.* McGraw-Hill, 1978.

Flesch, Rudolf. *Look It Up: A Deskbook of American Spelling and Style.* Harper & Row, 1977.

Furness, Edna. *Spelling for the Millions.* Nelson, 1977.

Gehlmann, John and Eisman, Philip. *Say What You Mean.* Odyssey Press, 1968.

Gibaldi, Joseph. ed. *MLA Handbook for Writers of Research Papers.* 6th ed. New York: The Modern Language Association of America, 2003.

Godshalk, Fred I. *Measurement of Writing Ability.* College Board, 1966.

Goldstein, Norm, ed. *The Associated Press Stylebook and Briefing on Media Law.* Perseus Publishing, 2000.

Gorrell, Robert and Gorrell, Laird. *Modern English Handbook.* Prentice-Hall, 1976.

Graves, Harold F. and Hoffman, L. *Report Writing.* Prentice-Hall, 1965.

Hake, Rosemary. *Mapping the Model: A Basic Rhetoric for the Basic Writer.* Kendall Hall, 1978.

Hook, J.N. *English Today: A Practical Handbook.* Wiley, 1976.

Hoy, John C. "The Candidate Speaks for Himself," *The Journal of the Association of College Admissions Counselors.* 12, No. 3.

Hubbell, George Shelton. *Writing Term Papers and Reports.* Barnes and Noble, 1958.

Hugon, Paul D. *Modern Word Finder.* Gale, 1974.

Hutchinson, Helene. *Hutchinson Guide to Writing Research Papers.* Glencoe, 1973.

Inglish, Joyce and Jackson, Joan. *Research and Composition.* Prentice-Hall, 1977.

Janis, Jack Harold. *Writing and Communicating in Business.* Macmillan, 1973.

Kearney, Ellizabeth I. *How to Write a Composition.* Lucas, 1972.

Kirszner, Lauries G., Stephen R. Mandell, Feroza Jussawalla, eds. *The Holt Guide to Documentation and Writing in the Disciplines.* 2nd ed. Fort Worth: Holt, Rinehart and Winston, Inc., 1989.

Kirszner, Lauries G, Larry G. Mapp, and Stephen R. Mandell, eds. *Harcourt Brace Guide to Documentation and Writing in the Disciplines.* 7th ed. New York: Harcourt Brace, 2001.

Knowles, Lyle. *A Guide for Writing Research Papers, Theses, and Dissertations.* Tam's Books, 1973.

Kreirsky, Joseph and Linfield, Jordan. *The Bad Speller's Dictionary.* Random House, 1967.

Lester, James D. *Writing Research Papers: A Complete Guide.* Scott, Foresman, 1976.

Lindblom, P. *Writing the Theme: A Practical Guide I.* Winthrop, 1973.

Marius, Richard and Harvey S. Wiener, eds. *The McGraw-Hill College Handbook.* 4th ed. New York: McGraw-Hill, Inc., 1994.

Markman, Roberta H. and Waddell, Marie L. *Ten Steps in Writing the Research Paper.* Barrons, 1971.

McLeod, Susan and Margot Soven. *Writing Across the Curriculum: A Guide to Developing Programs.* New York: Sage Publications, Inc., 1992.

Miles, Leland. *Guide to Writing Term Papers.* University of Iowa, 1959.

Mitchell, S. *How to Write Reports.* Watts, 1975.

Mulkerne, Donald J. D. and Kahn, Gilbert. *The Term Paper Step by Step.* Doubleday, 1977.

New York Times. *The New York Times Style Book for Writers and Editors.* The New York Times, 1962.

Perrin, Porter G. *Writer's Guide and Index to English.* Scott, Foresman, 1965.

Polanski, Virginia G., ed. *The Holt Guide to Documentation and Writing in the Disciplines.* 5th ed. Fort Worth: Holt, Rinehart and Winston, Inc., 2001.

Polgar, Caroline and Cathy White. "Chocolate," Colby Environmental Coalition. Waterville, ME.: Colby College, August 1, 2003. (December 18, 2003).

Publication Manual of the American Psychological Association. 5th ed. Washington, D.C.: American Psycholgical Association, 2001.

Pugh, Griffith T. *Guide to Research Writing.* Houghon Mifflin, 1968.

Ranald,, Margaret. *A Style Manual for College Students.* Queens College Press, 1975.

Ross, Charles. *Richard III*. Berkeley: University of California Press, 1981.

Roth, Audrey J. *Research Papers: Form and Content*. Wadsworh, 1978.

Schneider, Ben R., Jr. and Tjossem, Herbert. *Theses and Research Papers*. Macmillan, 1962.

Sears, Donald A. *Harbrace Guide to the Library and the Research Paper*. Harcourt Brace Jovanovich, 1973.

Short, Raymond W. and DeMaria, Robert. *Subjects and Sources for Research Writing*. Norton, 1963.

——————————. *Student Writer's Guide*. Everett Edwards, 1975.

Stegner, Wallace E. *Effective Theme*. Holt, Rinehart & Winston, 1967.

Stein, M. L. *How to Write Better Compositions, Term Papers and Reports*. Cornerstone, 1978.

Strunk, William, Jr., and White, E. B. *The Elements of Style*. Macmillan, 1959.

Swanson, Richard. *For Your Information: A Guide to Writing Reports*. Prentice-Hall, 1974.

Tanabe, Gen S. and Kelly Y. Tanabe. *Money-Winning Scholarship Essays and Interviews: Insider Strategies from Judges and Winners*. Palo Alto, CA: Supercollege, 2002.

Teitelbaum, Harry. *How to Write Book Reports*. Simon and Schuster, 1975.

Tey, Josephine. *The Daughter of Time*. New York: The MacMillan Company, 1951.

Turner, R. P. *Technical Report Writing*. Holt, Rinehart & Winston, 1971.

Yancey, Kathleen Blake and Brian Huot, eds. *Assessing Writing Across the Curriculum*. Greenwich, CT: Ablex Publishers, 1997.

Internet

Biggs, Brooke Shelby. "Slavery Free Chocolate?," Independent Media Institute, February 7, 2002. http://www.alternet.org/story.html?StoryID=12373 (December 18, 2003).

Donnelly, Fred. "The Titanic's Humanist Paradox.," *Humanist,* July 2000. http://www.findarticles.com/cf_dls/m1374/4_60/63257727/p1/article.jhtml (April 5, 2004).

Eedle, Arthur and Rosalind." The Loss of the Titanic," *Recognising the Hand of Judgment*, nd, http://www.oxleigh.freeserve.co.uk/rhj19.htm (April 5, 2004).

EssayEdge.com. CyberEdit Network Site. 2004.http://www.essayedge.com. (April 26, 2004).

Hall, Mark F. "*Titanic* Treasure Trove: Reference Bonanza on Ill-Fated 'Unsinkable' Ship," *LC INFORMATION BULLETIN*, May 1998. http://lcweb.loc.gov/loc/lcib/9805/titanic.html (December 22, 2003).

Halladay, Jim and Robin Halladay "Shipwrecks in Lake Erie," *Aquatic World*, September 22, 2003. http://www.aquatic-world.com/ErieWrecks.htm (April 8, 2004).

Howard, E. D. "Morgan Andrew Robertson, September 30, 1861–March 24, 1915." http://members.tripod.com/~rhazz/frobertson.html (April 8, 2004).

Kanigel, Robert. Taylor-Made. (19th-Century Efficiency Expert Frederick Taylor). *The Sciences*, May 1997, v. 37, i 3, pl 8(1), 4. http://216.239.53.104/search?q=cache:uaC2LfOL1XEJ:www.ams.sunysb.edu/~weinig/Taylor-made.pdf+Gantt+%2B+Gilbreth+%2B+%22driver%22&hl=en&ie=UTF-8, (April 21, 2004).

Kerr, Justin. "All About Chocolate: History of Chocolate," (Chicago: The Field Museum, 2001).

http://www.fmnh.org/chocolate/history.html (December 18, 2003).

Khamsi, Roxanne. "GREEN LIVING: EATING RIGHT:Enlightened Indulgence. Organic Chocolate Companies Help Make Calories Count Toward Conservation." *emagazine*, July/August 2001, 4:Vol. XII. http://www.emagazine.com/july-august_2001/0701gl_eating.html (April 9, 2004).

———————————————"Medieval Science, the Church and Universities." *Bede's Library*. http://www.bede.org.uk/university.htm (March 31, 2004).

Pippey, Ralph. Now, Where Did The Twirling Part Come From? *No-Mystery Majorette History*: 2 of 5, 2004. http://www.majorettes.ca/hist2.html (April 9, 2004).

Simpson, Jacqueline. "The Wreck of the *Titanic* Foretold." *Folklore Society*, 2001. http://www.findarticles.com/cf_dls/m2386/2_111/69202920/p1/article.jhtml, 2001 (April 5, 2004).

Swayze, David D. "The Great Lakes Shipwreck File: Total Losses of Great Lakes Ships 1679-1999." Lake Isabella, MI: June 2001. http://www.boatnerd.com/swayze/shipwreck (April 8, 2004).

———————————"Titanic—A Voyage of Discovery," *Sail on Titanic*. http://www.euronet.nl/users/keesree/intro.htm (April 5, 2004).

Warburton, David. Beyond the Gantt Chart: New Methods for Measuring Product Development." *Medical Device & Diagnostic Industry*, January 2003. http://www.devicelink.com/mddi/archive/03/01/014.html (April 21, 2004).

———————————————"Welcome to the tour of Olympia!" Quick TimePerseus Project, Tufts University. http://www.perseus.tufts.edu/Olympics/site.html (July 18, 2001).

Interviews

Harris, Maleah. 2003. Interview by author. October 14. Oregon State University, Corvallis.

Sandlin. Michele. 2003. Interview by author. October 14. Oregon State University. Corvallis.

Sawicki, Kristine. 2003. Interview by author. October 16. Reed College, Portland, OR.

Sickinger, Ted. 2004. Interview by author. June 29. Portland, OR.

Sleppin, Wendy. 2004. Interview by author. May 6. Hauppauge, NY.

Institutions

Auburn University. 2004. Auburn AL. http://www.auburn.edu/student_info/student_affairs/admissio/admissform.pdf (April 28, 2004).

Augsburg College. 2004. Minneapolis MN. http://www.augsburg.edu/irb/forms.html (April 29, 2004).

Bob Jones University. 2004. Greenville, SC. http://www.bju.edu/admissions/application.pdf (April 28, 2004).

Carroll College. 2004. Helena, MT. https//www.carroll.edu/prostudents/application/images/ccapp.pdf (April 27, 2004).

Common Application to 193 Private U.S. Colleges and Universities. 2003-2004. Harvard University, Cambridge, MA. http://www.admissions.college.harvard.edu/prospective/tools/download/HarvTsfrSupp.pdf (April 25, 2004).

Common Application, University of Maine System. 2004. Augusta ME. http://www.usm.maine.edu/admit/application.pdf (April 28, 2004).

Grambling State University. 2004. Grambling LA. www.gram.edu/departments/ admissions/ Documents/admission_app.htm (April 28, 2004).

Louisiana State University. 2004. Baton Rouge LA. https://appl010.lsu.edu/ admissions\admappl.nsf/AdmAppl/1E4174E8C182176986256E84007C4E7 2?EditDocument (April 28, 2004).

Oregon State University. 2004. Corvallis OR. http://oregonstate.edu/admissions/pdf/UGApp2004.pdf (April 28, 2004).

Purdue University. 2004. West Lafayette IN. http://www.ipfw.edu/admissions/ apply/application.shtml (April 28, 2004).

Reed College. 2004. Portland OR.

University of Alaska. 2004. Fairbanks AK.http://www.uaf.edu/admissions/apply/ undergrad_app.pdf (April 28, 2004).

University of Florida. 2004. Gainesville FL. http://www.reg.ufl.edu/pdf/freshmen-undergrad-app.pdf (April 28, 2004).

University of Georgia. 2004. Augusta GA. www.reg.uga.edu/or.nsf/html/soc (April 29, 2004).

University of Hawaii. 2004. Manoa HI. https://apply.hawaii.edu:9326/index.jsp (April 28, 2004).

University of Minnnesota. 2004. Minneapolis MN. 2004. http://admissions. tc.umn.edu/Apply(April 25, 2004).

University of Mississippi. 2004. Oxford MS. https://secure.olemiss.edu/services/ appl_index.html (April 27, 2004).

University of Southern California. 2004. Los Angeles CA.

http://afaweb.eds.usc.edu/USCAFA/upload_images/UGApplication0405.pdf (April 23, 2004).

University of Tennessee. 2004. Knoxville TN. http://admissions.utk.edu/under-graduate/AdmissApp04.pdf (April 27, 2004).

University of Texas. 2004. Austin TX http://bealonghorn.utexas.edu/bal/ essays.WBX (April 28, 2004).

University of West Virginia. 2004. Institute WV. http://www.collegeview.com/college/applications/netapply/appdocs/3301399/3301399_0.pdf (April 27, 2004).

Newspapers

Cohen, Richard. Washington Post News Service, reprinted in *The Oregonian*, November 6, 1988.

Kosseff, Jeff. "Options debate framed outside party lines." *The Oregonian*, June 29, 2004, C-1, 3.

The Oregonian. 2004. Editorial, "Ask your doctor about..." June 24.

Sickinger, Ted. "Oregon firms weigh options." *The Oregonian*, July 1, 2004, B-1,3.

Tripp, Julie. "Dr. Know: A Coos Bay neurologist's passion for investment wisdom produces highly rated books full of clear and informative advice." *Oregonian*, March 21, 2004, E-8

INDEX

NOTES

NOTES

NOTES

ASPIRE HIGHER WITH THE POWER... OF WORDS!

504 ABSOLUTELY ESSENTIAL WORDS, 4th Edition
$10.95, Can. $14.50 (0-8120-9530-8)
Builds practical vocabulary skills through funny stories and cartoons plus practice exercises.

VOCABULARY SUCCESS, 3rd Edition
$13.95, Can. $19.50 (0-7641-0311-3)
Covers all the methods of evaluating words to improve communication skills.

1001 PITFALLS IN ENGLISH GRAMMAR, 3rd Edition
$12.95, Can. $18.95 (0-8120-3719-7)
Examines the most common errors in the English language.

1100 WORDS YOU NEED TO KNOW, 4th Edition
$11.95, Can. $16.95 (0-7641-1365-8)
This book is the way to master more than 1100 useful words and idioms taken from the mass media.

WORDPLAY: 550+ WORDS YOU NEED TO KNOW
CD Pkg. $19.95, Can. $28.95 (0-7641-7750-8)
Based on **1100 Words You Need to Know**; included are five CDs presented in comedy-drama form to add in the dimension of dialogue and the spoken word.

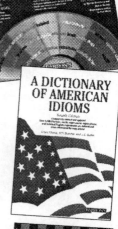

A DICTIONARY OF AMERICAN IDIOMS, 4TH EDITION
$14.95, Can. $21.95 (0-7641-1982-6)
Over 8,000 idiomatic words, expressions, regionalisms, and informal English expressions are defined and cross-referenced for easy access.

HANDBOOK OF COMMONLY USED AMERICAN IDIOMS, 4th Edition
$7.95, Can. $11.50 (0-7641-2776-4)
With 1500 popular idioms, this book will benefit both English-speaking people and those learning English as a second language.

BARRON'S EDUCATIONAL SERIES, INC.
250 Wireless Boulevard
Hauppauge, New York 11788
Canada: Georgetown Book Warehouse
34 Armstrong Avenue
Georgetown, Ont. L7G 4R9
www.barronseduc.com

Prices subject to change without notice. Books may be purchased at your bookstore, or by mail from Barron's. Enclose check or money order for total amount plus sales tax where applicable and 18% for postage and handling (minimum charge $5.95). NY State, New Jersey, Michigan, and California residents add sales tax. Books listed are paperback editions.
$ = U.S. Dollars   Can. $ = Canadian Dollars

No One Can Build Your Writing Skills Better Than We Can...

Essentials of English, 5th Edition
$9.95, Can. $13.95 (0-7641-1367-4)
The comprehensive program for effective writing skills.

Essentials of Writing, 5th Edition
$11.95, Can. $17.50 (0-7641-1368-2)
A companion workbook for the material in *Essentials of English*.

10 Steps in Writing the Research Paper, 6th Edition
$10.95, Can. $15.50 (0-7641-1362-3)
The easy step-by-step guide for writing research papers. It includes a section on how to avoid plagiarism.

Creative Writing The Easy Way
$12.95, Can. $18.95 (0-7641-2579-6)
This title discusses, analyzes, and offers exercises in prose forms.

The Art of Styling Sentences: 20 Patterns for Success, 4th Edition
$8.95, Can. $12.50 (0-7641-2181-2)
How to write with flair, imagination and clarity, by imitating 20 sentence patterns and variations.

Writing The Easy Way, 3rd Edition
$14.95, Can. $21.00 (0-7641-1206-6)
The quick and convenient way to enhance writing skills.

Basic Word List, 3rd Edition
$6.95, Can. $8.95 (0-8120-9649-5)
More than 2,000 words that are found on the most recent major standardized tests are thoroughly reviewed.

BARRON'S EDUCATIONAL SERIES, INC.
250 Wireless Boulevard • Hauppauge, New York 11788
In Canada: Georgetown Book Warehouse
34 Armstrong Avenue • Georgetown, Ontario L7G 4R9
Visit our web site at: www.barronseduc.com